THEORIES OF DEVELOPMENTAL PSYCHOLOGY

PATRICIA H. MILLER

University of Florida

Third Edition

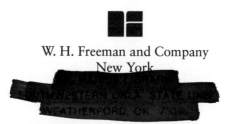

W. H. Freeman and Company
New York

Library of Congress Cataloging in Publication Data

Miller, Patricia H.
    Theories of development psychology / Patricia H. Miller.—3d ed.
        p.   cm.
    Includes bibliographical references and indexes.
    ISBN 0-7167-2308-5. — ISBN 0-7167-2309-3 (pbk.)
    1. Developmental psychology—Philosophy. 2. Child
psychology—Philosophy. I. Title.
    BF713.M55   1983
    155'.01—dc20   92-37252
                                                             CIP

Printed in the United States of America

1 2 3 4 5 6 7 8 9 0   VB   9 9 8 7 6 5 4 3

To Scott, Erica, and Kevin

A Series of Books in Psychology

Editors:
Richard C. Atkinson
Gardner Lindzey
Richard F. Thompson

CONTENTS

PREFACE

"What is your theory of psychological development?" As an undergraduate I faced that very essay question on my final exam in introductory child psychology. Drawing on all the theories I had ever heard of, I modestly generated a 6 (age) x 20 (developmental tasks) matrix—a Havighurst-gone-wild theory of development—and my interest in theories was launched. Perhaps if I had been given a multiple choice test this book would address a different topic.

In *Theories of Developmental Psychology* I have tried to show the "big picture" of psychological development. Sometimes students are frustrated by fact-laden textbooks that do not provide the theoretical frameworks in which to fit the facts. It is often not made clear, for example, why a Swiss philosopher would be interested in children's numerical judgments after a row of objects is spread out or why it is noteworthy that infants cry when their mother leaves the room. In this book, seven theories, or approaches, provide frameworks for understanding and perceiving the significance of the research findings in developmental psychology.

Theories of Developmental Psychology can be used as a primary or supplementary text in undergraduate or graduate courses. In addition, it can provide perspectives on children's behavior for those who interact with children in any capacity. I hope that both developmental psychologists and readers from other disciplines will find something of interest in these pages.

I have used a parallel structure in the various chapters to help the reader compare the theories. To provide continuity, four central issues of development are addressed in each chapter. In addition, I have tried to convey what is most exciting about each of the theories. The theories included are those that in my view are of most interest to developmental psychologists and professionals in related disciplines. Many important theories were necessarily excluded because of length restrictions. And some of the "theories" included are not formal theories, but they function as theories by identifying what to study, what questions to ask, and how to answer these questions.

The third edition updates the second. I have tried to show how each theory has changed in its emphasis, its data base, and its influence on developmental psychology over the last few years. The major change in this edition was the addition of a chapter on Vygotsky's theory and the contextualists. The recent influence of this approach mandated its inclusion. Other additions are recent notions about capacity, knowledge, and strategies in information-processing approaches, and new Piagetian work. Issues such as domain-specific reasoning and the social context of development are given more attention. To keep the book at its present length, it was necessary to present certain theories more concisely.

I am grateful to a number of people who read and offered comments for one or more editions: Patricia Ashton, William Charlesworth, Michael Cole, Jeffrey Farrar, Bridget Franks, Eleanor Gibson, Harry Grater, Richard Griggs, Gardner Lindzey, Jack Meacham, Stuart Miller, Joy Osofsky, Anne Pick, Robert Siegler, Addison Stone, and Robert Watson. Several undergraduate and graduate students also made helpful suggestions. Most of all, I want to thank Scott Miller, who provided valuable feedback on all editions. I am also grateful to John Flavell, who guided my meanderings into theories when I was a graduate student and has continued to be a source of inspiration. Finally, I want to thank Jonathan Cobb at W. H. Freeman and Company, who expertly guided the second and third editions.

Patricia H. Miller
Gainesville, Florida
November, 1992

INTRODUCTION

Give us theories, theories, always theories. Let every man who has a theory pronounce his theory.
[JAMES MARK BALDWIN]

Never trust an experimental result until it has been confirmed by theory.
[SIR ARTHUR EDDINGTON]

Archimedes is said to have run naked through the streets, shouting "Eureka, eureka!" (I have found it, I have found it!) after discovering the principle of hydrostatics. This joy and excitement of discovery, although usually more restrained than Archimedes', is the driving force behind every theoretical advance. The purpose of this book is to tell the story of theory building in developmental psychology. We will meet the grand old theories of Jean Piaget, Sigmund Freud, and Erik Erikson, rapidly changing social learning theory, and several approaches with more recent influence on developmental psychology—information processing, ethology, Eleanor Gibson's perceptual learning, and Vygotskian–contextual theory. These theories have saved developmental psychology from drowning in the sea of data on children. They have helped psychologists keep their faith that development is a comprehensible process and a legitimate area of study.

To understand the contribution of these developmental theories, we must first look at the general nature of theories. In this introductory chapter, we ask the following questions about theories:

1. What is a theory?

2. What is a developmental theory?

3. Of what value is a developmental theory?

4. How are facts and theories related?

5. What are the main issues of developmental psychology?

WHAT IS A THEORY?

This is a deceptively simple question. In fact, a philosopher of science might "answer" our question by asking two more:

1. Are we asking what theories should be or what they typically are?

2. Are we asking about theories as they are stated formally or as they operate in a scientific community?

The philosopher's first question concerns the distinction between ideal and real theories and expresses the sad fact of scientific life that our theories fall short of their goal. Especially in the social sciences, theories usually do not reach a complete, formal state. An ideal, complete, formal scientific theory is a set of interconnected statements—definitions, axioms, postulates, hypothetical constructs, intervening variables, laws, hypotheses, and so on. Some of these statements, which are usually expressed in verbal or mathematical form, are deduced logically from certain other statements. The function of this set of interconnected statements is to describe unobservable structures, mechanisms, or processes and to relate them to each other and to observable events. Perhaps the best way to contrast these types of statements is to show that they occupy different levels within a theory. That is, they vary in their distance from observable behavior. The "farther" a statement is from observable behavior, the less likely it is to be supported by empirical data.

At a point farthest from observable behavior are certain assumptions (axioms, postulates) that are accepted without being tested. (For example, in Piaget's theory, an assumption is that thinking is organized.) These assumptions may be so self-evident to the theorist that he is not even aware of them. As we move to a less general level, we find hypothetical constructs—concepts that posit relations among events, objects, properties, or variables. These constructs (such as "mental scheme" and "mental reversibility" in Piaget's theory) are unobservable themselves, but they refer to behavior that can be observed. Theorists infer what they cannot see. Hypothetical constructs are translated into testable hypotheses, which are tentative statements about the relations among events, objects, properties, or variables. (One Piagetian hypothesis is that the infant tends to repeat interesting actions, such as shaking a rattle.) A hypothesis becomes a fact when it is sufficiently supported by research. As facts accumulate, they are tied together by a law: a relatively well established general statement concerning the relationship among a set of facts.

All of these formal elements should meet certain requirements. A theory should be logically sound, that is, internally consistent, with no statements that contradict each other. A theory should also be empirically sound, that is, not contradicted by scientific observations. Furthermore, it should be testable and parsimonious, relying on as few constructs, propositions, and the like, as possible. Finally, a theory should cover a reasonably large area of a science, and it should integrate previous research.

Psychology has had few formal theories in its history, and no current theory of development falls into this category. However, the above requirements give us a context for judging whether each theory of development is headed in the right direction. We can ask whether each theory could eventually reach the status of a formal, testable theory. In their present form, developmental "theories" serve as frames of reference for examining changes in behavior over time. (For example, Piaget's theory directs our attention to the organization of thought rather than to specific pieces of knowledge, to stagelike changes during development rather than to a gradual accumulation of knowledge, and to children's active construction of knowledge rather than to their passive processing of information.)

Our philosopher of science would probably urge us to continue to build theories, despite their imperfect state, but to keep in mind that we are far from the promised land of formal theory. The young science of developmental psychology, with its informal theories and growing pains, may yet develop into a mature science with formal theories.

The philosopher's second question distinguishes between theories as they are stated (in books such as this one) and how they actually operate in a scientific community. A theory, in its tidy and polished form in a textbook, bears only a faint resemblance to the way the theory guides the behavior of real people doing real research. A theory is both a static formulation and a social and psychological phenomenon. When a person develops or adopts a particular theory, she takes on a whole set of beliefs concerning what questions about development are worth asking, what methods for studying these questions are legitimate, and what the nature of development is. A Freudian is not likely to study how rats learn to press bars in tightly controlled experiments, and a learning theorist is not likely to ask people to describe their dreams or memories of childhood. There are unwritten rules of the game that are very much a part of the theory as it is practiced.

WHAT IS A DEVELOPMENTAL THEORY?

Thus far we have seen that developmental theories are somewhat informal at present and, like all theories, have a dynamic, nonpublic role as well as a static, public one. Our next step is to ask what makes these theories developmental. Simply studying children does not make a theorist a developmental theorist. For example, studying learning in 6-year-olds does not necessarily lead to conclusions about development. What is critical about a developmental theory is that it focuses on *change over time*. Although developmental theories have nondevelopmental theoretical concepts such as id, mental representation, and attention, they diverge from nondevelopmental theories by emphasizing changes over time in these concepts.

This concern with change presents developmental theories with three tasks. These tasks are (1) to *describe* changes *within* one or several areas of behavior, (2) to *describe* changes in the relations *among* several areas of behavior, and (3) to *explain* the course of development that has been described. Let us look more closely at each of these three tasks.

1. A developmental theory describes changes over time in one or several areas of behavior or psychological activity, such as thought, language, social behavior, or perception. For example, a theory might describe changes in the rules of grammar underlying language in the first few years of life. Although developmental theories tend to stress changes over months or years, an adequate theory must ultimately describe changes over seconds, minutes, and days. For example, the object concept, the notion that objects exist even when we do not see them, may develop over many months, but a full description would include many "minidevelopments" that occur during the child's moment-to-moment encounters with objects.

Many people believe that description is based on neutral, objective observation and is prior to theory building. However, even direct observation is guided to some extent by theoretical notions that distort the flow of behavior in some way. Observers record certain behaviors and ignore others. They divide the stream of behavior into units. They encode the behavior into words that add connotations. They allow inference to creep into their observations. The following descriptions of the same behavior demonstrate that several degrees of inference are possible.

a. The baby's hand came closer and closer to the spinning top.

b. The baby reached for the spinning top.

c. The baby wanted to pick up the spinning top.

d. The baby applied his grasping scheme to the spinning top. (A scheme, according to Piaget, is an organized sequence of behavior that reflects an infant's knowledge in a particular area, such as grasping.)

Later in the chapter, we have more to say about the relationship between observation and theory.

Much of the early work in developmental psychology was almost exclusively concerned with description. In the 1930s, Arnold Gesell's maturational theory of development was directed toward establishing norms of physical, cognitive, and motor development through description. Although description is not sufficient for an adequate theory of development, it certainly is necessary. Without a data base, we have an "edifice without a foundation," in B. L. White's (1969) words.

2. A second task for a theory of development is to describe changes over time in the relations among behaviors or aspects of psychological activity within one area of development and, ideally, among several areas of development. A developmental theory tries to deal with the simultaneous changes in thought, personality, and perception that we observe. Developmental theorists are "specialized generalists" in that they are knowledgeable about many areas of psychology, but they specialize in the developmental approach to studying these content areas.

In the case of the object concept described above, a theory might describe how the concept relates to children's developing memory system and their social relationship with one particular object, their mother. A theory would outline the temporal relations among these areas of development. For example, a theory might claim that a certain degree of memory capacity must be developed before the object concept can emerge, that the mother is the first permanent object, and that subsequent developments within the object concept are correlated with changes in the memory system and children's attachment to their mother. Another example concerns the relationship between thought and language. One position, that of the Russian psychologist Lev Vygotsky, is that thought and language are relatively independent until they merge to produce symbolic thought. Both examples describe the organization within children at various points in time. The descriptions refer to certain sequences (first A, then B) and concurrences (A and B at the same time) that occur during development.

Of course, any attempt to divide behavior into parts is somewhat arbitrary because there is an interrelated system, or the famous "whole child." Nevertheless, since scientists are not superhumans, everything about the child cannot be studied at once. They break down the child before they can build it up again.

3. Even if a theory provides a full description of development, it has not accounted for the transitions from point to point during development. Thus, a third task for a developmental theory is to explain the course of development that the other two tasks describe. In fact, the sequences and concurrences identified in the first two tasks often suggest particular explanations. If skill B always appears shortly after the development of skill A, a psychologist may hypothesize that A causes B.

With respect to the third task, a developmental theory offers a set of general principles or rules for change. These principles specify necessary and sufficient antecedents for each change and identify variables that modify or modulate the rate or nature of each change. For example, Freud proposed that the biologically based drives "move" from the oral to the anal area and that the degree of the child's accompanying anxiety depends somewhat on the parents' child-rearing practices. In addition, principles of change hypothesize a set of processes for producing the change. These processes have been as diverse as dynamic equilibration in Piaget's theory, physical maturation in Freudian and ethological theory, and the strengthening of a response by reinforcement in learning theory.

One way to interpret developmental change is to hypothesize a continuity underlying the apparent change. For example, a theory might claim that dependency is expressed in different ways at different ages but that the underlying trait is the same. Or a theory might emphasize the underlying continuity in cognitive development by pointing to the gradual change in the understanding of number and by hypothesizing that what can be learned is limited by what number concepts the child already has. In more general terms, a theory may claim that concept, trait, skill, or behavior A is transformed into B, is replaced by B, combines with B to form C, and so forth. Most of the developmental theories we examine in this book posit an underlying continuity to the superficial changes during development.

When a theory explains why development proceeds in a certain way, it at the same time explains why certain other possible courses of development did not occur. Why did A lead to B rather than X? The significance of nonoccurrences is expressed by Sherlock Holmes:

" . . . the curious incident of the dog in the nighttime."

"The dog did nothing in the nighttime."

"That was the curious incident," remarked Sherlock Holmes.

[Sir Arthur Conan Doyle]

The discussion so far has avoided the question of exactly *what* should be described and explained. Should developmentalists emphasize universal change or individual differences? On the one hand, Piaget emphasizes concepts acquired in all racial and cultural groups. On the other hand, social learning theory emphasizes differences in various children's behavior that derive from the particular models, feedback, and learning situations to which the children are exposed. Throughout this book, we ask whether theorists should strive to describe and explain general, universal acquisitions or the acquisitions of any particular child or both.

It should be pointed out that listing the three tasks for developmental theories in a particular order should not imply that a theory approaches them in that order. Most commonly, a theory of development weaves back and forth among the three tasks. Progress on one of the tasks stimulates progress on another, which in turn feeds back to the first task or the third. A related point is that description and explanation are not as separate and independent as the list might imply. Attempts to describe change often bring in explanatory concepts, and the type of explanation that theorists offer is somewhat constrained by how they have described behavior.

These three monumental tasks, even if incompletely met in the near future, provide us with goals by which to measure the success of current theories of development. A more realistic expectation for the near future is that we can have theories that succeed in a more limited way. Theories may successfully describe and explain one particular area of development, such as language development, but not all areas. Or they may cover several areas but achieve only one or two of the three tasks. For example, a theory might competently describe changes in several areas but unsuccessfully explain these changes.

By the end of this book, it will have become clear that most theories are not equally concerned with these three tasks. Piaget is much more successful at describing the development of thought than explaining this development. In contrast, learning-theory and Vygotskian–contextual approaches have focused on mechanisms of change rather than the content of this change. No one theory has satisfactorily handled all three tasks, but each theory has contributed to at least one. As we examine each theory, we judge how well it has accomplished each of these tasks.

OF WHAT VALUE IS A DEVELOPMENTAL THEORY?

What does a developmental theory actually do when it describes and explains development? A theory makes two contributions: (1) it organizes and gives meaning to facts; (2) it guides further research. We examine each of these contributions in turn.

ORGANIZING INFORMATION

A developmental theory organizes and gives meaning to facts of development. Facts do not speak for themselves. As Jules Henri Poincaré (1908) said, "Science is built up of facts, as a house is built of stones; but an accumulation of facts is no more a science than a heap of stones is a house." Just as stones need an architect or a blueprint to become a house, so do facts need a theorist to give the facts structure and show their relation to the overall design. Thus, a theory gives meaning to facts, provides a framework for facts, assigns more importance to some facts than others, and integrates existing facts. One byproduct is that by summarizing and organizing information we are saved from "information overload." It is easier (but perhaps more dangerous) for us to refer to "defense mechanisms" than to state all the separate behaviors to which they refer.

Just as the same stones can be used to make different houses, so can a set of facts be given different meaning by different theories—by organizing them differently, emphasizing different behaviors, and inferring different hypothetical constructs. Consider the following example from McCain and Segal (1969). At one time, two theories explained the tendency of a falling rock to increase its speed as it approaches the earth. According to a popular Greek theory, rocks and earth like to be with each other because they are made of the same elements. As the rock gets closer to the earth, it travels faster because it becomes increasingly excited. The facts can also be explained by Newton's theory of universal gravitation. All particles attract each other with a force directly proportional to the product of their masses and inversely proportional to the square of their distances. These two theories are based on the same set of observations, but they assign different meaning to these facts.

When we view development through the lenses of first one theory and then another, we experience a gestaltlike shift. We see the child as seething with sexual energy or reflecting on the origins of the universe. We see the child as a bundle of conditioned responses or a highly organized system. At times, we may wonder if we are looking at the same child in these different perspectives. These theoretical shifts have been likened to shifts in the perception of ambiguous figures (Averill, 1976), such as the sudden perceptual shift of young woman to old woman in the illustration on the following page. The information has not changed, but our organization of it has.

The explosion of research on children in the last two decades makes it especially important to look at current theories or develop new

The lines in this drawing can be perceptually organized to form an old woman or a young woman.

theories to make sense of our information about children. All too often, textbooks on developmental psychology list empirical findings, much as a telephone book lists names and numbers. Although they briefly describe theories, they typically do not use these theories to organize facts other than those directly associated with the development of each theory.

GUIDING RESEARCH

In addition to giving meaning to facts, a theory serves a second function. It is a heuristic device, a tool to guide observation and to generate new information. A theory's abstract statements predict that certain empirical statements should be true. These empirical statements then must be tested. For example, Gibson's theory of perceptual development hypothesizes that attention to features that differentiate objects underlies much of perceptual development. In addition to organizing and giving meaning to a variety of previous research findings, this theory has led investigators to examine the roles of attention and the structure of objects and events in perceptual development. A further example comes from ethology, an approach borrowed from biology. This theory stimulated developmental psychologists to search for innate social behaviors that have contributed to the adaptation of the species to the environment.

Theories not only stimulate new observations but in some cases also cause us to reexamine familiar behavior and pay more attention to variables we have slighted. Piaget certainly was not the first person to watch babies play, but he suggested a new way of looking at this behavior: the actions themselves are creating thought, according to Piaget.

Theory's dual role as a stimulator and interpretor of data is nicely illustrated in a 22-year longitudinal study of aggression (Eron, 1987). Traditional learning theory, with its emphasis on drive reduction, guided the selection of the original variables in 1960. In later years, as new learning theories emerged, investigators interpreted the data first in terms of Skinnerian operant learning (early 1970s), then social learning (mid-1970s), and finally cognitive theory (mid-1980s). Thus, in these four phases of learning-theory development, investigators sought the causes of aggression in frustration (drive reduction), reinforcement of aggression (Skinner), aggressive models (social learning), and finally the child's attitudes and interpretation of potential instigators of aggression (cognition).

HOW ARE FACTS AND THEORIES RELATED?

The psychologist is never sure that what he does is "science." And if what he does is "science" he is never sure that it is psychology.

[Greco, 1967, p. 937]

Facts typically are defined as statements that are based on observations and are generally agreed on by several people. We accept this definition for the present, but it has many pitfalls, as we shall see later.

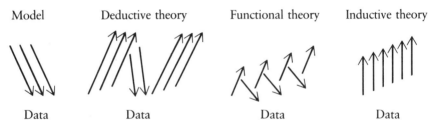

The relationship between theory and data defines four types of theory construction. [From "Formal Theory," by Melvin H. Marx. Reprinted with permission of Macmillan Publishing Co., Inc., from *Theories in Contemporary Psychology,* 2nd ed., edited by Melvin H. Marx and Felix E. Goodson. Copyright © 1976, Macmillian Publishing Co., Inc.]

Perhaps the best way to show the relation between facts and theories is to look at how facts are involved in theory construction. M. H. Marx (1976) has described four modes of interaction between theories and facts (data) that characterize theory construction. These are shown schematically in the accompanying illustration. The arrows show the direction of the relation between theory and data. The vertical lines indicate that the theory does little more than summarize the data. The diagonal lines indicate that data, theory, or both play a more dynamic role. The longer the line, the more removed the theory is from the data. Finally, the horizontal dimension represents the passage of time. We now examine the four basic ways of relating data and theory: models, deductive theories, functional theories, and inductive theories.

THE MODEL

A model is a framework, structure, or system that has been developed in one field and is then applied to another, usually less well-developed, field. The model stands for or represents something other than itself. It serves as an analogy or a metaphor to guide research and thinking. Examples are the early image of the nervous system as a telephone switchboard or the eye as a camera and the later notion of an instinct as a hydraulic system. More recently, thinking has been likened to an equilibration system (Piaget) or a computer (information-processing approach).

Since the model serves a heuristic function, there is a one-way influence between theory and data. The model suggests and guides research, but there is little interest in using the results of that research to modify the general model. More specific models, however, may be modified as a result of research. This is particularly true of information-processing theory, which takes the computer as a general model of thinking. This general model is not modified as a result of research, but the specific features of the processing model may change as a result of new data. These specific models often take the form of schematic diagrams consisting of boxes and arrows to represent the flow of information. The diagrammatic models are modified as a result of research.

In current usage, the term *model* has been used in another way that should not be confused with the use of the term here. *Model* sometimes replaces *theory* and connotes an undertaking that is more specific and limited than a general theory.

DEDUCTIVE THEORY

The earlier description of a formal theory refers to the deductive type of theory. A deductive theory is a logically organized set of propositions, stated in a formal way. These propositions include basic assumptions and definitions from which are deduced further propositions. There is a two-way relation between data and the theory in that theoretical propositions are continually tested and the results in turn modify the theory. Deductive theories are attractive because they are elegant and spell out all assumptions and implications of these assumptions. Good deductive theories are vulnerable simply because they cannot hide anything.

FUNCTIONAL THEORY

Most present-day theory construction falls into this category. Functional theory is much more informal and modest than deductive theory. Its propositions are closely related to data (as represented by the short arrows in the illustration on the facing page) and are often restricted to a particular experimental problem. There is a continual, rapid interplay between theory and data. General statements, or hypotheses, are suggested by a set of research findings. These general statements and their implications are then tested by further research. The general statements are then modified, and the process continues. For example, one might choose smiling in infancy as an experimental problem. A first hypothesis might be that recognition of an object causes smiling. Research, however, may show that this hypothesis is true only for certain ages and particular types of situations. The hypothesis is continually refined through modification and further testing.

Inductive Theory

An inductive theory consists of descriptive statements that summarize sets of data. Little inference is involved. An inductive theorist is someone who demands "just the facts." A one-way relation holds between data and theory: data lead to theory. Inductive theorists argue that collecting facts unbiased by interpretation eventually leads to statements that tie together the data. The best contemporary example of inductive theory is Skinner's operant conditioning theory (despite the fact that Skinner claims to have no theory at all). Statements in Skinner's inductive theory take the following form: If a response is followed by a reinforcer for several trials, the frequency of that response increases. Because of their belief in making minimal inferences from the data, inductive theorists are likely to react to more grandiose theories with "What's a nice fact like you doing in a theory like this?"

An Overview

These four modes of theory construction demonstrate that theories can generate research either by analogy, as in the model, or by deduction, as in deductive and functional theories. Data, in turn, generate theories by induction, test the deductions or specific models that are derived from theories, and ultimately modify theories, except in the case of general models. Empirical observation can never completely prove that a theory is true because future observations could provide disconfirming evidence.

The history of science shows that there may be a considerable lag between the gathering of data and the production of a theory. Data may not immediately suggest a particular theory. Darwin's *Origin of Species* was published more than 20 years after his voyage on the HMS *Beagle*. It took Kepler over 30 years to produce the three laws of planetary motion.

The four types of theories vary in how far the empirical observations are from the theoretical statements. Functional and inductive theories are closer than deductive theories or models to the data. For example, a learning theorist might refer to "stimulus," "response," and "punishment"—terms that are very close to observable objects or events. At the other extreme, Freud's "unconscious" or Piaget's "equilibration" process bears at best an uncertain and distant relationship to observable behavior.

The distance between theory and behavior is of considerable importance for two reasons.

1. The greater this distance, the more difficult it is to either support or weaken the theory. Much of scientific progress comes from showing that particular theories are wrong and correcting them. If a theory is so far from possible data that it can be neither confirmed nor disconfirmed (even in the future), it is of little value for science.

2. A second, related point is that the farther the distance between data and theory, the greater the number of theories that can be produced to explain the same set of facts. As we saw earlier, two theories were offered to explain observations about falling objects. Because of the distance between these theories and their observations, neither could be disproved. Sometimes theories are retained for years because their central claims are so far from possible observations that they cannot be tested and refuted.

To some extent, this section on theory building has presented a half-truth. In it, we have seen the conventional view of theory building presented. Theory building was pictured as an orderly, objective, logical process that involves four types of relations between facts and theories. This is a picture of scientists in their "dress clothes." Although science sometimes does proceed in this way, more often it proceeds in a much messier, irrational fashion to produce a polished final product.

More specifically, the conventional view of theory building implies that empirical observations are objective bits of information that we can use to make more general statements or to test statements derived from a theory. In reality, observations themselves are somewhat constrained by the observer's theoretical orientation, expectations based on previous research, beliefs about "human nature," and personal motivations. Facts do not simply present themselves to eager scientists for the purpose of developing a new theory or evaluating an existing one. For example, scientists hold certain assumptions that lead them to see certain facts more easily than others; in fact, it is difficult to see what we are not looking for. As an illustration, radio signals from Jupiter had been heard—but ignored—for many years before two young American astronomers "discovered" these signals in 1955 and recognized their significance.

The scientist's social and political beliefs can be especially biasing in a field such as psychology, in which people are studying people. The psychologist holds a mirror rather than a telescope. If a psychologist assumes that humans are basically rational, he is more likely to study thought than emotions, more likely to become a Piaget than a Freud. Developmental psychologists do not escape their culture's views. As Scarr observed, "We pose questions to fit our place and time; we get answers to fit our theoretical niches" (1985, p. 204). She argued that we change our scientific lenses as the culture changes. Scarr noted that in the 1950s and 1960s social scientists expected, and thus looked for, evidence that boys in "broken homes" were affected negatively by the lack of a father. The finding that these boys, when young, were observed to be low in aggression was taken as evidence for poor sex-role development. After the women's movement and the emergence of nontraditional families, it is no longer automatically assumed that negative effects accompany a father's absence. With today's less rigid view of desirable masculine and feminine traits or behavior, low aggression in a boy may not be seen as a deficit.

Individual psychologists' personality and motivations also influence the particular direction their research takes, a point demonstrated by learning theorist E. C. Tolman:

> I started out . . . with considerable uneasiness. I felt that my so-called system was outdated and that it was a waste of time to try to rehash it and that it would be pretentious now to seek to make it fit any accepted set of prescriptions laid down by the philosophy of science. I have to confess, however, that as I have gone along I have become again more and more involved in it, though I still realize its many weak points. The system may well not stand up to any final canons of scientific procedure. But I do not much care. I have liked to think about psychology in ways that have proved congenial to me. Since all the sciences, and especially psychology, are still immersed in such tremendous realms of the uncertain and the unknown, the best that any individual scientist, especially any psychologist, can do seems to be to follow his own gleam and his own bent, however inadequate they may be. In fact I suppose that actually this is what we all do. In the end, the only sure criterion is to have fun. And I have had fun.

> *[1959, p. 152]*

Because of all these influences on scientists, when they make an observation or discover a fact, they are not neutral fact finders. As mentioned earlier in the discussion about the task of describing in developmental psychology, investigators do not simply record reality. They have, often unconsciously, already made decisions about what facet of behavior to study, what measures to use, how to divide up the "stream of behavior," how to collect the data, and how to score the data. Each decision further constrains what facts can be observed. A one-minute episode of a baby playing could be described or measured in thousands of ways. There are different levels of behavior, from heart rate to pattern of manual exploration, and different behavioral temporal units, from a fraction of a second to an entire minute. Which facts or observations the psychologist chooses from the thousands of candidates tells us as much about the psychologist or her theory as about the episode of behavior itself. These constraints on what is observed are necessary, of course, because it is not feasible to record everything.

This discussion of facts, theories, and theory construction was intended to prepare the reader for the specific theories that follow, not to serve as a crash course in the philosophy of science. It should be kept in mind that this simplified account ignores many controversies in the history of ideas. Also, we have given little attention to the disagreement among philosophers of science about the distinctions between such terms as *hypothetical constructs, laws, hypotheses,* and *postulates*. These controversies and the more subtle aspects of metatheory can be found in the suggested readings at the end of this chapter. The reader is encouraged to explore these problems.

WHAT ARE THE MAIN ISSUES OF DEVELOPMENTAL PSYCHOLOGY?

Although the theories to be covered differ in their content, methods of investigation, and formal nature, they share the need to take a position on certain core issues of development. Developmental change, by its very nature, leads to these issues. There are four critical issues:

1. What is the basic nature of humans?

2. Is development qualitative or quantitative?

3. How do nature and nurture contribute to development?

4. What is it that develops?

These issues, which serve as a way of summarizing and contrasting the theories, reappear at the end of each chapter. First, however, some discussion of each issue is in order.

WHAT IS THE BASIC NATURE OF HUMANS?

A theorist's view of development is closely tied to his view of human nature. His view of human nature, in turn, is closely tied to his world view, or his notion about how the universe works. In the history of the Western world, there have been three basic world views of great relevance to the study of psychology (Overton, 1984; Reese, 1991): the mechanistic, the organismic, and the contextual. We examine each of these.

In the mechanistic view, the world is like a machine composed of parts that operate in time and space. For example, the world could be likened to a watch. Forces are applied to the parts and cause a chain reaction that moves the machine from state to state. In principle, then, complete prediction is possible because complete knowledge of the state and forces at one point in time allows us to infer the next state. This mechanistic view has its roots in Newtonian physics. It is also related to the empiricist philosophy of Locke (1632–1704) and Hume (1711–1776), which pictures the human as inherently at rest—a passive robot, motivated by external sources. Development, consequently, is caused by external forces and events acting on a passive, machinelike mind composed of interlocking parts. One can almost see the wheels turning in the child's head!

In contrast, the organismic world view is modeled on living systems, such as plants or animals, rather than machines. This image derives from Leibniz (1646–1716), who believed that substance is in "a continuous transition from one state to another as it produces these states out of itself in unceasing succession" (Cassirer, 1951, p. 29). Leibniz pictured the world as composed of organized "wholes" that are inherently and spontaneously active and self-regulating. This organization is necessary, or natural, given the nature of the organism. This view emphasizes the whole rather than its parts, the relations among the parts, and how the whole gives meaning to its parts. In the realm of psychology, visual perception, for example, cannot be understood by looking only at the processes of the retina, optic nerve, visual areas of the cortex, and so on. The whole must be considered, including other perceptual systems and higher cognitive functions.

Rather than look for antecedent causes, as the mechanistic world view has done, the organismic view considers inherent properties and goals. The human, by nature, is an active, organized whole and is constantly changing, not randomly but in a particular direction. Development, then, is inherent in humans. Self-initiated behavior and thought lead to changes in both the structure and the content of behavior and thought. S. H. White describes an active organism:

> Let us define an active organism as one that gives form to its experience, a passive organism as one that receives form from its experience. Active organisms have purposes and they attend, reason, and selectively perceive. All this enables the active organism to select, modify, or reject environmental influences pressing upon it.
>
> *[1976, p. 100]*

Because so many examples of the organismic and mechanistic world views will emerge throughout this book, a single one will serve us at this point. With respect to acquiring knowledge about the world, the organismic view is that children "construct" their knowledge by actively formulating and testing hypotheses about categories of objects and the causes of events. In contrast, the mechanistic view is that children passively acquire ("soak up" like a sponge) a copy of reality. Organismic, unlike mechanistic, theories are usually stage theories, which posit qualitative rather than gradual change.

According to the third world view, contextualism, a behavior has meaning (and can be "explained") only in terms of its social–historical context. The pragmatist philosophers such as William James and George Herbert Mead provide the philosophical inspiration. As Pepper describes contextualism, it

> takes for its root metaphor the textured event, with its richly qualitied strands fading into a past that dies and guiding the changing pattern of a present duration into a future that dawns. The event through its texture extends sidewise in its present duration into neighboring contexts which are themselves textures extending into still other contexts. And the texture of each event is internally analyzable into strands, which have individual tensions and references into other textures.
>
> *[1934, p. 183]*

Thus, the metaphor is not a machine or a living system but a tapestry extending from the distant past to the distant future and from the proximal to the distal. These horizontal temporal and vertical spatial threads intermesh into a pattern of a human life.

We study this tapestry of development by looking at ongoing action–event units consisting of meaningful goal-directed activities. As Reese explains it, "Writing is not an act; but writing something with something on something in some situation at some time is an act"

(1991, pp. 191–192). Reese lists other components of the contextual metaphor: the meaning of a behavior varies from context to context; a math problem may involve feelings of competence in the school environment but spell survival for a homeless child street vendor. Moreover, behavior has a purpose that reaches into the past (some proximal "cause") and into the future (some goal). Finally, like the organismic view, the contextualist view is wholistic. Not only is a unit greater than the sum of its parts, but a unit-in-context is greater than the sum of a unit and its context. To continue the writing example, writing a sentence "is an act but is also a part of the larger act that includes writing about the act of writing the sentence, which in turn is part of the larger act that includes writing an entire paper, which in turn is part of the larger act that is the writer's lifetime, which in turn is part of the larger act that includes others' lifetimes, etc." (Reese, 1991, p. 194).

In addition to these three metaphysical views of humans, the world, and causality are more specific and limited views based on particular economic and political ideologies. For example, Riegel (1972) relates views of childhood and development to the capitalistic and mercantilistic politicoeconomic systems in the seventeenth to nineteenth centuries.

The capitalistic system, largely Anglo-American, saw humans as competitive, as struggling for success. Thomas Hobbes' (1588–1679) pronouncement of humans as selfish and competitive and of life as "nasty, brutish, and short" expressed this notion. The roots continue through Charles Darwin, who stressed the survival of the fittest. In the economic arena, the emphasis was on free trade, competition, and entrepreneurship. The standard of success (as a result of struggle and competition) was the white, middle-class adult male engaged in manufacturing or business. By this standard, children, the elderly, mental defectives, and women were considered inferior. Childhood, considered a state of incomplete adulthood, was a "disability." Normative descriptions of each age were developed to detect "abnormal" development and chart children's progress toward the adult standard of success. Society saw children as passive beings who must be molded ("socialized") into appropriate adult roles.

The mercantilistic ideology, in contrast, was found primarily in continental Europe in the seventeenth through the nineteenth centuries. The economy was based on land ownership and state-controlled trading more than on manufacturing and free trade. Distinct social classes enjoyed specified duties and privileges, and little competition between classes occurred. Society emphasized cooperation more than competition; differences between groups were tolerated. The main philosophical spokesman, Jean Jacques Rousseau (1712–1778), saw the child as a "noble savage," basically good but ruined by the adult world. Children were not to be judged by adult standards; children and adults were seen as qualitatively different. From this point of view, the goal of education was self-realization. Consequently, a child-oriented education was developed by Maria Montessori, Eduard Spranger, and others.

From even this brief account of changing history, it is easy to see how each theory of developmental psychology always has a view of the human being that reflects philosophical, economic, and political beliefs. This view is often implicit, and sometimes theorists themselves are not even aware of these assumptions. The view influences not only theory construction but also decisions about which research problems are meaningful, what method should be used, and how data should be interpreted. Even the meanings of the terms "explanation" and "fact" are different in theories with different world views. For these reasons, it is sometimes claimed that it is impossible to integrate or reconcile theories or make crucial tests that support one or the other if they have different world views.

IS DEVELOPMENT QUALITATIVE OR QUANTITATIVE?

Closely related to these views of humans is the issue of the basis of developmental change: is it qualitative or quantitative? The mechanistic and capitalistic views emphasize quantitative change, the organismic and mercantilistic approaches emphasize qualitative change, and contextualism permits both. Qualitative changes refer to changes in kind or type. An example from nature is the following sequence: egg → caterpillar → cocoon → butterfly (Spiker, 1966). New phenomena or characteristics emerge that cannot be reduced to previous elements. Qualitative changes typically involve changes in structure or organization. In contrast, quantitative changes refer to changes in amount, frequency, or degree. In some cases, the behavior becomes more efficient or consistent. The change is gradual and occurs in small increments. Bits and pieces of knowledge, habits, or skills are acquired during development.

An example of the contrast between quantitative and qualitative change can be found in the development of memory. If a 4-year-old can recall three objects and a 7-year-old can recall seven objects from a set of objects seen several minutes earlier, we might infer a quantitative difference in their mental functioning: the older child can remember more. However, if the 7-year-old uses strategies such as organizing the objects into classes and rehearsing them, whereas the 4-year-old does not, we would infer a qualitative difference in their mental functioning: they process the information in a different way.

At a more general level, the issue of qualitative versus quantitative change becomes an issue of stage versus nonstage development. When there are similarities in a number of new abilities or behaviors during a period of time, a theorist often infers that the child is in a particular "stage." For example, Piaget posits stagelike qualitative changes in the structure of thought from birth to adolescence. Stage theorists disagree about the possibility of being in more than one stage at the same time or of regressing to an earlier stage, and they argue about what causes children to differ in how fast they pass through the stages.

Stagelike, qualitative changes have been identified by scholars other than developmental psychologists. Historians identify periods in history, such as the "industrial age" or the "age of reason"; Shakespeare saw seven ages of man from the "mewling and puking" infant to the old person "sans teeth, sans eyes, sans taste, sans everything."

Despite their arguments about which developmental changes are qualitative and which quantitative, most developmentalists agree that both types of changes occur. Some behaviors involve both qualitative and quantitative changes. In some cases the periods of quantitative and qualitative change appear to alternate. Using the memory example presented earlier, one might find an increase in the number of items rotely memorized (quantitative change). This increase in memory may eventually be followed by the development of a strategy (qualitative change) of putting together items from the same category, say, foods, furniture, and toys. Subsequent increases in the speed and accuracy of this clustering would involve quantitative change.

How Do Nature and Nurture Contribute to Development?

Regardless of the extent to which development is qualitative or quantitative, a theorist must refer to the underlying causes of development. The basic issue is whether knowledge and behavior are derived from one's genetic endowment or from experience in the world. The nature–nurture issue is known by several other labels, such as "heredity versus environment," "nativism versus empiricism," "biology versus culture," "maturation versus learning," and "innate versus acquired abilities."

This controversy has raged not only within psychology but also within philosophy. The controversy began in classical Greek times when philosophers asked whether ideas are innate or acquired through the experience of the senses. For example, Plato (427–347 B.C.) believed that ideas are innate because the soul, which exists before birth in the realm of ideas, is trapped by the body at birth. Later, medieval Christian philosophers proclaimed the innate depravity of man, and later still the French philosopher Rousseau (1712–1778) proclaimed innate goodness. On one side, Descartes (1596–1650) believed that certain ideas are innate, while on the other side the British empiricist Locke (1632–1704) argued that the newborn's mind is a blank slate *(tabula rasa)* on which experience writes. The debate continued through the history of psychology. In developmental psychology today "nature" theorists are represented by the ethologists and psychobiologists (Chapter 5) and modularity theorists (e.g., Fodor, 1983). According to the latter, the mind is a collection of *mental modules*, which are specialized innate mental abilities devoted to a single domain. Examples are processing language, recognizing faces or facial expressions, and concepts of physical causality, number, and the mind. The strongest "nurture" developmental approaches today are social learning theory and Vygotsky–contextualism.

Anastasi (1958) points out that we did not ask the right question in the past. We should not have asked *which* (heredity or environment) causes a behavior or *how much* of each is needed for a given behavior. Instead, we should ask *how* (in what manner) nature and nurture interact to produce development. This is an interesting illustration of how progress in a field sometimes simply means learning how to ask the right question.

Today nearly everyone agrees that the interaction of innate and environmental factors accounts for both the development of a trait or behavior in an individual and the variations in a trait or behavior among individuals. Nature and nurture are inextricably intertwined. Both nature and nurture are fully involved in the development of any behavior. Hebb (1980) concluded that behavior is determined 100 percent by heredity and 100 percent by environment. Genes are never expressed directly in behavior. There is a long chain of events involving genes, physiological processes, and the environment. The way that heredity is expressed depends on the specific environment in which this expression occurs. In other words, a given hereditary influence can have different behavioral effects in different environments. And, conversely, a given environment can have different effects on people with different genetic makeups. A jack-in-the-box might delight a placid baby but disturb a nervous, reactive infant who is upset by sudden change. Moreover, intense stressful events that cause disturbances in most children have little effect on so-called resilient children (Garmezy & Tellegen, 1984). To complicate matters even further, environmental influences actually can have a genetic basis. For example, an innately active, exuberant child and a passive, quiet, reflective child will select different types of play settings. Thus, they are exposed to different types of experiences. Finally, genes and the environment can be correlated, as when shy parents both pass on a tendency toward shyness genetically and provide an environment that encourages shyness (Plomin, DeFries, & Loehlin, 1977).

The theories presented in this book differ in whether they emphasize the nature or the nurture part of the interaction. In addition, they disagree about the process by which either environmental or innate factors have their influence. For example, the environment can "stamp in" associations, provide models to be imitated, or supply information to be assimilated.

There are several possible ways in which experience can have an influence. Wohlwill (1973) has proposed four models.

1. In the first, or "hospital-bed," model, people are acted on by the environment, as if they were helpless hospital patients. This condition is most likely in the first few months of life.

2. In the "amusement-park" model, people select certain features of the environment to experience. However, once they select certain stimuli, they have little control over their effect on them: "Once he has decided to partake of the roller-coaster ride, there is little he can do to alter the experience he will derive from it" (p. 101).

3. The third, or "swim-meet," model likens experience to a swimming race in which "from the sound of the gun the individual's behavior takes its course in virtual independence from environmental stimuli" (p. 101). The environment is merely a supportive context for the person's behaviors.

4. In the "tennis-match" model, there is an interaction between the influences of the environment and the person. Tennis players must adapt to the way their opponent (the environment) returns the ball. However, they influence the opponent's behavior by hitting a lob or volleying.

As these four models demonstrate, a theory's conception of the influence of the environment is closely related to the theory's view of humans as active or passive, a distinction we noted earlier.

Finally, theories differ in how much importance they place on the timing of a particular experience. Are there "critical periods" in which the child is especially sensitive to a particular experience? Is early experience more influential than later experience?

WHAT IS IT THAT DEVELOPS?

Each theorist makes a claim concerning the "essence" of development, or at least the proper unit of analysis. Throughout this book, we encounter various phenomena, such as cognitive structures, psychic structures (id, ego, superego), strategies of information processing, fixed action patterns, perceptual exploration, and psychological tools. What theorists see as the essence of development depends on where their theoretical assumptions and methods of study place them along several dimensions.

1. Their level of analysis (from molecular to molar).

2. Whether they focus on structure (organization of behavior, thought, and personality) or process (dynamic, functioning aspects of the system).

3. What content they emphasize (for example, personality or cognition).

4. Whether they emphasize overt behavior or covert thought and personality.

5. What methodology they use to study development.

These five dimensions have a chicken-and-egg relationship: Which came first, ethologists' decision to study complex, molar behavior acquired by species in their struggle to adapt to the environment or their choice of a methodology, namely, observations in natural settings? This interrelationship among the dimensions will become more obvious as we examine each theory.

SUMMARY

The traditional view of an "ideal" scientific theory is that it should be a hypotheticodeductive system and include a set of logically interconnected statements. It formally describes psychological structures and processes and relates them to each other and to observable events. However, in several ways, this picture of psychological theories is incomplete. In addition to deductive theories, there are models, functional theories, and inductive theories, which are less elaborate and formalized. Most psychological "theories" have failed to achieve the status of a theory in the strict definition of the term. Another way in which the traditional view of theories is incomplete is that a theory has not only a public, formal, static nature but also a private, informal, dynamic nature. Theory building is objective and subjective, orderly and disorderly. A theory plays an important informal role as it guides the behavior of psychologists doing research. It helps the psychologist formulate questions, choose what to study, and decide how to study a problem.

We need developmental theories. They help us describe and explain developmental changes by organizing and giving meaning to facts and by guiding further research. Developmental theories have taken a stand on four issues that are of special importance to the study of development:

1. What is the basic nature of the human?

2. Is development qualitative or quantitative?

3. How do nature and nurture contribute to development?

4. What is it that develops?

We now have a framework for viewing each of the theories in turn.

A WORD ABOUT THIS BOOK

The following seven chapters describe seven major theories of development. Piaget's theory is presented first because many of the current issues in developmental psychology were raised by his theory. Next come the other two big theories of development: psychoanalytic theory and social learning theory. The next three theories are directed toward more limited areas of development. The information-processing approach examines thinking, particularly memory, ethology focuses on early social behavior, and Gibson's theory analyzes perceptual development. Vygotskian–contextualist theory is presented last because it has had the most recent impact on the field of developmental psychology. Each chapter follows roughly the same organization, in order to make comparisons among the theories easier. At the end of each chapter, the theory is evaluated in terms of its strengths and weaknesses, according to the current state of developmental psychology. That is, we ask what each theory can contribute to today's developmental researchers, professionals who work with children, and parents.

Suggested Readings

The following books serve as helpful guides to philosophical issues in theory construction.

Bergmann, G. (1957). *Philosophy of science.* Madison: University of Wisconsin Press. Bergmann discusses issues of theory construction in various sciences.

Hempel, C. C. (1966). *Philosophy of natural science.* Englewood Cliffs, NJ: Prentice-Hall. This book is a useful simple introduction to the nature of scientific theories.

Marx, M. H., & Goodson, F. E. (Eds.). (1976). *Theories in contemporary psychology* (2nd ed.). New York: Macmillan. This collection of reprinted papers and new essays covers a wide range of issues and problems in theory building and evaluation, especially in the field of psychology.

The following sources are oriented to issues in developmental theories.

Lerner, R. M. (1986). *Concepts and theories of human development* (2nd ed.). Reading, MA: Addison-Wesley.

Horowitz, F. D. (1987). *Exploring developmental theories.* Hillside, NJ: Erlbaum.

Overton, W. F. (1984). World views and their influence on psychological theory and research: Kuhn–Lakatos–Laudan. In H. W. Reese (Ed.), *Advances in child development and behavior* (Vol. 18). Orlando, FL: Academic Press.

Thomas, R. M. (1992). *Comparing theories of child development* (3rd ed.). Belmont, CA: Wadsworth. Chapters 1 and 2.

1

PIAGET'S COGNITIVE-STAGE THEORY

[At 7 months, 28 days] Jacqueline tries to grasp a cel-luloid duck on top of her quilt. She almost catches it, shakes herself, and the duck slides down beside her. It falls very close to her hand but behind a fold in the sheet. Jacqueline's eyes have followed the movement, she has even followed it with her outstretched hand. But as soon as the duck has disappeared—nothing more! It does not occur to her to search behind the fold of the sheet, which would be very easy to do (she twists it mechanically without searching at all).
[PIAGET, 1937 (1954, p. 36)]

Hub (age 6 1/2): Is the moon always round?—No.— What's it like?—Sometimes a crescent, it is very worn out.—Why?—Because it has done a lot of lighting.— How does it come round again?—Because it is made again.—How?—In the sky.
[PIAGET, 1926 (1929, p. 281)]

ntriguing glimpses of children's behavior and thought, such as those on the preceding page, fired Piaget's imagination. In these unremarkable daily events, Piaget saw a remarkable process of cognitive development. In Piaget's view, moment-to-moment specific encounters with objects or people lead to general ways of understanding the world. This understanding changes during development as thinking progresses through various stages from birth to maturity. Moreover, children themselves actively construct this knowledge.

Piaget's theory is the most widely known theory of cognitive development. His influence has spread not only throughout the disciplines of psychology but also into areas such as education and philosophy. Moreover, his theory raised issues of development that the other theories must address. It is appropriate, then, to begin our look at theories with the cognitive-structural theory of Jean Piaget.

This chapter can only hint at the complexity of Piaget's theory. We first delve into Piaget's life in some detail in order to clarify his theory and to illustrate the close relationship between the personality of a theorist and the nature of his theory. After this biography comes a general orientation to the theory, then a description of the stages and other developmental changes, followed by a discussion of the mechanisms of development. The next section relates cognitive-structural theory to the critical issues of development and to the characteristics of theories presented in the introduction. Near the end of the chapter, Piaget's theory is evaluated in a contemporary context. The chapter ends with a description of Piaget's own modifications of his theory to supplement the more traditional version presented in the chapter, along with an overview of work of the neo-Piagetians.

BIOGRAPHICAL SKETCH

Jean Piaget was born in 1896 in Neuchâtel, Switzerland.* Piaget described his father, a historian devoted to medieval literature, as "a man of a painstaking and critical mind, who dislikes hastily improvised generalizations, and is not afraid of starting a fight when he finds historic truth twisted to fit respectable traditions" (1952, p. 237). Piaget

---

* Most of the material in this biographical sketch comes from Piaget's autobiography, which appears in a book edited by E. G. Boring et al., *A history of psychology in autobiography*, Vol. 4 (Worcester, MA: Clark University Press, 1952).

remembered his mother as intelligent, energetic, and kind, but with a neurotic temperament that drove him to both imitate his father and escape to what Piaget called a "private and nonfictitious world," a world of serious work. Piaget acknowledged that the turbulent family situation aroused his interest in psychoanalytic theory.

It would be easier to list what did not interest the boy Piaget than what did. A sampling of his interests includes mechanics, seashells, birds, and fossils. One of his early writings was a pamphlet (written in pencil because he was not yet allowed to write in ink) describing an "autovap," an intriguing union of a wagon and a locomotive. Piaget's first publication was a one-page article about a partly albino sparrow he had observed in a park. This achievement came at age 10—long before he had heard of "publish or perish"! Piaget's interest in the exhibits in the local natural history museum led to an invitation to assist the director with his mollusk (shellfish) collections. In this way Piaget entered the field of malacology, the study of mollusks, which captivated him for years to come. Piaget's publications on mollusks attracted notice among natural historians. He was offered, sight unseen, the curatorship of mollusks at a natural history museum in Geneva. He had to decline the offer, however, because he had not yet finished secondary school!

Piaget did not escape the typical social and philosophical crises of adolescence. Conflicts between his religious and scientific teachings stimulated him to read hungrily through Bergson, Kant, Spencer, Comte, Durkheim, and William James, among others. This philosophical turmoil is expressed in his philosophical novel published in 1917. That this novel did not become a best-seller can be surmised from passages such as these: "Now there can be no awareness of these qualities, hence these qualities cannot exist, if there are no relationships among them, if they are not, consequently, blended into a total quality which contains them while keeping them distinct," and "positive theory of quality taking into account only relationships of equilibrium and disequilibrium among our qualities" (1952, p. 243). Piaget observed that "no one spoke of it except one or two indignant philosophers" (1952, p. 243).

Piaget continued to write on a variety of philosophical issues. He noted: "I wrote even if it was only for myself, for I could not think without writing—but it had to be in a systematic fashion as if it were to be an article for publication" (1952, p. 241). In these writings, one finds themes that are central in Piaget's later writings, for example, the logical organization of actions and the relationship between the parts and the whole.

Piaget continued his formal studies in the natural sciences and took his doctoral degree with a thesis on mollusks at the University of Neuchâtel in 1918 at age 21. Although he had published twenty papers by this time, he was not eager to devote his life to malacology. After visiting psychological laboratories in Zurich and exploring psychoanalytic theory briefly, Piaget spent two years at the Sorbonne. There he studied psychology and philosophy. By luck (for the field of developmental psychology), Piaget met Theodore Simon, a pioneer in the development of intelligence tests. Simon, who had at his disposal Alfred Binet's laboratory at a grade school in Paris, suggested that Piaget standardize Binet's reasoning tests on Parisian children. Piaget began the work with little enthusiasm. However, his interest was aroused when he began questioning children about the reasons underlying both their correct and their incorrect answers. He became fascinated with the thought processes that appeared to lead to the answers. In these "conversations," Piaget used psychiatric techniques he had learned while interviewing mental patients for his courses at the Sorbonne. Without Simon's knowledge, Piaget continued this research for two years. Piaget summed up this experience:

> At last I had found my field of research. First of all it became clear to me that the theory of the relations between the whole and the part can be studied experimentally through analysis of the psychological processes underlying logical operations. This marked the end of my "theoretical" period and the start of an inductive and experimental era in the psychological domain which I always had wanted to enter, but for which until then I had not found the suitable problems. . . . my aim of discovering a sort of embryology of intelligence fit in with my biological training; from the start of my theoretical thinking I was certain that the problem of the relation between the organism and environment extended also into the realm of knowledge, appearing here as the problem of the relation between the acting or thinking subject and the objects of his experience. Now I had the chance of studying this problem in terms of psychogenetic development.
>
> *[1952, p. 245]*

The subsequent publication of three articles based on this research in Binet's laboratory led to an offer in 1921 to become director of studies at the Institut J. J. Rousseau in Geneva. Piaget planned to spend only five years studying child psychology (a plan that, happily, went awry). The freedom and research facilities of this position nurtured Piaget's productive tendencies and led to the publication of five books: *The Language and Thought of the Child* (1923), *Judgment and Reasoning in the Child* (1924), *The Child's Conception of the World* (1926), *The Child's Conception of Physical Causality* (1927), and *The Moral*

Judgment of the Child (1932). To his surprise, the books were read and discussed widely. He became known as a child psychologist, even though he had no university degree in psychology. He was much sought after as a speaker, and his fame grew rapidly in Europe. This public attention was somewhat disquieting to Piaget, in part because he considered his ideas in these books to be quite preliminary and tenuous, rather than the final statement that many people considered them to be.

In the following few years, Piaget continued his research at the Institut Rousseau, taught philosophy at the University of Neuchâtel, learned about Gestalt psychology, observed his own babies, and even performed some research on mollusks in his free time. From 1929 to 1945, he occupied several academic and administrative positions at the University of Geneva, as well as international posts, such as President of the Swiss Commission of UNESCO. There were productive collaborations with Alina Szeminska, Bärbel Inhelder, and Marcel Lambercier on the manipulation of objects, the development of perception, and the notions of number, physical quantity, and space. Hearing of Piaget's work, Albert Einstein encouraged him to study the concepts of time, velocity, and movement. Two provocative books emerged from this suggestion: *The Child's Conception of Time* (1946a) and *The Child's Conception of Movement and Speed* (1946b).

The 1940s and 1950s were marked by research on an amazing range of topics: various aspects of mental development, education, the history of thought, logic, and his old passion, epistemology, or theory of knowledge. His titles included Professor of Psychology at the University of Geneva and the Sorbonne, Director of the Institut des Sciences de l'Education, and Director of the Bureau International de l'Education. In addition, he founded the Centre d'Epistémologie Génétique, a meeting ground for philosophers and psychologists. In 1969, the American Psychological Association gave Piaget the Distinguished Scientific Contribution Award "for his revolutionary perspective on the nature of human knowledge and biological intelligence" (Evans, 1973, p. 143). He was the first European to receive this award.

Piaget pursued the riddle of children's thinking until his death in 1980, at the age of 84. Even in his final years, books and articles continued to stream from his home, the Center for Genetic Epistemology. His flowing white hair, pipe, beret, and bicycle were a familiar sight in Geneva. We have the following description of Piaget at age 70: "He moves deliberately, but his blue eyes sparkle with youth, good humor and zest. Benevolent enough, but not heavy enough, to look like Santa Claus, he reminds one faintly of the pictures of Franz Liszt that have come down to us" (Tuddenham, 1966, p. 208).

One cannot help but be struck by Piaget's amazing productivity. A conservative estimate of his writing is over 40 books and more than 100 articles on child psychology alone. Adding publications in philosophy and education swells these numbers even more. Piaget attributed his productivity, in part, to his helpful colleagues, but he also gave us the following interesting glimpse into his personality:

> And then, too, I owe it to a particular bent of my character. Fundamentally I am a worrier whom only work can relieve. It is true I am sociable and like to teach or to take part in meetings of all kinds, but I feel a compelling need for solitude and contact with nature. After mornings spent with others, I begin each afternoon with a walk during which I quietly collect my thoughts and coordinate them, after which I return to the desk at my home in the country. . . . it is this dissociation between myself as a social being and as a "man of nature" (in whom Dionysian excitement ends in intellectual activity) which has enabled me to surmount a permanent fund of anxiety and transform it into a need for working.
>
> *[1952, p. 255]*

GENERAL ORIENTATION TO THE THEORY

The wise tourist begins to explore an unfamiliar city by setting out on a guided tour, with map in hand. This experience gives the tourist a "feel" for the city—its general structure, tempo, and major landmarks. Similarly, Piaget's theory is best approached by an overview that presents the Piagetian landscape. The quick guided tour that follows attempts to give the reader a "feel" for Piaget's theory before exploring the nooks and crannies—and perhaps becoming lost. Because Piaget's theory is complex and notoriously difficult to understand, we approach it first at a general level, then at a more specific level. We examine the following salient characteristics of the theory: genetic epistemology, the biological approach, structuralism, the stage approach, and methodology. The orientation both describes these characteristics and relates them to Piaget's interests and goals.

As a preface to the rest of this chapter, it should be noted that Piaget acknowledged the contributions of his coworkers. Although this is a chapter on Piaget's theory, much of the work it describes was done in collaboration with a number of people, especially Bärbel Inhelder.

GENETIC EPISTEMOLOGY

Perhaps the most incomprehensible thing about the world is that it is comprehensible.

[Albert Einstein]

Piaget might well have agreed with Einstein, for he had a lifelong fascination with how humans comprehend the world. The branch of philosophy concerned with the study of knowledge is called epistemology. As Piaget viewed it, epistemology is "the problem of the relation between the acting or thinking subject and the objects of his experience" (1952, p. 245). Piaget tackled the same questions that have engaged philosophers for centuries: How do we come to know something? Is objective knowledge, unbiased by the nature of the knower, even possible? Are there certain innate ideas, or must all knowledge be acquired? All of Piaget's writings can be seen as attempts to answer these questions in different content areas, for example, mathematics, moral reasoning, and language. As we saw in our biographical sketch of Piaget, his philosophical quest led him through various schools of philosophy, biology, history, mathematics, and psychology. His search finally stopped at developmental psychology, which was not even an organized field of study at the time.

Piaget's journey to developmental psychology brings us to the "genetic" part of the term *genetic epistemology*. "Genetic" refers not to what is innate, the more common meaning of the term today, but to "development" or "emergence." By studying developmental changes in the process of knowing and in the organization of knowledge, Piaget felt that he could find answers to the traditional questions of epistemology. His concern with the classical issues in epistemology explains his concern with what philosophers have considered the basic categories of thought: time, space, causality, and quantity. These categories of thought are obvious to an adult but, in Piaget's way of thinking, may not be obvious to children. Piaget wondered how and when children understand that no two objects can occupy the same place, that two contiguous events can have a causal relationship, and that a specific event cannot occur both before and after some other event. It may be as difficult for young children to understand these concepts as it is for adults to understand black holes in space or the theory of relativity.

Piaget could be called an experimental epistemologist. Unlike most epistemologists, who used logical arguments to support their views, Piaget rejected the armchair approach and formulated empirical hypotheses that could be tested. For example, he examined the question of how humans acquire concepts of time, space, and causality by tracing the development of these concepts. Thus, Piaget's brand of epistemology is a marriage of philosophy and the scientific method, of logic and fact.

Piaget's solution to the problem of epistemology involved the simple but revolutionary claim that knowledge is a process rather than a state. It is an event or a relationship between the knower and the known. A child knows or understands a ball or a rattle by acting on it—physically or mentally. In a sense, people "construct" knowledge. They have an active part in the process of knowing and even contribute to the form that knowledge takes. Cognitive humans actively select and interpret information in the environment. They do not passively soak up information to build a storehouse of knowledge.

Children's knowledge of the world changes as their cognitive system develops. As the knower changes, so does the known. A concrete example is the knowledge of relationships in space. Infants construct a practical knowledge of near and far, up and down. Older children construct a more abstract "cognitive map" of the relations among objects in their environment. Infants "know" space by crawling in it and reaching for objects, whereas older children know space by manipulating mental symbols in particular ways. Note that in both cases there is a constant interaction between the knower and the external world.

One implication of Piaget's theory of knowledge is that knowledge is biased. Experience is always filtered through the child's current ways of understanding. A child's mind is not a camera that takes faithful pictures of reality. However, as the mind develops, it becomes more in tune with reality.

BIOLOGICAL APPROACH

Beginning with the early boyhood interest in shells and birds, Piaget's thinking was firmly rooted in biology. Piaget's distinction is that he saw more in mollusks than did most biologists. In the humble mollusk he saw general principles of how living organisms adapt to the world. Mollusks both adjust themselves to the environment and actively assimilate it in ways allowed by their biological structure. Piaget felt that these principles also apply to human thought. His most general definition of intelligence is that it is adaptation to the environment. Just as human and nonhuman organisms adapt physically to the environment, so does thought adapt to the environment at a psychological level. Piaget hypothesized that the modes of psychological functioning involved in this adaptation are universal.

Borrowing another concept from biology, Piaget proposed that cognitive growth is much like embryological growth: an organized structure becomes more and more differentiated over time. In fact, Piaget (1970) sometimes referred to cognitive development as "mental embryology."

Adaptation, organization, and structure, as well as such other biological concepts as equilibration, assimilation, and accommodation, are discussed later in the chapter, when we turn our attention to processes of development. At this point, however, it should be emphasized that these biological concepts serve as analogies for the way intelligence works. Biology did not lead Piaget to a physiology of intelligence.

STRUCTURALISM

Along with such other luminaries as anthropologist Claude Lévi-Strauss and linguist Ferdinand de Saussure, Piaget belongs to an approach called *structuralism*. Structuralists look at the organizational properties of whatever they are studying. Piaget proposed that a small set of mental operations underlies a wide variety of thinking episodes. Thus, there is an underlying structure to the apparent diversity of the content. Structuralists look at how parts are organized into a whole, and they abstract patterns of change. In particular, they are concerned with relationships—between parts and the whole and between an earlier and a later state. For example, the thinking of younger and older children has similar elements, but these elements are combined in different ways to form the organized whole of thought.

According to Piaget the structuralist, the nature of mental structures changes as the structures develop. An infant's cognitive structures are labeled "schemes" (sometimes translated "schemas" or "schemata"). A *scheme* is an organized pattern of behavior; it reflects a particular way of interacting with the environment. For Piaget, a scheme is whatever is repeatable and generalizable in an action. The sucking scheme, then, describes the way children put various objects into their mouths and suck them. As the scheme becomes more differentiated, children classify objects into "suckables" and "nonsuckables," with various subcategories such as hard suckables, soft suckables, pliant suckables, and hairy suckables (daddy's leg).

In contrast, the cognitive structures of the older child, from roughly age 7 on, are described in terms of organized abstract mental operations similar to logicomathematical systems. The structuralist framework can be seen in the way these schemes and operations organize themselves into an organized whole and can be applied to various content. For example, addition, subtraction, multiplication, and division are operations that are coordinated in a concept of number that underlies (mediates) much mathematical behavior. (We return to the notion of cognitive structures later.)

STAGE APPROACH

Milestones, phases, and ages
render general gauges
While periods, levels, and stages
require pages and pages.

[Leland van den Daele*]

Perhaps the boldest and most controversial of Piaget's claims was that cognitive development proceeds through a series of stages. For Piaget, a *stage* is a period of time in which the child's thinking and behavior in a variety of situations reflect a particular type of underlying mental structure. Piaget's emphasis on stages is not surprising, considering his years of careful observing and classifying while a student of zoology. The stages can be thought of as sequential levels of adapting. Just as various species have different ways of adapting to the environment, so do various cognitive levels provide different ways of adapting to the environment. Because stage theories abound in developmental psychology, it would be well to characterize Piaget's particular brand of stage theory. There are five salient characteristics.

1. *A stage is a structured whole in a state of equilibrium.* Piaget the structuralist sees a stage as an integrated whole that organizes the parts. The schemes or operations of each stage are interconnected to form an organized whole. Each stage has a different structure, which allows a different type of interaction between the child and the environment, and consequently provides fundamentally different views of the world. The essence of Piaget's stage approach is that movement through the stages involves structural changes that are qualitative (changes in type or kind)

---

* From "Qualitative models in developmental analysis" by Leland van den Daele, *Developmental Psychology, 1*, 303-310. Copyright © 1969 by the American Psychological Association.

rather than quantitative (change in degree, amount, speed, or efficiency). For example, there is a qualitative change when the child moves from structures based on actions in infancy to structures based on mental representation in the preschool years. At the *end* of each major period of development, the cognitive structures are in a state of balance, or equilibrium. (More on the equilibration process appears later in this chapter.)

2. *Each stage derives from the previous stage, incorporates and transforms that stage, and prepares for the next stage.* The previous stage paves the way for the new stage. In the process of achieving this new stage, the previous stage is reworked. Thus, once children achieve a new stage, they no longer have the previous stage available. Although previous skills remain, their position or role in the organization changes. For example, elementary schoolchildren can still roll or hit a ball (a skill acquired during infancy), but they now imbed this skill in a number of other skills. Furthermore, a more advanced level of thought controls the old skills of rolling and hitting. Rolling and hitting are now combined with other actions to win the game. One implication of this characteristic is that regression to an earlier stage is impossible because the previous stage is no longer present. This notion is in contrast to Freud's theory of stages, in which a person overwhelmed with anxiety may regress to an earlier stage.

3. *The stages follow an invariant sequence.* The stages must proceed in a particular order. No stage can be skipped. In other words, since the first stage does not have all the building materials needed for the third stage, the second stage is required. This claim that stages follow an invariant sequence is implied by the second claim that each stage is derived from the preceding stage.

4. *Stages are universal.* Because Piaget was interested in how humans as a species adapt psychologically to their environment, he focused on the structures and concepts acquired by humans everywhere. Of course, because of mental retardation from brain damage, severe deprivation, or other sources, some people may not progress through all the stages or may progress through them more slowly. And even people who are not retarded vary in how fast they proceed through the stages. However, the crucial claim is that the same order is found universally—in children of the African jungle, the American suburb, or the Swiss mountainside.

5. *Each stage includes a coming-into-being and a being.* There is an initial period of preparation and a final period of achievement in each stage. Unstable, loosely organized structures mark the initial period of transition from the previous stage. The description of each stage later in this chapter refers to the final, stable, generalized, tightly organized structure of each stage.

In summary, stages are structured wholes that emerge from and transform a previous stage, follow an invariant and universal sequence, and proceed from an unstable period of transition into a final stable period.

METHODOLOGY

One message from the introductory chapter was that the scientist, the theory, and the methods for gathering data both facilitate and constrain one another. The three develop together in particular directions. Piaget the sparrow watcher and mollusk collector used his observation and classification skills when watching infants master the objects around them and when observing toddlers struggle to express their thoughts in spontaneous speech. Piaget as the Sorbonne student interviewing mental patients soon became known as the man who asked questions about dreams, the origin of the universe, and quantity. Piaget's early work with preschool and school children typically involved the *clinical method*, which refers to a chainlike verbal interaction between the experimenter and the child. The experimenter begins by posing a problem or asking a question, but his subsequent questions are guided by the answer the child gave to the previous question. Through this interchange, the experimenter tries to understand the line of reasoning underlying the child's answers. A talented interviewer avoids biasing the child's answers by giving too much suggestion.

The following exchange between Piaget and a 5-year-old illustrates the clinical method:

> Where does the dream come from?—*I think you sleep so well that you dream.*—Does it come from us or from outside?—*From outside.*—What do we dream with?—*I don't know.*—With the hands? . . . With nothing?—*Yes, with nothing.*—When you are in bed and you dream, where is the dream?—*In my bed, under the blanket. I don't really know. If it was in my stomach(!) the bones would be in the way and I shouldn't see it.*—Is the dream there when you sleep?—*Yes, it is in my bed beside me. . . .* Is the dream in your head?—*It is I that am in the dream: it isn't in my head(!). When you dream,*

you don't know you are in the bed. You know you are walking. You are in the dream. You are in bed, but you don't know you are. . . . Where do dreams come from?—*I don't know. They happen.*—Where?—*In the room and then afterward they come up to the children. They come by themselves.*—You see the dream when you are in the room, but if I were in the room, too, should I see it?—*No, grownups (les Messieurs) don't ever dream.* . . . When the dream is in the room, is it near you?—*Yes, there!* (pointing to 30 cms. in front of his eyes).

[1926 (1929, pp. 97-98]*

In Piaget's later work, these interviews were often combined with the manipulation of objects by the experimenter or child. This was especially likely when Piaget studied numerical and physical concepts or perceptual development. For example, Piaget might spread out a row of objects and ask whether the number had changed.

Infants, of course, cannot fruitfully be questioned about their thoughts. Piaget carefully observed his own infants as they went about their normal activities. At times he became a participant-observer by inventing little experiments on the spot, such as hiding a toy and observing whether the infant searched for it.

Because these verbal protocols and behavioral observations were seen through the eyes of Piaget the philosopher and theoretical biologist, their description became more and more abstract. Piaget saw general structures of thought in these varied, concrete behaviors. This process of abstraction, or generalization, is evident in his writings, which often have a high proportion of theoretical interpretation compared with actual observation.

One of the challenges to someone encountering Piaget's theory for the first time is to relate the many elusive, abstract features of the theory to the abundant specific behaviors found in each stage. For the moment the reader may simply have to have faith that the abstract and the concrete actually fit together somehow. Perhaps the best way to grasp the relationship between the abstract and the concrete is to swing back and forth between the two. Following this strategy, we now swing from the preceding abstract orientation to a description of specific stagelike changes, then swing back to a new set of abstract features: the mechanisms of change.

---

* The references to Piaget's works in this chapter are to the publication dates of the original works, usually in French. The page numbers are those of the translations (given in parentheses).

DESCRIPTION OF THE STAGES

In the introductory chapter of this book, it was proposed that a developmental theory should both describe and explain development. This section describes the prototypic Piagetian child making her way through the stages of cognitive development. The subsequent section tackles the questions of how and why this particular course of development occurs.

To understand each stage, we need to know not only where it came from but also where it is going. Each stage holds both the fruits of the past and the seeds of the future. Here, then, is an overview of the stages, followed by a more detailed account. The ages listed with each stage are approximate because children vary somewhat in the ages at which they proceed through the stages.

1. *Sensorimotor period* (roughly birth to 2 years). Infants understand the world in terms of their overt, physical actions on the world. They move from simple reflexes through several steps to an organized set of schemes (organized behaviors).

2. *Preoperational period* (roughly 2 to 7 years). No longer do children simply make perceptual and motor adjustments to objects and events. They can now use symbols (mental images, words, gestures) to represent objects and events. They use these symbols in an increasingly organized and logical fashion.

3. *Concrete operational period* (roughly 7 to 11 years). Children acquire certain logical structures that allow them to perform various mental operations, which are internalized actions that can be reversed.

4. *Formal operational period* (roughly 11 to 15 years). Mental operations are no longer limited to concrete objects; they can be applied to purely verbal or logical statements, to the possible as well as the real, to the future as well as the present.

The following description of the stages of development should be prefaced by a word about Piaget's terminology. Although Piaget refers to "stages" of development, each of the four major stages is designated a "period," for example, the "sensorimotor period." When Piaget identifies substages within one of these four major periods, they are designated "stages."

SENSORIMOTOR PERIOD (ROUGHLY BIRTH TO 2 YEARS)

In Piaget's view, a human starts life with a set of reflexes, a particular physical makeup unique to the human species, and inherited ways of interacting with the environment. These inherited ways of interacting refer to the tendency of thought to be organized and adapted to the environment. The thinking of even an Einstein has these humble beginnings. Although infants know almost nothing about the world, they have the potential to know everything. Indeed, one of Piaget's books on infancy is aptly titled *The Origins of Intelligence in Children* (1936). We now trace the infant's construction of a model of the world by means of the sensory (perceptual) and motor (physical movement) systems. The infant progresses through six stages in the construction of a sensorimotor system of thought.

Stage 1: Modification of Reflexes (Roughly Birth to 1 Month)

A newborn is a bundle of reflexes, or "wired-in" responses that are triggered by particular stimuli. Touch a newborn's lips and she sucks, prick her foot and her knee flexes, place a finger in her hand and she grasps it. As these reflexes are activated a number of times, they very gradually are modified. The infant adjusts them slightly to meet the requirements of slightly different circumstances. For example, the infant's mouth must search out the nipple from different angles on different occasions. In addition, the way the mouth and tongue fit around a hard, plastic rattle differs from the way they fit around a finger.

As an expanding number and type of objects serve as "grist" for the reflex, the category of "suckables" grows to include objects ranging from nipples to blankets to bars of the crib. However, at the same time that infants are generalizing their sucking behavior to many objects, they are also increasing their discrimination between objects. Hungry infants never confuse a finger with a nipple. In a sense, they "recognize" objects.

Behaviors such as sucking, grasping, and looking do not remain reflexes; they can be produced spontaneously. In fact, the baby sometimes sucks when there is nothing to suck. Piaget claimed that there is an innate tendency for humans to exercise their skills. Babies suck because they *can* suck. Sucking strengthens the sucking skill and leads to further sucking in a like-begets-like fashion.

In short, in stage 1 the baby strengthens, generalizes, and differentiates behaviors that began as reflexes. At this point, Piaget begins to use the term "scheme," which was introduced in the earlier section on structuralism. These schemes—organized patterns of behavior—continue to strengthen, generalize, and differentiate throughout the rest of the sensorimotor period. The infant is constructing a world of things to suck, grasp, look at, hit, feel, listen to, and so on. The primitive schemes of the first stage are a small but significant step in this construction.

Stage 2: Primary Circular Reactions (Roughly 1 to 4 Months)

The behaviors in stage 1 can be called schemes only in a very limited sense because there is so little modification of the reflex. In stage 2, there is widespread and rapid development of schemes because primary circular reactions can now occur. A circular reaction is a behavior that is repeated over and over again and thus becomes circular. By chance, the baby discovers an interesting result from some behavior and then attempts to recapture this result. As the behavior and its results are successfully repeated, it can be said that a "habit" is formed. These circular reactions are called "primary" because they involve response consequences that are centered on or around the infant's body rather than other objects.

Piaget observed many cases of primary circular reactions in his own infants. Consider the following example (the three numbers express the child's age in years, months, and days):

> From 0;2(3) Laurent evidences a circular reaction which will become more definite and will constitute the beginning of systematic grasping; he scratches and tries to grasp, lets go, scratches and grasps again, etc. On 0;2(3) and 0;2(6) this can only be observed during the feeding. Laurent gently scratches his mother's bare shoulder. But beginning 0;2(7) the behavior becomes marked in the cradle itself. Laurent scratches the sheet which is folded over the blankets, then grasps it and holds it a moment, then lets it go, scratches it again and recommences without interruption. At 0;2(11) this play lasts a quarter of an hour at a time, several times during the day. At 0;2(12) he scratches and grasps my fist which I placed against the back of his right hand. He even succeeds in discriminating my bent finger and grasping it separately, holding it a few moments. At 0;2(14) and 0;2(16) I note how definitely the spontaneous grasping of the sheet reveals the characteristics of circular reaction—groping at first, then regular rhythmical activity (scratching, grasping, holding and letting go), and finally progressive loss of interest.

> *[1936 (1952, pp. 91-92)]*

One primary circular reaction that is probably universal is thumb sucking. Although thumb sucking has occurred since (or before) birth, it now has developed into a systematic, coordinated behavior. The infant efficiently brings the thumb to the mouth and keeps it there. Other examples of primary circular reactions include active visual exploration of objects and listening to one's own vocalizations.

The performance of the circular reactions seems to be accompanied by feelings of pleasure. Piaget describes a baby who "played with his voice, not only through interest in the sound, but for 'functional pleasure,' laughing at his own power" [1945 (1951, p. 91)].

Stage 3: Secondary Circular Reactions (Roughly 4 to 8 Months)

Infants are never content with the status quo; they continue to expand their world. This expansion is especially striking in the movement from primary to secondary circular reactions. Whereas primary circular reactions are centered around the infant's body, secondary circular reactions are oriented to the external world. By chance, the infant does something that leads to an interesting effect in the environment: he shakes a rattle, which produces a noise; he slaps a ball, which causes it to roll. In the previous stage, the shaking or slapping itself was of interest; now the environmental consequences are.

When the secondary circular reactions generalize, Piaget calls them "procedures for making interesting sights last." If kicking their legs vigorously leads to a jiggling mobile a number of times, infants may make this kicking procedure a part of their repertoire. On future occasions when an interesting movement occurs, they may make kicking movements in an attempt to sustain or recreate this movement. Sometimes these procedures produce the desired result; sometimes they do not. On one occasion, after watching, in fascination, his father drum on a tin box, 7-month-old Laurent first stares at it, then shakes his arm, raises himself, strikes his covers, and shakes his head in an attempt to capture the box—all to no avail!

One of Piaget's novel observations was the "motor recognition" that emerges during this stage:

What happens, in effect, is that the child, confronted by objects or sights which habitually set in motion his secondary circular reactions, limits himself to outlining the customary movements instead of actually performing them. Everything takes place as though the child were satisfied to recognize these objects or sights and to make a note of this recognition, but could not recognize them except by working, rather than thinking, the schema helpful to recognition.

[1936 (1952, pp. 185–186)]

For example, when Piaget's infant daughter, Lucienne, sees a doll that she has often swung in the past, she simply opens and closes her hands or shakes her legs; this is a reduced, effortless version of the original behavior.

During stages 2 and 3, the infant achieves some simple coordinations of his schemes. The integration of vision and grasping is especially useful for developing circular reactions. Now the infant can see an object, reach for it, and run through his repertoire of "things to do to objects." This coordination of the schemes of looking, grasping, sucking, hearing, and so forth continues throughout the sensorimotor period. In this way, the cognitive structures are becoming increasingly integrated and organized.

Stage 4: Coordination of Secondary Schemes (Roughly 8 to 12 Months)

In this stage, infants can combine their schemes in complex ways. In particular, planning and intentionality emerge. This new behavior sequence is made up of an instrumental (or means) behavior and a goal behavior. Infants know what they want and can use their skills to achieve that goal. They have differentiated between means and end. In contrast, in stage 3, infants' discovery of interesting results was fortuitous; only *afterward* did they try to achieve the outcome again. A special feature of the means–end behavior found in stage 4 is that it is applied to *new* situations. The schemes are now mobile; they are freed from their original contexts and can be used at will to achieve a variety of goals.

Piaget relates various occasions on which he placed his hand in front of a desirable matchbox. Whereas in stage 3 Laurent simply applied (unsuccessfully) his familiar grasping scheme toward the matchbox, in stage 4 he hit his father's hand (means) and grasped the box (end). Laurent had removed a barrier in order to achieve a goal.

In addition to coordinating schemes to remove barriers, the infant can now use objects as instruments to obtain a goal. A modern example is the infant who places his mother's hand on the television knob in order to see the dark screen come alive.

Another outcome of the differentiation between means and ends is the anticipation of events:

> At 0;9(16) . . . she likes the grape juice in a glass, but not the soup in a bowl. She watches her mother's activity. When the spoon comes out of the glass she opens her mouth wide, whereas when the spoon comes from the bowl, her mouth remains closed. Her mother tries to lead her to make a mistake by taking a spoon from the bowl and passing it by the glass before offering it to Jacqueline. But she is not fooled.
>
> *[1936 (1952, p. 249)]*

Stage 5: Tertiary Circular Reactions (Roughly 12 to 18 Months)

In this stage, we see infant scientists at work. The environment is their laboratory. They perform miniature experiments in which they deliberately vary an action in order to see how this variation affects the outcome. They exploit each object's potential. They seem to be asking, "Is there anything new about this object?" As in earlier circular reactions, there is repetition with variation.

Again Laurent thoughtfully provides us with a nice example:

> At 0;10(11) Laurent is lying on his back but nevertheless resumes his experiments of the day before. He grasps in succession a celluloid swan, a box, etc., stretches out his arm and lets them fall. He distinctly varies the positions of the fall. Sometimes he stretches out his arm vertically, sometimes he holds it obliquely, in front of or behind his eyes, etc. When the object falls in a new position (for example on his pillow), he lets it fall two or three times more on the same place, as though to study the spatial relation; then he modifies the situation. At a certain moment the swan falls near his mouth: now, he does not suck it (even though this object habitually serves this purpose), but drops it three times more while merely making the gesture of opening his mouth.
>
> *[1936 (1952, p. 269)]*

Through deliberate trial-and-error exploration, infants extend the means–end behavior of the previous stage to develop new means. They no longer simply coordinate old schemes. In fact, Piaget often characterizes stage 5 as "the discovery of new means through active experimentation." Examples of new means might include pulling a blanket to obtain an object resting on the blanket or positioning a long, thin object in such a way that it can be slipped through the bars of a crib.

Stage 6: Invention of New Means Through Mental Combinations (Roughly 18 to 24 Months)

Stage 6 both closes the curtain on the sensorimotor period and raises it on the preoperational period. The achievements of one period always make it possible for the child to begin the next period. In stage 6, thought begins to go underground. Up to this time, children have displayed their thinking to the world; now the overt is becoming covert. External physical exploration gives way to internal mental exploration. All of this is possible because the child now can use mental symbols to *represent* objects and events.

Let us see how this mental representation leads to a new way of solving problems:

> At 1;6(23) for the first time Lucienne plays with a doll carriage whose handle comes to the height of her face. She rolls it over the carpet by pushing it. When she comes against a wall, she pulls, walking backward. But as this position is not convenient for her, she pauses and without hesitation, goes to the other side to push the carriage again. She therefore found the procedure in one attempt, apparently through analogy to other situations but without training, apprenticeship, or chance.
>
> *[1936 (1952, p. 338)]*

This episode illustrates the critical features of stage 6 behavior:

1. Children abandon overt trial and error because it no longer is necessary.

2. They create new solutions (means to an end) on the spot.

3. They manipulate mental images that correspond to (stand for, represent) external events.

The emergence of a mental symbol can be seen in one of the most stunning of Piaget's observations. Piaget has been playing a game with Lucienne at age 1 year, 4 months, in which he hides from her a watch chain inside an empty matchbox. Lucienne has attained the chain by applying old schemes—turning the box upside down so that the contents spill out through the opening or, with a smaller opening, sliding her fingers into the slot to grasp the chain. (It should be noted that Lucienne has not observed her father sliding the box to change the size of the opening.) Then Piaget slips the chain through an even smaller opening, which, as Lucienne discovers, is too small to permit her fingers to reach the chain. Now we see the behavior of interest:

She looks at the slit with great attention; then, several times in succession, she opens and shuts her mouth, at first slightly, then wider and wider! Apparently Lucienne understands the existence of a cavity subjacent to the slit and wishes to enlarge that cavity. The attempt at representation which she thus furnishes is expressed plastically, that is to say, due to inability to think out the situation in words or clear visual images she uses a simple motor indication as "signifier" or symbol.

[1936 (1952, p. 338)]

When faced with a problem that past methods do not solve, Lucienne thinks through the problem, partly by means of movements of the mouth and partly by thinking. She is in transition to a true use of mental symbols. The movements of the mouth represent the idea of widening the opening of the matchbox.

One achievement of this stage is that an event that has been represented can be evoked at a later time. This absent event is reproduced in part, as seen in the following observation:

At 1;4(3) J. had a visit from a little boy of 1;6, whom she used to see from time to time, and who, in the course of the afternoon got into a terrible temper. He screamed as he tried to get out of a play-pen and pushed it backwards, stamping his feet. J. stood watching him in amazement, never having witnessed such a scene before. The next day, she herself screamed in her play-pen and tried to move it, stamping her foot lightly several times in succession. The imitation of the whole scene was most striking. Had it been immediate, it would naturally not have involved representation, but coming as it did after an interval of more than twelve hours, it must have involved some representative or pre-representative element.

[1945 (1951, p. 63)]

Comment

The sensorimotor period has been presented in some detail because it provides a concrete illustration of the following general characteristics of all four periods:

1. The child learns about properties of objects and relations among them. In the sensorimotor period, the child achieves this knowledge through overt actions, thus, a "logic of action."

2. Cognitive structures become more tightly organized. The child coordinates schemes and applies them as solutions to new situations.

3. Behavior gradually becomes more intentional. The child differentiates between means and ends, invents new means, and applies them to new ends in new situations.

4. The self is gradually differentiated from the environment. Children discover the boundaries of their own body and see themselves as one object in a world of objects.

If this book were devoted entirely to Piaget's theory, the next step would be to show how various important concepts develop as a result of the six stages of the sensorimotor period. Because we still have many theorists to meet, there is time only to hint at some of these developments. A description of these developments would not seem unfamiliar, however, because the concepts are simply extended applications of the general sensorimotor abilities of each stage already outlined.

Perhaps the most important concept acquired during the sensorimotor period is the notion of *object permanence*. This concept is the knowledge that there are entities that have a reality of their own, independent of the child's actions. Thus, an object continues to exist even when the child cannot see, hear, or feel it. Piaget proposed that the essence of the development of the object concept is that children gradually come to understand that their actions on an object are separate from the object itself. The assumption that objects exist even when not seen is without doubt one of the most basic assumptions in the adult's conception of a stable, predictable physical world. Briefly, according to Piaget, the concept develops as follows. During the first few months of life, if an object disappears, infants do not search for it (stages 1 and 2). Their behavior follows the rule "out of sight, out of mind." Later, they search if the object is only partially hidden or if they were doing something with the object when it disappeared (stage 3). However, they give up easily if the object does not reappear quickly. They still think of the object as an extension of their actions on it. Still later, as schemes are coordinated, children have the skills needed to look for hidden objects (stage 4). However, they persist in searching in the place where they searched previously. Thus, when Piaget hides a toy parrot twice under a mattress to his daughter's left, then hides it to her right (as she watches), she immediately searches to the left—in the original hiding place. Piaget's interpretation of her persistence is that she defines an object partly in terms of its position—a "parrot-under-the-mattress."

The next advance is that children can appropriately search for an object even if there are several displacements, but only if they are visible (stage 5). There is a problem with invisible displacements, as when Piaget puts a coin in his hand and moves it under a cushion, then under a coverlet, then out again. However, in the final stage, Jacqueline continues to search for the coin because she now knows that it has to be somewhere (stage 6). She can represent the object mentally, so she is not dependent on seeing or otherwise acting on the object. At last she understands that objects, including herself, are things that exist in and of themselves.

In addition to the object concept, Piaget traced the development of concepts of time, space, and causality. This should come as no surprise, given Piaget's interest in these classical philosophical problems of epistemology. The details of the sensorimotor evolution of these concepts can be found in Piaget's *Construction of Reality in the Child* (1937). The concepts of time, space, and causality are closely linked to the object concept because objects exist, move, and affect other objects in a spatiotemporal field. As in the case of the object concept, these concepts are variations on a (sensorimotor) theme by Piaget.

PREOPERATIONAL PERIOD (ROUGHLY 2 TO 7 YEARS)

Ending the first period and beginning the next can be likened to climbing a mountain, only to discover that it is merely a foothill to Mt. Everest. The achievements of the sensorimotor period, although monumental, are also preparation for what is to come. In a sense, children start all over again. What they have achieved in the realm of actions on the world is redeveloped, now in the realm of mental representations. They transfer notions about objects, relations, causality, space, and time to a new medium (mental representation) and a more highly organized structure.

Semiotic Function

As we noted earlier, the emergence of mental representations in stage 6 of the sensorimotor period provides a bridge to the preoperational period. These mental representations are made possible by a more general developmental milestone: the *semiotic function*, or ability to use one object or event to stand for another. Stated more formally, a *signifier* evokes a *significate*. Words, gestures, objects, and mental images can serve as signifiers. A 4-year-old may use the word "airplane," a swooping hand, a mental picture of an airplane, or a toy airplane to stand for a real airplane.

There are precursors to the true use of signifiers. One precursor, which was mentioned in the description of stage 6, is imitation. Lucienne's solution to the problem of the watch chain in the matchbox illustrates the transition between overt behavior and a mental symbol. These reduced imitations become internal symbols during the course of development.

There are two types of signifiers: *symbols* and *signs*. Symbols bear some similarity to the objects or events they stand for. They have lingering traces of their origins in imitation. Symbols often appear in *symbolic play*, as when Jacqueline pretends that a cloth is a pillow and feigns sleep, laughing hard all the while.

In contrast to symbols, signs are arbitrarily related to certain events or objects. There is no relationship between the word "table" and the four-legged thing at which we sit, except that our language has assigned a relationship between them. This notion that words or other signs are arbitrarily assigned to objects is not easy for a child to grasp. Young children think that an object's name is as intrinsic to the object as are its color and form. When asked why spaghetti is called spaghetti, a young child may say that it looks like spaghetti and feels like spaghetti and tastes like spaghetti, so we call it spaghetti!

Representational thought has some obvious advantages over sensorimotor thought. It is faster and more mobile. It can deal with the past, present, and future in one grand sweep and can recombine its parts to create ideas that refer to nothing in reality (for example, monsters that go bump in the night). In contrast, Piaget described sensorimotor intelligence as a motion picture in which the action is slowed down so that "all the pictures are seen in succession but without fusion, and so without the continuous vision necessary for understanding the whole" [1947 (1950, p. 121)].

It should be noted that Piaget did not hold the common view that the source of representational thought is the ability to use words. He believed that the opposite is true. The development of representational thought makes it possible to use words as well as other signifiers. Thus, thought is both prior to language and broader than language. Language is primarily a mode for expressing thought. Throughout development, thought is prior to language. For example, teaching a child to use the words "more," "taller," and "same" does not teach him the quantitative concepts underlying these utterances.

Although thinking is not dependent on language, language can aid cognitive development. Language can direct children's attention to new objects or relationships in the environment, introduce them to conflicting points of view, and impart abstract information that is not easily acquired directly. Language is one of many tools in our cognitive "toolkit" (Wertsch, 1991).

Characteristics of the Period

Although thinking through symbols and signs is a tremendous advance over sensorimotor thought, such thinking is limited in a number of ways. As the term *preoperational* suggests, children in this period have not yet acquired reversible mental operations, which characterize the thinking of the next period, called concrete operations.

In many ways, this period is a time of preparation for the next stage, and Piaget himself described preoperational children in terms of what they cannot do, rather than what they can do. However, he also identified a number of positive acquisitions such as identity, functions, and regulations, all described later. The main characteristics of preoperational thought are egocentrism, rigidity of thought, semilogical reasoning, and limited social cognition.

1. *Egocentrism.* Egocentrism does not refer to selfishness or arrogance, and Piaget does not use it in a derogatory way. Rather, the term refers to (a) the incomplete differentiation of the self and the world, including other people, and (b) the tendency to perceive, understand, and interpret the world in terms of the self. One implication is that the child cannot take another person's perceptual or conceptual perspective. For example, preoperational children do not realize that a person viewing a display from a position different from their own sees the display from a different perspective. A child holding a book upright points to a picture and asks, "What is this?" He is unaware that his mother, who is facing him, can see only the back of the book. Egocentrism makes it difficult to take the role or point of view of another person. This can be seen in a card game when a 5-year-old giggles upon receiving the "old maid" card. A 5-year-old does not perceive the need for a "poker face" as card-playing strategy.

Because children cannot easily take another person's role, they make little effort to tailor their speech to meet the needs of the listener. In fact, Piaget noted that the child "feels no desire to influence his hearer nor to tell him anything; not unlike a certain type of drawing-room conversation where everyone talks about himself and no one listens" [1923 (1926, p. 9)]. He may tell his mother that at a birthday party "he hit her with it," without bothering to explain to what "he," "her," and "it" refer. He may omit essential events, so that his mother cannot understand how "he cried" and "he blew out the candles" are related.

Egocentric speech is rampant in children's play groups. Children who apparently are talking together while playing in a group may actually be talking, but not necessarily together. Each child's remarks are unrelated to anyone else's. There is a collective monologue, of sorts, rather than a conversation. For example, one child's statement, "I think I saw Superman in a phone booth yesterday," might be followed by "This sweater makes me itch" from another child.

Although preoperational children are considered egocentric, they are less egocentric than they were in the sensorimotor period. Early sensorimotor functioning reflects a lack of differentiation between one's own actions and properties of objects. After the preoperational period, egocentrism continues to decline, but it never disappears completely, even in adulthood.

2. *Rigidity of thought.* Piaget characterized preoperational thought as frozen. One example is *centration*, the tendency to attend to or think about one salient feature of an object or event and ignore other features. If two identical containers have equal amounts of water and the contents of one container are poured into a taller, thinner container, children center on the heights of the liquids, while ignoring their widths. Consequently, they erroneously conclude that there is now more liquid because the water level is higher. Centration and egocentrism are similar in that they both reflect an inability to deal with several aspects of a situation at the same time and that they both cause a biased view of the world.

We also find a rigidity, or lack of flexibility, of thought in the tendency to *focus on states* rather than on the transformations linking the states. When faced with the question concerning quantity of liquid in the containers, the child thinks about the "before" and "after" states but ignores the process of changing from A to B as the liquid is poured. Relatedly, children *focus on appearance* rather than reality. If a stick looks as if it bends when it is plunged into a body of water, young children assume that this perception is true. Interest in the *appearance–reality* distinction made a "comeback" within the recent study of children's concepts about the mind (Flavell, 1986).

Perhaps the clearest example of the rigidity of thought is its *lack of reversibility*. Preoperational children cannot mentally reverse a series of events, transformations, or steps of reasoning. For example, they are unable to return the poured liquid to its original container mentally. Their ability to internalize action is not yet complete because it is not bidirectional.

Toward the end of the preoperational period, we begin to see "the great thaw," as the child partially corrects the tendency of thought to be centrated, focused on states, and irreversible. We now see three positive achievements of the preoperational period: function, regulation, and identity. These cognitive skills serve as transitions to the mental reversibility of the concrete operational period.

A *function* is the notion that there is a relation between factors, as expressed in the equation $y = f(x)$. For example, the more one pulls a curtain, the farther a curtain opens. Or when the rope on a pulley is pulled, there is an increase in the length of one section of rope as the other section decreases in length. However, the child cannot yet work out the precise and quantitative nature of the relationship.

A *regulation* is a mental act that is partially decentered. Again using the test of liquid quantity, we find that the child switches back and forth between using liquid height and width to make his judgments about quantity. A glass may contain more than another glass because it has a higher water level, or it may contain less because it is thinner.

The third achievement, *identity*, is the notion that an object can change its appearance without changing its basic nature, or identity. Water may look different after it is poured from one container to another, but it is the same water. Putting on a Halloween mask does not change a person into a witch, contrary to the belief of younger children. Thinking has become less rigid because a concept can be maintained despite superficial physical changes.

3. *Semilogical reasoning.* As a young psychologist, Piaget questioned children about their beliefs concerning the world. These interviews reveal various fascinating characteristics of preoperational reasoning. The conversations provide many examples of egocentrism and rigidity of thought. We treat them separately because they demonstrate some specific and somewhat surprising properties of semilogical reasoning. The following protocol illustrates several facets of semilogical reasoning in a 6-year-old child.

How did the sun begin?—*It was when life began.*—Has there always been a sun?—*No.*—How did it begin?—*Because it knew that life had begun.*—What is it made of?—*Of fire.*—But how?—*Because there was fire up there.* — Where did the fire come from? —*From the sky.* —How was the fire made in the sky?—*It was lighted with a match.*—Where did it come from, this match?—*God threw it away.* . . . How did the moon begin?—*Because we began to be alive.*—What did that do?—*It made the moon get bigger.*—Is the moon alive?—*No . . . Yes.*—Why?—*Because we are alive.*

[1926 (1929, pp. 258-259)]

The child tries to explain the mysterious natural events of everyday life. One solution is to explain natural events in terms of human behavior. The sun and moon, like people, are alive, are created by a humanlike action (a god lighting a match) and are tied to human activities (the moon began because people began to exist). Similarly, a preoperational child may assert that snow is made for children to play in and clouds move because they are pulled when people walk.

Thoughts are often linked together in a loose way rather than in a logical relationship. For example, one afternoon when Lucienne had no nap, she reasoned that it could not be afternoon because she had not had her nap. Or a child might say that his friend fell down because he got hurt. The child reasons from the particular to the particular.

4. *Limited social cognition.* Piaget argued that his description of thought applies to social objects and events as well as physical ones. Our description of preoperational thought hints at this parallel between the physical and the social realms. Examples are deficits in role taking and communication resulting from egocentrism, confusions between natural events and human events, and notions about the identity of persons when physical appearances are changed. In addition, Piaget specifically examined social thought in his work on moral judgments. A preoperational child judges the wrongness of an act according to external variables, such as how much damage was done and whether the act was punished. He ignores internal variables, such as the person's intentions. Thus, a boy who breaks fifteen cups while trying to help his mother set the table is considered guiltier than a boy who breaks only one cup while trying to steal cookies from the cabinet.

CONCRETE OPERATIONAL PERIOD (ROUGHLY 7 TO 11 YEARS)

Piaget sometimes combined ages 2 to 11 and labeled this period as "preparation for and achievement of concrete operations." Despite the considerable accomplishments in the preoperational period, in many ways the period is simply preparation for the pinnacle of cognitive development: the operation. Regulations, functions, and identities turn into operations as they become more complete, differentiated, quantitative, and stable. Let us now turn to these operations.

An *operation* is an internalized action that is part of an organized structure. With the ability to use these operations, or concepts, the child's representations are no longer isolated, rigid, or simply juxtaposed, as in the preoperational period. They are brought to life.

We can most easily see operations at work in Piaget's famous *conservation* task, which we described as the problem of liquid quantity. Let us consider this task in more detail. The child sees two identical containers equally filled with water and judges them to contain the same amount of water. As the child watches, one container is poured into a container with different dimensions or into several small containers. A "nonconserver" claims that the amount has changed, usually because the water level has changed. Since the water rises higher in a taller, thinner container, the child concludes that the amount has increased. In contrast, a "conserver" believes that the amount has not changed. He realizes that quantity remains the same despite changes in appearance. Piaget usually required the child to give a logical explanation for this judgment before he considered the child to be a true conserver.

Both the nonconserver and the conserver have a basis for their answers. Both think their conclusions are quite reasonable. In fact, if a tester happens to test the same child twice—once when the child is a nonconserver and later when she is a conserver—he may face the child's scorn on both occasions. The child on both occasions is likely to think that the tester is dumb to ask a question when the "correct" answer is so obvious!

Conservation is an important concept because it gives a certain stability to the physical world. In addition, Piaget assigned a great deal of importance to the conservation task because it reveals the presence or absence of mental operations. It is a diagnostic tool that probes the cognitive structures. Piaget asserted that children cannot conserve unless they have certain mental operations. These operations can be illustrated by the explanations the children give:

"If you pour it back where it was, they will have the same amount." *(reversibility)*

"The water goes up higher, but the glass is thinner." *(compensation)*

"You didn't add any water or take any away." *(addition–subtraction)*

The preoperational child who lacks these operations centers on states, especially the water level.

Other examples of operations are the common mathematical operations of multiplying, dividing, ordering (greater than, less than), and substituting (one thing equals another thing). Each operation is related to and obtains its meaning from the entire structure of which it is a part. Thus, addition is coordinated with subtraction, multiplication, and division to form a system of mental actions. Piaget's interest in logic and mathematics appeared in his attempt to describe these systems of operations in terms of logicomathematical structures. These structures serve as a model for characterizing concrete operational thought. (We examine Piaget's use of this model when we discuss the formal aspects of the theory.)

The various operations are applied to a wide variety of physical and social situations, of which only a few can be described here. For example, various properties are conserved in addition to liquid quantity. The number of objects in a collection remains the same when they are spread out; the total length of a stick remains the same if the stick is pushed ahead of another stick; the weight of clay remains the same if the clay is broken into pieces.

Operations are evident in another basic acquisition: *class inclusion*. The experimenter shows the child 20 wooden beads, 17 of them brown and 3 white. He asks whether the child could make a longer necklace with the brown beads or the wooden beads. The preoperational child claims that there are more brown beads than wooden beads. She can deal only with the parts (brown or white beads) or the whole (wooden beads), but not with both of them simultaneously. She does not understand that the parts and the whole are reversible. In contrast, the concrete operational child has the underlying operations necessary to derive the correct answer.

Operations apply not only to classes but also to *relations*. If a concrete operational child knows that John is taller than Bill, and Bill is taller than Henry, she can infer that John has to be taller than Henry. In addition, she can order a row of dolls according to height and give the dolls sticks ordered according to length.

Operations are also applied to *temporal–spatial representations*. For example, preoperational children draw liquid in a container in such a way that it remains parallel to the base or a side (as in the illustration on the facing page). Their perceptions are influenced by the immediate surroundings. In contrast, concrete operational children keep the liquid parallel to the larger context, the surface of the earth.

Turning to the social realm, we see that children are overcoming many of the limitations in their reasoning about the social world. They

A typical error on the water-level problem during the preoperational period.

are less egocentric, but they sometimes still have difficulties with role taking and communication. They are beginning to take intentions into account in their moral judgments. They are increasingly aware of the subtle social relationships in the family, peer group, and larger society.

This list of acquisitions could continue to the end of this book, but the examples we have considered are representative. Two observations about these acquisitions should be kept in mind. First, the various concepts or operations do not develop at the same time. In fact, some concepts, such as conservation of weight, often do not appear until near the end of the period. Second, each cognitive acquisition develops over a period of time. At first, it is transitional in nature and is demonstrated only part of the time. It gradually strengthens, stabilizes, and generalizes to a variety of situations.

We have seen the child move from an understanding of the world based on action schemes to one based on representations to one based on internalized, organized operations. Thought now is decentered rather than centered, dynamic rather than static, and reversible rather than irreversible. For the first time, the lawful nature of the world seems to be reflected in a logical system of thought. Thought is in tune, in equilibrium, with the environment. However, the concrete operations are still "concrete. " They can be applied only to concrete objects—present or mentally represented. They deal with what "is" rather than what "could be." The final step is to apply the operations to purely verbal or logical statements and to the possible as well as the actual. This story unfolds as we turn to formal operations.

FORMAL OPERATIONAL PERIOD
(ROUGHLY 11 TO 15 YEARS)

During the concrete operational period, mental operations are applied to objects and events. Children classify them, order them, and reverse them. During formal operations, adolescents carry concrete operations one step farther. They can take the results of these concrete operations and generate hypotheses (propositions, statements) about their logical relations. Thus, we now have operations on operations; thought has become truly logical, abstract, and hypothetical.

Formal operational thought resembles the kind of thinking we often call the scientific method. Children formulate a hypothesis about a present or potential event and test this hypothesis against reality. If necessary, they can generate all possible outcomes or all possible combinations at the beginning. Piaget typically presented a problem from physics or chemistry and observed how the adolescent goes about solving it. The problem-solving process, rather than the correct answer itself, is what is of interest.

A prototypic task is the pendulum problem. An adolescent observes an object hanging from a string and attempts to discover what determines how fast the object swings. He is shown how to vary the length of the string, the height from which the pendulum is released, the force of the push on the pendulum, and the weight of the object. One or several of these variables could control the speed of the swing. A concrete operational child experiments with the variables and may even arrive at the correct answer, but his approach is haphazard; he has no overall plan. He does not vary one factor while holding the other factors constant. For example, he may compare a long, light pendulum with a short, heavy one and conclude that both factors are important. In fact, the length of the string is the main determinant of the rate of oscillation.

In contrast to concrete operational children, formal operational adolescents imagine all possible determinants of the rate of oscillation before they begin, systematically vary the factors one by one, observe the results correctly, keep track of the results, and draw the appropriate conclusions (they identify which factor controls the rate of oscillation). They systematically isolate the critical factor and deal all the while with propositions, not objects. By testing predictions from each hypothesis, they demonstrate hypotheticodeductive thought. More generally, as Flavell expressed it, "Reality is thus conceived as a special subset within the totality of things which the data would admit as hypotheses; it is seen as the 'is' portion of a 'might be' totality, the portion it is the subject's job to discover" (1963, pp. 204–205).

Piaget posed several other problems.

1. Determine which mixture of five colorless liquids produces a yellow color.

2. Discover which variables (for example, weight, length, types of material) cause a rod suspended over water to bend down far enough to touch the water.

3. Discover and state the law governing the relationship between the angle at which a billiard ball hits the table wall and the angle of its rebound.

4. Solve a geometric proof.

5. Discover proportional relationships (for example, 16 is to 4 as 4 is to 1).

6. Evaluate syllogisms, such as "All children hate spinach; girls are children; therefore, girls hate spinach."

It should be noted that direct instruction in scientific thought is not necessary for the development of formal operations. Years of common, unremarkable experiences contribute to this achievement. As Einstein remarked: "The whole of science is nothing more than a refinement of everyday thinking."

As in the concrete operational period, Piaget applied logico-mathematical models to the child's thought. He identified 16 underlying mental operations that he believed are necessary for solving the various problems he presented to adolescents. This *system of 16 binary operations* forms a tightly knit organization of logical relations. Although his complex model is beyond the scope of this chapter, we look at two examples: conjunction and disjunction. *Conjunction* is an operation that refers to the simultaneous occurrence of x and y. Another operation is *disjunction*, which refers to three possible outcomes: x and y, x and *not* y, and y and *not* x. In the problem of discovering what causes rods to bend, we consider two of many possible outcomes: (1) great length, great bending (conjunction) and (2) great length, great bending; short length, great bending; great length, little bending (disjunction).

In addition to the binary operations, a system of rules for manipulating the logical relations identified by the binary operations is included in Piaget's logical model. For example, in a weight-balance problem, an imbalance can be negated by subtracting the extra weight from the heavier side or adding more weight to the lighter side.

The ability to consider abstract ideas, the future, and various possibilities is evident in adolescents' social world. They dream about their future and imagine themselves in various occupational and social roles. They may experiment with some of these roles just as they experiment with hypotheses about physical events. They are concerned with the world of ideas. In sessions with friends, they debate various moral and political issues, such as whether wars can ever be moral, whether abortions should be legal, whether there are basic inalienable human rights, and what an ideal community would be like. They can consider these issues from a number of different perspectives and see how the issues are related to a larger set of social relationships. However, there is still a lingering egocentrism. Adolescents are impressed with the power of thought and naively underestimate the practical problems involved in achieving an ideal future for themselves or for society. They feel that the sheer force of their logic will move mountains. Piaget noted that this starry-eyed egocentrism is squelched when adolescents undertake their first real job!

One further difference between concrete and formal operational thought has implications for both social and physical development. Adolescents can reflect on their own thinking (and that of others). For example, they can think about propositions, which are thoughts. Or, in the social realm, we find the following line of thought: "He's thinking that I'm thinking that he's thinking about her."

By achieving formal operations, adolescents complete their cognitive structures. The various concrete operational logical systems have been combined to create a single, tightly organized system of thought—a unified whole. Thought is logical, abstract, and flexible. Thinking continues to develop throughout adulthood as formal operations are applied to more and more content areas and situations. Egocentrism continues to decline as people broaden their experiences in the world of work and social relationships. However, these changes after age 15 entail a change not in the structure of thought but only in its content and stability.

AN OVERVIEW

Now that we have reached the height of Piaget's theory, it would be well to look back over our climb. Perhaps the best way to highlight the differences between periods is to see how a typical child in each period would understand several aspects of reality. First, what is an "object" for a child in each stage? During the sensorimotor period, an object that at first is simply a stimulus for feeding a reflex becomes something on which one can act. Then an object becomes an independently existing entity that is separate from one's actions and can be mentally represented. For a preoperational child, an object can represent other objects, can undergo physical changes while maintaining its identity (if not its amount), and can be joined with other objects to form a class of objects. During the period of concrete operations, various operations manipulate the representation of an object; for example, any changes in the object can be reversed, and the object can be fitted into a series of objects ordered according to some dimension. Finally, during the period of formal operations, higher-order operations allow further mental manipulations of the representation of the object. All the object's possibilities can be examined scientifically.

Another way of slicing the periods vertically is to consider how a child in each period would attack a specific problem. Consider what would happen if we gave children in each stage a tub of water and various small objects of various densities, sizes, weights, shapes, and colors. Infants would immediately splash, throw the objects, push the objects to the bottom of the tub, and probably attempt to eat the objects. Toward the end of the sensorimotor period, children might drop the objects from various heights and note that the bigger, heavier objects make bigger splashes than do the smaller, lighter objects. They might also notice that some objects sink, while others do not.

Preoperational children might imagine that the objects are boats or fish. They would notice that some objects float, while others sink, but they would be content to change their reasons from case to case. They might claim that one object floats because it is little, another because it is dry, another because it is a boat, and so on.

Concrete operational children are bothered by inconsistencies that did not bother them in the previous stage, such as the fact that some small objects sink, while other small objects float. They make comparisons between objects, but they are neither systematic nor exhaustive. For example, they do not hold amounts constant while varying weights. However, they do develop several categories of "sinkability," for example, always floats (light weight), always sinks (heavy), and sinks or floats depending on the circumstances (small objects, lids).

Formal operational adolescents have both a plan and the necessary operations to solve the problem. They systematically vary the factors to determine their influence and use the results to test their hypotheses.

They know that density is the proportion of weight to volume and that the relative density of the object to the water is the critical factor. Adolescents are able to form a proportion made up of two other proportions: the density for the objects and for the water. These are operations on operations. This general law allows them to predict whether any particular object will sink or float.

MEMORY

Some of Piaget's most dramatic claims stemmed from his work on memory. Consider the following typical experiment by Piaget and Inhelder (1968). They showed children an array of 10 sticks of various sizes that were ordered according to size. A week later they asked the children to draw from memory the array of sticks they had seen. Developmental differences emerged. In general, 3- and 4-year-olds lined up a few sticks having the same length. The 5- and 6-year-olds tended to draw some tall and some short sticks. By 7 years of age, most children could draw the original array correctly. Piaget and Inhelder concluded that the children had processed and interpreted the original array in terms of their present understanding of ordered relations. Only when this understanding is fully achieved can the child accurately remember the array. Thus, memory reflects and depends on the entire cognitive structure. Memory is active understanding rather than a static, passive state.

Although this is an interesting set of results, it is less surprising than that found 6 months later when the children returned. Although the children were not shown the sticks again, this time 75 percent of the children drew arrays that were more advanced cognitively than those they had produced 6 months earlier. For example, a child who originally lined up three tall sticks of the same height and three short sticks of the same height later made a row of three tall sticks, three medium-size sticks, and three short sticks. Piaget's interpretation is that such improvements are reasonable if one assumes that the children have developed cognitively during those 6 months. If the child's cognitive structures are expressed in his memory, then changes in these structures should produce changes in memory.* Note that improvement in

---

* It should be mentioned that there are many methodological problems involved in this type of study. Furthermore, other researchers have not always replicated Piaget's results (see Liben, 1977, for a review).

memory over time is the *opposite* of what one would expect from most theories of memory or from common sense. The typical view is that a memory trace fades over time and its recall is blocked by newer memories.Piaget's claim that memory is not always reliable is seen in the following intriguing account of a memory from his second year of life:

> I was sitting in my pram, which my nurse was pushing in the Champs Elysées, when a man tried to kidnap me. I was held in by the strap fastened around me while my nurse bravely tried to stand between me and the thief. She received various scratches, and I can still see vaguely those on her face.

> *[1945 (1951, p. 188)]*

When Piaget was 15, his parents received a letter from the nurse shortly after she had joined a religious order. She said she wanted to return the watch that had been given to her as a reward for protecting little Jean from the kidnapper. The truth was that she had made up the story and had even faked the scratches that Piaget so vividly "remembered"! Piaget believes that what he remembered was a visual memory that he created from the story his parents had told him as a child.

In addition to studying memory performance, Piaget examined children's concepts of memory. This topic was rediscovered by American and English psychologists 50 years later and labeled "metamemory," which is described in Chapter 4. A sample of Piaget's work is the following interview with an 8-year-old innatist:

> *Memory is something in the head which makes us think.*—What do you think this memory is like?—*It is a little square of skin, rather oval, and inside there are stories (les histoires).*—What are they like?—*They are written on the flesh.*—What with?—*Pencil.*—Who wrote them?—*God, before I was born, he put them there.*

> *[1926 (1929, p. 52)]*

MECHANISMS OF DEVELOPMENT

A previous section described the stages of cognitive development. We now turn to Piaget's explanation of the development through those stages. In other words, by what processes does the child's thinking progress? What are the rules of transition from step to step? Our attempt to answer these questions both expands our coverage of Piaget's theory and integrates the earlier sections that oriented us to the theory and described developmental changes. The abstract and the specific ultimately do fit together—at least for Piaget.

Emphasizing the grand stages, which span several years each, can make us forget that thought actually develops in the moment-to-moment, everyday encounters between children and their environments. Stagelike changes ultimately are due to millions of these minidevelopments. An adequate theory of cognitive development must explain these small but significant steps.

In Piaget's theory, these small steps are spurred by certain *functional invariants*. The functional invariants are intellectual functions that do not change during development. The two basic functional invariants are organization and adaptation. In yet another tie to biology, these invariants are also found in physiological activities. In both physiological and intellectual functioning there are certain abstract properties (functional invariants) that define the relationship between the organism and the environment. These functional invariants are part of the general heredity of living organisms. We are born with tendencies to organize our thinking into structures and to adapt to our environment. With apologies to Descartes, it could be said that "I am, therefore I think."

COGNITIVE ORGANIZATION

Cognitive *organization* refers to the tendency for thought to consist of systems whose parts are integrated to form a whole. These systems, in turn, are coordinated; there are interrelationships among cognitive activities. The mind is not a grab bag of facts. Rather, it is a coherent view of the world. This view becomes more and more coherent and interrelated as the child develops. For example, the young infant has separate structures for sucking objects and for grasping them. Only later are these two structures organized into a higher-order structure that allows coordinated reaching for an object and bringing it to the mouth to suck.

Again, Piaget saw parallels between psychological and physiological activity. The human body is composed of systems, such as the digestive system, circulatory system, and nervous system. Each is organized within itself and interacts with other systems. A change in one system has repercussions for other systems. For example, digesting a meal changes not only the temporary state of the digestive system but also the flow of blood and body temperature.

Development through the stages involves changes in the nature of cognitive organization as the structures of thought change from stage to stage. As development proceeds, thought may be organized into schemes, regulations (partial reversibility), functions, concrete operations, or formal operations. Thus, an infant's sucking on a toy and Einstein's insights into relativity both reflect cognitive organization. In principle, one could trace a line of development from the former to the latter.

COGNITIVE ADAPTATION

We do not live to think, but, on the contrary, we think in order that we may succeed in surviving.

[José Ortega y Gassett]

The other basic functional invariant, cognitive *adaptation*, refers to the interaction between the organism and the environment. Piaget claimed that all organisms have an innate tendency to adapt to the environment. Intelligent behavior is behavior that is appropriate to the demands of the environment. The following passage by Piaget expresses the close relationship between adaptation and organization:

Organization is inseparable from adaptation: They are two complementary processes of a single mechanism, the first being the internal aspect of the cycle of which adaptation constitutes the external aspect. . . . The "accord of thought with things" and the "accord of thought with itself" express this dual functional invariant of adaptation and organization. These two aspects of thought are indissociable: It is by adapting to things that thought organizes itself and it is by organizing itself that it structures things.

[1936 (1952, pp. 7–8)]

Adaptation involves two complementary processes: assimilation and accommodation. *Assimilation* is the process of fitting reality into one's current cognitive organization. In every cognitive encounter with objects or events, there is a degree of "bending" or distorting of experience as people attempt to incorporate, understand, or interpret this experience. In other words, people apply what they know in order to understand properties of objects and events as well as relationships between properties and events.

The four types of assimilation occur in all the periods and stages, but they are observed most easily in the sensorimotor period:

1. *Reproductive (or functional) assimilation.* Infants exercise their schemes by repeating them again and again. Consequently, the schemes become stronger.

2. *Generalizing assimilation.* The range of stimuli that can be assimilated to a scheme increases.

3. *Recognitory assimilation.* Various objects are differentiated even as the schemes generalize. Infants "recognize" an object when they assimilate it appropriately; they suck a nipple when they are hungry and suck a rattle when full.

4. *Mutual assimilation of schemes.* Schemes can assimilate each other (become coordinated) to form a larger, more organized scheme.

We can see these four kinds of assimilation in the sucking scheme. Babies tends to suck repeatedly *(reproduction)* fingers, nipples, blankets, and toys *(generalization)* but suck each one in a slightly different way *(recognition)* and often combine sucking with watching objects, reaching for them, grasping them, and bringing them to the mouth *(coordination)*.

Accommodation is the other side of the coin. This term refers to adjustments in cognitive organization that result from the demands of reality. Every object or event has special characteristics that must be taken into account sooner or later. In a sense, accommodation occurs because the current structures have failed to interpret a particular object or event satisfactorily. The resulting reorganization of thought leads to a different and more satisfactory assimilation of the experience. A particular stimulus is never again experienced in quite the same way. As Oliver Wendell Holmes told us, "Man's mind stretched to a new idea never goes back to its original dimensions."

Assimilation and accommodation are closely intertwined in every cognitive activity from birth to death. Attempts to assimilate reality necessarily involve slight changes in the cognitive structures as these adjust to the new elements. Assimilation and accommodation are so related, in fact, that Piaget sometimes defined adaptation as an equilibrium between assimilation and accommodation. In a state of equilibrium, neither assimilation nor accommodation dominates.

In true Piagetian style, both a biological example and a psychological example are needed. In the biological realm, food is assimilated into the body as it is changed into a form the body can use. As Piaget expressed it, "A rabbit that eats a cabbage doesn't become a cabbage; it's a cabbage that becomes rabbit—that's assimilation" (Bringuier, 1980, p. 42). The digestive system accommodates to food by adjusting the mouth opening, chewing, secreting digestive juices, contracting the muscles of the stomach, and so on. Thus, the digestive system both changes and is changed by an environmental event, the presentation of food.

In the psychological realm, consider an infant who has happened onto a sheet of newspaper for the first time. In an attempt to make sense out of this new experience, she runs through her repertoire of actions on objects. She applies her current structures (habitual patterns of behavior). She grasps the paper, hits it, sucks it, turns it over, shakes it, puts it over her head, and so on, in her attempts to fit this new object into something she already knows. However, a newspaper has certain characteristics foreign to her existing schemes. She is forced to stretch or reorganize (accommodate) these schemes in small ways. Her ideas about the way things sound when they are shaken must be altered to include the rustle of a newspaper. Similarly, the light weight and the new feel and sight make further demands on her comprehension of the world.

Most of the characteristics to be assimilated and accommodated to in our example are at least related to previous experiences, but some characteristics (for example, ripping the paper) may be quite foreign and startling. These varying degrees of discrepancy between current schemes and the experience at hand raise the issue of what the limitations are to accommodation. Piaget's answer was that only moderately discrepant events or characteristics can be accommodated to; great leaps are not possible. If reality is too different from the person's current level of understanding, she cannot bridge the gap. There can never be radical departures from the old. Thus, development necessarily proceeds in small steps.

To illustrate this gradual, continual development, consider what would happen if children of various ages were given a metal magnet for the first time. Six-month-olds might accommodate to the unfamiliar metallic taste, the peculiar (horseshoe) shape, and the sound of the magnet being dropped. However, they cannot accommodate such features as magnetic properties. Three-year-olds, if given an assortment of objects, might accommodate to the fact that some of the objects cling to the magnet and might entertain explanations such as "stickiness" and "wanting to stay together." Nine-year-old children might hypothesize that only objects with certain characteristics are attracted to the magnet and might test out the conditions in which magnetism occurs—through glass, water, and certain distances. Only in adolescence could children accommodate by formulating an abstract theory of magnetism and simultaneously consider all of the variables involved, such as the size and shape of the magnet and the distance from the object. Thus, accommodation always occurs in small steps and is relative to the present cognitive level. Infants do not accommodate to the property of magnetism.

In summary, the functional invariants of assimilation and accommodation are simultaneously present in every act and stimulate cognitive development. Attempts to apply one's current intellectual structures typically are only partially successful because most encounters with the environment are new in some way. As a result of this failure to "understand" the object or event, minor cognitive adjustments or accommodations are made. These push children to a slightly more advanced cognitive level. They are one step closer to reality. However, this new level of understanding makes them aware of other discrepancies in experience, and again assimilation presents new elements and again accommodation occurs. Each accommodation makes new accommodations possible in the future. This spiral continues in our moment-to-moment encounters with the environment throughout development.

COGNITIVE EQUILIBRATION

The two basic functional invariants, organization and adaptation, imply a third functional invariant: equilibration. In Piaget's view, every organism strives toward *equilibrium* with the environment and equilibrium within itself (among cognitive elements). When assimilation and accommodation are in balanced coordination so that neither one is dominant, equilibrium is achieved. This balance is achieved through the development of organized structures that provide ways of interacting with the world. A change in either the organism or the environment leads to a state of disequilibrium, which must be corrected. It should be clear from other parts of Piagetian theory that equilibrium is dynamic rather than static. There is constant activity, but there is a balance, a pattern, to this activity.

Piaget often used the liquid-conservation task to illustrate the equilibration process. Children proceed through four steps:

1. Centering on the heights of the liquids.

2. Centering on the widths of the liquids and eventually switching back and forth between heights and widths.

3. Considering heights and widths at the same time.

4. Applying mental operations such as compensation of height and width, which lead the child to assert that the amount is conserved. Children achieve equilibrium by bringing several pieces of information into balance. Their interaction with the world is no longer distorted by centration.

Equilibration, while one of the most important concepts in the theory, is probably also the most difficult and evasive. Part of the difficulty may lie in the fact that equilibration can refer to several spans of time, ranging from a fraction of a second to a number of years. In each case, there is a period of equilibrium, followed by a state of disequilibrium, followed by equilibration, which leads again to equilibrium.

Piaget seems to have had at least three spans of time in mind when he applied the notion of equilibrium. In each span one can consider equilibrium between the child and the external world or among concepts within the child.

1. The moment-to-moment equilibration process occurs as assimilation and accommodation operate in the course of adaptation. Temporary disequilibrium occurs when children encounter new properties of objects that do not fit into their present cognitive structures. Once the assimilation–accommodation process occurs and discrepancies are resolved, equilibrium is once again achieved. Assimilation and accommodation are brought into balance once again. At this level, the equilibration process is continually operating in the child's daily activities, no matter how mundane the activities.

2. Equilibration refers to moving toward the final level of achievement of each period or stage. A child enters a new period in a state of relative disequilibrium because the new cognitive organization is in the process of formation and therefore is incomplete and unstable. By the end of this new period, the child has achieved equilibrium with respect to the structures of the period. For example, at the end of the sensorimotor period, a child is in equilibrium with the environment in terms of action schemes but not in terms of operations. Each period achieves a different kind of equilibrium state. Equilibrium is reachieved in each period at a higher and higher level of abstraction.

3. The entire course of cognitive development can be seen as a process of equilibration as the child proceeds through increasingly "better" forms of equilibrium. The most complete equilibrium is achieved when formal operations bring fully reversible and abstract thought. Piaget saw a directionality to development toward a generalized, mobile, stable set of relations between the subject and the object. The earlier states of equilibrium, because they are incomplete, inevitably break down at some point. In a sense, each period or stage eventually self-destructs.

For Piaget, equilibration is the grand process that puts together all of the elements of development. Equilibration integrates and regulates the other three main factors of development: physical maturation, experience with the physical environment, and the influence of the social environment. All of these factors together propel the child through the stages. These factors are stage-independent forces that make cognitive development possible.

COMMENT

Perhaps the best way to summarize this section on mechanisms of development is to relate it to the earlier sections of this chapter. Knowledge of the world develops through a series of discrete states of equilibrium (stages) between the organism and the environment. This is the essence of Piaget's genetic epistemology. Mental structures, in equilibrium, are acquired as the organism interacts with objects in an organized way. Here we see Piaget's structuralism. In the innate tendencies toward organization and adaptation (assimilation and accommodation), we see Piaget the biologist. Finally, the particular stages that characterize human cognitive development are an inevitable outcome, given the nature of the human organism (its physical structures and cognitive functions) and the nature of the environment.

POSITION ON DEVELOPMENTAL ISSUES

The introductory chapter identified four basic developmental issues on which each theorist takes a stand. Using these issues, we can view Piaget's theory from a new perspective. The issues also provide a means for cutting across the diverse theories covered in this volume.

HUMAN NATURE

Piaget's world view clearly fits into the organismic rather than the mechanistic view. He posited an inherently active organism. Children tirelessly explore, hypothesize, test, and evaluate; they do this either overtly (particularly in the sensorimotor period) or covertly (as in the manipulation of symbols, concrete operations, and formal operations).

No external motivation is necessary. The motivation for this activity is intrinsic to the organism. Schemes are used simply because they exist. Once activated, they tend to be repeated. In other words, "to be is to do." The Piagetian child is a self-regulating, organized whole as he strives to maintain an equilibrium within himself and with the environment. He corrects any cognitive imbalance to the extent he is capable. The tendencies toward inherent activity and self-regulation produce an organism that is constantly changing.

Finally, the organismic world view can be seen in the fact that the parts can be understood only in terms of the whole. Any one behavior, scheme, or operation is influenced by and derives its meaning from the whole structure. The same behavior (for example, swinging a pendulum) obviously has a different meaning when observed in a 2-year-old than when observed in a 12-year-old.

QUALITATIVE VERSUS QUANTITATIVE DEVELOPMENT

Although Piaget saw both qualitative and quantitative changes, he emphasized the qualitative changes that occur when the overall cognitive structure changes. These structural changes occur, of course, when the child moves from period to period or from stage to stage. Just as the colored fragments rearrange themselves when a kaleidoscope is turned, so does the organization of thought change to form new patterns as the child develops.

In contrast to qualitative change, quantitative changes occur as schemes, operations, or other cognitive skills become stronger, more easily activated, more efficient, and more consistent. One could also say that there is quantitative development in the increase in the number of schemes or habits in the child's repertoire or the number of "facts" available. The child who can name the capitals of all the states has more information at hand than the child who can name only five capitals. Of course, it should be kept in mind that this information is always assimilated into structures that undergo qualitative changes. Thus, qualitative and quantitative changes go hand in hand.

Qualitative and quantitative changes build on each other during development. A qualitative change in structure makes possible certain quantitative changes. For example, once class inclusion is understood, the child can quickly learn about the classifications and relationships in many different content areas, such as animals, people, trees, shapes, and colors. Quantitative increases in amount of information, in turn, may pave the way for further qualitative change as new information challenges the present structures. For example, talking with peers and adults rapidly expands children's knowledge and challenges their present understanding. This new information can stimulate subsequent qualitative change as the system attempts to resolve the contradictions in children's knowledge.

Whether we see quantitative or qualitative change in Piaget's theory depends, in part, on the unit of time we select. If we look at changes over minutes, days, and weeks, we are struck by the gradual nature of development. If we look at changes over months and years, we are struck by the qualitative changes from stage to stage or period to period. For example, from age 4 to 4 1/2, children may become more consistent in their grouping of objects according to shape. That is, during those six months they are increasingly likely to keep the same basis of sorting from the beginning to the end of the task. This gradual improvement contrasts with the qualitative change in the basis of sorting, as when these children at age 7 can sort objects into hierarchies of classes—for example, animals, mammals, brown mammals, and so forth.

NATURE VERSUS NURTURE

Piaget was an interactionist through and through. All psychological phenomena, from the most specific and concrete sensorimotor behavior to the most general and abstract formal thought, are a result of the inextricable influences of innate and experiential factors. Innate factors include physical structures (for example, the structure and positioning of the particular species' eyes), reflexes, physical maturation, and the invariant functions (organization and adaptation). Given these innate factors and the nature of the physical and social world, development inevitably proceeds in the way it does. It could not be otherwise.

Piaget would have agreed with Anastasi (1958) that the proper question to ask is *how* innate and environmental factors interact. Piaget proposed the following four-factor "formula" for development:

Development = Physical maturation + Experience with the physical environment + Social experience + Equilibration

1. It is obvious that physical maturation—of the nervous system, the muscular system, and the like—creates new possibilities for the cognitive system and requires certain adjustments of that system. For example, when physical maturation permits walking, new vistas open up for toddlers. As children actively exploit this new skill, they are forced to assimilate and, whenever possible, accommodate to new experiences. Also, recent neuropsychological research (e.g., Diamond, 1991; Thatcher, Walker, & Giudice, 1987) has identified cerebral changes during development that appear to be linked to Piagetian qualitative changes in cognition.

2. Regarding experience with the physical environment, Piaget emphasizes *logicomathematical experience*. This term refers to reflecting on one's own actions on the objects rather than on the objects themselves. To illustrate, Piaget referred to a friend's recollection from childhood:

He was seated on the ground in his garden and he was counting pebbles. Now to count these pebbles he put them in a row and he counted them one, two, three up to 10. Then he finished counting them and started to count them in the other direction. He began by the end and once again found he had 10. He found this marvelous. . . . So he put them in a circle and counted them that way and found 10 once again.

[1964, p. 12]

The child considered the results of repeatedly counting and arranging the pebbles and concluded that number is constant despite physical rearrangements. He discovered something (number) that is not intrinsic to the objects themselves. He went beyond simply noting the color, shape, size, and weight of the pebbles.

3. The third factor, social experience, refers to the effect of the cultural or educational environment. For example, other people transmit knowledge, either directly or through books, television, and so on. In this way, a child can benefit from the experience of others. Of course, as always, the child must be cognitively advanced enough to assimilate the information if it is to be of value.

These three factors, taken together, can address the question of what is universal about cognitive development. Given the similarities among cultures in the course of physical maturation, the nature of the physical world, and, to a lesser extent, the nature of the social environment, it is not surprising that the four major periods proceed in the same order in all cultures studied. However, it is not clear whether the development of steps *within* the major periods occurs in an invariant sequence in all cultures. The methodological problems in doing cross–cultural research cloud the issue (see Ghuman, 1981, for a review). Even if some or all of the sequences identified by Piaget prove to be universal, we would still expect some variation in the *rate* of progress through the cognitive stages. This variation can arise from differences in physical maturation, physical experience, or social experience. We would expect some variation within a culture and some overall differences between cultures. An example of how experience in particular cultural settings can influence development comes from a study by Price-Williams, Gordon, and Ramirez (1969). They found that experience with clay promotes the development of conservation of substance (in which clay is the medium). Mexican children aged 6 to 9 who had grown up in pottery-making families were more likely to be conservers of substance than were Mexican children who had grown up in families engaged in other activities. In addition, Piaget recalled that his daughter Jacqueline, who was born in the winter, was often bundled up in a carriage, so she did not have as much opportunity as children born in warmer weather to develop eye–hand coordination.

4. The fourth factor, equilibration, ties together and controls the interaction of the innate and experiential factors. Maturation, experience with the physical environment, and the influence of the social environment constantly cause momentary disequilibrium. In this way, they force the cognitive system to change, to adjust. Through reestablishing equilibrium, the cognitive system reaches a higher level. Thus, it is in the interplay of forces within the equilibration process that experiential and innate forces together finally have their effect on cognition.

From this account, it is obvious that experience does not write upon a passive, blank slate. Intelligence is always active and self-regulating, from the first modification of a reflex to the formal operations of adolescent thought.

A final claim about the role of experience is that the timing of the experience is important. Here we see the notion of "readiness." A child can profit from a given experience only if she is ready for it. She must be able to assimilate it to her present cognitive structures or accommodate her structures to the experience. Instruction in calculus would not be successful with most 5-year-olds.

What Develops

For Piaget, the essence of cognitive development is structural change—change in the schemes, regulations, functions, and various logico-mathematical structures of the concrete and formal operational periods. Structural change gives meaning to and influences change in the content of thought. Thus, Piaget emphasized change on a molar level, which leads to change at various more molecular levels.

The question of what develops is tied to Piaget's methodology. He relied on observations, interviews (the clinical method), and assessment situations in which the experimenter participates. In this way, he kept the organization of the thought processes as intact as possible; too much experimental interference or control would distort the child's normal line of reasoning.

THEORETICAL NATURE OF THE THEORY

We have essentially completed our description of Piaget's theory. It is now time to look back to our discussion of the nature of theories in the introductory chapter and see what kind of theory Piaget had. This meta-theoretical overview prepares us for the final section, which is an evaluation of the theory.

Did Piaget deduce, induce, model, or describe functional relationships? The best answer to this multiple-choice question is "all of the above." At one time or another in his life, Piaget could be found doing each kind of theory building. Let us look at what aspects of the theory could be classified as a model, a deductive theory, a functional theory, and an inductive theory.

There are two main models in the theory: the equilibration model and the logicomathematical model. Both were described earlier in this chapter, and they are now examined in terms of what they do for the theory. Recall from the Introduction that a model is a framework, structure, or system that has been developed in one field and is applied to another field. A model is a heuristic device that guides research and theory building, but is not itself modified by the outcome of this research and theorizing.

Of the many types of equilibration systems in nature, Piaget chose a system that maintains a dynamic rather than a static balance. The dynamic model of equilibrium comes from the fields of physics (thermodynamics and mechanics) and biology. For example, a thermostat and a mollusk are self-regulating equilibration systems. For Piaget, systems of psychological actions maintain equilibrium, despite constant activity and change, to maintain a steady state. Built-in corrective devices counteract new forces acting on the system. In contrast to Piaget's active system is a static system, exemplified by a balance scale with equal weights on the two pans. It is a closed system at rest, with no method of exchange between the system and the environment. If someone adds more weights to one side, the scale has no inherent, internal mechanism for achieving balance again; re-equilibration occurs only by means of an external force, such as a human who adds weights to the other side.

The equilibration model has been used by many theorists, including Freud, Gesell, and the cognitive-dissonance theorists. However, Piaget more than anyone else gave it a central, unifying role in cognitive development. Equilibration unifies the theory by providing a general, overall regulatory function. The various experiential and maturational forces are tied together and organized by the process of equilibration. The model also unifies the theory by outlining the causes and nature of the transitions from state to state. Cognitive imbalance motivates the system to activate cognitive actions, and these move the system to a higher state of equilibrium. A final way in which the model unifies the theory is that it gave Piaget a way to compare and contrast the various cognitive levels or various domains within a cognitive level. Cognitive levels or domains can vary in their stability and mobility.

The second main model is the logicomathematical model, which is most clearly seen in the logicomathematical structures applied to concrete and formal operational thought. Logic and algebra are purely formal, nonpsychological systems. However, Piaget felt that cognitive structures approximated these abstract logicomathematical structures and that it would be fruitful to look for various types of thinking suggested by the model. Furthermore, logical models are often clearer and more specific than verbal statements.

Since a complete description of the various logicomathematical structures is beyond the scope of a single chapter on Piaget, an example may illustrate how the model is used. In the concrete operational period, there are nine groupings—logical structures that describe certain logical operations and relationships among these operations. Let us look at the psychological concept of class inclusion, which corresponds to what Piaget called grouping I. This grouping describes the primary addition of classes and is the simplest grouping. For example, modes of transportation form a classification hierarchy, in which modes of transportation (C) at the top of the hierarchy have two subheadings: ground vehicles (B) and other classes of vehicles (B'). B, in turn, contains cars (A) and other ground vehicles (A'). The system's elements (A, A', B, B', C) can be manipulated according to certain rules. In the case of grouping I, the rules refer to the following properties of the grouping: composition $(A + A' + B)$; association $[(A + B) + C = C]$; general identity $(A + 0 = A)$; negation $(A - A = 0)$; and special identities $(A + A = A$ or $A + B = B)$. These properties, stated in formal, nonpsychological terms, serve as a model for the properties of thought that underlie the concept of class inclusion. They are logical representations that describe the essence of thought.

The grouping probably should be considered an idealized version of what cognitive structures the child must have in order to solve class-inclusion problems. As Flavell (1963) expressed it, a child who understands class inclusion is like a computer with a grouping program. The grouping supplies the necessary operations for the computer to solve the problem, and children solve the problem in an analogous way. The actual process of thinking, however, may differ in various ways from that expressed by the grouping. Several different computer programs can produce the same answer. In other words, grouping I is a logically possible cognitive structure, but it is not necessarily the child's actual cognitive structure. In short, this is the nature of models. They are heuristic devices. They tell us what to look for, and they provide a framework for interpreting behavior. However, they may or may not reflect reality.

Next, regarding deductive theories, it is clear that Piaget's theory as a whole does not meet the requirements. Recall that a deductive theory is a formalized network of logically related propositions. Hypotheses, which are derived from the propositions, are subjected to empirical tests, and the outcomes of these tests serve to support or modify the theory. At best, Piaget's theory provides a set of loosely connected verbal propositions. For example, we could translate his claims about stages into a set of propositions and derive certain hypotheses about behavior during each of these stages. However, we cannot trace a logically tight series of steps from the general propositions about stages all the way down to specific hypotheses. Certain steps in the logical progression are missing, and certain propositions are vague (for example, claims about equilibration). As a result, we only know in general what to predict about behavior in each stage. The consequence is that the empirical results do not always clearly support or refute the more general claims about stages. This state of affairs does not mean that the theory can never be presented in a deductive fashion. It merely means that at present, like most developmental theories, Piaget's theory is not satisfactorily formalized. Thus, the more general claims are difficult to test.

It should be noted that in more limited ways the theory could be considered a deductive system. The logicomathematical model, in particular, may play this deductive role. Most models do not have a hierarchic, organized structure that lends itself to making deductions. The logicomathematical model, however, consists of sets of logically interrelated formal propositions. Because the various logical operations are logically interconnected, if certain logical operations are found in the child's thought, then one can predict (deduce) that the child should possess certain other logical operations. For example, Piaget's model would predict a particular type of logical relationship between the operation of classifying objects and the operation of ordering them along some dimension.

Regarding functional theories, if we were to leaf through developmental research journals, we might conclude that Piaget's theory is of this type. American psychologists have focused on certain Piagetian tasks such as conservation, object permanence, and perceptual perspective taking. In the case of conservation, Piaget claimed that conservers should demonstrate certain concrete operations, such as mental reversibility and compensation, and that conservation training should be most successful for children who are "ready" to develop conservation naturally. These claims and others have been tested in hundreds of experiments. In these experiments, there is a close interplay between the explanatory hypotheses and the data.

Finally, there is little in Piaget's theory that can be termed inductive theory building: developing descriptive statements that merely summarize sets of data and involve little inference. It is true that the theory includes some low-level descriptive statements that are closely tied to the data. However, as we have seen, Piaget constantly leapt from empirical observations to the abstract upper levels of the theory. Inductive theorists simply do not talk about cognitive structures, equilibration, and the like. Moreover, unlike inductive theorists, Piaget moved from theory to data as easily as from data to theory.

EVALUATION OF THE THEORY

As we saw earlier, when Piaget's first writings on children appeared, he was appalled that people evaluated them as though they were final statements on certain cognitive problems rather than the tentative solutions he intended them to be. Even in his final years, over half a century later, Piaget probably would have reacted to evaluations of his theory in much the same way. The theory continued to expand and undergo modifications as Piaget continued to work into his mid-eighties. We should keep the theory's potential for change in mind as we sit in judgment. We now look at the most salient strengths and weaknesses of the theory.

STRENGTHS

We focus on five strengths of Piaget's theory: its recognition of the central role of cognition in development, its value as an integrative and heuristic theory, its discovery of surprising features of young children's thinking, its wide-ranging scope, and its ecological validity.

Recognition of the Central Role of Cognition

Piaget transformed the field of developmental psychology. If a developmental psychologist were somehow plucked out of the 1950s and set down today, he would be bewildered by the talk around him. He would hear psychologists discussing strategies, rule-governed behaviors, cognitive structures, schemes, plans, and representations, instead of stimulus generalization, mean length of utterance, mental age, conditioning, discrimination learning, and learning set. To a great extent, Piaget was responsible for this change. He altered the course of psychology by asking new questions that made developmentalists wonder why they had ever asked the old questions in the first place. Once psychologists looked at development through Piaget's eyes, they never again saw children in quite the same way. Before we go into the specific notions that transformed developmental psychology, we must glance at the state of the field that received and assimilated Piaget.

Both the state of academic psychology and the history of developmental psychology in the United States provided fertile ground for change in the 1950s and 1960s. Academic psychology had pushed behaviorism in general and learning theory in particular to their limits and found them wanting. Even when learning theory was modified by such notions as verbal mediation, social reinforcement, modeling, intrinsic reinforcement, and attention, it did not completely satisfy psychologists. There was dissatisfaction with the notion of drives, with the explanation of language development in terms of imitation, practice, and reinforcement, and with the formal theory building of Hullian psychology. Along with these dissatisfactions, there were promising approaches from several directions: Noam Chomsky's transformational grammar, Donald Broadbent's filter model of attention, and computer scientists' work on information processing. All these were cognitive approaches. The winds of change were sweeping the field of psychology. America was ready for Piaget.

We must look at not only the readiness of American academic psychology for cognitive theories but also the particular history of developmental psychology in the United States. Until the 1950s, researchers interested in children could be found less often in departments of psychology than in "child institutes" or departments of home economics, pediatrics, public health, education, clinical psychology, and nursing. The real-life problems of children's physical and mental welfare often meant that developmentalists worked in child institutes that were physically and ideologically isolated from departments of psychology. At the very least, most developmental psychologists were forced to keep one foot in real-life settings and one foot in the laboratory. Thus, concern with poor nutrition, physical and mental retardation, learning disabilities, and emotional disturbances prevented many developmental psychologists from becoming completely immersed in the behaviorist–experimental zeitgeist of academic psychology of the 1940s and 1950s. In addition, developmental psychologists at that time were primarily interested in collecting normative data—descriptions of the behaviors that could be expected at each age. For all these reasons, there was room for Piaget's naturalistic, descriptive approach. For developmentalists, problems resulting from Piaget's lack of uniform testing procedures and statistical analysis and his small number of subjects were more than offset by his remarkable naturalistic observations.

A newcomer to developmental psychology might wonder why Piaget had produced almost a lifetime of work before American academics became interested in him. Certainly the state of academic psychology at that time provides part of the answer. A further reason is the language barrier. Until the 1960s, much of Piaget's work had not been translated into English. An additional language problem is that Piaget's writings are difficult to understand in any language! Fortunately, John Flavell, David Elkind, Hans Furth, and Joachim Wohlwill, among others, served as psychological translators of Piaget's work in the late 1950s and early 1960s. In particular, Flavell's timely book, *The Developmental Psychology of Jean Piaget* (1963), made Piaget understandable to English-speaking psychologists.

The rest, as they say, is history. Psychology witnessed both a flurry of Piagetian replication studies and an attempt to fit Piaget into the existing field of developmental psychology. For example, Berlyne (1965) attempted to integrate learning theory and Piagetian theory. Next came efforts to train children to acquire various Piagetian concepts, especially conservation. At the same time, there emerged American-style laboratory studies of variables such as the nature of task materials and instructions, the scoring criteria, and the socioeconomic level of the children. In fact, interest in Piaget's theory became so intense that nearly 20 percent of all articles published in the journal *Developmental Psychology* from 1969 to mid-1972 cited books by or about Piaget (Looft & Svoboda, 1971). Later came an extension of Piaget's theory into areas such as social development, clinical psychology, and education. For example, educators applied Piaget's notions that learning is most likely to occur when the child actively participates, when problems are approached in a concrete rather than an abstract way, and when the child is cognitively ready to learn. In short, the 1960s and 1970s became the "Piagetian stage" of developmental psychology.

The purpose of this historical side trip has been to show the impact of a theory that recognized the central role of cognition in development. Piaget searched for the modes of thinking underlying the overt behavior studied by behaviorists and by child psychologists constructing norms of development. This focus on cognition provided a new perspective for a generation of developmental psychologists.

Value as an Integrative and Heuristic Theory

The introductory chapter asserted that a theory has two functions. First, it should integrate and give meaning to facts. Second, it should serve as a heuristic device for further research. Piaget's theory passes both tests. With respect to its integrative function, it postulates an underlying continuity and organization to a range of seemingly unrelated behaviors. Continuity and organization exist at any one point in time by means of stages and at different points in time by means of the invariant functions. For an example of the integrative nature of the stage notion, we can turn to the logical structures that underlie notions about number, time, causality, and people in the concrete operational period. For an example of the integrative nature of the invariant functions, we turn to the gradual, selective changes in the concept of spatial relations. There is moment-to-moment continuity over time as schemes or operations are slowly stretched to incorporate new information. Longer, cross-stage continuity occurs as the understanding of spatial relations is transformed from physical actions to symbols, then concrete operations, and finally formal operational systems.

Piaget's theory has also served well in its second function, as a heuristic device for the generation of new research. One influential notion is Piaget's view that children actively construct knowledge. This view has colored research not only in general cognitive development, but also in memory, attention, learning, language, and social cognition. Researchers in these areas are sensitive to children's strategies, hypotheses, and plans. The "active child" has become a cliché.

A second notion that has had heuristic value is that development follows an invariant sequence, in which later forms use and build on earlier forms. Psychologists studying Piagetian-inspired concepts, such as classification, number, and causality, search for intellectual precursors to the mature forms of these concepts. A psychologist studying number automatically looks for earlier subskills, such as counting or attending appropriately, that eventually lead to a mature understanding of number.

Other influential heuristic ideas about development include the following:

1. Children inherently seek stimulation rather than passively await it (as proposed by the stimulus–response learning and Freudian theories).

2. The thinking of elementary schoolchildren resembles that of logicomathematical structures.

3. The "wrong" or "cute" notions that preschool children have about the world are a symptom of a complex, probing intellectual system that is trying to understand reality.

4. Much of cognitive development does not depend on our ability to use language.

5. To a great extent, children teach themselves.

The list could go on.

Discovery of Surprising Features of Children's Thinking

Piaget's main legacy may be his rich description of what it is we develop. The thousands of observations by Piaget himself, combined with the thousands of studies inspired by him, constitute a remarkable body of information. Regardless of the final judgment on his theoretical claims, his detailed, sensitive, and astute observations remain with us.

Piaget revealed new developmental phenomena, many of which strike people as surprising or counter to common sense. Especially notable are the following: Infants apparently do not expect objects to be permanent. Preschoolers believe that rearranging objects can change their number and assert that the wrongness of an act depends on how much damage resulted. More generally, most concepts not only take longer to develop than we might think but also go through a number of interesting steps along the way. A further surprise is that children think about such a wide variety of things. Children's thinking ranges from pondering the origin of the universe to solving the problem of how to open doors without dropping what they are holding, from penetrating the nature of society's moral system to determining the speed of the swing of a pendulum. In a discipline that has few real "discoveries" to rival the discovery of a new planet or the structure of DNA, Piaget's surprises about cognitive development are refreshing and his observations remarkable, considering that they came from seemingly mundane, everyday behavior. He showed us that developmental descriptions can be profoundly intriguing.

Wide-ranging Scope

Piaget's theory is ambitious, drawing its net over behavior ranging from playing with pebbles to causal reasoning, from the sucking reflex to formal operational structures. The theory attempts to describe and explain both cognitive states and transitions between those states. Piaget not only tackled cognitive development, he also followed up on its implications for other areas of development, such as social and emotional development and learning. In addition, he spoke to other disciplines, such as epistemology, philosophy of science, and education. In Piaget we catch a glimpse of how a complete theory of development might look.

The theory's wide scope obviously increases its attractiveness. At the same time, it increases its vulnerability. The theory may have tried to do too much too soon.

Ecological Validity

Every psychologist has an intuitive list of what a good theory should do. Many lists would include the requirement that the theory tell us about the real world of children. Although even the most basic research in laboratories has some relevance for day-to-day behavior, some approaches have a closer relationship than others to common, everyday behavior. Piaget's theory seems to rate well in this respect. The focus is on children's adaptation to the world they encounter every day. Infants try to grasp a rattle just out of reach, replace a pacifier, and figure out where a ball has rolled. Preschoolers divide their cookies with friends, try to express their ideas to others, and chastise those who break the rules of games. School children struggle with math problems, try to make sense of social rules, and find their way around their neighborhood or city.

The ecological validity of the theory is more striking for infancy than for the later stages of development. When studying children beyond infancy, Piaget tended to interrupt the flow of behavior with questions or even pose problems from the beginning. The reason is that infants' thinking is expressed in their overt actions, whereas older children's thinking is more covert and must be prodded.

WEAKNESSES

The excitement and inspiration generated by Piaget's theory have faded into a feeling that the theory is not all that it could be. Although it broke much new ground, several serious weaknesses have been exposed. Piaget provides an easy target in many ways. His unusual methodology, his wide scope, and his ties to biology and philosophy encourage psychologists to find the inadequacies in the theory. The goal in this section is to point out these inadequacies and determine which are most easily corrected. We examine the following weaknesses: inadequate support for the stage notion, inadequate account of mechanisms of development, need for a theory of performance, slighting of social and emotional aspects of development, and methodological and stylistic inadequacies. In addition, we review some of the recent research, particularly in North America, stimulated by the recognition of these weaknesses.

Inadequate Support for the Stage Notion

The strongest attacks on Piaget's theory concern his notion of stages, the heart of the theory. Are there, in fact, broad stretches during development that have characteristics that apply to all the psychological events during that period? Or does the notion of stages simply confuse and mislead by oversimplifying development and claiming more coherence among concepts than there actually is? A basic issue here is how stages are related to the child's actual intellectual functioning. Although Piaget sometimes treated the stages, particularly their logical structures, as idealized models of thought, he usually claimed that the stages have a psychological reality. They are not merely models or heuristic devices. That is, the stages describe the actual psychological organization of the child's knowledge and predict the child's knowledge about a range of objects and events. His main evidence for the reality of stages was the similarity in thought over a variety of content areas and the feeling of necessity that accompanies the acquisition of a cognitive structure. For example, he quoted a child who said, "Once one knows, one knows forever and ever" (1971, p. 5). Piaget asserted that the logical structures give this feeling of logical necessity.

The evidence certainly does not support a strong structural version of stages, in the sense of concurrent changes across all content areas. In fact, Piaget himself acknowledged that a structure may apply only to a particular content area and may have to be constructed anew in various domains during a stage. He referred to *horizontal décalages* that occur when a general concept emerges earlier on some tasks than others. For example, in the case of conservation, the conservation of substance typically develops a year or two before conservation of weight. He also would probably not have been bothered by child prodigies whose cognitive achievements in one particular area, such as math, are much more advanced than they are in other areas of thinking. Thus, a weaker structural version of stages may be still viable; some unevenness across domains would even be expected. However, inconsistency in applying even a content-limited concept, such as conservation of substance, poses a problem even for this weaker version. For instance, Uzgiris (1968) assessed conservation of substance, using plasticine balls, metal cubes, wire coils, or plastic wire. Conservation emerged earlier on some materials or types of transformations than others. Moreover, as described later, a concept is demonstrated with simpler task demands earlier than with more complex ones. In addition, "formal operational" adults who can test hypotheses like a scientist in some situations often are poor at testing hypotheses regarding matters about which they have intuitive, often erroneous, theories (Kuhn, 1989). They even ignore or distort data that contradict their beliefs. Is the mind simply a "collection of different and unrelated mindlets" (Flavell, 1992) devoted to different contents?

Even if one accepts a weaker stage notion, the problem remains that Piaget did not provide a satisfactory account of what determines whether a structure will be applied to a particular content area. When should we expect generalization and when should we not? Piaget's claim that décalages are caused by differences in how various stimuli "resist" the application of the cognitive structures was not worked out satisfactorily.

It is difficult to decide whether the notion of stages is wrong or simply incomplete. Are the logicomathematical structures a philosopher's dream or, as described at present, are they simply too vague, general, and distant from behavior? Looft and Svoboda voice some of these doubts:

> While reading Piaget's most recent writings one sometimes acquires an eerie, cold feeling that something very strange is going on in this man's work. In his early writings we read about delightful children playing on the banks of Lake Geneva, expressing their surprise and exhilaration as they make new discoveries about their little worlds. Today we are presented with some sort of cybernetic automata, regulating themselves and pushing themselves to ever higher levels of differentiation and complexity. In short, it would seem that as Piaget's theory has evolved over the past five decades to higher and higher levels of abstraction, people have somehow dropped out and have been replaced by sterile logicomathematical structures.
>
> *[1971, p. 15]*

Analyses of the stage notion by Flavell (1971b, 1982) demonstrate both its incompleteness and the potential for revision within the theory. Flavell suggested several modifications of Piaget's conception of stages:

1. Stagelike, qualitative changes appear to be causally linked to more gradual, quantitative sorts of developmental changes, such as an increasing attentional capacity or an increasing stability and generality of concepts.

2. The development of a cognitive skill is an extended process. In fact, children may not achieve the "full functional maturity" of a stage until after that stage has officially ended.

3. Concepts or structures that characterize a stage are often only roughly synchronous in their development. For example, two concepts might begin their development at the same time but complete it at different times. Or they might begin and end their development at different times but have a considerable temporal overlap. There are other possible temporal relationships as well. The temporal relationships among various developments are especially important for an adequate account of the logicomathematical structures. In what sense are they a simultaneously developing, tightly knit system of structures?

4. The cognitive items of a particular stage may *eventually* become tightly organized and interrelated into a true stage even if there is not synchrony throughout the stage.

5. In cognitive performance, there are several different types of homogeneity and heterogeneity, and these vary in their implications for Piaget's theory. For example, there may be more cognitive homogeneity in spontaneous, everyday thinking than in testing situations and more in some cognitive domains than in others.

Although Flavell revealed the ambiguity and complexity of the notion of stages, he also showed that Piaget's theory can generate interesting and testable hypotheses. Even though the stages may be less coherent units than Piaget would have us believe, they are still useful ways to organize a large number of diverse behaviors. They are convenient points of reference for accounting for the orderliness of thought. As Flavell and Wohlwill concluded, "To paraphrase Voltaire's dictum concerning the deity: if there were no such structures in the mind of the child, we should have to invent them, to account for the degree of consistency and orderliness that we do find in his cognitive development" (1969, p. 94).

As suggested earlier, the most reasonable way to use Piaget's notion of stages may be to look for stagelike changes limited to a particular content area (Feldman, 1980). Each domain may develop somewhat independently of the others, and thus we would have domain-specific knowledge. This possibility was explored by the neo-Piagetians, to be discussed later. Domain-specific knowledge also is emphasized by knowledge-based approaches (e.g., Chi, Glaser, & Farr, 1988; and see Chapter 4). In this view a child shifts from novice to expert status after experience in a particular domain such as chess, soccer, or dinosaurs. Domain-specific knowledge also is posited by the modularity approach (see the Introduction) and certain other biological approaches (Carey & Gelman, 1991). Similarly, the recent "theory-based" approach (e.g., Carey, 1985; Keil, 1989) proposes that knowledge about a particular domain consists of an informed, intuitive "theory"—a coherent, interrelated, causal–explanatory set of concepts. Examples of such domains are biology, physics, and psychology (Wellman & Gelman, 1992). One of the most active areas of such research currently is children's "theory of mind" (Premack & Woodruff, 1978). This knowledge involves a sequence of concepts, namely, that the mind (1) exists, (2) is connected to the external world, (3) is separate from and differs from the external world, (4) can represent objects and events accurately or inaccurately, and (5) actively mediates how a person interprets reality (Flavell, Miller, & Miller, 1993). For example, 3-year-olds, because of their limited understanding that representations affect behavior, do not understand that a person acts on the basis of beliefs—true or false. That is, they do not realize that a person would look for an object in the place he last saw it rather than in the place it is in reality—where it was moved to in the person's absence and without his knowledge (Perner, Leekam, & Wimmer, 1987).

Inadequate Account of Mechanisms of Development

We need clarification not only of the criteria for stages but also of the transitional mechanisms both within a stage and from stage to stage. Piaget more successfully described than explained the course of development. The functional invariants, such as assimilation and accommodation, provide at best a general framework with which to examine cognitive change. There are no specific, precise statements as to how sensorimotor thought becomes preoperational thought or how preoperational thought becomes operational thought. Furthermore, although the equilibration process is an intuitively appealing idea, it is not clear how children's awareness of a contradiction would lead them to the solution that resolves the contradiction (Bryant, 1986). Simply knowing that something is wrong does not identify the cause of the problem.

One way to study mechanisms of change is to supply certain experiences and see whether they cause cognitive change. Piaget was dubious about the value of trying to intensively teach concepts to children and cautioned that "each time one prematurely teaches a child something he could have discovered for himself, that child is kept from inventing it and consequently from understanding it completely" (1983, p. 113). However, Piagetians, especially Inhelder, attempted to provide empirical support for the mechanisms of change by studying how training studies stimulate learning (Inhelder, Sinclair, & Bovet, 1974). In addition, hundreds of training studies were conducted by American and British psychologists. Many of these successfully taught a new concept by creating cognitive conflict, teaching underlying operations such as reversibility or compensation, verbalizing the rule for the child, or providing a model who illustrates the new concept. Other approaches focused on removing barriers to the child's performance by redirecting attention to the relevant feature, such as number, or by ensuring memory of relevant information.

Unfortunately, training studies only minimally illuminated mechanisms of development. First of all, even if we find that training based on one of Piaget's mechanisms of development (for example, cognitive conflict) causes the child to acquire the concept, there is no guarantee that children progress by this mechanism in real life. Spontaneous, natural development may proceed in other ways. Secondly, when a training study does succeed, that success may be based on mechanisms other than those the investigators thought they were providing. Gelman's (1969) training procedure was intended to redirect the child's attention from irrelevant dimensions (e.g., length of a row of objects) to the relevant dimension (number). However, as Beilin (1971) pointed out, this procedure's success could have stemmed from cognitive conflict created when the child's initial answer did not consistently lead to reinforcement. Third, there is no specific account of why a particular training experience stimulates change in some children but not others. In general, the older children are, the more likely they are to acquire the concept as a result of training, presumably because they are closer to acquiring the concept naturally. However, more refined predictions are more difficult because it is not clear how to assess degree of readiness in children of the same age.

Need for a Theory of Performance

Piaget created an elaborate system of cognitive structures that represent children's knowledge about the world. He also provided a rich description of behavior. There is, however, a missing link: a detailed account of exactly *how* the structures are translated into behavior. This account could be called a theory of performance—a theory of how a child's knowledge is expressed in her behavior at any particular time. A theory of performance takes heed of cognitive processes such as memory, attention, mental capacity, and verbal comprehension. In this undertaking, the theory must deal with variables that influence these processes. This list of variables would include, for example, the salience of each attribute (shape, color) in the materials, familiarity of the materials, the amount of information to remember, and the complexity of instructions about the task. These performance factors may account, in part, for the extended, gradual development described in the papers on stages by Flavell (1971b, 1982) mentioned earlier. For example, it may be that the early, fragile form of a concept can be used only if there are not large demands on the child's memory, attentional capacity, and verbal ability.

The conservation-of-number task can supply us with a concrete example of how a theory of performance would analyze the way children use their cognitive structures. A test of conservation of number requires that the child proceed through a number of steps as the stimuli (objects and instructions) make contact with the mental operations relevant to conservation. Some of the steps are as follows: (1) understanding that the task concerns the number of the objects rather than some other feature and (2) attending to the relevant attribute (number) while ignoring irrelevant attributes (color, length, and orientation). Other steps might be (3) counting the objects, (4) encoding information about the number of objects, (5) observing the experimenter move the objects, and (6) remembering the initial equality and the lack of addition or subtraction during the transformation. In addition, the child may (7) recall previous experiences with counting or moving objects, (8) search for an appropriate rule or mental operation, and (9) carry out the appropriate operation, for example, mentally reversing the transformation. Final steps involve (10) inferring the correct answer and (11) translating this answer into words, including a logical explanation. It should be noted that some of these steps may occur at the same time rather than in sequence.

Piaget did not deny the importance of these cognitive activities. He simply was less interested in them than in the more general cognitive structures. In contrast, other theoretical approaches, such as information processing, Gibson's perceptual learning, learning theory, and contextualism, focus on the nature of performance. We encounter these theories in later chapters; they may eventually provide the missing link between structures and behavior in Piaget's theory.

In his later years Piaget and his colleagues [Inhelder & Piaget, 1980; Piaget, 1981 (1987)] began to give more attention to a performance model, as seen in their work on procedural knowledge. Piaget saw procedural knowledge as distinct from but complementary to structural knowledge. Procedures, or mental actions carried out in a sequence, provide the means used to reach a goal. They include strategies for gathering relevant information or processing it further during problem solving. Thus, procedures help children use their structures.

Developmental psychologists have given some attention to performance variables in Piagetian cognitive development. Flavell and

Wohlwill (1969) made a distinction between competence (knowledge) and performance in cognitive development and outlined a set of issues involved in this distinction. Empirical research revealed the importance of memory (Trabasso, 1977), attention (Gelman, 1969), stimulus complexity (Gzesh & Surber, 1985), encoding (Siegler, 1978), language used in the testing procedures (S. A. Miller, 1976), stimulus variables (P. H. Miller, 1978), and information-processing capacity (Case, 1985). For example, with respect to stimulus variables, materials for conservation have included even classmates and live crickets (S. A. Miller, 1982).

Slighting of Social and Emotional Aspects of Development

Piaget gave relatively little attention to (1) how sociocultural–historical influences and emotions shape cognitive development and (2) the nature of the development of cognitions concerning people and social events. With respect to the first criticism, it has been said that Piaget's epistemic subject has no social class, sex, nationality, culture, or personality—and also has no fun (Murray, 1983, p. 231). Later chapters on social learning theory and contextualism will show that social influences must be addressed. Piaget's neglect of social factors reflected his lesser interest in such factors compared to other factors. We can hardly say that Piaget was lazy! However, this inattention to social influences may have affected even his assessment of physical concepts. For example, the standard Piagetian procedure, in which an adult asks children about quantity twice (before and after the transformation), may cause children to think that they should change their answer because of the adult's actions on the materials or because they were asked the question twice, which may imply that their first answer was wrong. More conservation is revealed when the question is asked only once (Samuel & Bryant, 1984).

Curiously, emotional influences continue to be slighted by contemporary developmentalists. Piaget considered cognition and emotion to be parallel and interdependent: "Feelings express the interest and value given to actions of which intelligence provides the structure" [1945 (1951, pp. 205–206)]. He suggested that, in a sense, emotions provide the energetic force behind behavior. For example, feelings influence the content to which structures are applied (see Renninger, Hidi, & Krapp, 1992, for recent research on the role of interests). A child with a passion for airplanes is likely to learn a great deal about them.

Regarding children's thinking about social objects and events, Piaget claimed that the development of cognitive structures can be seen in the realm of social as well as physical objects and events. However, his philosophical and biological interests led him mainly toward physical concepts such as time, space, and causality. His main contributions to social development are his work on moral judgments, egocentrism, and communication. Kohlberg (1969) adopted Piaget's stage approach to moral judgments and expanded and modified the model considerably. Inspired by Kohlberg and Piaget, psychologists publish studies on moral judgments at a steady rate. In recent years, there has been a flurry of interest in what is called "social cognition." This term refers to how children understand (a) the thoughts, intentions, feelings, points of view, and behavior of other people and (b) social relationships such as friendship. The inspiration for this work comes from both Piaget and social attribution theory based primarily on research with adults. To some extent, then, others are correcting Piaget's omissions in the area of social development.

Methodogical and Stylistic Inadequacies

Critics of Piaget have identified certain inadequacies in how he conducted and reported his research. With respect to his infancy research, Piaget observed his own three children. Unfortunately, he did not have 40 or 50 children of his own for a more respectable sample size! The small number of subjects, the possible biases in interpreting the behavior of one's own children, the absence of measures of reliability by having two independent observers, and the lack of control over the children's immediate environment, possible only in a laboratory, did not endear Piaget to American experimental psychologists. However, subsequent studies, with more subjects and better-controlled testing situations, generally have replicated the sequence of development within infancy, if not always the exact ages at which the changes occur.

In his work with older children, Piaget usually employed the clinical method. Although the clinical method has certain advantages, such as flexibility in tailoring questions to the particular answers given by each child, it also has a number of disadvantages. Two main disadvantages are the danger that examiners may be too leading in their questions or not leading enough and that different children may be asked slightly different questions. Uniform instructions, stimuli, and measures of response are the backbone of testing in experimental psychology. We are asked to make the leap of faith that Piaget was in fact a sensitive and accurate observer. Piaget himself seemed aware of these problems:

It is so hard not to talk too much when questioning a child, especially for a pedagogue! It is so hard not to be suggestive! And above all, it is so hard to find the middle course between systematization due to preconceived ideas and incoherence due to the absence of any directing hypothesis!

[1926 (1929, p. 9)]

With respect to the verbal nature of the testing, one concern has been that children may not completely understand the instructions, for example, the meaning of "same number" and "amount." Another concern is that children may not be able to express in words their ideas about quantity, the origin of the universe, the nature of dreams, and so forth. Moreover, children may have the concept of conservation but not be able to give an adequate reason for their answer—one of Piaget's criteria for conservation. Children's knowledge may, therefore, be underestimated.

This concern with the considerable verbal requirements has led to a number of interesting attempts to devise nonverbal or at least less verbal procedures. Psychologists have cleverly devised ways of using expressions of surprise (Gelman, 1972), heart rate (Bower, 1974), and choice of candy (S. A. Miller, 1976) to test for the presence or absence of certain concepts. For example, Gelman (1972) found that 3-year-olds notice and are surprised when the number of toy mice changes (because the experimenter has surreptitiously removed one).

Similarly, Piaget's requiring infants to search for a hidden object before being credited with the concept of object permanence may have caused underestimations of their competence as well. Baillargeon (1987) found that 4-month-old infants, who should not yet possess the concept of object permanence, were surprised when a screen falling away from them seemed to pass through a now out-of-view box they had seen there earlier. Other studies find infant precocities in areas such as understanding physical concepts (Spelke, 1991), causal understanding (e.g., Leslie, 1988), problem solving (e.g., Willatts, 1989), and representation (Mandler, 1990). There is considerable debate whether these studies demonstrate that some of Piaget's concepts develop earlier than he thought or whether the nonverbal or motorically less demanding procedures are revealing earlier, less advanced versions of these concepts. Some theorists who interpret these studies as showing sophisticated knowledge in infants go on to argue for powerful biological constraints that permit the rapid acquisition of certain knowledge about language, mental states, and objects and their behaviors (Carey & Gelman, 1991). It should be noted that even if concepts are developed earlier than Piaget found, this finding is not necessarily damaging to his theory. His concern was with the order in which concepts are acquired, not the particular ages.

Another basic concern with Piaget's methods is that his procedures may be too complex and consequently underestimate the child's knowledge. One way to simplify the task is to use simpler materials. For example, young children demonstrate more knowledge about counting when there are only a few objects than when there are many (Gelman & Gallistel, 1978). The importance of such modifications of Piaget's methodology may lie less in the fact that the concepts may be acquired earlier than Piaget thought than in the unearthing of precursors to the concepts examined by Piaget. Gelman and Gallistel found a sequence of simple principles of counting, such as the principle that numerals must always be used in the same order. That is, children who say "1, 2, 6, 9" follow this counting principle correctly if they always use these numerals in this order for counting. These early principles supplement Piaget's account of the full-blown concept of number acquired several years later. Techniques that simplify the Piagetian tests are more sensitive to earlier forms of concepts than are Piaget's procedures.

The differences in the methodology of Genevan Piagetians on the one hand and North American and British psychologists on the other reflect different goals of assessment. Piaget especially wanted to avoid "false positive errors," namely, concluding that children have the concept when in fact they do not. Thus, he sometimes even considered it desirable to have complex materials, a misleading visual array, and heavy verbal demands. In contrast, the other camp is more concerned about "false negative errors"—concluding that children do not have the concept when in fact they do.

The inadequacies of Piaget's methodology carry over to his reporting of his experiments. His reports do not allow the reader to evaluate the research. He typically did not report the number of subjects, the exact ages and socioeconomic level of the children, and details of the testing procedure. Sometimes it is even difficult to tell whether Piaget was referring to hypothetical children or children he actually tested! He was not impressed with statistical analysis. In his words, "Acute observation, especially when made by [a good observer] . . . , surpasses all statistics" [1936 (1952, p. 72)]. Instead of presenting statistical summaries of the findings, Piaget provided sample protocols, which he interpreted at great length. The reader has no idea whether these protocols are representative of all children tested. The data from the entire group of subjects are needed to evaluate Piaget's claims that children typically go through stages of cognitive development.

What are we to make of these shortcomings in Piaget's methodology? Flavell (1963) concluded that Piaget was primarily interested in satisfying his own curiosity, not the requirements of the scientific community. Consequently, he played by his own rules when doing research and wrote almost as though he were talking to himself.

Although the inadequacies in Piaget's methodology and reporting are annoying to anyone trying to understand and evaluate his theory, they may be somewhat responsible for Piaget's success. It could be argued that when psychologists explore new areas and develop tentative hypotheses to guide their research, they should be flexible in their methods. If Piaget had used standardized procedures from the beginning, he might have missed some fascinating facets of cognitive development. In fact, as Ginsburg and Opper suggested, "If Piaget had attempted to establish every point with the maximum of certainty, then he probably would not have advanced beyond the study of children's verbal communication (one of his first research topics)" (1979, pp. 94–95).

PIAGET'S OWN MODIFICATIONS OF HIS THEORY

As Piaget's later works are translated, the "classic Piaget" presented in this chapter must be modified. Many of these changes in Piaget's thinking are described in recent chapters by Beilin (1989, 1992). Three main areas are discussed below: equilibration, the logicomathematical model, and the stage notion.

In his later years, Piaget [1978 (1985)] increased his attention to mechanisms of cognitive change, especially the equilibration process. He emphasized "possibilities" (the way things might be) and "procedures" (strategies) in this process. This contrasts with his earlier emphasis on logical necessity. A new cognitive structure generates new possibilities, which cause the child to try out new procedures on objects. Through accommodation to these new experiences, the child can establish equilibrium again. In this process possibility and necessity are intertwined because new possibilities may lead to a new necessity, which in turn may lead to new possibilities, and so on, back and forth.

Over a longer period of time, development involves an increasing awareness of possibilities. Piaget (1981) showed children a box with only one side visible under a cloth. At age 5 or 6, children would accept only a single possibility for the color of the hidden side of the box—the same color as the visible side. Thus, a sense of necessity occurs in young children because they can imagine only a single possibility. By age 7 to age 10, children recognized multiple though limited possibilities: the hidden side might be "green, violet, blue, white, yellow . . . that's all" (1981, p. 44). At age 11 or 12, children realize that the number of possibilities is essentially unlimited. One reason that this development is interesting is that the concept of unlimited possibilities cannot be observed in the environment. It must be constructed internally.

An important aspect of equilibration is contradiction. An example of Piaget's [1974 (1980)] research in this area involved a row of seven disks, each of which was slightly, but imperceptibly, larger than the one before it. Because the last and largest disk was unattached, it could be moved to and compared with each of the six disks attached to the board. Thus, the contradiction facing the child was that any two adjacent disks appeared to be equal in size, but the disk at the end of the series was obviously larger than the first disk. Three stages of understanding contradiction emerged. In the first stage, young children were unaware of the contradiction. Next, children had some awareness of the contradiction but their attempted solutions were not satisfactory. For example, a child might categorize the disks as small ones and large ones, thereby accounting for some of the perceived equivalences between adjacent disks (both are "small") and also explaining the difference in size of the first ("small") and last ("large") disk. Finally, by age 11 or 12 children resolved the contradiction and reestablished equilibrium by creating a new structure—quantified seriation of size.

Researchers have had trouble finding support for Piaget's logico-mathematical-based model of thinking. Piaget in fact introduced changes in the model in his later years. He tried to incorporate a "logic of meanings" and "category theory," a branch of mathematics developed since the 1960s. A logic of meanings is described in a posthumous publication (Piaget & Garcia, 1991). Briefly, Piaget emphasized that logic comes from the meanings of objects. Specifically, infants learn that one action on an object is related to other actions. That is, one action can be inferred from another, in a sort of "logic of meaning in actions." For example, an infant who pushes an object away from himself may infer that the object can be pulled toward himself. Other examples are that grasping a rattle implies relations between grasping and seeing and the reasoning that "if I release the car down the ramp it will crash into the house at the bottom." This action-based logic later leads to a logic of operations, such as when the pushing–pulling relation leads to the reversal or negation of a mental action. The meaning of an object comes not only from what can be done with the object but also from children's description of the attributes of an object and their classification of it.

In category theory, Piaget's previous emphasis on action in the form of mental transformations was supplemented with "correspondences" between two static states (1979). Comparisons of static states are central, as when a child sees the similarity between a currently perceived object and a previously encountered one, and thereby assimilates the current one. The current object or event is recognized, categorized, or characterized; it therefore "corresponds" (is seen as similar) to other objects or events. Detecting correspondences can lead the child to notice a transformation. For example, when a picture corresponds to the same picture hung upside down, a mental rotation links the two states and underlies their correspondence.

A final modification concerns the stage notion. In his last years, Piaget put less emphasis on stages. He began to view development as less steplike, with longer transition periods between stages. In fact, Vuyk concluded that Piaget "now considers development a spiral and though one may call a stage 'a detour of the spiral,' this indicates that periods of equilibrium are relatively unimportant" (1981, p. 192).

Piaget's final contributions concerning equilibration, the logico-mathematical model, and stages raise enough important questions to occupy cognitive theorists and researchers for years to come. Only after this critical examination will we be able to judge the ultimate value of these new ideas.

THE NEO-PIAGETIANS

Many of the problems and limitations in Piaget's theory have been addressed by a group of developmental psychologists labeled "neo-Piagetians." They are Piagetian in their belief in the active construction of some sort of stages, sequences, and structural change. In particular, they believe that lower-level concepts are integrated to form higher-level concepts. However, they are "neo" in their inclusion of constructs such as skills, limited memory capacity, and automaticity and in their focus on domain-specific concepts. Domain-specific concepts or stages are those that pertain only to a particular area or areas, such as role taking or number. In contrast, Piaget tended to emphasize the domain-general application of cognitive structures.

The neo-Piagetians are represented here by Robbie Case (1985, 1992), a major theorist and researcher. The interested reader is urged to read the work of other neo-Piagetians such as Fischer (1980), Halford (in press), Pascual-Leone (1987), and Demetriou, Efklides, and Platsidou (in press).

Case's work draws heavily on the construct of memory capacity or, in his words, *executive processing space*: "the maximum number of independent schemes a child can activate at any one time" (1985, p. 289). Capacity is emphasized by information-processing psychologists. In fact, because Case attempts to integrate Piagetian and information-processing theory, his views could have been presented instead in the later chapter on information processing. For Case, an increase in the efficiency of using one's capacity, rather than the equilibration process, is the major mechanism for development. Practice with a skill, such as counting, makes it faster and more automatic. Consequently, counting becomes less effortful and more efficient. Children in effect increase their capacity by increasing their speed of processing information and freeing previously needed capacity. A given amount of capacity goes a lot farther if many elements can be processed, rather than a few. This increase in available capacity also can be used for new or additional cognitive activities, for example, both counting and remembering. The faster a child can count objects, the better she is at remembering the number of objects in sets in a counting span test (Case, 1985).

The increase in available mental capacity is also due to neurological maturation. Case hypothesizes that increased myelinization (insulation of neurons) during development increases the efficiency of the conduction of neural impulses. He presents evidence that different systems of the brain are myelinated at different times during development. Thus, changes in biological maturation could partially account for the transitions from one stage to another because these changes tend to occur at the ages of the movement from one stage to another.

Case differs from Piaget in his view of how children's mental structures can be modeled. Case remarks that "it seemed that Piaget's theory was better equipped for representing the structure in the mind of logicians than the structure in the minds of young children" (1992, p. 6). Rather than draw on symbolic logic, Case uses constructs from the information-processing framework, particularly *executive control structures*, which are devices for dealing with specific problem situations. They represent the existing state in the problem situation, the desired goal state, and strategies for achieving the goal. He views children as problem solvers, with these control structures as their tools. These structures use processes such as setting goals, activating procedures (scheme sequences) in novel ways for reaching the goals, and evaluating the results of the procedures. Other processes include restructuring successful procedures so that they later can be produced intentionally and practicing and integrating successful procedures until they are consolidated. For example, with respect to counting, children set a goal (determining the number of objects), generate counting procedures for attaining it, evaluate their success, "mark" the successful sequence, and integrate the successful counting procedures.

When children experiment during attempts to solve problems, they use these general processes: they explore objects, observe and imitate other people, and interact with others as together they solve a problem. For example, children might learn about counting by using their own verbal labels as they touch each object during problem solving, counting different types of objects during exploring, observing others count, and trying to count a large set with the help of an adult.

As stated earlier, if children have the necessary processing capacity, they can use their innate processing abilities to take advantage of these experiences to construct more advanced executive control structures (for example, procedures for determining quantity). This occurs in the following way. Case proposes a multilevel cognitive system, with levels ranging from the very general to the specific. Children's capacity (general systemwide change), along with the particular experiences offered by their culture, permits certain central conceptual structures. These structures are at an intermediate level of generality; each is a representational system of a domain of knowledge such as number or space. These structures interpret specific tasks and assemble problem-solving procedures for these tasks (specific-level change). These multilevel systems contribute to both the evenness and the unevenness of cognitive development. Children's processing capacity sets an upper limit on their thinking at a given developmental point, which gives a uniform or stage-like cast to their thinking across domains. Even performance across tasks also occurs when tasks are of equal complexity and require similar executive control structures and central conceptual structures. In contrast, uneven performance across tasks results when these factors differ.

Although Piaget and Case offer very different mechanisms for change and propose different models for mental structures, they both view development as structural change resulting in a series of stages. In both theories, lower-order concepts are differentiated and coordinated into higher-order concepts. Case proposes four stages, which will sound very familiar to someone who has just read a description of Piaget's theory. Each stage has a different type of executive control structure.

Also, each stage begins with the most advanced cognitive skill of the previous stage.

1. *Sensorimotor* (birth to 1 1/2 years). Infants' mental representations are linked to physical movements. By the end of the stage they understand the relation between two action–reaction units. For example pushing a beam downward and seeing it go down is the reverse of pushing it upward and seeing it go up.

2. *Interrelational* (1 1/2 to 5 years). Children detect and coordinate relations among objects, events, or people. For example, children eventually understand the relation between the difference in weight of two objects and the effect of this difference on the arms of a balance scale; that is, the heavy object makes the arm go down more than the light one does. For a child, this dimension is bipolar, for example, heavy and light. In contrast to Piaget, who sees this stage primarily as preparation for the concrete operational stage, Case sees a distinct stage, equal to the others in importance.

3. *Dimensional* (5 to 11 years). Children extract the dimensions of significance in the physical and social world. They learn to compare two dimensions, such as height and width in a logical quantity task, in a quantitative way: liquid poured into a narrower container rises proportionately higher.

4. *Vectorial* (11 to 19 years). Children acquire abstract systems of thought that allow them to use proportional reasoning, solve verbal analogy problems, and infer psychological traits in other people. Children's dimensional control structures serve as a foundation for this final stage.

Case also is interested in changes within a stage. His analysis of Noelting's (1980) orange juice problem for the third stage will serve as an illustration. There are two sets of small glasses. In each set some glasses contain orange juice and some contain water. Children must predict which pitcher would taste more strongly of orange juice if the liquid were poured from one set of glasses into one pitcher and that of the other set into a second pitcher. Thus, children must determine which pitcher would have the higher proportion of orange juice.

Three sequential substages differ in the number of elements represented and the way in which these elements must be organized: (1) Assemble a new structure by coordinating two structures already in the repertoire; this new structure can be applied only in isolation. (2) Apply two such units in succession. (3) Integrate two or more units into a coherent system that forms the basic unit for the next stage. Each stage involves these three substages. At the end of the previous stage, 3- to 5-year-olds judged solely on a perceptual basis, on whether one set looked as if it had a lot of juice and the other set did not. In substage 1, 5- to 7-year-olds judged on a single quantitative basis and believed that the pitcher of whichever set had more glasses of juice would taste more strongly of juice. Thus, they were correct when there was an equal total number of glasses in the two sets but were incorrect when, for example, set A contained four glasses of juice and four of water and set B contained three glasses of juice and two of water. That is, the children chose set A. In substage 2, 7- to 9-year-olds attended to the numbers of both types of glasses and said, for example, "the same, since there's more juice here but more water here." In substage 3, 9- to 11-year-olds noted the difference in the number of water glasses in the two sets and the difference in the number of juice glasses in each set. If the juice difference was greater, they picked the set with more juice as "juicier," and if the water difference was larger they picked the set with more water as less juicy.

With this task, as well as others used by Case, what changes during the stage is that (1) more elements are considered (because processing capacity has increased) and (2) these elements become more organized into a structure. These changes are made possible by an increase in mental capacity. In addition to tasks that are similar to those in Piaget's research, Case has examined a variety of tasks, such as eating with utensils in infancy, using vocalizations for social purposes, manipulating other people's feelings, story telling, and judging intelligence in others.

Case's theory is an exciting attempt to integrate a structural and a processing model of development. That is, he shows how limits in processing capacity limit logical reasoning and constrain what the child can learn at any developmental level. By the same token, increases in capacity create a new opportunity for the further development of logical thinking. Because Case's theory is still being developed, criticisms generally point to the need for more supporting evidence, for example, on the role of myelinization in increasing mental efficiency. He also needs a clearer criterion for assessing how much capacity a particular strategy requires (Flavell, 1984). Case (1992) is continuing to develop his theory, most recently in areas such as emotional development, learning disabilities, spatial representation, and social cognition.

The two main contributions of the neo-Piagetians have been to propose a promising set of processes to account for developmental change and to clarify and refine the notion of stages, for example, by attempting to differentiate domain-general and domain-specific achievements. As Flavell has observed, "Cognitive development might appear to be more general-stagelike than many of us believed, if only we knew how and where to look" (1982, p. 1).

Although many psychologists claim that the influence of Piaget's theory is waning, this decline may be more apparent than real. Even though there are fewer studies with such Piagetian tasks as conservation and class inclusion, many Piagetian concepts are still studied, for example, object permanence, number, space, causality, moral judgments, and perspective taking. Moreover, so many of Piaget's assumptions about the nature of cognitive development are assimilated into the thinking of researchers that Piaget's ongoing influence often is not recognized. For example, the search for a general concept underlying several different behaviors and for the process by which a new concept arises from a previous one continues in most cognitive developmental research. Also, it is assumed that children actively construct their knowledge.

SUMMARY

Piaget's theory is the most influential stage theory in developmental psychology. The invariant stages describe changes in how children acquire knowledge about the world (genetic epistemology). In the first two years of life, children construct sensorimotor schemes based on physical action upon the world. The schemes become more intentional and more intercoordinated during that time. During the preoperational period, approximately ages 2 to 7, children exploit their newly acquired symbolic ability. Despite the limitations of egocentrism, rigid thought, and limited role-taking and communication abilities, children combine symbols into semilogical reasoning. During the concrete operational period, roughly ages 7 to 11, children acquire logicomathematical structures. Now thought is operational and consequently more flexible and abstract. Finally, during the formal operational period, ages 11 to 15, these operations are no longer limited to concrete objects. Operations can be performed on operations, verbal propositions, and hypothetical conditions.

These stagelike changes involve changes in the structure of thought. Thought becomes increasingly organized, always building on the structure of the previous stage. Evidence for these structural changes comes from observations of infants and from interviews or problem-solving tasks with older children.

Movement through the stages is caused by four factors: physical maturation, experience with physical objects, social experience, and equilibration. Experience brings cognitive progress through assimilation and accommodation. These functional invariants help children adapt to the environment by strengthening and stretching their current understanding of the world.

Piaget viewed children as active and self-regulating organisms that change by means of interacting innate and environmental factors. He emphasized qualitative change, but identified certain quantitative changes as well. The essence of cognitive development is structural change.

With respect to the theoretical nature of the theory, it is possible to discern all four types of theory building: models, deductive theory, functional theory, and inductive theory. In particular, Piaget drew on the equilibration model and the logicomathematical model.

The theory's main strengths are its recognition of the central role of cognition in development, value as an integrative and heuristic theory, discovery of surprising features of young children's thinking, wide scope, and ecological validity. The main weaknesses include its inadequate support for the stage notion, inadequate account of mechanisms of development, need for a theory of performance, slighting of social and emotional aspects of development, and methodological and stylistic inadequacies. Some of these problems have been addressed by the neo-Piagetians. In addition, Piaget himself continued to modify his theory in his later years.

What should be our final judgment on Piaget's theory? This flawed but amazingly productive theory gives us a framework for viewing the richness and complexity of cognitive development. Even when it has failed, for example, where an adequate explanation for conservation cannot be found despite hundreds of studies, the theory has revealed interesting facets of development, such as rudimentary numerical skills that may lead to conservation. Furthermore, the theory has raised issues that all theories of development must address. All new theories for years to come will inevitably be compared to Piaget's theory. In short, we have not made a mistake by paying attention to this "giant in the nursery" (Elkind, 1968).

SUGGESTED READINGS

A vast number of books have been written about Piaget. Especially notable efforts are the following.

Ginsburg, H., & Opper, S. (1988). *Piaget's theory of intellectual development* (3rd ed.). Englewood Cliffs, NJ: Prentice-Hall. This book presents a readable account of the theory.

Chapman, M. (1988). *Constructive evolution: Origins and development of Piaget's thought*. Cambridge: Cambridge University Press. This book about Piaget's theory is for the more advanced student.

The following books by Piaget are two of his more readable and clearly written publications.

Piaget, J. (1967). *Six psychological studies*. New York: Random House.

Piaget, J., & Inhelder, B. (1969). *The psychology of the child*. New York: Basic Books.

Piaget's research has stimulated a number of thoughtful publications on issues raised by his theory. Three are listed here.

Case, R. (1985). *Intellectual development: Birth to adulthood*. Orlando, FL: Academic Press.

Chandler, M., & Chapman, M. (Eds.). (1991). *Criteria for competence: Controversies in the conceptualization and assessment of children's abilities*. Hillsdale, NJ: Erlbaum.

Beilin, H., & Pufall, P. (1992). *Piaget's theory: Prospects and possibilities*. Hillsdale, NJ: Erlbaum.

2

FREUD'S AND ERIKSON'S PSYCHOANALYTIC THEORIES

*I dreamt that it was night and that I was lying in my
bed. . . .Suddenly the window opened of its own accord, and I was terrified to see that some white wolves
were sitting on the big walnut tree in front of the window. There were six or seven of them. The wolves
were quite white, and looked more like foxes or sheep-
dogs, for they had big tails like foxes and they had
their ears pricked like dogs when they pay attention to
something. In great terror, evidently of being eaten up
by the wolves, I screamed and woke up.*
[FREUD, 1918 (1955, p. 29)]

*The most significant sex difference was the tendency of
boys to erect structures, buildings, towers, or streets. . .
the girls tended to use the play table as the interior of a
house, with simple, little, or no use of blocks. . . .
Simple enclosures with low walls and without orna-
ments were the largest item among the configurations
built by girls. However, these enclosures often had an
elaborate gate. . . . A blocking of the entrance or a
thickening of the walls could on further study be
shown to reflect acute anxiety over the feminine role.*
[ERIKSON, 1950a, pp. 102–105]

P sychoanalytic theory and Piagetian theory are the giant theories of developmental psychology. To meet the source of psycho-analytic theory, we move from Geneva to Vienna, where Freud spent most of his life. The development of the theory followed a tortuous course, full of dazzling insights, diverging ideas, and clashing personalities. Although many figures are responsible for the psycho-analytic movement, we must limit our attention to Sigmund Freud, who began the movement, and Erik Erikson, who more recently constructed a life-span view of development. Both proposed that personality dev-elopment proceeds through a series of stages. In each stage, the child copes with certain conflicts, stimulated to a great extent by biological changes in development. The presentation of these theories follows the order of Chapter 1: a biography, a general orientation, a description of stages of development, an account of mechanisms of change, the theory's stand on critical issues, the theoretical characteristics of the theory, and an evaluation.

FREUD

BIOGRAPHICAL SKETCH

Sigmund Freud was born in Freiberg, Moravia, in 1856.* When he was 4, his family moved to Vienna, where he lived for nearly 80 years. He was the eldest of eight children born to a wool merchant and his wife. Freud believed that he was a favored child and that great things were expected of him. As he expressed it, "A man who has been the indis-putable favorite of his mother keeps for life the feeling of a conqueror, that confidence of success that often induces real success" (Jones, 1961, p. 6). He had a voracious appetite for books on history and philosophy, as did Piaget. He and a friend taught themselves Spanish so that they could read *Don Quixote* in the original. In secondary school, he read an essay by Goethe on nature that awakened an interest in science. He entered medical school with the expectation that he would devote his life to scientific research. In retrospect, it is interesting, given the even-

---

* Much of the material in this section comes from Ernest Jones's biography, *The life and work of Sigmund Freud*, in three volumes (1953, 1955, 1957), abridged in 1961 by L. Trilling and S. Marcus (New York: Basic Books).

tual focus of his theory, that his first major research project was on the structure of the testes in eels.

The goal of becoming a research scientist had to be set aside when his poor economic situation and the barriers against advancement for a Jew in academia forced him to enter private practice. Freud's longstanding interest in neurology led him naturally into the treatment of nervous disorders. At the time, this branch of medicine was at a very primitive level, and its practitioners could give little help for the mentally ill. Patients typically received hydrotherapy (various types of baths) and electrotherapy (mild electric currents passed through the body).

Freud was fascinated with hysteria, a disorder characterized by such symptoms as paralysis, numbness, squinting, and tremors. His interest in a possible new treatment, hypnosis, was aroused by his contact with the French neurologist Jean Charcot and the Viennese physician Josef Breuer. The fact that Charcot could produce symptoms of hysteria in people by means of hypnotic suggestion was evidence that the malady had a psychological basis. As Freud began to use hypnosis with his patients, he was impressed that they could recall important incidents and feelings while under hypnosis that were otherwise inaccessible. Despite the general belief among neurologists that hypnotism was both fraudulent and dangerous, Freud enthusiastically experimented with this technique: "There was something positively seductive in working with hypnotism. For the first time there was a sense of having overcome one's helplessness; and it was highly flattering to enjoy the reputation of being a miracle-worker" [1925a (1959, p. 17)].*

Freud was also influenced by Breuer's discovery that symptoms of hysteria could be alleviated simply by having his patients talk about (and "relive") their emotion-laden experiences from early life. It eventually became clear that hypnosis was often not even necessary in order to remove hysterical symptoms. With a sense of excitement, Freud experimented with what Breuer called the "talking cure." In a letter to his friend Wilhelm Fliess in 1895, he described how psychology possessed him: "A man like me cannot live without a hobbyhorse, a consuming passion—in Schiller's words a tyrant. I have found my tyrant, and in his service I know no limits. My tyrant is psychology."

Freud's study of his patients' dreams and childhood memories led to his first major publication, *The Interpretation of Dreams*, in 1900.

---

* The references to Freud's works in this chapter are to the publication dates of the original works in German. The page numbers are those of the translations (given in parentheses): J. Strachey, ed. and trans., *The standard edition of the complete psychological works of Sigmund Freud*. 24 vols. (London: Hogarth Press, 1953–1966).

Although this book was ignored by medical and scientific circles, as well as the general public, Freud was not discouraged. A succession of fascinating books appeared in the following years. Although he worked almost completely in isolation for years, he eventually began to attract a small following.

Carl Jung and Alfred Adler, in particular, strengthened the new psychoanalytic movement even while the European medical establishment spurned it. This rejection drew the psychoanalysts closer together, and they formed the International Psycho-Analytical Association, which exists even today. A turning point came in 1909, when the eminent American psychologist G. Stanley Hall invited Freud to speak at the twentieth-anniversary celebration of the founding of Clark University in Worcester, Massachusetts. Freud described his feelings on this occasion: "In Europe I felt as though I were despised; but over there I found myself received by the foremost men as an equal. As I stepped on to the platform at Worcester to deliver my *Five Lectures on Psycho-Analysis* . . . it seemed like the realization of some incredible daydream: psychoanalysis was no longer a product of delusion, it had become a valuable part of reality" [1925a (1959, p. 52)].

Freud began to achieve international recognition, especially in the years following World War I. Psychoanalysis began to influence not only psychiatry and the social sciences, but also fields such as literature, art, ethics, and education. "Subconscious" and "ego" became household words. It should be noted that much of the reaction was far from positive. Many people were shocked at the claim that children have a sexual nature. The attacks on psychoanalytic theory continued throughout Freud's lifetime. In addition, Freud's success was marred by the later defections of Jung and Adler and other prominent leaders within psychoanalysis.

Freud continued to develop his theory over the years. In fact, he made some basic changes in his views when he was in his seventies. By the end of his life, his psychoanalytic writings filled 23 volumes. In his last years, he worked while in considerable pain from cancer of the jaw. When the Nazis took over Austria in 1937, he was forced to flee to England. He died in 1939 in London.

GENERAL ORIENTATION TO THE THEORY

The neophyte faces frustration when attempting to understand Freud's theory because various sources give contradictory accounts. The problem stems from the fact that Freud revised his ideas over the years. Although revision is a sign of a healthy theory, it is discouraging to anyone struggling to understand the theorist's writings. Fortunately, despite certain changes in the details of the system, there is constancy in the general approach. Six general characteristics emerge from the details of Freud's work: a dynamic approach, a structural approach, a topographic approach, a developmental stage approach, a normal–abnormal continuum, and the psychoanalytic methods. We look at each of these characteristics and, when useful for clarifying the theory, compare them with those of Piaget's theory.

DYNAMIC APPROACH

Freud described his theory as "a sort of economics of nervous energy" (Jones, 1953, p. 345). This nervous energy is variously termed *psychic energy, drive energy, libido*, and *tension*. In an analogy to energy in the field of physics, nervous energy builds up and can be distributed, tied to certain images, transformed, and discharged. Just as mechanical, electrical, or thermal energy performs physical work, so does psychic energy perform psychological work.

It is possible to identify several laws of energy in Freud's system with its commonsense physics. For example, in the same way that physical energy is transformed but not destroyed, psychological energy is transformed into anxiety, displaced into a physical structure that causes a symptom, such as paralysis, transformed into a thought, such as an obsession, and so on. Another law of energy comes from the famous *pleasure principle*, which states that whenever possible, energy is discharged without delay. The organism strives toward the immediate, direct reduction of tension, which reduces pain and produces pleasure. Hunger leads to eating; the need to suck leads to sucking one's thumb. A final example is the *principle of least action*, in which small amounts of energy are discharged, but only after a delay and only after following an indirect route. The *reality principle* rules here. The mental apparatus scans reality and evaluates various possible courses of action before allowing energy to be discharged. For example, an angry child may tell his friend that he is angry with him rather than hit him and risk punishment.

Where does this psychological energy come from? The human body has certain instincts that make demands on the mind. Instincts (or biological drives, as they often are called) involve excitation in some region of the body. This internal excitation stimulates the mind and creates a "need." Thus, psychic energy is derived from biological energy. Freud maintained that "mind" and "body" have a constant interplay: an instinct is "a concept on the frontier between the mental and the somatic" [1915 (1957, p. 121)].

In Freud's final account, the two basic instincts were *Eros* (sex, self-preservation, love, life forces, striving toward unity) and the *destructive instinct* (aggression, undoing connections, the death instinct, hate). Freud assigned the term *libido* to the available energy of Eros. There is no analogous term for the energy of a destructive instinct. His interest in the destructive instinct came late in life and is attributed to his horror at the atrocities of World War I and the anti-Semitic feelings of his times. In Freud's words, "the aim of all life is death" [1920 (1955, p. 38)].

We can use the sex drive to illustrate four characteristics of an instinct: source, aim, object, and pressure.

1. The sex drive has its *source* in bodily needs, as described above. Sexual excitation arises from erogenous zones in the body, particularly the oral, anal, and genital areas. The change in the site of excitation underlies the movement from stage to stage, as we shall see later.

2. The *aim* of the sex drive, or of any instinct, is to remove this bodily need. This ultimate goal is achieved through such subordinate goals as finding and investing energy in sexual objects. An instinct, in Freud's words, is "an urge inherent in organic life to restore an earlier state of things" [1920 (1955, p. 36)]. The return to a state of mental and physiological equilibrium (or lack of excitation) is achieved by satisfying the need.

3. Tension mounts, an appropriate sex *object* is found, tension is discharged, and the person experiences pleasure. The object may be a real person (the self or another) or object or a representation of a person or an object. There are many ways to satisfy a drive. Libido becomes attached or, in Freud's terminology, "cathected" to an object. Infants cathect their mother and other objects that satisfy their needs.

4. Finally, the *pressure* of the sex drive is determined by the degree of force (amount of sexual energy). The more energy, the stronger the drive.

Diverse human behaviors can ultimately be traced to the two general instincts, with their various subinstincts. Freud would claim that writing a book, jogging, watching television, and making a bookcase have their origins deep in human needs. The route between the instinct and the behavior may be very indirect because of the mobility of the instincts. Psychic energy is a general energy source that can be likened to an electricity supply, which can be used to toast bread, shave, bake, and so forth (Hall, 1954, p. 84). Freud spoke of the many ways that instincts can be expressed and combined. Drives can be fused; for example, playing soccer may satisfy both aggressive and cooperative needs, or eating, both hunger and destructiveness (by biting and chewing). Drives can be satisfied in a partial and roundabout way, as when a person gossips about an enemy instead of physically attacking him. Freud believed that da Vinci's interest in painting Madonnas was a way of partially satisfying his desire for his mother, from whom he had been separated early in life. Drives also may be substituted, as intense hate turns into love or sexual desire becomes platonic love. Finally, one object can substitute for another object, as when an adult's oral needs are satisfied by playing a trumpet. In some cases, a culturally or morally "higher" goal object is substituted for the truly desired object. This is labeled *sublimation*. An angry person might sublimate his desire to attack other people by painting violent scenes. Another common type of object substitution is *compensation*, in which people make up for their failure in one area by applying themselves in another area. A five-foot, six-inch basketball player may eventually become a sports announcer.

Both Freud and Piaget had a dynamic approach, but in different ways. Freud was concerned with drive *forces* that energize behavior, whereas Piaget was concerned with mental actions—schemes, operations, assimilation, and accommodation. Piaget contended that emotions are the energizers behind thought, but he did little to develop this idea further. Both Piaget and Freud were enamored of another aspect of dynamics: the notion of equilibrium from physics. The process of equilibrium, followed by disequilibrium and subsequently by equilibrium again, is central in both theories. However, crucial differences in the nature of equilibrium divide the theories, as we shall see in the section on mechanisms of development.

STRUCTURAL APPROACH

The previous section creates the image of a human hydraulic system with powerful forces surging through the body and the mind. We now look at the psychological structures through which these forces flow. These structures mediate between the drives and behavior; drives do not lead directly to behavior. There is, then, an architecture of the mind. Mental processes take place within the structures, between the structures, and by means of the structures. There are three major structures: id, ego, and superego. Roughly speaking, the *id* is the seat of biologically based drives, the *ego* is the mechanism for adapting to reality, and the *superego* is analogous to the conscience. We examine each "province of the mind" [1933a (1964, p. 72)] in turn and then portray their overall organization.

Id

As the novelist Peter De Vries humorously expresses it in *Forever Panting*, "'Id' isn't just another big word." The id is the seat of innate desires and is the main source of psychic energy. It is the "dark, inaccessible part of our personality . . . a chaos, a cauldron full of seething excitations" [Freud, 1933a (1964, p. 73)]. The id wants immediate satisfaction, in accordance with the pleasure principle described earlier. The energy of the id is invested either in action on an object that would satisfy an instinct or in images of an object that would give partial satisfaction. For example, infants may satisfy their oral-hunger drive directly by sucking a nipple and receiving milk or partially and indirectly by imagining a bottle of milk. This hallucinatory wish fulfillment is called *primary-process thought*. The id's energy is so mobile that it is easily discharged or transferred from object to object or image to image.

In contrast to young infants, older infants, children, and adults have an ego and a superego in addition to an id. The id, however, continues to operate throughout life, especially in our nighttime dreams, daydreams, imagination, and impulsive, selfish, and pleasure-loving behavior. The id has been called the "spoiled child of the personality" (Hall, 1954, p. 27). Deep down inside us, we want total satisfaction—a state of nirvana.

Much of Freud's knowledge about the id came from his study of dreams. The desires of the id appear in dreams in either an obvious or a disguised fashion. One does not need psychoanalytic training to interpret a hungry person's dream about a thick steak. However, some urges are so threatening that they must be rendered less obvious. According to Freud, clothes and uniforms sometimes represent nakedness; water can stand for birth; a journey can mean death. (The interpretation of dreams is discussed in a later section.)

Ego

In the beginning, there is id. The id, armed with primary-process thought (hallucinatory wish fulfillment), makes its demands. However, babies soon discover that thinking something does not make it so. The image of the mother and milk and the memory of warmth do not quiet the pangs of hunger. They learn that there is a difference between images and reality, between the self and the outer world.

The id's inability to always produce the desired object leads to the development of the ego.* The ego, the mind's avenue to the real world, is developed because it is needed for physical and psychological survival. It aids in survival because it possesses *secondary-process thought*. Secondary-process thought is rational. It is more organized, integrated, and logical than primary-process thought, in which contradictions abound. The ego's activities include such intellectual ones as perception, logical thought, problem solving, and memory. Most of the intellectual abilities studied by Piaget would fall into Freud's ego domain. The ego is the director who must make the tough, high-level decisions. It evaluates the present situation, recalls relevant decisions and events in the past, weighs various factors in the present and future, and predicts the consequences of various actions. The ego's decisions are aided by feelings of anxiety, which signal that certain actions would be threatening. Above all, the ego's decision making involves the *delay* of energy discharge, the reality principle mentioned earlier. Freud described the thinking of the ego as "an experimental action carried out with small amounts of energy, in the same way as a general shifts small figures about on a map before setting his large bodies of troops in motion" [1933a (1964, p. 89)].

These small quantities of energy at the disposal of the ego come from the id. As the ego acquires more and more energy and gains experience using secondary-process thought during development, it becomes stronger and more differentiated. Of course, the ego, with its secondary-process thought, does not replace the primary-process thought of the id. Rather, it simply adds another level to thought. Gratification can be achieved either by finding appropriate real objects in the environment after a delay or by hallucinating and dreaming. Throughout life, we use a mixture of primary- and secondary-process thought. However, as development proceeds, the secondary-process aspects of thought become more dominant.

---

* Near the end of his life, Freud softened his claim that the ego developed out of the id. He began referring to an early, undifferentiated ego–id.

The ego serves "three tyrannical masters": id, superego, and external world [1933a (1964, p. 77)]. Freud described the ego's position in an analogy:

> The ego's relation to the id might be compared with that of a rider to his horse. The horse supplies the locomotive energy, while the rider has the privilege of deciding on the goal and of guiding the powerful animal's movement. But only too often there arises between the ego and the id the not precisely ideal situation of the rider being obliged to guide the horse along the path by which it itself wants to go.
>
> *[1933a (1964, p. 77)]*

The ego mediates between the id and the external world:

> Thus the ego is fighting on two fronts: it has to defend its existence against an external world which threatens it with annihilation as well as against an internal world that makes excessive demands. It adopts the same methods of defence against both, but its defence against the internal enemy is particularly inadequate. As a result of having originally been identical with this latter enemy and of having lived with it since on the most intimate terms, it has great difficulty in escaping from the internal dangers. They persist as threats, even if they can be temporarily held down.
>
> *[1940 (1964, p. 200)]*

These constant threats and dangers from the id and the environment arouse anxiety. When possible, the ego tackles the problem in a realistic way, using its problem-solving skills. However, when the anxiety is so strong that it threatens to engulf the ego, *defense mechanisms* come into play. They control and thereby alleviate anxiety by distorting reality in some way. Although defense mechanisms allow only partial satisfaction of the drives, for the organism in a state of tension some satisfaction is better than none at all. Freud's list of defense mechanisms changed in number from time to time as they were combined or further differentiated in his writings or those of his daughter, Anna Freud. We limit our discussion to five main defense mechanisms: repression (denying or forgetting the danger), reaction formation (acting the opposite from the way one feels), projection (attributing one's unacceptable impulses to others), regression (returning to an earlier form of behavior), and fixation (remaining at the present level).

1. *Repression* is preventing a threatening thought from emerging into awareness. The principle seems to be "What we don't know can't hurt us" (Hall, 1954, p. 85). If anxiety-arousing thoughts cannot surface, we do not experience anxiety. A thought may be anxiety-arousing because it threatens a breakdown in self-control or arouses frustration or guilt. To avoid anxiety, we forget the name of someone who has hurt us or forget to pay a bill that would put a severe strain on the budget and cause worry.

Often a whole constellation of memories must be repressed because recalling neutral memories would elicit associated painful memories. One of Freud's patients feared going out in the street because it aroused her earlier fear that she would become a prostitute, which in turn was related to her desire for sexual experience. Furthermore, according to Freud, there is massive repression of memories of childhood sexuality once children reach grade-school age. Only with great difficulty could Freud help his adult patients recover these memories.

Freud's ideas about repression developed from his observations in therapy. When a patient freely reported her thoughts during "free association," she would often stop abruptly and claim that her mind had suddenly gone blank, just at the moment when important memories of the past seemed about to emerge. Perhaps Friedrich Nietzsche was correct in his remark, "One's own self is well hidden from oneself: of all mines of treasure one's own is the last to be dug up."

If a person depends too heavily on this defense mechanism, she may develop a repressed personality: withdrawn, inaccessible, nonspontaneous, and rigid. Also, there can be some loss of contact with reality as the person makes serious and frequent mistakes in remembering, speaking, and perceiving or develops symptoms of hysteria. For example, hysterical deafness may prevent a person from hearing something she does not want to hear.

2. In *reaction formation*, the ego masks an unacceptable emotion by focusing on its opposite, often in an exaggerated way. A child's jealousy and hatred for a newborn sibling is experienced as love, extravagantly displayed. A toddler who wants to soil his diapers and do "dirty" things may become compulsively clean, frequently washing his hands. Chastity may hide unacceptable sexual desires; purity may hide evil.

3. *Projection* is the attribution of anxiety-arousing thoughts to people and objects in the external world, rather than to the self. "I want to kill him" is changed to "He wants to kill me." Consequently, any violence against the other is permissible because it is done in self-defense. It is easier for the ego to handle objective, external dangers than internal dangers.

4. In *regression*, a person reverts to an earlier level of development. If the anxiety of the present is too much to handle, one retreats to simpler times, when there were fewer controls. Thus, people act in childish ways. They fight, play practical jokes, eat too much ice cream, yell obscenities at the referee at a football game, seek cuddling, and get drunk.

5. In *fixation*, one component of personality development comes to a halt. A portion of the libido remains tied to an earlier period of development and does not allow the child to proceed fully to the next stage. Fixation can occur when the present mode of satisfaction, for example, sucking a breast or bottle, is so gratifying that the child does not want to give it up, even under pressures to become weaned. Fixation can also occur when the next step appears to be too frightening or demanding or unsatisfying. The initiation of toilet training, if too harsh, may cause the toddler to remain partially in the oral stage rather than progress through the anal stage. The toddler may be fixated on a particular mode of satisfaction (sucking), object (mother), or type of thinking (primary process). Fixation is tied to regression in that a person is more likely to regress in the face of a barrier if there has been fixation at an earlier point in development.

Other psychological processes discussed elsewhere in the chapter are sometimes considered defense mechanisms. These include sublimation of an unacceptable desire to a more socially accepted activity, identification with the aggressor (usually a boy's father), and displacement of drives.

Defense mechanisms are a necessary evil. We need them to deal with high anxiety, but we pay the price of "wasting" our energy when it could be put to better use in ego development, for example, for creative thought or the development of problem-solving skills. Furthermore, if too much energy is tied up in the defense mechanisms, personality may not develop normally because the person distorts reality and deceives himself. This situation makes subsequent adjustments to reality even more difficult.

Superego

The superego is the last to develop. It arises when children resolve their Oedipus complex and develop identification with their parents. That story is told in the section on stages.

The superego is composed of two parts: the conscience and the ego ideal. In general, the conscience is negative and the ego ideal is positive. The *conscience* is composed of the parents' prohibitions, their "Thou shalt nots." Just as the parent has punished the child for his transgressions, so does the conscience punish the person with feelings of guilt, "accidentally" cutting one's finger, or intentionally self-destructive behavior. Curiously, the superego often becomes even more severe than the parents were. People with a particularly strong conscience may lead a "strait-jacket existence" (Hall, 1954, p. 46) or be extremely moral-idealistic rather than realistic in their thinking.

The term *ego ideal* refers to standards of conduct toward which the child strives. Just as the child has been rewarded for certain behavior by her parents, she is rewarded by the ego ideal with feelings of self-esteem and pride. These are echoes of early years when a parent said "Good girl!" to the young child.

The superego opposes both the id and the ego. It rewards, punishes, and makes demands. It tries to do away with both the pleasure principle and the reality principle. The superego watches over not only behavior but also the thoughts of the ego. Thinking is as bad as doing, from the superego's point of view. As in the case of the id, the superego does not distinguish between the subjective and the real.

The superego is society's way of achieving order. Unrestrained sexual and aggressive behavior would destroy the always tenuous social structure. Freud noted that if the ego represents the "power of the present" and the id represents the "organic past," then the superego represents the "cultural past" [1940 (1964, p. 206)].

Structural Relationships

We have dissected the personality into id, ego, and superego. However, personality is an organized whole—a unique constellation of forces and structures. Freud sketched out the relationship among the mental "areas," as seen in the illustration on the following page. He cautioned that we should not regard the id, ego, and superego as sharply defined areas. Rather, they are "areas of color melting into one another as they are presented by modern artists" [1933a (1964, p. 79)]. The superego, for example, blends into the id and, in fact, is intimately related to the id. This close relationship is most clearly seen in the Oedipus complex, discussed later, in which strong urges in the id necessitate the development of the superego and are subsequently controlled by the superego. Or in another instance, the id and superego may join forces in attacking

In Freud's sketch of the structure and topography of the mind, which also depicts the process of repression, the label "pcpt.-cs." refers to the perceptual-conscious, usually termed the conscious. [Reproduced from *New Introductory Lectures on Psycho-Analysis*, by Sigmund Freud, translated and edited by James Strachey, with the permission of Hogarth Press and W. W. Norton & Company, Inc. Copyright © 1965, 1964 by James Strachey.]

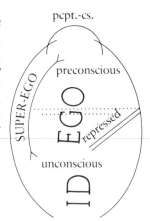

supposedly "immoral" persons, as in witch-burning or the cruelty of the Inquisition (Hall, 1954, p. 48).

The energy of the three structures is also not rigidly separated. If the id's energy cannot be discharged, it can be used to energize the ego or superego. Sexual energy might be transformed into artistic activities, creative scientific thought, or piety. In fact, the ego has no energy of its own; all energy is derived from the id. Just as the energy can go from the id to the ego, it can return to the id if the ego does not successfully satisfy the needs of the id. This return of energy to the id is common in normal personalities during dreams or during wishful thinking when awake.

These structures contain a closed energy system, in which a certain amount of energy is distributed to the three parts. A gain in energy in one part strengthens that part but at the same time weakens the other parts.

Finally, the id, ego, and superego lack separation, in that they combine to produce a behavior or a thought. Nearly every activity reflects the combined action of the id, ego, and superego. Licking an ice-cream cone reflects the hunger and oral-sucking drives of the id, the successful search for a suitable object by the ego (adults do not normally suck on lollipops in public), and a reward for good behavior by the superego. Under ordinary circumstances, the three systems work together as a team in relative harmony rather than war against each other.

The ego is central in this structural relationship. It is brought into all conflicts between the id and superego because each is trying to use the ego to meet its own needs. The ego must both obey and control the id, superego, and external reality. It survives by compromising. If the id says "yes" and the superego says "no," then the ego says "wait" (Hall, 1954, p. 47). Freud summed up this relationship as follows:

Thus the ego, driven by the id, confined by the super-ego, repulsed by reality, struggles to master its economic task of bringing about harmony among the forces and influences working in and upon it; and we can understand how it is that so often we cannot suppress a cry: 'Life is not easy!'

[1933a (1964, p. 78)]

Yet Freud remained optimistic about human reason:

The voice of the intellect is a soft one, but it does not rest till it has gained a hearing. Finally, after a countless succession of rebuffs, it succeeds. This is one of the few points on which one may be optimist about the future of mankind, but it is in itself a point of no small importance.

[1927 (1961, p. 53)]

There are two possible misconceptions of Freud's model that should be corrected. The reader may be struck by the anthropomorphizing of the id, ego, and superego. Freud spoke of them as if they were three homunculi, or little men—one passionate and spoiled, one rational, and one moral—constantly at each other's throat. He was displeased with these humanlike images, but he felt that they helped give both the clinician and the layman an intuitive understanding of the three systems: "Analogies, it is true, decide nothing, but they can make one feel more at home" [1933a (1964, p. 72)]. The other possible misinterpretation is that the three systems refer to particular physical regions of the brain. The structures are simply a way of summarizing three aspects of the personality.

TOPOGRAPHIC APPROACH

Everyone is a moon and has a dark side which he never shows to anybody.

[Mark Twain]

Freud's early writings portrayed a geography (or topography) of the mind. In a metaphorical sense, the "parts" of the mind have spatial relations to each other. This geography was later supplemented by the structural notions of id, ego, and superego described earlier. Turning again to the illustration on the following page, we see that the map of the mind displays three topographic regions: the unconscious, preconscious, and conscious (or perceptual conscious, as labeled in the illustration at left). The unconscious is largely unknown territory; the preconscious and especially the conscious have familiar terrains.

1. The *unconscious* refers primarily to thoughts and feelings that are repressed and therefore unknown. This material is incapable of breaking into consciousness without certain changes or interventions, such as an increase in the drive, a weakening of ego defenses, or the guidance of a therapist.

2. The *preconscious* is capable of becoming conscious because it is not actively barred from consciousness. It is a great deal closer to the conscious than is the unconscious. Preconscious thought becomes conscious by forming mental images or linking up with language.

3. The *conscious* (or perceptual conscious) is synonymous with what a person is aware of at the moment. It is a "highly fugitive state" [Freud, 1940 (1964, p. 159)] because thoughts can rapidly slip back and forth between the preconscious and the conscious. Since energy is required for a thought to enter into consciousness, only a few thoughts can be conscious at any one time.

Freud used a metaphor to describe the relationship between the unconscious and the preconscious and conscious:

> Let us therefore compare the system of the unconscious to a large entrance hall, in which the mental impulses jostle one another like separate individuals. Adjoining this entrance hall there is a second, narrower, room—a kind of drawing-room—in which consciousness, too, resides. But on the threshold between these two rooms a watchman performs his function: he examines the different mental impulses, acts as a censor, and will not admit them into the drawing-room if they displease him.
>
> *[1917 (1963, p. 295)]*

Returning to Freud's sketch, we see how the id, ego, and superego (structures) are related to the unconscious, preconscious, and conscious (topography). All the id resides in the unconscious. The unconscious id is a large area, and in fact Freud corrected his drawing by noting that the space taken up by the unconscious id should have been much greater than that of the ego or the preconscious. If the mind is like an iceberg, then the conscious is only the exposed tip of the iceberg; most of the iceberg (the unconscious) remains hidden. Both the ego and the superego span the three layers. For example, the ego is unaware of the action of its defense mechanisms.

Developmental changes also occur in the relative size of the unconscious, preconscious, and conscious. The infant's mind is almost completely unconscious. With increasing age, the preconscious and conscious occupy more and more of the mental territory. Even among adults, however, the unconscious is the largest area.

Although Freud described the unconscious, preconscious, and conscious as though they were separate entities, he constantly noted that no such separation exists. Rather, he was simply abstracting three aspects of mental functioning. These three aspects of functioning operate together in a holistic fashion to produce behavior. Reading obituaries in the newspaper can be traced to both unconscious (fear of death) and conscious (keeping track of elderly friends) motivations.

Freud placed great importance on the role of the unconscious: "For the property of being conscious or not is in the last resort our one beacon-light in the darkness of depth-psychology" [1923 (1961, p. 18)]. The notion that there is a vast unconscious that controls behavior emerged from Freud's early psychoanalytic sessions with his patients. Patients had sexual fantasies or impulses of which they were unaware but which led to certain inexplicable behavior. For example, a patient with a healthy visual system was unable to see because seeing was too painful; seeing activated painful memories in the unconscious. Additional evidence for the existence of an unconscious came from posthypnotic suggestion, in which patients perform some action that was suggested to them while under hypnosis, or from slips of the tongue, accidents that were not really accidental, selective forgetting (as when someone forgets a dental appointment), and dreams.

STAGE APPROACH

Freud made two bold claims about human development. One is that the first few years of life are the most important years for the formation of personality. The other claim is that this development involves psychosexual stages.

The notion that early experience is crucial seems obvious and noncontroversial to the modern student of development. This idea, however, had not really been taken seriously until Freud systematically developed it. According to Freud, a behavior can be understood only if one knows how it developed in the person's early history. Both normal behavior and abnormal behavior have their roots in the early years, when the basic structure of the personality is laid down. The early interactions between children's drives and their social environment set the pattern for later learning, social adjustment, and coping with anxiety.

It is interesting that a therapist who studied and treated adults would develop a theory of child development. Early in his work, Freud discovered that tracing the cause of a disturbed personality usually led to traumatic, unresolved sexual experiences of childhood. The distant past was very much alive in his patients' current lives in dreams, anxiety from repressed childhood desires, and defense mechanisms acquired in childhood. From information revealed in sessions with patients, Freud was able to reconstruct the sequence of stages of childhood.

Freud and Piaget are the grand stage theorists of developmental psychology. Freud, like Piaget, focuses on qualitative changes during development. We look at the general nature of the stages here and leave a description of the content of each stage for later.

Four distinct stages and a period of latency mark developmental time. Each stage is defined in terms of the part of the body around which drives are centered. The eye of the storm shifts from the oral to the anal to the phallic area during the first five years. Then a period of latency in middle childhood is followed by the genital stage of adolescence. Each stage presents new needs that must be handled by the mental structures. The way in which these needs are met (or not met) determines not only how sexual satisfaction is achieved, but also how children relate to other people and how they feel about themselves. Children develop characteristic attitudes, defenses, and fantasies. Unresolved conflicts in any stage may haunt people throughout their lifetime.

Because the movement from stage to stage is biologically determined, it occurs whether or not there is unfinished business in the stage that is ending. This notion of stage development is very different from Piaget's, in which one stage must be essentially completed before the next stage may begin. The two theories, however, coincide in their claim that the stages follow an invariant order. For Freud, the invariant order comes almost entirely from physical maturation. For Piaget, it comes not only from physical maturation but also from physical and social experiences and innate ways of functioning mentally.

The two theories differ in the relationship between the stages. In Freud's theory, each stage is characterized by one dominant trait (for example, anal concerns) but does not form a tightly knit, structured whole, as does a stage in Piaget's theory. Freud's stages form layers, with each stage only loosely integrated into the next. The reorganization of previous knowledge that characterizes each of Piaget's stages is much less apparent in Freud's stages. Furthermore, one stage does not contain the germ of the next, as it does in Piaget's theory. The oral stage does not *become* the anal stage, in the way that concrete operations become (are transformed into) formal operations.

Although a stage builds upon and is dominant over the previous stage, it does not completely replace that stage, according to Freud. No stage is ever given up entirely. Freud offered a simile of an army that advances into new territory but leaves forces en route to send on supplies or provide a place to retreat if difficulties arise. In the same way, a child can escape unbearably tense experiences by regressing to earlier behavior, such as sucking the thumb or hallucinating the desired object.

We can see many remnants of earlier stages in later stages. Earlier modes of satisfaction may be retained, as when thumb sucking persists throughout the preschool years. Or these earlier modes of gratification may be integrated into later sexual gratification, as when kissing becomes a subordinate part of adult sexuality. Anal concerns may still be present, but they are suppressed, sublimated, and displaced until they bear little resemblance to their earlier form (for example, giving gifts in adulthood). There is a partial integration in the last stage, the genital, when the component instincts (oral, anal, and phallic) merge to form adult genital sexuality.

Normal–Abnormal Continuum

Psychologists often study the unusual or exotic in order to understand the usual or mundane. The unusual may include the mentally ill, the retarded, another culture, or impoverished environments. And Freud's profession, medicine, studies diseased or malfunctioning organisms in order to understand normal organisms. Strokes and injuries to various areas of the brain cause characteristic changes, such as paralysis of one side of the body, loss of speech, or loss of balance. These data clarify the role of each area of the brain in its undamaged stage.

Freud's first evidence about the normal functioning of the unconscious arose from his early study of hysteria. Much more evidence came later. For example, certain patients suffered from delusions of being observed by unknown persons who distrusted them and expected them to transgress and be punished. This abnormal behavior revealed the workings of the conscience in normal people. The only difference was that the internal was projected to the external in abnormal cases. Freud explains the value of studying abnormal behavior:

Pathology, by making things larger and coarser, can draw our attention to normal conditions which would otherwise have escaped us. Where it points to a breach or a rent, there may normally be an articulation present. If we throw a crystal to the floor, it breaks; but not into haphazard pieces. It comes apart along its lines of cleavage into fragments whose boundaries, though they were invisible, were predetermined by the crystal's structure. Mental patients are split and broken structures of this same kind. . . . They have turned away from external reality, but for that very reason they know more about internal, psychical reality and can reveal a number of things to us that would otherwise be inaccessible to us.

[1933a (1964, pp. 58–59)]

So far, we have followed Freud's argument that his study of the abnormal heightens our understanding of the normal. Freud, however, makes a further claim. He sees no sharp cleavage between the abnormal and the normal. Instead, abnormal and normal personalities obey the same principles and merely occupy different positions along a continuum ranging from the very disturbed to the very healthy. In an abnormal personality, psychological processes are exaggerated or distorted. A melancholic patient has an overly strong superego. A sadistic killer has a strong, uncontrolled aggressive drive. An amnesiac must repress all of a painful past. Yet every normal personality has traces of melancholia, sadism, and unaccountable forgetting, as described in a publication appropriately titled *The Psychopathology of Everyday Life* [1901 (1960)]. When reality becomes too painful or impulses of the id intensify, the ego's frantic attempts to keep in touch with reality or fortify the barriers against the id or superego ultimately fail. Neurotic symptoms or even a psychosis results. In Freud's words, "The threatened ego throws itself into the arms of the unconscious instinctual forces in a desperate revolt" [1933a (1964, p. 16)].

METHODOLOGY

It might seem odd that Freud did not study children directly as he built a theory of development. His rationale was that our childhoods remain with us always, in that our adult personalities are residues of our childhoods. In addition, his patients happened to be adults rather than children. For these reasons, he devoted his efforts to developing methods for eliciting information about childhood from adults.

Freud's methodology has aroused as much interest and controversy as has the content of the theory. Free association, dream analysis, and transference at first shocked the psychiatric profession and the public but eventually won the acceptance of many therapists.

The method of *free association* requires that patients verbally report their ongoing stream of thought. During Freud's free-association sessions, the patient relaxed, usually on the famous couch, in a quiet room. Freud sat near the patient's head but out of sight. He instructed his patients to report every thought, regardless of how trivial it seemed, omitting or censoring nothing. This relaxed, accepting state promoted the relaxation of control by the ego over unconscious thoughts. Repressed thoughts might then emerge, though often in disguise. Occasionally, if the patient fell silent, Freud would ask a question or even "lay on hands"—put his hand on the patient's forehead—and tell him that new memories would come!

The theoretical rationale for the free-association technique is as follows. Freud believed that every psychological event has a meaning. That is, a thought or feeling is caused; it does not occur randomly. If one thought typically leads to another, there is a reason for it. If a patient talked about her deceased father, then abruptly changed the subject to a trip she was thinking about taking, Freud might have inferred that she was troubled by her father's death. (Freud found that a journey is often a symbol for death.) The patient might not be aware of these anxious feelings. In this way he abstracted common themes underlying seemingly unrelated thoughts or behaviors. More generally, he tried to describe the organization of the patient's mind.

The central concepts of Freud's theory arose from the free-association sessions. Freud found that patients' thoughts often turned to sexual memories of childhood. At first, Freud thought that these early sexual experiences had actually happened. Eventually, however, he concluded that it was unlikely that so many Viennese parents had sexually abused their children. Freud then viewed the sexual memories as fantasies or perceptions distorted by sexual desire. This issue was never resolved. Even if the experiences were not based on fact, they were still quite important because our early perceptions and memories, true or false, affect the course of development of our personality. Furthermore, the way in which patients distort memories provides the therapist with a clue about their personality.

It might seem difficult for a therapist to elicit repressed thoughts and correctly infer the connections between sentences during free-association sessions. Freud, however, claimed that the task is not so difficult:

> I thought the task was a harder one than it really is. He that has eyes to see
> and ears to hear may convince himself that no mortal can keep a secret. If his
> lips are silent, he chatters with his finger tips; betrayal oozes out of him at

every pore. And thus the task of making conscious the most hidden recesses of the mind is one which it is quite possible to accomplish.

[1905a (1953, pp. 77–78)]

A final comment about Freud's use of free association is that he conducted a self-analysis, beginning in 1897 and continuing throughout his life. He devoted the last half hour of each day to this purpose. This increased his confidence, if not that of the scientific community, in his theory of personality.

A second method is *dream analysis*. If all thoughts are causally related and significant, then psychologists cannot ignore dreams. In fact, Freud concluded that more unconscious material may emerge when one is asleep than awake. During dreams, the usual psychological controls are "sleeping" and allow disturbing thoughts to be expressed and wishes to be fulfilled. These thoughts, however, are often disguised until they are unmasked during psychoanalysis. A house with smooth walls stands for a man, a house with balconies and ledges represents a woman, kings and queens are parents, little animals or vermin are siblings or other children, water refers to birth, and snakes and trunks stand for the sex organs [Freud, 1916 (1963, pp. 153–157)].

Third, *transference* refers to a particular type of relationship that develops between the patient and the analyst during therapy. In the analyst the patient sees some important figure from childhood, often a parent. He consequently transfers to the analyst feelings and reactions that he felt toward this person. Transference helps the analyst discover the nature of patients' relationships with their parents in childhood. Certain patterns of social interaction are repeated throughout life in various settings, including the therapist's office. The patient acts out these interactions from childhood instead of giving a verbal account, which might be inaccurate.

In summary, Freud's methodology was to listen to troubled adults talk. He did not perform controlled experiments and, unlike Piaget, did not observe children's behavior in natural situations. Instead, he studied single individuals in depth, sometimes spending hundreds of hours with a single patient. As if putting together a jigsaw puzzle, he put together pieces of information from patients' free associations, dreams, expressions of emotion, use of defense mechanisms, slips of the tongue, and so on.

Freud organized this information into a coherent picture in his case studies. Several long case studies were published and became well known. For example, the "Rat Man" (1909b) had the obsession that his father and girlfriend would be punished with hungry rats fastened to their buttocks. The "Wolf Man" (1918) reacted to viewing the "primal scene" (sexual intercourse between his parents) by dreaming about wolves (see the dream report at the beginning of this chapter).

DESCRIPTION OF THE STAGES

Earlier we saw that Freud's stage approach is based on the belief that development through the psychosexual stages early in life lays the foundations of personality. This claim was startling because it challenged the common belief that children are sexually innocent until puberty. According to Freud, oral sexuality (birth to 1 year) changes to anal sexuality (1 to 3 years), which in turn becomes phallic sexuality (3 to 5 years). After a period of latency, in which sexual feelings are repressed (5 years to the beginning of puberty), adult "true" genital sexuality emerges. Each stage except latency centers on a particular *erogenous* zone, an area of the body that, when stimulated, produces sexual tensions that need to be relieved. This section describes each of the psychosexual stages. As in Piaget's theory, the ages are approximate.

ORAL STAGE (ROUGHLY BIRTH TO 1 YEAR)

During infancy the mouth rules. Oral experiences introduce the baby to both the pleasure and the pain of the world. Pleasure flows from the satisfaction of the oral drives. Sucking, chewing, eating, and biting give sexual gratification by relieving uncomfortable sexual excitations. The oral activities cause pleasant sensual feelings in the lips, tongue, and membranes of the mouth. These pleasant feelings need not be linked with the satisfaction of hunger because the oral activities themselves are satisfying. The outcome of all of this, in Freudian terminology, is that libidinal energy is cathected (invested) in the oral erogenous zone. The salient social and nonsocial experiences in the oral stage center around oral concerns.

In addition to experiencing oral pleasure, the infant meets pain from frustration and anxiety. Sexual tensions are pleasant if they are satisfied but painful if they are not and continue to intensify. A preferred object, such as a nipple, may not be present at the moment the infant wants it. She must wait, which she finds frustrating and anxiety arousing. She may lapse into hallucinatory wish fulfillment as she imagines the desired nipple. Or she may suck her fingers, a blanket, or a soft toy. Still, satisfaction is not complete. Other frustrations come when parents demand that the nighttime feeding be given up, that certain objects not be chewed because they are unsanitary or unsafe, and especially that the breast or bottle be given up for the cup. The cultural demands of one's society are expressed through the parents. Parents teach the infant how to satisfy her drives in ways that are acceptable to the society. Conflict is inevitable. In small ways, the infant discovers that life has its frustrations as well as its pleasures, its "downs" as well as its "ups." She develops ways of coping with these frustrations that will form the basis for her later personality.

As babies seek gratification and valiantly struggle to overcome barriers to this satisfaction, there is an important psychological principle at work: infants are in trouble if they obtain either too little or too much oral gratification. The side effects of too little gratification are obvious: frequent anxiety, continual seeking of oral gratification in later years, and pessimism. The outcome of too much gratification is less obvious. If oral satisfaction is especially gratifying, children may find it difficult to shift their cathexes to new objects, as demanded by a new stage. In this case, fixation can occur. Furthermore, relatively minor anxiety in a later stage may cause regression to highly cathected objects of the oral stage. For example, the initiation of toilet training during the anal stage may cause a child to return quickly to thumb sucking. The goal, then, is to achieve an optimal level of oral gratification so that he need not carry unfulfilled needs into later stages or feel unwilling to move on to a new stage.

This description of the oral stage has emphasized infants' search for objects that satisfy their oral needs. During the oral stage, however, we also have our first glimpse of the negative side of human nature. Young infants pass from the oral passive–receptive phase to the oral sadistic phase when teeth appear. Biting and spitting out unpleasant substances are destructive, rejecting behaviors. As we shall see later, these behaviors have their counterparts in adult aggressive behavior. In infancy and throughout life, people often feel ambivalence toward other people and objects. Both positive and negative emotions arise, often in quick succession. Just as an infant both sucks and bites a nipple, a man both loves and hates his wife.

Freud claims that the way that infants develop during the oral stage forms the foundation for their personality as an adult. This claim is now elaborated. There are at least five oral "modes of functioning": (1) taking in, (2) holding on, (3) biting, (4) spitting out, and (5) closing

(Hall, 1954, p. 104). Each of these modes forms a prototype (model, plan, or blueprint) for later personality characteristics. Infants learn certain oral reactions to situations they encounter. These characteristic reactions lead to certain attitudes, behaviors, and life goals in adulthood:

1. The infant who found pleasure in taking in food becomes an adult who voraciously "takes in," or acquires, knowledge or power and who incorporates or identifies with significant other people.

2. Holding on to the nipple when it is removed may lead to determination and stubbornness.

3. Biting is the prototype for destructiveness, "biting" sarcasm, cynicism, and dominance.

4. Spitting out becomes rejection.

5. Closing the mouth firmly leads to rejection, negativism, or introversion.

Note that these adult behaviors range from the literally oral, as in smoking, nail biting, and eating, to the metaphorically oral, as in being gullible (swallowing anything) and obstinate (holding on).

All these characteristics are found in every personality to some degree. However, some people have a personality structure that is dominated by one or several of these prototypes from the oral modes. In particular, certain traits may dominate because of extremely pleasant or unpleasant experiences in infancy. For example, an infant with an unaffectionate mother may become an adult who seeks to "take in" love symbolically by acquiring power or vast amounts of money.

Perhaps the most momentous event of the oral stage is the formation of attachment to the mother. Freud proclaims that the mother's importance is "unique, without parallel, established unalterably for a whole lifetime as the first and strongest love-object and as the prototype of all later love-relations" [1940 (1964, p. 188)].* Because it is the mother who typically satisfies needs such as food, sucking, and warmth, she becomes the primary love object in the infant's life. The infant invests a good deal of libidinal energy in her. The notion of an emotional

---

* The obsession with mothers, which characterized not only Erikson and Freud but most developmental psychologists before the 1970s, is fading somewhat as fathers are beginning to be given some attention (for example, M. Lamb, ed., *The father's role: Cross cultural perspectives*, Hillsdale, NJ: Erlbaum, 1987).

attachment to the mother is one of Freud's main legacies to the field of developmental psychology. This work inspired Spitz's (1945) work on disturbed mother–infant relationships. After observing that many infants left in foundling homes became depressed and that some even died, Spitz concluded that lack of mothering contributes to psychological and health problems in infants. Bowlby's (1958) seminal work on attachment led to subsequent research by many other investigators. (Research on attachment is discussed in detail in Chapter 5.)

Although it may seem counterintuitive, attachment seems to lead to the infant's healthy sense of separateness from his mother. Winnicott (1971) stresses that this gradual differentiation is necessary for a clear sense of self and for normal interpersonal relations later. Before this differentiation, an infant–mother matrix gives little sense of a separation of the self and the world. What Winnicott calls "good-enough mothering" involves a synchrony, or match, between the infant's needs and spontaneous behaviors and the caretaker's activities. Consequently, the infant feels omnipotent because he can magically obtain his every desire. Gradually, the baby's ego develops as he encounters delays in gratification, interacts with various "not-me" objects, and discovers his own resources for interacting with the world. The "holding environment" with the mother provides a secure base for this threatening process of individuation. Mothers also design "play dialogues," which involve a mutual regulation of the interaction between themselves and their infants. The mother uses the infant's gaze and state of arousal as cues for the timing and intensity of her facial expressions and talking (Stern, 1974; 1985). Thus, the ideal mother tries to avoid both stimulus overload and boredom. The important outcome is that in the context of a social relationship, the child uses feedback regarding his effect on the mother to construct his self-concept. In other words, the baby expresses and defines his true self by being with his mother and seeing the effects of his spontaneous actions toward the mother.

The individuation process continues during development as children use "security blankets" or other cuddly, comforting objects to ease their separation from their mother (Winnicott, 1953). In addition, Mahler, Pine, and Bergman (1975) describe a series of steps in the differentiation of the self from the mother. The toddler has ambivalent feelings about this growing independence and, in severe cases, child psychosis results from a faulty individuation process. These and other psychoanalysts have identified object loss, particularly the real or perceived loss of the mother, as one of the most significant events that can occur in early life.

Attachment is a vital process for development because it serves as a building block for later social relationships. Furthermore, it facilitates the mother's attempts to socialize the child by using her attention to reward desirable behavior. However, in Freud's somewhat pessimistic theory, all silver linings are covered by clouds. Thus, attachment has its dangers. If the attachment is too strong, the infant may become overly dependent on the mother or anxious about her possible rejection of him. Then, later in life, he may depend on others to do things for him and even do his thinking for him. He may develop a generally passive personality.

ANAL STAGE (ROUGHLY 1 TO 3 YEARS)

By the end of the oral stage, infants have developed the rough outlines of a personality. This personality consists of attitudes toward themselves and other people, mechanisms for achieving gratification within the demands of reality, and interests in certain activities and objects. As maturation moves infants to the anal stage, the concerns move from the oral area to the anal area. The new needs of this stage set in motion new conflicts between children and the world. The way in which children resolve these new conflicts further differentiates and crystallizes the rudimentary personality structure. The expression of oral needs does not stop, of course. Children simply face a new set of needs and demands that require their immediate attention.

The physiological need to defecate creates tension, which is relieved by defecation. This anal stimulation and subsequent reduction of tension produces pleasure. As in the oral stage, the erogenous zone brings frustration and anxiety as well as pleasure. Society, as represented by the parents, demands that involuntary expulsion be replaced by delayed, voluntary expulsion. Thus, children face toilet training. Their desire for immediate gratification is frustrated. In a small but momentous way, children enter into conflict with authoritarian adult society. Children all over the world face and resolve this conflict in some way. Obviously, many variables affect how much conflict the child feels and how she adapts to the demands placed on her. These variables include the age at which toilet training is begun, how strict or relaxed the training is, and the parent's attitude toward defecation, control, and cleanliness.

If toilet training is particularly harsh or premature or overemphasized by the parents, defecation can become a source of great anxiety for children. This anxiety can generalize to other situations in which an external authority makes demands or children must control their own impulses. Some children react to strict toilet training by holding back elimination and becoming constipated or by defecating at inappropriate times or places, such as the supermarket.

Activities and events surrounding the anal area serve as prototypes for a variety of behaviors during both this stage and subsequent stages. Explosive, uncontrollable elimination is a prototype for temper tantrums or vigorous, demanding, physical exercise. In reaction against overly strict toilet training, the child may become messy, dirty, and irresponsible. Or, at the other extreme, the child may become a compulsively neat, frugal, and overly controlled adult. Freud's term *anal character* describes people who are orderly, pedantic, and obstinate. Such people have a distorted perception of the world as they try in vain to make everything clearcut, neat, and unambiguous. Another possible outcome is that the parent's praise of the child's success at the toilet may create a link between giving a gift (feces) and receiving love. In this case, the child may become "giving" and generous. If the parent places great value on the child's productions at the toilet, the child may become creative and productive, or, on the other hand, become depressed due to a feeling of loss. If the child balks at giving up his prized possessions at the toilet, he may become retentive and stingy and may gain pleasure from collecting objects. This list of personality characteristics reflects the child's ambivalence between giving and retaining.

The list of potential negative outcomes in the anal stage certainly is not comforting to the prospective parent! As in the oral stage, the goal is to allow enough but not too much gratification, and to develop enough but not too much self-control. If this goal is adequately achieved, the child will have developed a more mature ego because it has been sharpened by its confrontation with reality. The child who survives the anal period relatively unscathed is ready to tackle the third stage, the phallic stage, when it arrives.

PHALLIC STAGE (ROUGHLY 3 TO 5 YEARS)

The child's solution to problems of the oral and anal stages sets a pattern for solving later problems of adjustment. This development is continued in the phallic stage, so named because the possession of the phallus in boys and its absence in girls is a major concern of children, according to Freud. In this stage, pleasures and problems center on the genital area. Stimulation in the genital area brings tensions and, if the tensions are relieved, pleasure. The problem of the stage arises when the sexual urge is directed toward the parent of the opposite sex. This situation is the well-known *Oedipus complex*. (In Greek mythology, Oedipus killed his father and married his mother.)

Since the Oedipus complex is somewhat different for boys than girls, each sex is considered separately here. Freud emphasized the development of boys more than girls in the phallic stage because he believed that the conflict is more intense for boys. A young boy has sexual desires for his mother and does not want to share her with his father. At the same time, the boy fears that the father, in retaliation, will castrate him. As a way out of this highly anxious situation, the boy represses both his desire for his mother and his hostility toward his father.

The most important outcome of the Oedipus complex is that the boy comes to identify with his father. That is, he develops a strong emotional bond with the father, strives to be like him, and "internalizes" him—his beliefs, values, interests, and attitudes. Identification serves as a basis for much of socialization. In particular, the development of the superego and behavior considered appropriate to one's sex are by-products of this identification. The superego increases the child's self-control and adherence to the parents' morality.

Identification is a reasonable solution to the demands of the ego and id in this stage. The ego is partially satisfied because anxiety is reduced. The id is partially satisfied because the child can "have" the mother vicariously through the father. Again, as the child tries to cope with both his drives and the prohibitions of society, he achieves a compromise solution that advances his psychological maturity.

In comparison with boys, girls face a similar but much less intense conflict during the phallic stage. The father, of course, is the object of the girl's sexual longings. Freud argues that part of this longing involves penis envy as the girl realizes that the father has a prized object that she does not have. In Freud's words, "She makes her judgment and her decision in a flash. She has seen it and knows that she is without it and wants to have it" [1925b (1961, p. 252)]. The girl begins to prefer her father to her mother. She feels that she has been castrated and blames her mother for this loss because she "sent her into the world so insufficiently equipped" [1925b (1961, p. 254)]. This anger toward the mother weakens the cathexis with her.

As in the case of boys, society does not allow the full expression of the sexual desire for the parent. However, the girl feels less threat from the mother than the boy does from the father. The girl has less to fear because castration is not possible. Freud claims that since there is less anxiety and consequently less repression, the girl has a weaker identification with the mother than does the boy with the father. Freud then concludes that girls have a weaker conscience than do boys, a claim that is not supported by research. In girls, the Oedipus complex usually continues to some extent for many years but may slowly weaken or be repressed.

It should be noted that there is a basic difference in the role of feelings about castration in boys and girls. In boys, fear of castration leads to the abandonment of the Oedipus complex. In girls, the belief that castration has already occurred partially causes the Oedipus complex, through penis envy.

This account of the Oedipus complex is somewhat oversimplified. In actuality, there is always identification with both parents. The relative strengths of the two identifications vary from child to child, depending on variables such as the balance of feminine and masculine components in the physiological makeup of the child (because all people are bisexual to some extent, according to Freud) and the intensity of the castration anxiety or penis envy. In addition, both sexes retain a strong cathexis for the mother because she is the most important object in the two previous psychosexual stages.

In psychoanalytic sessions, Freud found powerful and lasting influences from the phallic stage. For example, women often had disturbing sexual fantasies about their fathers that had never been resolved. Another common problem was the inability to overcome one's attachment to one's parents and establish independence. More generally, lasting attitudes toward the opposite sex and toward people in authority could be traced to this stage.

With the achievement of identification and the waning of the phallic stage, the influential early years come to an end. Thereafter, conflicts are resolved in characteristic ways. Personality changes, but primarily by further differentiation of the basic structure. It is rather awesome that these important early years are only dimly remembered by the adult because of massive repression.

PERIOD OF LATENCY
(ROUGHLY 5 YEARS TO THE BEGINNING OF PUBERTY)

After the *Sturm und Drang* of the first three stages, there is a period of relative calm, when sexual drives are repressed and no new area of bodily excitement emerges. Children conveniently "forget" the sexual urges and fantasies of their earlier years. They turn their thoughts to school activities and play primarily with children of the same sex. This is a time for acquiring cognitive skills and assimilating cultural values as children expand their world to include teachers, neighbors, peers, club leaders, and coaches. Sexual energy continues to flow, but it is channeled into social concerns and into building defenses against sexuality. Thus, the ego and superego continue to develop. The small amount of space allotted to describing this period and the next stage reflects Freud's emphasis on the first three stages.

GENITAL STAGE (ADOLESCENCE)

The sexual impulses, which were repressed during the latency stage, reappear in full force as a result of the physiological changes of puberty. These sexual impulses are fused with the earlier ones but are now directed toward a peer of the opposite sex. The goal is mature, adult sexuality, with the biological aim of reproduction. Love becomes more altruistic, with less concern for self-pleasure than in earlier stages. The choice of a partner is, of course, not independent of the person's earlier development. A woman may choose a "father figure," a passive man she can dominate, a sadistic male, and so on, depending on the attitudes and social patterns developed in the early years.

Although some internal conflict is inevitable throughout life, a relatively stable state is achieved by most people by the end of the genital stage. Typically, the individual achieves a fairly strong ego structure that makes coping with the reality of the adult world possible. One important achievement is a balance between love and work.

CASE STUDY OF "LITTLE HANS"

The above outline of the psychosexual stages cannot capture the vivid, powerful conflicts that operate in an individual child's life. Thus, we turn to one of Freud's most famous case studies, the "Analysis of a Phobia in a Five-Year-Old Boy" (1909a) or, as it is more commonly known, "Little Hans." This case study was unique because it was Freud's only analysis of a child and because Freud conducted the analysis by mail in a series of letters with the boy's physician-father, who made the observations. Nevertheless, the study was a central force in the formation of one of Freud's most important developmental concepts: identification.

When Hans was 5 years old, anxiety attacks, a phobia, and a fantasy appeared. His phobia, the fear that a horse would bite him or fall down, was so strong that he would not leave his house. He was especially afraid of horses that pulled heavy loads in carts or vans or were white with a black muzzle and wore blinders. In Hans's fantasy, during the night "there was a big giraffe in the room and a crumpled one; and the big one called out because I took the crumpled one away from it. Then it stopped calling out; and then I sat down on top of the crumpled one" [1909a (1955, p. 37)].

After sifting through this evidence, Freud identified three themes: an Oedipus conflict, sibling rivalry, and fear of punishment for masturbation. Thus, in the phobia, the horse represented Hans's father, who had a mustache (a black muzzle around the horse's mouth) and eyeglasses (blinders) and was, as Hans remarked, "so white" (like the white horse). Hans feared that the horse would bite (castrate) him because of his sexual longing for his mother and his masturbating. Anxiety about masturbation may have been prompted by his mother's threat that if his masturbation continued, she would send him to the doctor to cut off his "widdler." The fear that a horse might fall down was interpreted as a fear that his father might die or go away, as he sometimes wished when he wanted his mother alone. Significantly, Hans had remarked, "Daddy, don't trot away from me" (p. 45). The giraffe fantasy might be interpreted as a wish for possessing the mother, as Hans imagined he sat on the smaller giraffe (mother), which he had taken from the larger giraffe (father). Note the phallic symbol in the giraffe's long neck.

Hans's feelings of loss of attention and love after the birth of his sister were expressed in the fear that a cart might be upset and spill its contents (his mother might give birth again). In the fantasy, Hans destroyed his younger sister when he sat on her (the small giraffe).

Hans eventually identified with his father, thereby resolving his conflicts and recovering from his fear of horses. He continued to develop a healthy personality.

MECHANISMS OF DEVELOPMENT

The section on psychosexual stages presented the "what" of development, but not the "how" or "why." Our next task is to examine the mechanisms that propel the child through the stages. One similarity between the theories of Freud and Piaget is striking in this respect. Both had a "trouble" theory of development. Development proceeds because of disturbances or perturbations to the system. Development is hard work. The child must continually try to reestablish a state of relative calm. There are, however, important differences in how the two theorists conceptualize the disturbances and their removal. Piaget posited a dynamic equilibration system that orchestrates and brings into harmony three inputs: physical maturation, social experience, and physical experience. These inputs produce new information that may contradict, or at least not fit into, current schemes. Equilibrium is reachieved when actions (operations or schemes) are in balance once again. Although Freud also saw equilibration as a process of reducing disturbing elements, he stressed different inputs: emotion-laden thoughts rather than objective information about the physical world. He was more concerned with psychological pain than logical inconsistency, with energy in repose than mental actions in balance.

Another difference between the theorists is that Freud's equilibration system is less open (less responsive to external information) than Piaget's. Piaget spoke of continual assimilation and accommodation as new experiences are encountered. In Freud's system, there is more resistance to change. The system is also closed in that there is a certain amount of energy that can be changed in form but never amount.

Now that we have examined the general nature of equilibration in Freud's theory and compared it with Piaget's use of the term, we look more specifically at how equilibration is a mechanism of development. Freud identified several sources of conflict or psychological disruption: physical maturation, external frustrations, internal conflicts, personal inadequacies, and anxiety (Hall, 1954, p. 72).

1. *Maturation* refers to changes in the nervous system, motor development, hormonal changes, drives, and so on. Each maturational change brings new possibilities and new problems. As we saw earlier, the drives are particularly important. Maturational forces both propel children into activity as they try to satisfy the drives and move them from stage to stage as the bodily site of pleasure changes.

2. *External frustrations* come from people or events that do not allow the immediate expression of needs. These cause a painful buildup of tension and force children to delay and detour their discharge of energy.

3. *Internal conflicts* arise from the battle among the id, ego, and superego or, more specifically, between drives and forces of repression.

4. *Personal inadequacies* refer to certain skills, knowledge, expertise, or experience that the person needs but lacks. For example, a child may want to join a peer group but be too shy to enter the group or too clumsy at the game they are playing.

5. Finally, *anxiety* is an unpleasant feeling that occurs when the child anticipates physical or psychological pain. The fear of losing a valued love object is a common example.

All these elements cause an unpleasant state of tension, which the child attempts to rectify in accordance with the pleasure principle and the reality principle. These disturbances, however, merely initiate change. Other mechanisms actually accomplish change. The ego has the primary responsibility for guiding the course of change. Its perceptual and cognitive systems gather relevant information about the current situation, recall useful information from past experiences, and use whatever defense mechanisms are most appropriate. The ego develops methods for keeping distressing sexual thoughts from becoming conscious and placates the id and superego. The ego, then, mediates change from moment to moment. The accumulation of these small changes adds up to long-term change. Over time the ego gathers strength, and personality crystallizes and becomes further differentiated into complex attitudes, interests, and behaviors.

Several developmental "products" also serve as mechanisms of development. The most notable are attachment and identification. As mentioned earlier, both lead to other important acquisitions, such as sex typing and moral development in the case of identification.

POSITION ON DEVELOPMENTAL ISSUES

HUMAN NATURE

Hall and Lindzey summarize Freud's view of the person as

a full-bodied individual living partly in a world of reality and partly in a world of make-believe, beset by conflicts and inner contradictions, yet capable of rational thought and action, moved by forces of which he has little knowledge and by aspirations which are beyond his reach, by turn confused and clear-headed, frustrated and satisfied, hopeful and despairing, selfish and altruistic; in short, a complex human being.

[1957, p. 72]

This description of the conflicted, contradictory nature of humans stands in sharp contrast to Piaget's rational human, calmly searching for epistemological truth in a predictable world. Freud's theory is concerned with emotions, particularly their role in forcing the development of personality and thought as children strive to cope with them. By nature, people have strong passions that color their perceptions throughout life.

Although not all interpreters of Freudian theory would agree, Freud's world view seems to fit more comfortably into the organismic than the mechanistic camp. The classification, however, is less clear than for Piaget. For Freud, a psychological being is a loosely organized whole that is, in most ways, active and self-regulating. Freud's holistic approach is clearest in his claim that a given behavior is caused by several aspects of personality. The id, ego, and superego, organized into a structured whole, together cause a particular behavior. An action is not "pure" id, ego, or superego. Of course, the relative influence of each varies from behavior to behavior.

Although human beings are passive, in that drives force them into action, they are active in their attempts to cope with the drives and maintain a state of equilibrium. The ego, in its executive role, is the most active agent of the personality. It organizes incoming information from the self (for example, anxiety about some impending event) and the social environment and directs the behavior chosen.

Although both Freudian and Piagetian theory can be considered organismic theories, two important differences should be noted. First, it is clear that Freud's psychological whole is not the tightly knit, integrated, equilibrated whole described by Piaget. Freud posits a looser organization. Still, his thinking is in line with the Gestaltists' claim that the whole is more than the sum of the parts. Second, for Piaget children act because they are inherently active and self-regulated; for Freud children act because drives force them to act.

QUALITATIVE VERSUS QUANTITATIVE DEVELOPMENT

As in Piaget's theory, the stagelike changes proposed by Freud imply that development involves qualitative change. There is a change in which aspect of the sexual drive is dominant: oral, anal, phallic, or genital. There is also qualitative change in the psychological organization as new acquisitions, such as defense mechanisms and the superego, appear.

Although Freud emphasized qualitative change, he did not slight quantitative change. The developing child exhibits a gradual strengthening of the ego, superego, and various defense mechanisms.

NATURE VERSUS NURTURE

It is sometimes claimed that Freud had a biologically based theory of development. Although he emphasized maturation and the biologically based drives, he was, in fact, an interactionist: "The constitutional factor must await experiences before it can make itself felt; the accidental factor must have a constitutional basis in order to come into operation" [1905b (1953, p. 239)]. Although drives derive from a person's biological nature, their expression is always modified by the social milieu. The people or objects available and the behaviors allowed by parents or other authorities direct the satisfaction of the drives. The demands of civilization are as real as the demands of the body.

Within the category of nurture, not all experiences make an equal impact. The experiences of the first five years of life are especially important. These experiences need not be traumatic in order to be influential. In fact, many intense, violent events of childhood have only a fleeting effect. In Freud's words, "harsh rulers have short reigns" [1905b (1953, p. 241)]. The recurrent, day-to-day enduring patterns of satisfying one's drives in a socially and psychologically acceptable way have the most influence on later life.

Variations in either the social environment or the physical constitution can cause personality differences among people. Although it is easy to imagine the former, the latter may be less obvious. Freud suggested that there are innate differences from person to person in the strength of the various components of the sex drive (oral, anal, phallic) and in the time at which each psychosexual stage emerges.

WHAT DEVELOPS

The essence of development is the emergence of structures—the id, ego, and superego—that channel, repress, and transform sexual energy. These structures and their dynamic processes are both affective (emotional) and cognitive. The tendency to criticize Freud for slighting cognition is somewhat unfair. Thought—whether unconscious, preconscious, or conscious and whether primary or secondary process in nature—always accompanies feeling.

THEORETICAL NATURE OF THE THEORY

Freud was a practicing therapist concerned with the real problems of real people. He entered a field that offered few tools for helping him solve these problems. Therefore, he had to develop ideas about personality that helped him develop therapeutic tools. This pragmatic concern left little time for formal theory building. Nevertheless, we can sort out various theoretical characteristics of the theory.

There have been attempts to systematize Freud's theory, for example, the fruitful efforts of Rapaport (1960). However, there is no organized, formal, axiomatic account of his theory. Thus, it certainly is not a deductive theory. The theory was only modestly functional. Freud's "observations" (usually patients' reports of thoughts, dreams, and behavior) modified his theory, which in turn suggested new hypotheses to be "tested" by further observations. The theory, however, is most marked by the use of models. Rapaport (1960) describes four models implicit in Freud's theory: reflex arc, energy, Darwinian (genetic), and Jacksonian (neural-integration hierarchy).

1. *The reflex-arc model* comes from neurology, Freud's original field. A reflex refers to an innate connection between a particular type of stimulation and a particular response. For example, when an infant's foot is pricked, the knee flexes. The path to and from the spinal cord forms a curve, or arc. The model, then, refers to the tendency for organisms to respond when stimulated. This simple "in-and-out" or S–R (stimulus–response) model is useful for describing the relation between various types of stimuli and various types of responses. Stimulation can come from the external world or the internal world, particularly the unconscious. Drive excitations in the unconscious usually lead to behavior but may stop in the preconscious or conscious.

2. The *energy model* was outlined in the earlier sections on Freud's dynamic approach and mechanisms of development. In an attempt to reduce drive tension, people are forced to do something. As tension associated with hunger mounts, the baby may act (suck a bottle), hallucinate (imagine a bottle of milk), or discharge affect (cry). As the internal pressure builds up, the release of energy becomes more and more necessary. If one possible outlet is "plugged," the person seeks another. This model, of course, comes from physics and draws on many physical laws concerning the distribution, transformation, and discharge of energy. The goal of this energy system is to maintain a homeostatic (equilibrated) state, in which energy buildup is corrected by energy discharge.

3. The *Darwinian*, or *genetic, model* presents the biological, evolutionary viewpoint. In Freud's interpretation of the model, development proceeds according to instincts, which we share with animals. These instincts express themselves in the psychosexual stages. Both evolution over many generations and developmental changes within a lifetime are due to organisms' attempts to adapt to the environment. Modes of adaptation developed early in life influence personality and behavior later in life. Psychological adaptation can parallel physical adaptation. For example, mental flight from a dangerous thought or impulse can be likened to physical flight from a dangerous predator.

4. Freud borrowed the *Jacksonian*, or *neural-integration hierarchy, model* from the study of the nervous system. According to this model, the nervous system is organized into a hierarchy. Higher levels control (facilitate or inhibit) lower levels. If the higher levels are unable to function, because of injury or other problems, the lower levels run unchecked. In the same way, higher psychological levels (for example, the ego) control lower psychological levels (the id) unless the higher levels are unable to function, for example, because anxiety has overwhelmed the ego.

EVALUATION OF THE THEORY

Although clinical psychology is still influenced by psychoanalytic theory, an anti-Freudian attitude has pervaded experimental psychology for many years. The world of academic developmental psychology has its fads and fashions, as does the larger world. The psychoanalytically oriented developmental psychologist is now an endangered species. To illustrate, if one looks through the major journals of developmental research, it is clear that "tests" of the theory are almost nonexistent and references to psychoanalytic work are scarce. There are many reasons for the theory's falling stock in recent years. Some of these are discussed in the section on weaknesses and include an inadequate methodology for identifying developmental processes, the uncertain testability of central claims concerning development, and the overemphasis on sexuality. In addition, the theory's incorporation into "pop culture" and the recent focus on cognition in developmental research surely contributed to the trend.

Although rejection of certain aspects of Freud's theory is reasonable, experimental psychologists' overall rejection of the theory may have deprived the field of a valuable perspective on development. In the belief that the Freudian approach can provide some insights into current concerns of developmental psychologists, the following section presents some strengths of the theory. The focus is on contemporary relevance.

STRENGTHS

Of the many strengths of Freud's theory, two seem most central to present-day developmental psychology: the introduction of new psychological phenomena to Western culture, and the theory's relevance for contemporary research on cognitive development.

Introduction of New Psychological Phenomena to Western Culture

Freud's notion that behavior and development are directed by powerful unconscious drives struck twentieth-century thought with force. Concepts such as infantile sexuality, the anal personality, and the teeming desires of the unconscious jarred a Victorian society that covered piano legs to hide their nakedness. That the theory eventually was partially accepted may reveal more about changes in society than about the theory itself. Freud's view of the human potential for destructive behavior could not be so easily dismissed after two world wars and the political crimes of the times. It was a theory whose time had come.

Regardless of one's judgment about the scientific merit of the theory, it is without doubt the most widely influential psychological theory in history. Its impression on society may equal that of Marx and Darwin. The theory's influence reaches into nearly every area of twentieth-century thought. Freud described unconscious motivation in the areas of anthropology (*Totem and Taboo*, 1913), art ("The Moses of Michelangelo," 1914), religion (*The Future of an Illusion*, 1927), literature ("Dostoevsky and Parricide," 1928), sociology (*Civilization and Its Discontents*, 1930), and history (*Why War?*, 1933). Freud also touched these disciplines indirectly in his more general writings. Many neo-

Freudians developed further the implications of psychoanalysis for other disciplines. For example, Ernst Kris drew fascinating conclusions in *Psychoanalytic Explorations in Art* (1952). In addition to professionals in the various areas, the general public became familiar with many of his ideas. Slips of the tongue became more embarrassing than before, and millions of people began to take their dreams seriously. The belief that weaning and toilet training should not be sudden and harsh is often attributed to Freud's ideas.

Within psychology and psychiatry, the influence of Freud's work on emotional and nonrational aspects of personality was also far-reaching. He left his mark on every area from social psychology to sensory processes, from adult therapy to child therapy. The diversity of viewpoints among psychoanalysts today can be traced to the various followers of Freud who further developed his theory and in some cases broke away from Freud. Some of the best-known neo-Freudians were Carl Jung, Otto Rank, Alfred Adler, Karen Horney, Harry Stack Sullivan, Erik Erikson, Melanie Klein, Anna Freud, Heinz Hartmann, and David Rapaport.

Since Freud's theory is thoroughly developmental, it is not surprising that it deeply influenced developmental psychology. There was considerable interest in the theory, in part because of the growth of child-guidance clinics in the 1920s and 1930s. It became clear that emotional forces are an important part of development. Salient psychoanalytic developmental work in the 1940s and 1950s included Erikson's stages of psychosocial development; direct observations of children by Anna Freud, Ernst Kris, Sybill Escalona, and Rent Spitz; John Whiting and Irvin Child's cross-cultural work; and John Bowlby's early studies on infant social attachment. Psychoanalytic theory also touched the early work of social learning theorists, especially Robert Sears, Neal Miller, and John Dollard, who began to incorporate psychoanalytic content. For instance, a concern with unconscious motivation was very clear in Sears's work on defense mechanisms, dependency, identification, and parent–child relations. Although Freud's influence is rarely acknowledged explicitly in current developmental research, many core concepts are his: developmental stages, psychological structures, unconscious motivation, and the importance of early experience. In addition, the theory stimulated research in the areas of moral development, sex typing, identification, parent–child relations, attachment, aggression, and dependency. These remain active areas of research even today. Although a number of Freud's specific claims may be inaccurate, he told us what is important in development. Researchers have found something of value in the theory, even if they have not accepted it in its entirety.

Freud's theory remains a vital force within child clinical psychology, child psychiatry, and counseling psychology. Both the therapeutic techniques and the theoretical notions, such as the normal–abnormal continuum, the unconscious–conscious distinction, and the psychic structures (id, ego, superego) are very much alive.

Relevance for Contemporary Research on Cognitive Development

The major change in developmental psychology from the late 1960s to the present has been the tremendous interest in cognitive development. This trend may be responsible, in part, for the waning interest in Freudian theory in recent years. After surveying the results of this era of research on cognitive development, we may conclude that certain shortcomings could be remedied by a renewed interest in psychoanalytic theory. The theory's relevance for the current research scene in cognitive development is outlined here.

In the last 20 years, cognitive developmentalists have focused on rational problem solving: how thought becomes increasingly organized, efficient, abstract, and objective. This type of thought characterizes that of an adult scientist. It is assumed that this is the goal of cognitive development. This viewpoint emerges clearly in Piaget's emphasis on logical operations and on concepts of the physical world. The information-processing approach, described in a later chapter, also pictures a developing child as an organism that relentlessly searches for truth in an increasingly efficient and rational way. Although this view characterizes part of cognitive development, it does not tell the whole story. Humans probably are not as rational as these theories propose. As Wason and Johnson-Laird express it, "At best, we can all think like logicians; at worst, logicians all think like us" (1972, p. 245).

Psychoanalytic theory's focus on "irrational" thought processes can expand and enrich our current concepts of children's thinking. Freud's work suggests that much thought is motivated by reasons unknown to the child. She may be intellectually capable of inferring that she hates her younger brother for the attention he receives from her parents; yet, because of the psychological pain and guilt that such knowledge would produce, she may instead believe that she feels only love for her brother. Even intelligent adults are guided by emotions when they buy resort property without seeing it first, daydream, support corrupt politicians on faith, and marry someone they know has a personality incompatible with theirs. In other words, thought distorts reality and ignores relevant information.

Irrational thought processes are as important as the more frequently studied rational ones; in fact, the former may occur more frequently than the latter. Thus, Freud's theory poses two challenges for developmentalists. One challenge is to study how emotions affect thinking in children. Do children reason differently when angry or frustrated than when calm? A second challenge is to examine whether the mental processes underlying primary- and secondary-process thought and the defense mechanisms (such as projection, reaction formation, repression, and sublimation) differ from the mental processes described by Piaget and the information-processing psychologists. For example, how is Piaget's notion of mental reversibility related to Freud's notion of reaction formation, in which a negative attitude toward a person or an object is transformed into a positive attitude? Are conflicting feelings and logically contradictory ideas resolved in the same way? What are the mental processes underlying self-deception? What cognitive acquisitions are necessary for understanding displaced aggression (taking one's anger out on an innocent person)? Do the notions of repression and the preconscious have any relevance for the distinction between short-term and long-term memory?

So far, the suggestion has been that the processes of thought identified by psychoanalytic theory could fruitfully become an object of developmental research. They could supplement and perhaps modify our view of logical thought. A further suggestion is that the *content* of children's thought is more wide-ranging than recent research would indicate. Freud would point out that children do not think only about quantity, spatial relationships, justice, objects, and causality. They also try to understand and mentally adjust to the violence on television or in their home, hunger, their parents' physical and emotional relationship, their own sexual or aggressive feelings, the tendency of adults to say one thing and do the opposite, rejection by their peers or parents, failure in social interactions, and so on. Other psychological content given little attention by current cognitive research includes dreams and fantasies. Adding this content to that considered by cognitive developmentalists would give a more balanced view of children's thinking.

This suggested new direction for research on cognitive development is particularly promising because it is compatible with two new interests within the field: *social cognition* and *theory of mind*. Social cognition, thinking about people and their behavior, obviously should take into account the problematic or troublesome content of thought just described. Thus far, social-cognitive research has given almost no attention to this area. As described in Chapter 1, *theory of mind* refers to a person's understanding of the nature of mental states, particularly representations. A child's theory of mind would influence his understanding of the psychological defenses used by others as well as himself, desires, the nature of dreams, the distinction between fantasy and reality, and so forth.

WEAKNESSES

Freud made it difficult for anyone to criticize his theory: "No one has a right to join in a discussion of psycho-analysis who has not had particular experiences which can only be obtained by being analyzed oneself" [1933a (1964, p. 69)]. Nevertheless, we now critically look at several weaknesses of the theory: inadequate methodology for studying development, uncertain testability of central claims concerning development, and overemphasis on childhood sexuality.

Inadequate Methodology for Studying Development

The scientific community requires that theories be based on empirical observations that can be replicated by other scientists. Freud's methodology makes this type of data gathering nearly impossible. His primary methods—free association, dream analysis, and transference—pose three major difficulties.

1. According to Freud, these methods require that the experimenter be trained in psychoanalysis. Because such training is a long, expensive process, few people are even qualified to test the theory. Furthermore, those who are psychoanalytically trained tend to be "believers," who can hardly be expected to supply objective data. (Of course, this criticism can be leveled against any researcher who has a theoretical bias.) If one believes that there are strong psychosexual forces in childhood, one can see them in every word or action.

2. Freud's methods lend themselves to experimenter error. Freud made notes about the psychoanalytic sessions after they occurred, often hours later. It is ironic that someone who demonstrated the distortions of memory in his patients should be so oblivious to that possibility in himself. There is a danger that he selectively remembered only that which fit into his theory. Another source of experimenter error is the possibility that the patient's line of thought is influenced by the nature of the therapist's questions or even the timing of his grunts and silences.

3. Adults' recollections of childhood and recent dreams are unlikely to be completely accurate. Introspection has a poor reputation in psychology. It is not easy to report objectively even one's current mental state or recent dream states; mental states from 50 years earlier pose even more difficulties. Childhood and dream experiences are filtered through the patient's memory, which is selective, and his cognitive-linguistic system, which supplies a structure. Freud himself knew that these verbal reports are not reliable, but he felt that even fantasies and distortions are revealing. The patient's experience of these earlier events, whether accurate or distorted, is what is most relevant to therapy. Still, the fact that therapists usually do not have the means to discern when the reports are real and when they are not limits their assessment of the patient's perception of reality.

Uncertain Testability of Central Claims Concerning Development

Perhaps the most common criticism leveled against Freud's theory is that it is inherently untestable or at least difficult to test. In part, this problem stems from the methodological inadequacies outlined above. An involved, possibly biased participant–observer, who records only a portion of the patient's responses, is a dubious source of objective data for testing the theory. In addition, it is uncertain whether the critical developments during childhood can be clarified by data coming from adults. Furthermore, the problem of definition poses a challenge to the experimental psychologist. There are many vague, imprecise, poorly defined terms. Because Freud relies heavily on analogies to communicate the meaning of the terms, the meaning conveyed is intuitive. Freud's reply to this criticism was that terms are imprecise in the early years of any science. For example, when physics was a young science, the notions of force and mass were elusive.

One facet of the problem of definition is that many of Freud's notions have an uncertain relationship to observable behavior, in part because of the considerable distance between the two. The therapist takes verbal reports and, to a lesser extent, nonverbal behavior (e.g., facial expressions, crying, and physical accidents) and interprets them in terms of distant theoretical concepts, such as defense mechanisms, drives, and unconscious motivation. In particular, the evidence for the unconscious from dreams, forgetting, and puns sometimes seems rather farfetched. For example, Freud made a large jump from a report of a dream about an oven to the interpretation that this image represents the uterus. One way to state the problem is that in Freud's system a psychological attribute can refer to several different behaviors or, conversely, a particular behavior can stem from several different psychological attributes. As an example of the former, an "anal personality" can be expressed in either a compulsively neat or an overly messy person. Or a patient's problem can be diagnosed as an Oedipus complex if he either talks constantly about his mother or never mentions her (due to repression). As an example of the case in which a behavior can have several possible causes, the inability to eat can stem from hysteria (perhaps caused by a fear of seeming to be pregnant) or paranoia (perhaps a fear of being poisoned). It is unclear how one would "test" these notions. The theory must be stated more systematically before it is clearly testable. Rapaport (1960) took a significant step in that direction.

There have been numerous attempts to test Freud's theory either clinically, often with hypnosis or projective tests in which the subject must interpret inkblots or pictures, or experimentally.* The latter approach, however, has been criticized for not adequately testing the theory. For example, exposing a boy to an aggressive, hostile male adult and subsequently observing how much the boy imitates the male's behavior is not a fair test of the notion that the Oedipus complex leads to identification with the aggressor. The long-term, emotionally powerful experiences of real life may not be translated easily into brief, simplistic, experimental episodes. In short, psychologists are in a bind. They cannot adequately test the most crucial theoretical notions outside the psychoanalytic session, but the psychoanalytic session does not lend itself to experimental procedures.

If the theory itself cannot be tested scientifically, perhaps the best use of the theory is as a springboard for more limited, testable hypotheses. For example, in the 1950s, learning theorists took Freudian notions such as sex typing, dependency, identification, and defense mechanisms and studied their development within a learning framework. More recently, hypnosis has been used to test hypotheses concerning the unconscious (Hilgard, 1965). Reyher (1967) provides an example. Hypnotized college students were told a story designed to arouse unconscious Oedipal feelings. They were told that they would not remember anything about the story after awakening but would have strong sexual feelings when certain words were mentioned after they awakened. As predicted, the critical words, but not neutral words, aroused sweating, trembling, and guilt. Thus, it is possible to test hypo-

---

* For reviews of research on Freudian theory, see S. Fisher and R. P. Greenberg, *The scientific credibility of Freud's theories and therapy* (New York: Basic Books, 1977) and M. N. Eagle, *Recent developments in psychoanalysis: A critical evaluation* (New York: McGraw-Hill, 1984).

theses about unconscious conflicts. Finally, there have even been attempts to formulate computer models based on information-processing constructs (see Chapter 4) of Freud's notions concerning the repression of painful memories (Wegman, 1985).

It should be recognized that Freud's notion of the scientific approach differed from that of the scientific community. He looked for converging evidence for a particular interpretation. If dream reports, memories from childhood, physical symptoms, slips of the tongue, and accidents all suggested that the patient had not resolved her feelings of sibling rivalry in childhood, then Freud believed he had proved his case. He integrated facts from several sources to form a consistent picture. He felt that his interpretations were further bolstered if several patients illustrated the same relationship between variables. For example, patients with paralysis of a limb (hysteria) often reported unresolved sexual conflicts from childhood. We are not, however, told how many patients exhibited these two behaviors. Furthermore, we cannot know whether the association of the variables would be statistically significant or was simply coincidental. However, this lack of experimental rigor was not of great concern to Freud. His goal, after all, was to provide clinical insights that would help him formulate a theory that would improve therapy.

Overemphasis on Childhood Sexuality

Freud's emphasis on sexuality brings to mind the greeting card that begins, "SEX—Now that I have your attention." Not surprisingly, claims about childhood sexuality both captured the attention of psychologists and the public and alienated many. Freud's answer to those who saw little evidence that sexuality pervades childhood was that his critics were repressing their own strong sexual memories from childhood! If we criticize the theory, we risk being recast as a patient.

For most developmental psychologists, claims about infantile sexuality in normal children strain the theory's credibility. The bulk of the developmental research of the last 20 years portrays infants and children as curious, self-motivated, social creatures who seek stimulation, rather than driven, anxiety-ridden beings who seek the reduction of tension. Recent research on attention and thinking in infants demonstrates that even a young infant is much more than id. Of course, the Freudian and cognitive views are not necessarily incompatible. Decarie's (1965) study of parallels in the development of Freud's object relations and Piaget's object permanence, neo-Freudian advances in ego psychology (for example, Hartmann, 1958), and Furth's (1987) integration of Freudian and Piagetian theory are particularly notable attempts to bridge the two areas.

Developmentalists certainly would not deny that most children are curious about sex, just as they are curious about much of their world. The issue is how much emphasis to place on sexuality. Freud's theory demonstrates the mutual constraints among method, data, and theory mentioned in the Introduction. His data on the sexual fantasies of neurotic middle- and upper-class adults during the sexually repressive Victorian era may have little generality to children developing today. Furthermore, the specific claims about sexuality may reflect the biases of a male-oriented society. For example, Horney (1967) suggests that one could find as much evidence for womb envy in boys, due to their inability to have children, as for penis envy in girls.

Freud's emphasis on sexuality slights the social influences on development. Although he believes that social factors are important, he did not work out their role in any detail. Erikson and other neo-Freudians have remedied this oversight to some extent. Even this work, however, pays little attention to children's prosocial behavior, such as empathy and altruism, which is an active topic of research today. It should be mentioned that some of the early research on social factors stimulated by Freud's theory did not totally support the theory. For example, among the Trobrianders, Malinowski (1927) found little evidence of the type of Oedipus conflict described by Freud.

It is possible to reject Freud's focus on sexual content without rejecting the entire theory. The structures (id, ego, superego), processes (repression, unconscious motivation), and stage notion can retain their validity even if replaced with other content.

COMMENT

What is Freud's heritage for developmental psychology? He began by asking why his patients suffered and ended by giving us a new perspective on human development. The theory has been a rich source of hypotheses for developmental research and has untapped relevance for today's research on cognitive development. The breadth and richness of the theory is impressive; it includes what other psychologists have ignored: dreams, slips of the tongue, humor, and fantasies. Freud's loose, informal manner of gathering data and developing the theory poses problems, but that style is typical of pioneering theorists in many of the sciences. Hall and Lindzey note that whereas Freud may not have been the most rigorous scientist or theorist, "he was a patient, meticulous, penetrating observer and a tenacious, disciplined, courageous, original thinker" (1957, p. 72).

ERIKSON

Powerful theories spawn "neo"s: neo-Piagetians, neo-Freudians, neo-behaviorists, and so on. Freud's theory, despite its limitations, inspired a diverse group of brilliant and creative theoreticians, researchers, and therapists. They stretched, patched, and rearranged Freud's vision in two main ways that had consequences for developmental psychology.

First, several neo-Freudians, especially Hartmann (1958), stressed the development of conflict-free ego functions, such as perception, memory, and logical thought. Whereas Freud's ego defends and inhibits, the neo-Freudian's ego integrates and organizes personality. Hartmann described an ego that is partly independent of the id and its drives. The ego derives not from the id but from an undifferentiated matrix from which both the id and the ego develop. The emphasis on the ego's cognitive processes as a way of adapting to reality can be found in works by Rapaport (1960), Gill (1959), and Klein (1970). Furthermore, White (1963) identified such ego satisfactions as exploration and competence at performing tasks well. These satisfactions are independent of satisfactions of the id. It is clear that psychoanalytic theory can address normal as much as abnormal behavior.

Second, many neo-Freudians moved away from Freud's biological approach and considered the vast influence of society on development. These trends toward ego and social concerns came to developmental psychology largely through the work of Erik Erikson, who now commands our attention.

BIOGRAPHICAL SKETCH

Erik Erikson was born in 1902 in Frankfurt, Germany, and grew up in Karlsruhe. His wanderlust and desire to be an artist drew him away from formal schooling. After several years of drifting, studying art, and painting children's portraits, Erikson was hired to teach art and other subjects to children of Americans who had come to Vienna for Freudian training. This accidental entry into the vigorous Freudian circle resulted in his admittance into the Vienna Psychoanalytic Institute. His own psychoanalysis, part of the usual training program, was conducted by Anna Freud. Erikson also learned from Freud himself, Heinz Hartmann, Ernst Kris, Helene Deutsch, and other gifted analysts.

The threat of fascism brought Erikson to the United States in 1933. He became Boston's first child analyst and obtained a position at the Harvard Medical School. Later he held positions at several eminent institutions, including Yale, Berkeley, and the Menninger Foundation. During the McCarthy era, Erikson's (1951) concern that California's loyalty oath was a danger to personal and academic freedom precipitated his move back to the East Coast and to the Austen Riggs Center at Stockbridge, Massachusetts, Harvard, and several other eastern universities. Finally, he returned to California to the Center for Advanced Study in the Behavioral Sciences at Palo Alto and later the Mount Zion Hospital in San Francisco to serve as a clinician and psychiatric consultant.

These diverse settings, from clinicians's chair to professor's podium, fueled an energy that spread Erikson's interests over a remarkable area. He studied combat crises in troubled American soldiers in World War II, child-rearing practices among the Sioux in South Dakota and the Yurok along the Pacific Coast, the play of disturbed and normal children, the conversations of troubled adolescents suffering identity crises, and social behavior in India. These observations molded his ideas, which he expressed in many publications, including the well-known *Childhood and Society* (1950a) and *Identity: Youth and Crisis* (1968). He was constantly concerned with the rapid social changes in America and wrote about issues such as the generation gap, racial tensions, juvenile delinquency, changing sexual roles, and the dangers of nuclear war. It is clear that psychoanalysis had moved far from a doctor's couch in Vienna.

GENERAL ORIENTATION TO THE THEORY

Erikson accepted the basic notions of Freudian theory: psychological structures, the unconscious and conscious, drives, psychosexual stages, the normal–abnormal continuum, and psychoanalytic methodology. Because this orientation is described earlier in the chapter, this section concentrates on Erikson's additions to psychoanalytic theory. Erikson expanded Freud's theory by developing a set of eight psychosocial stages covering the lifespan, by studying the development of identity, and by developing methods that reach beyond the structured psychoanalytic setting used with adults. A look at these three contributions serves as an orientation to the theory. When reading the following account of his theory, keep in mind Bruner's observation that "there are two Eriksons: one a surprisingly doctrinaire psychoanalyst, embracing the received doctrines of the master; the other a moralist, artist, and intellectual trying to deal with a culture that has begun to lose its power as an instrument for fulfilling the potential and the aspirations of those who live within it" (1987, p. 8).

PSYCHOSOCIAL STAGES

Erikson's work in various cultures convinced him of the need to add a psychosocial dimension to Freud's theory of psychosexual development. In the table on the facing page, columns A to D describe several aspects of Erikson's theory, and column E names the Freudian psychosexual stage corresponding to each of Erikson's psychosocial stages. To illustrate the psychosexual and psychosocial components, Erikson (1959, p. 115) contrasted a toddler's oral pleasure when making speech sounds (psychosexual component) with the role of speech communication in shaping his relationship with his parents and significant others (psychosocial component). In the psychosocial view, physical maturation has personal and social repercussions. Maturation brings a new skill that opens up new possibilities for the child but also increases society's demands on him, in this case pressure to talk instead of cry when he wants something. There is a "fit" between the child and his culture. Societies have evolved agreed-upon ways of meeting the child's new needs in each step of his maturation. These include parental care, schools, social organizations, occupations, a set of values, and so on. Erikson spoke of a "cogwheeling" of life cycles, as when adults' needs to become caretakers coincide with children's needs for caretaking. In other words, each child is a life cycle in a "community of life cycles" (Erikson, 1959, p. 121). The child is surrounded by others who are also passing through various stages. While the culture, over many generations, has adapted itself to the child, the child in turn adapts himself to the culture, as when a new kindergartner adjusts to a bewildering new set of experiences called "school."

Erikson's "worksheet" summarizing the eight stages of development

Stage	A Psychological crises	B Radius of significant relations	C Related elements of social order	D Psychosocial modalities	E Psychosexual stages
1	Trust vs. mistrust	Maternal person	Cosmic order	To get / To give in return	Oral-respiratory, sensory-kinesthetic (incorporative modes)
2	Autonomy vs. shame, doubt	Parental persons	"Law and order"	To hold (on) / To let (go)	Anal-urethral, muscular (retentive-eliminative)
3	Initiative vs. guilt	Basic family	Ideal prototypes	To make (= going after) / To "make like"(= playing)	Infantile-genital, locomotor (intrusive, inclusive)
4	Industry vs. inferiority	"Neighborhood," school	Technological elements	To make things (= completing) / To make things together	"Latency"
5	Identity and repudiation vs. identity diffusion	Peer groups and outgroups; models of leadership	Ideological perspectives	To be oneself (or not to be) / To share being oneself	Puberty
6	Intimacy and solidarity vs. isolation	Partners in friendship, sex, competition, cooperation	Patterns of cooperation and competition	To lose and find oneself in another	Genitality
7	Generativity vs. self-absorption	Divided labor and shared household	Currents of education and tradition	To make be / To take care of	
8	Integrity vs. despair	"Mankind" "My kind"	Wisdom	To be, through having been / To face not being	

Psychosocial development is culturally relative in two ways. First, although children in all cultures go through the same sequence of stages, each culture has its own idiosyncratic way of directing and enhancing the child's behavior at each age. For example, Erikson observed that the Sioux allowed nursing for several years in the spirit of an overall generosity that pervaded the Sioux value system. They also thumped the teething male babies on the head for biting the mother's nipples in the belief that their crying rage would turn them into good hunters, and they trained their girls to be bashful and afraid of men in preparation for serving their hunter–husbands. Second, there is cultural relativity within a culture as it changes over time. Institutions that meet the needs of one generation may prove inadequate for the next. Industrialization, urbanization, immigration, the Depression, and the civil-rights movement brought changes in what children needed to be taught in order to develop a healthy personality at their time in history.

Psychosocial development proceeds according to the *epigenetic principle*, a term derived from *epi*, which means "upon," and *genesis*, which means "emergence." This principle is borrowed from fetal development:

> Somewhat generalized, this principle states that anything that grows has a ground plan, and that out of this ground plan the parts arise, each part having its time of special ascendancy, until all parts have arisen to form a functioning whole. At birth the baby leaves the chemical exchange of the womb for the social exchange system of his society, where his gradually increasing capacities meet the opportunities and limitations of his culture.
>
> *[Erikson, 1968, p. 92]*

Like the fetus, the personality becomes increasingly differentiated and hierarchically organized as it unfolds in and is shaped by a particular environment. As summarized in the table on page 157, this unfolding involves several dimensions. There is movement through a set of psychosocial "crises" or issues as the child matures, and there is an expansion of his radius of significant relations. Other dimensions include the translation into the child's terms of certain elements of social order or structure and the progression through a set of psychosocial modalities or ways of "being" and interacting in society. Put succinctly, the child has inborn laws of development "which create a succession of potentialities for significant interaction with those who tend him" (Erikson, 1968, p. 52).

We now look at the general nature of the eight stages and leave a specific description of each stage for a later section. Maturation and society's expectations together create eight crises, or issues, that the child must resolve. Each issue is most evident at a particular stage in the life cycle but appears in some form throughout development. For example, autonomy is the dominant concern of the second year of life, but it is prepared for in the first year and elaborated on in later stages.

Erikson described each crisis in terms of a dimension with both positive and negative outcomes possible, for example, autonomy versus shame and doubt. Ideally, the child develops a favorable ratio, in which the positive aspect dominates the negative. For instance, a person needs to know when to trust and when to mistrust but generally should have a trusting attitude toward life.

If the childhood crises are not handled satisfactorily, the person continues to fight his early battles later in life. Many adults are still struggling to develop a sense of identity. Erikson optimistically claimed that it is never too late to resolve any of the crises.

With respect to the integration of successive stages, Erikson's theory lies between that of Piaget, with his tight integration, and Freud, with his loose integration. Each stage builds on the previous stages and influences the form of later stages. As Erikson expressed it, "Each stage adds something specific to all later ones, and makes a new ensemble out of all the earlier ones" (Evans, 1967, p. 41).

EMPHASIS ON IDENTITY

In contrast to Freud's concern with how people defend themselves from unpleasant tensions—a somewhat negative approach—Erikson's concern was more positive. He held that a main theme of life is the quest for *identity*. This term refers to "a conscious sense of individual identity . . . an unconscious striving for a continuity of personal character . . . a criterion for the silent doings of ego synthesis . . . a maintenance of an inner solidarity with a group's ideals and identity" (Erikson, 1959, p. 102). Stated differently, identity is the understanding and acceptance of both the self and one's society. Throughout life, we ask "Who am I?" and form a different answer in each stage. If all goes well, at the end of each stage the child's sense of identity is reconfirmed on a new level. Although the development of identity reaches a crisis during adolescence, Erikson noted that it begins when the baby "first recognizes his mother and first feels recognized by her, when her voice tells him he is somebody with a name and he's good" (Evans, 1967, p. 35).

Thus, identity is transformed from one stage to the next, and early forms of identity influence later forms. This process is similar to the reworking of a concept (such as causality) in each successive stage in Piaget's theory.

Erikson, the wandering youth and the American immigrant, had lived with the need to establish an identity: "As an immigrant . . . I faced one of those very important redefinitions that a man has to make who has lost his landscape and his language, and with it all the 'references' on which his first sensory and sensual impressions, and thus also some of his conceptual images, were based" (Evans, 1967, p. 41). His conversations with Huey P. Newton (Erikson, 1973) demonstrate that he was particularly sensitive to the problems that minority groups have when trying to form an identity. He began using the term "identity crisis" to describe the loss of identity he observed in World War II soldiers. He saw a similar problem among troubled adolescents "who war on their society" (1968, p. 17). Eventually, Erikson realized that the problem of identity appears, though usually on a smaller scale, in all lives. Furthermore, he recognized that identity is a central problem of our times: "If the relation of father and son dominated the last century, then this one is concerned with the self-made man asking himself what he is making of himself" (Evans, 1967, p. 41).

Expansion of Psychoanalytic Methodology

Erikson contributed to three methods for studying development: direct observation of children, cross-cultural comparisons, and psychohistory. His early experiences with children and his contact with Anna Freud, who was developing child observations and play therapy, immersed him in the world of both normal and disturbed children from the beginning of his career. In moving from the couch to the playroom, he asserted that "we must study man in action and not just man reflecting on reality" (Evans, 1967, p. 91).

Erikson's writings are sprinkled with contrasts between cultures. He is fascinated with how the solutions to the universal stages vary from culture to culture. His forays into cultural anthropology point out the inherent limitations to basic Freudian theory, which was based almost completely on psychologically troubled patients in turn-of-the-century Vienna.

Some of Erikson's most interesting writing is found in his "psycho-histories." These are analyses of the psychosocial development of well-known people, based on their own writings and their conversations and behaviors as reported by others. Erikson (1950a) believed that Hitler's rise illustrated the meshing of an individual's particular needs for identity and a nation's need for a more positive identity. In *Young Man*

Erikson described a troubled youth who defied his strict [...] [...]hed him to study law, rebelled against the authority of the church, and followed a belief that gave him an honest sense of identity. Other historical "patients" include Maxim Gorky (1950a) and George Bernard Shaw (1968). His biography *Gandhi's Truth* (1969) won a Pulitzer Prize and the National Book Award in philosophy and religion.

DESCRIPTION OF THE STAGES

Erikson divided the entire life cycle into eight "ages of man." The eight stages refer to eight critical periods in which various lifelong ego concerns reach a climax. (The table on page 157 provides an overview of each stage.)

STAGE 1: BASIC TRUST VERSUS BASIC MISTRUST (ROUGHLY BIRTH TO 1 YEAR)

In the table on page 157, we see that the main task of infancy is to acquire a favorable ratio of trust to mistrust. If this balance is weighted toward trust, the child has a better chance of weathering the later crises than if it is weighted toward mistrust. Erikson defines *basic trust* as "an essential trustfulness of others as well as a fundamental sense of one's own trustworthiness" (1968, p. 96) and the sense that "there is some correspondence between your needs and your world" (Evans, 1967, p. 15).

Infants with an attitude of trust can predict that their mother will feed them when they are hungry and comfort them when they are frightened or in pain. They will tolerate having their mother out of sight because they are confident she will return. The mother, then, is all-important: "Mothers create a sense of trust in their children by that kind of administration which in its quality combines sensitive care of the baby's individual needs and a firm sense of personal trustworthiness within the trusted framework of their culture's life style" (Erikson, 1950a, p. 249). Babies develop trust in themselves from the feeling that others accept them and from increased familiarity with their bodily urges. This faith in themselves and their small world corresponds to religious faith in the "cosmic order" of the universe (column C).

From the mother's side of the interaction, there must also be trust—trust in herself as a parent and in the meaningfulness of her caretaking role. Erikson (1950b) refers to a remark from Benjamin Spock: "To be a good parent you have to believe in the species—somehow."

Some mistrust is necessary at all ages in order to detect impending danger or discomfort and to discriminate between honest and dishonest persons. However, if mistrust wins out over trust, the child, or later the adult, may be frustrated, withdrawn, suspicious, and lacking in self-confidence.

The specifically oral experiences—sucking, biting, teething, and weaning—are prototypes for the psychosocial modality of getting and giving (column D). The baby "takes in," or "incorporates," stimulation through all the senses, much as a Piagetian child "assimilates." By taking from the mother and the world, the baby is laying the foundation for her later role as a giver to others.

STAGE 2: AUTONOMY VERSUS SHAME AND DOUBT (ROUGHLY 2 TO 3 YEARS)

With further neurological and muscular development come walking, talking, and the potential for anal control. As the child becomes more independent physically and psychologically, there are new possibilities for personality development. At the same time, however, there are new vulnerabilities, namely, anxiety over separation from the parents, fear that anal control may not always be possible, and loss of self-esteem when failure does come.

A clash of wills is inevitable. Erikson refers to the "sinister forces which are leashed and unleashed, especially in the guerrilla warfare of unequal wills; for the child is often unequal to his own violent drives, and parent and child unequal to each other" (1959, p. 66). Ideally, parents create a supportive atmosphere in which the child can develop a sense of self-control without a loss of self-esteem.

While the positive component of this stage is autonomy, the negative components are shame and doubt: "Shame supposes that one is completely exposed and conscious of being looked at—in a word, self-conscious . . . 'with one's pants down.' Shame is early expressed in an impulse to bury one's face, or to sink, right then and there, into the ground" (1959, pp. 68–69). Doubt has to do with the unknown "behind" that the child cannot see, yet must try to control. Shame and doubt about one's self-control and independence come if basic trust was insufficiently developed or was lost, when bowel training is too early or too harsh, or when the child's will is "broken" by an overcontrolling parent.

The culture, expressed through the parents, shapes and gives meaning to the toddler's new competencies. For example, cultures vary in how seriously they take training for anal control. Erikson points to the machine age's ideal of a "mechanically trained, faultlessly functioning, and always clean, punctual, and deodorized body" (1959, p. 67), in contrast to the lack of concern with such matters in the Sioux culture. By simply imitating older children, Sioux children achieve bowel control by the time they begin school.

The psychosocial modality is holding on versus letting go, the counterpart to retention and elimination. This ambivalence pervades the child's behavior and attitude. For example, toddlers often zealously hoard toys or other objects and anxiously guard them in their hiding place, then casually throw them out the window of a moving car or give them to a friend. One morning a mother is late to work because her 2-year-old adamantly has insisted on buttoning every single shirt button himself, while the next morning the young Dr. Jekyll–Mr. Hyde screams with rage because his mother has not helped him get dressed. Failure to coordinate the opposing tendencies to hold on and let go can lead to the "anal personality" described by Freud—overcontrolled, compulsive, messy, stingy, or rigid.

In this second stage, the child encounters such rules as when he can have bowel movements or which areas of the house he is allowed to explore. These rules are an early hint of the "law and order" society he will face (column C of the table on page 157). The issue here, according to Erikson, is "whether we remain the masters of the rules by which we want to make things more manageable (not more complicated) or whether the rules master the ruler" (1959, pp. 72–73). In a well-functioning society, the sense of autonomy encouraged in children is maintained throughout their lives by that society's economic and political structures.

STAGE 3: INITIATIVE VERSUS GUILT (ROUGHLY 4 TO 5 YEARS)

"Being firmly convinced that he *is* a person, the child must now find out *what kind* of a person he is going to be. And here he hitches his wagon to nothing less than a star: he wants to be like his parents, who to him appear very powerful and very beautiful, although quite unreasonably dangerous" (Erikson, 1959, p. 74). The theme of this stage is children's identification with their parents, who are perceived as big, powerful, and intrusive. Erikson accepts the basic outline of Freud's account of how children achieve identification through the Oedipus complex, but he emphasizes the social components more than the sexual. As we saw in Freud's theory, identification brings with it a conscience and a set of interests, attitudes, and sex-typed behaviors.

The basic psychosocial modality is "making," namely, intrusion, taking the initiative, forming and carrying out goals, and competing. After T. S. Eliot, we might conclude that the stage-3 child dares to disturb the universe. The child intrudes "into other bodies by physical attack . . . into other people's ears and minds by aggressive talking . . . into space by vigorous locomotion . . . into the unknown by consuming curiosity" (Erikson, 1959, p. 76). This initiative is supported by advances in mobility, physical dexterity, language, cognition, and creative imagination.

The child settles somewhere along a dimension ranging from successful initiative to overwhelming guilt due to an overly severe conscience that punishes sexual fantasies and immoral thoughts or behavior. In addition to guilt, another danger is that the child may forever feel that he must always be doing something, always competing, always "making," in order to have any worth as a person.

For this stage the related elements of social order are "ideal prototypes" (column C). These refer to social roles, such as police officer, teacher, astronaut, president, and "hero."

STAGE 4: INDUSTRY VERSUS INFERIORITY (ROUGHLY 6 YEARS TO PUBERTY)

The "industrial age" begins. Children now want to enter the larger world of knowledge and work. Their theme is "I am what I learn" (Erikson, 1959, p. 82). The great event is the entry into school, where they are exposed to the technology of their society: books, multiplication tables, arts and crafts, maps, microscopes, films, tape recorders, and computers. Learning, however, occurs not only in school but also on the street, in friends' houses, and at home.

Successful experiences give the child a sense of industry, a feeling of competence and mastery, while failure brings a sense of inadequacy and inferiority, a feeling that one is a good-for-nothing. Children strive to make things well and complete what they have begun. The years spent establishing basic trust, autonomy, and initiative were preparation for this energetic entry into our technological society. Erikson noted that this stage differs from the first three in that "it does not consist of a swing from a violent inner upheaval to a new mastery" (1959, p. 88). It is a calmer period, a time of psychosexual latency.

STAGE 5: IDENTITY AND REPUDIATION VERSUS IDENTITY DIFFUSION (ADOLESCENCE)

Erikson quoted a saying that hangs in a cowboys' bar in the West: "I ain't what I ought to be, I ain't what I'm going to be, but I ain't what I was" (1959, p. 93). In an earlier section, we saw that the quest for identity is the undercurrent running through all the stages:

> The process of identity formation emerges as an *evolving configuration*—a configuration which is gradually established by successive ego syntheses and resyntheses throughout childhood; it is a configuration gradually integrating *constitutional givens, idiosyncratic libidinal needs, favored capacities, significant identifications, effective defenses, successful sublimations, and consistent roles.*
>
> *[1959, p. 116]*

Trust, autonomy, initiative, and industry all contribute to the child's identity. In the fifth stage, however, this concern reaches a climax. Rapid physiological changes produce a "new" body with unfamiliar sexual urges. These changes, along with social pressure to make occupational and educational decisions, force the youth to consider a variety of roles. The basic task for adolescents is to integrate the various identifications they bring from childhood into a more complete identity. Erikson emphasized that this whole (the identity) is greater than the sum of its parts (previous identifications). This reassembled identity is appropriate for the new needs, skills, and goals of adolescence. If adolescents cannot integrate their identifications, roles, or selves, they face "identity diffusion." The personality is fragmented, lacking a core. Erikson quoted Biff in Arthur Miller's *Death of a Salesman*: "I just can't take hold, Mom, I can't take hold of some kind of a life" (1959, p. 91). The problem may be exacerbated by one's minority-group status, uncertaintiy about one's sexual orientation, an overly strong identification with a parent, or too many occupational roles from which to choose.

The psychosocial modality of this stage is to be oneself or not to be oneself. Hamlet's "to be or not to be" soliloquy voices this alienation and role confusion (Erikson, 1968). Youths seek their true selves through peer groups, clubs, religion, political movements, and so on. These groups provide opportunities to try out new roles much in the way someone might try on jackets in a store until finding one that fits. The ideology of society, this stage's counterpart in the social order, guides this role playing by conveying which roles are valued by society.

STAGE 6: INTIMACY AND SOLIDARITY VERSUS ISOLATION (YOUNG ADULTHOOD)

Only if a reasonably well-integrated identity emerges from stage 5 can psychological intimacy with other people (or even oneself) be possible. If a youth fears that she may lose herself in someone else, she is unable to fuse her identity with someone else. Although young people usually form important relationships with the opposite sex during this time, their friendships with the same sex and even their access to their own intimate feelings and thoughts also mark this stage. These relationships, by enhancing one's own identity, further the growth of personality. One aspect of intimacy is the feeling of solidarity of "us" and the defense against "them," the threatening "forces and people whose essence seems dangerous to one's own" (Erikson, 1959, pp. 96–97). If a youth's attempts at intimacy fail, she retreats into isolation. In this case, social relationships are stereotyped, cold, and empty.

STAGE 7: GENERATIVITY VERSUS STAGNATION AND SELF-ABSORPTION (MIDDLE ADULTHOOD)

Generativity refers to "the interest in establishing and guiding the next generation" (Erikson, 1959, p. 97) through child rearing or creative or productive endeavors. Simply bearing children does not, of course, ensure that the parent will develop a sense of generativity. Faith in the future, a belief in the species, and the ability to care about others seem to be prerequisites for development in this stage. Instead of having children, one may work to create a better world for the children of others. Stage 7, then, provides the mechanism for the continuity of society from generation to generation. A lack of generativity is expressed in stagnation, self-absorption (self-indulgence), boredom, and a lack of psychological growth.

STAGE 8: INTEGRITY VERSUS DESPAIR (LATE ADULTHOOD)

In the final stage, people must live with what they have built over their lifetime. Ideally, they will have achieved integrity. *Integrity* involves the acceptance of the limitations of life, a sense of being a part of a larger history that includes previous generations, a sense of owning the wisdom of the ages, and a final integration of all the previous stages. The antithesis of integrity is despair—regret for what one has done or not done with one's life, fear of approaching death, and disgust with oneself. A recent book, *Vital Involvement in Old Age* (Erikson, Erikson, & Kivnick, 1986), describes the importance of a person's continuing to stimulate and challenge the environment as the environment simultaneously has that effect on the person.

COMMENT: CONTEMPORARY ERIKSONIAN RESEARCH ON STAGES

Marcia (1967, 1980) expanded two of Erikson's notions, crisis and commitment: "Crisis refers to times during adolescence when the individual seems to be actively involved in choosing among alternative occupations and beliefs. Commitment refers to the degree of personal investment the individual expresses in an occupation or belief" (1967, p. 119). The presence or absence of crisis or commitment defines four *identity statuses*. The *identity-diffused* person, because she has experienced neither an identity crisis nor a commitment, is easily influenced by others and changes her beliefs often. The *foreclosure* person has made commitments without experiencing an identity crisis. She unquestioningly accepts beliefs, attitudes, and an occupation based on the views of others. The *moratorium* person is in a severe state of identity crisis and is not yet able to make commitments. Finally, the *identity-achieved* person has successfully passed through an identity crisis and has made a set of personal commitments.

Erikson's sequences may not be universal. For example, the stage sequence may differ for men and women and across various cultures. Although identity may precede intimacy for men, Gilligan pointed out that "for women these tasks seem instead to be fused. Intimacy goes along with identity" (1982, p. 12).

A final example of contemporary Eriksonian work is the renewed interest in ego development. Snarey, Kohlberg, and Noam (1983) provided a useful framework for comparing theories of ego development; they saw three types of such theories. The first type includes structurally defined stages, such as Piaget's cognitive stages. In the second, stages are culturally defined in terms of ages, for example, starting school at ages 5 through 7. The third type, exemplified by Erikson's theory, has functionally defined stages that arise because of the interaction between structural and cultural factors. For example, children start school and are faced with the task of establishing their competence both because they generally have the requisite cognitive structures to deal with this task and because society says they are at the age when children must begin school. Other contemporary theoretical work aimed at refining or clarifying Erikson's stages of ego development includes that of Coté and Levine (1987) and Meacham and Santilli (1982).

MECHANISMS OF DEVELOPMENT

The epigenetic principle describes the forces that underlie movement through the stages. Physical maturation writes the general timetable for development. Within these limits, one's culture pushes, slows down, nurtures, and destroys. In Erikson's view, society exerts its influence on the developing organism at many levels, ranging all the way from its abstract ideology to a parent's caress. Many of Freud's mechanisms of development can join Erikson's list of mechanisms of development: drives, frustrations from external and internal forces, attachment, and identification. However, Erikson made little use of Freud's tension-reduction equilibration process. Instead, he viewed development as the resolution of conflict from opposing forces. The child integrates holding on and letting go, initiative and guilt, the biological and psychological, and so on.

Erikson (1977) elaborated on a more specific mechanism of development: play. Play is used in a broad sense to mean the use of imagination to try out ways of mastering and adapting to the world, to express emotions, to recreate past situations or imagine future situations, and to develop new models of existence. Problems that cannot be solved in reality can be solved through doll play, dramatics, sports, art, block play, "playing house," and so on. Play, however, is not limited to children. Play includes Einstein visualizing a model of time and space, an adolescent fantasizing about entering various occupations, or a lab technician rehearsing what to say to the boss the next day. Play is often ritualized and becomes a somewhat formal, enduring, culturally agreed-upon way of interacting with others. For example, an adolescent who is "hanging out" with friends is acquiring culturally approved patterns for interacting with other people. Or the child-care rituals of infancy pass on "proper" ways of recognizing and greeting other people. Rituals are mechanisms of development because they bring humans in every stage into the cultural mainstream and provide ready-made solutions to the problems of everyday life.

POSITION ON DEVELOPMENTAL ISSUES

Erikson's position on the four issues is close to Freud's, except for differences in emphasis. Erikson, like Piaget, had a more optimistic view of human nature. Children and adults not only seek to avoid pain but also actively seek to develop a positive sense of identity. The existential human is in a process of "becoming" throughout life. This development is primarily qualitative because changes are stagelike, but it is also somewhat quantitative in that one's identity becomes stronger and one's convictions solidify.

Unlike Freud's theory, Erikson's has elements of the contextualist world view. He saw a changing child in a changing world and a system of culturally constructed contexts devoted to the socialization of children into the culture. The nature of these settings contributes to and affects the resolution of the crisis of each stage.

Like Freud, Erikson believed that nature determines the sequence of the stages and sets the limits within which nurture operates. If heredity ensures that certain crises arise, then the environment determines how they are resolved. Erikson, however, more than Freud, emphasized the role of culture in nurturing and shaping the developing child or adult. Not only the person's past and present but also society's past and present influence the developing person. In addition, Erikson did not accept Freud's claim that development is essentially complete after the first five years of life. Development is a lifelong process; sometimes childhood conflicts are not resolved satisfactorily until adulthood. Finally, for Erikson, the essence of development is the formation of an identity that gives coherence to one's personality.

THEORETICAL NATURE OF THE THEORY

Erikson presented his theory as would a novelist or an artist rather than a scientist. At most, the theory is a loosely connected set of ideas and observations that could not, strictly speaking, be called a deductive, an inductive, or a functional theory. Two models are implicit in the theory. The Darwinian evolutionary model describes the development of social institutions that ensure the physical and psychological survival of the species. In addition, the dialectic model of history is evident in the resolution of opposing forces in each stage of development and the integration of each stage into the next.

EVALUATION OF THE THEORY

Because Erikson's theory is an extension of psychoanalytic theory, the earlier evaluation of Freud's theory is relevant here. Instead of reiterating those comments, this section focuses on the unique strengths and weaknesses of Erikson's theory.

STRENGTHS

Expansion of Psychoanalytic Theory

By widening the empirical base of psychoanalytic theory, Erikson increased its credibility and application. He added the psychosocial to the psychosexual, the cultural to the biological, the ego identity to the ego defenses, the normal to the abnormal, the cross-cultural to the culture-specific, child observations to adult reconstructions from childhood, and adult development to child development. The theory is remarkable in its power to integrate a wide variety of situations. Erikson's version of development seems well grounded in the everyday lives of the majority of people, as they struggle to find coherence and meaning in their lives. He "looks for the hopeful and active part of the person and for how human experience and human potential are organized in the communal environment, within a radius of significant social encounters" (Schlein, 1987, p. xxv). This broadened psychoanalytic framework has been a valuable heuristic for counseling and therapy, especially with adolescents. Erikson influenced the field of developmental psychology in a general way, in that he provided a new view of development. His emphasis on cultural factors and life-span development were especially important. However, his work stimulated little research on the specific claims of his theory, such as the ordering of the stages or, at a more concrete level, sex differences in children's play.

Broad Perspective

Erikson's relevance for contemporary views of development lies in the broad perspective he gives to a child's behavior. A specific behavior of a specific child is influenced by his past history, the present situation, and the past and present history of his own culture and even the world society. All levels of society, from international relations to the nation's political structure to the interaction within the family, influence behavior. Erikson's writings conjure up the image of a system of interlocking forces uniting the child and the universe, the distant past and the distant future. Although many developmentalists pay lip service to this position, with few exceptions (see Vygotskian–contextualist theories in Chapter 7) they do not seriously examine these social and historical variables. Instead, the behavior of children is typically studied in isolation.

WEAKNESSES

Lack of Systematicity

Erikson's theory is a loose connection of observations, empirical generalizations, and abstract theoretical claims. Consequently, it is difficult to state his claims in a way that can be tested or relate his empirical findings to the more abstract levels of the theory. As with Freud, much of the problem lies in the methodological inadequacies, particularly the lack of controlled experimentation. In Erikson's case, the observations are laden with interpretations that are difficult to evaluate. For example, in Erikson's observation at the beginning of this chapter, do boys build towers because of their phallic, intrusive orientation, as Erikson claimed, or simply because they like to knock tall things down? His psychohistories are fascinating but are necessarily speculative. A related problem is that the terms he selected often mislead rather than elucidate. For example, *generativity* and *integrity* do not have their usual meanings. It is not surprising, then, that many of Erikson's concepts are often misunderstood.

Lack of Specific Mechanisms of Development

It became clear in the earlier section on mechanisms of development that Erikson's theory does not explain in any detail how a child moves from stage to stage or even how he resolves the crisis within a stage. It states *what* influences the movement (for example, physical maturation, parents, cultural beliefs, to what extent earlier crises were resolved), but not specifically *how* the movement comes about. By what mechanisms does an infant learn when to trust and when to mistrust? Why does the resolution of the initiative–guilt polarity lead to the industry–inferiority conflict rather than to some other conflict? The validity of many of Erikson's notions, such as the conflict-resolution model, rests on the ability to describe in detail the mechanisms of development.

SUMMARY

Two of Freud's ideas have formed the backbone of developmental psychology. First, he proposed that the first few years of life are critical because the basic personality is formed during that time. Second, he believed that personality is developed as the child copes with an invariant sequence of conflicts. Each conflict involves a different domain: the oral, anal, phallic, and adult genital. The way children satisfy the drives in each stage forms the basis of their personality. Although Freud's psychosexual focus is less influential today in academic psychology, the notion of stages has greatly influenced research and therapy with children in this century.

Using an energy model from physics, Freud described a system of psychological energy that is distributed, transformed, and discharged within a psychological structure. This structure consists of the id, ego, and superego in a delicate balance. The ego considers its available defenses, its perceptions of reality, the demands of the id for drive reduction, and the prohibitions of the superego before deciding on a course of action. Most of the "mind" is unconscious because knowledge of the thoughts and wishes hidden in the id, ego, and superego would cause unbearable anxiety.

Most of Freud's evidence came from his patients' free associations concerning their childhood, dreams, and present concerns. Freud believed that the workings of the abnormal mind clarify the nature of normal personality because there is a continuum of behaviors ranging from the abnormal to the normal.

Freud viewed humans as being driven by instincts but actively trying to cope with various internal and external conflicts. He stressed qualitative, stagelike changes in development, but he also included quantitative change. Although he emphasized biological influences, especially drives, he also recognized the role of experience, particularly in the first five years of life. The essence of development is the emergence of psychological structures that mediate all experience and behavior. Freud's theory introduced new psychological phenomena to Western culture and has the potential to broaden future research on cognitive development by including emotion-laden thoughts and defense mechanisms. However, the theory has methodological inadequacies, and its claims may not be testable. In addition, its focus on infantile sexuality has limited its acceptance in academic psychology.

Erikson's psychosocial theory of development modified Freudian theory in two important ways. First, it identifies important social influences on development. Erikson's research in various cultures and various social settings within a culture suggests that every society tries to deal with the biologically based changes occurring during development. Ideally, there is a fit between the child's needs and the society's needs at each point in development. In each of eight stages, there is a psychosocial crisis in which there are two possible extreme outcomes: (1) trust versus mistrust, (2) autonomy versus shame and doubt, (3) initiative versus guilt, (4) industry versus inferiority, (5) identity and repudiation versus identity diffusion, (6) intimacy and solidarity versus isolation, (7) generativity versus stagnation and self-absorption, and (8) integrity versus despair.

Erikson's second major contribution to psychoanalytic theory is his notion that life is a quest for identity. Thus, it focuses on ego processes. The work on both social and ego processes greatly expanded psychoanalytic theory and provided a broad perspective on development. However, the theory is rather unsystematic and lacks specific mechanisms of development.

Freud and Erikson produced unique yet complementary perspectives on development. A remark by Kierkegaard expresses an integration of the two views: "Life can only be understood backwards; but it must be lived forwards."

Suggested Readings

This paperback is a short, lucid introduction to Freud's theory.

Hall, C. S. (1954). *A primer of Freudian psychology*. New York: World.

For a metatheoretical look at Freud's theory, the reader should consult David Rapaport's writings, especially the following.

Rapaport, D. (1960). *The structure of psychoanalytic theory: A systematizing attempt. Psychological Issues*, Monograph 6. New York: International Universities Press.

The following provides a nice integration of psychoanalytic theories of development and other developmental work.

Tyson, P., & Tyson, R. L. (1990). *Psychoanalytic thories of development*. New Haven, CT: Yale University Press.

Because Freud is a talented and provocative writer, his ideas should be explored in his own writings.

Strachey, J. (Ed. and Trans.) (1953–1966). *The standard edition of the complete psychological works of Sigmund Freud*. 24 vols. London: Hogarth Press. Particularly recommended are "An outline of psychoanalysis" (Vol. 23, pp. 144–207), "New introductory lectures on psycho-analysis" (Vol. 22, pp. 5-182), and any of the case studies.

The following is a comprehensive introduction to Erikson's theory.

Gross, F. L. (1986). *Introducing Erik Erikson: An invitation to his thinking*. Lanham, MD: University Press of America.

Two of Erikson's books and a fairly recent collection of his papers provide a comprehensive look at his ideas.

Erikson, E. H. (1950). *Childhood and society*. New York: Norton.

Erikson, E. H. (1968). *Identity: Youth and crisis*. New York: Norton.

Schlein, S. (Ed.). (1987). *A way of looking at things: Selected papers from 1930 to 1980. Erik H. Erikson*. New York: Norton.

Erikson's psychohistories are a source of fascinating reading. Especially recommended is the following.

Erikson, E. H. (1958). *Young man Luther*. New York: Norton.

A biography clarifies some of Erikson's ideas.

Coles, R. (1970). *Erik H. Erikson: The growth of his work*. Boston: Little, Brown.

3

SOCIAL LEARNING THEORY

Subjects were tested for the amount of imitative learning. . . . Three measures of imitation were obtained: Imitation of physical aggression: This category included acts of striking the Bobo doll with the mallet, sitting on the doll and punching it in the nose, kicking the doll, and tossing it in the air. Imitative verbal aggression: Subject repeats the phrases, "Sock him," "Hit him down," "Throw him in the air," or "Pow." Imitative nonaggressive verbal responses: Subject repeats, "He keeps coming back for more," or "He sure is a tough fella."
[BANDURA, ROSS, & ROSS, 1961, p. 33]

The experimenter introduced the training task as follows: "Now let's give this lady (model) a chance to play the game. Then you (child) can play the game. Here are some cards. Which ones are the same? Which ones go together?" The model grouped the stimuli according only to the size dimension. The experimenter queried the model, "Why are they the same?" and the model responded, "Because these two are pictures of big things (pointing) and these two are little things (pointing)." Then the same item was presented to the child in identical fashion (asking about only one dimension). "Now it's your turn to play the game. Play the game just like the lady did."
[ZIMMERMAN, 1974, p. 1035]

Mark Twain once remarked, "Training is everything. The peach was once a bitter almond; cauliflower is nothing but cabbage with a college education." This optimistic view of learning captures learning theorists' belief that development comes primarily from experience. Children acquire new behaviors and modify old behaviors as they encounter their social and physical world. As specific learning experiences accumulate, the child develops, but not in the stagelike way described by Freud and Piaget.

Chapters 1 and 2 presented theories flowing mainly from a single person. In contrast, learning theory came from many researchers working over a span of more than 60 years. More than any other theoretical approach, learning theory was responsible for bestowing scientific respectability on developmental psychology. The theory's rigorous, objective research methods made laboratory studies of children possible in the 1950s and early 1960s, developmental psychology's formative years. Thus, learning theory changed the course of developmental psychology. Developmental psychology remains quite experimental today, but the content of studies has shifted from learning to a wide range of cognitive processes, such as memory, attention, and representation (see Chapter 4).

Learning theory is the most truly American theory. Most of the theories in this volume began and developed in Europe and only later influenced North American psychology. Although early Russian work on reflexes and conditioning had already begun and Hermann Ebbinghaus's verbal-learning studies were already history, learning theory developed and had most of its influence on American soil. To a great extent, the history of American psychology and the history of learning theory were synonymous until the 1960s. Learning theory has become part of our culture and has entered our language as "behaviorism," "rat psychology," "behavior modification," "Skinner box," and "reinforcement."

This chapter focuses on social learning theory because it is the version of learning theory that most clearly influences current developmental thinking and research. Work by Albert Bandura (born 1925) will be highlighted. However, in order to understand the assumptions and goals of social learning theory, it is necessary to take an extended look at its heritage in "classical" learning theory. Therefore, the first section, the history of the theory, is more extensive than in other chapters. The next sections include a general orientation to social learning theory and its mechanisms of development. The final topics include the theory's position on developmental issues, its theoretical nature, and its strengths and weaknesses.

HISTORY OF THE THEORY

Learning theory up to the time of social learning theory raised many of the issues to which social learning theory responded. This history, then, is critical to our understanding of social learning theory. As Henri Bergson noted, "The present contains nothing more than the past, and what is found in the effect was already in the cause."

BEHAVIORISM

Early in this century, pychologists' attempts to examine systematically the structure of the mind and the nature of consciousness relied on introspection—verbalizing one's own thoughts or feelings. This unsatisfactory state of affairs led to John Watson's "declaration of behaviorism" in 1913. In this strongly worded statement, he asserted that the goal of psychology should be to predict and control overt behavior, not to describe and explain conscious states. Thus, Watson redefined the field of psychology. In 1917, he was awarded the grand sum of $100 to study reflexes in infants. In his most famous study, he conditioned a fear response in "Little Albert" (a feat described later). Watson, like Skinner and certain other behaviorists to follow, had visions of a better society. If changing the environment can change behavior, there are exciting possibilities for human society. Watson carried his ideas to the public, especially parents. The follow excerpt comes from his manual *Psychological Care of Infant and Child*:

> There is a sensible way of treating children. Treat them as though they were young adults. Dress them, bathe them with care and circumspection. Let your behavior always be objective and kindly firm. Never hug and kiss them, never let them sit in your lap. If you must, kiss them once on the forehead when they say goodnight. Shake hands with them in the morning. Give them a pat on the head if they have made an extraordinary good job of a difficult task. Try it out. In a week's time you will find how easy it is to be perfectly objective with your child and at the same time kindly. You will be utterly ashamed of the mawkish, sentimental way you have been handling it.

> *[1928, pp. 81–82]*

It speaks well for the wisdom and common sense of parents that they did not adopt his philosophy wholeheartedly. By the 1920s Watson had left academia and had become an advertising executive.

Behaviorism had its greatest influence on developmental psychology in the 1950s and early 1960s, following its tremendous influence on psychology in general. Learning theorists asked questions that could be answered and provided a fruitful methodology for examining these questions. Central questions included the following: Can learning occur if a stimulus and a response simply occur together, or is reinforcement always necessary? Why is a learned response more persistent if it has been reinforced only part of the time rather than all of the time? Is there "latent" learning—knowledge that is acquired simply by being in a particular environment without any immediate reinforcement? In Sheldon White's words, learning theories were so influential "because they found for Psychology a reasonable species of psychological reality, and because they then laid down a paradigm of cooperative research procedures which might search that reality with a hope of significant findings. . . . one could stop the hair-splitting and throat-clearing and one could move into intensive scientific development" (1970, p. 662). Thus, learning theory served a need at a particular point in history.

After several decades of great research activity, learning theory ran into trouble in the 1960s. Part of the discontent came from within; hundreds of studies of verbal learning had not led to a satisfactory account of memory or learning. In addition, new evidence suggested that biological predispositions limit or modify the laws of learning. For a given species, some kinds of learning are easier than others. For example, rats learn to associate nausea with a certain taste, but not with a light or a sound (Garcia & Koelling, 1966). At the same time, learning theory faced external challenges. Noam Chomsky's (1959) attack on Skinner's account of language acquisition was a serious blow because it showed that learning approaches could not explain the acquisition of a skill as complex as language. In addition, alternate conceptions of learning were developing. Information processing (see Chapter 4), Chomsky's transformational grammar, and Piaget's cognitive theory provided attractive opposing explanations of behavior: they characterized learning as a change in knowledge rather than as a change in the probability of response. Attempts to patch up learning theory by positing verbal mediation (associations involving verbal labels), generalized rules, and complex hierarchies of mental associations did not halt the declining influence of the theory. With the entrance of cognitive psychology, psychology began what Hebb (1960) called its second American revolution, the first being the elimination of any psychology based on introspection.

EARLY RESEARCH ON CHILDREN'S LEARNING

A parallel but delayed scenario unfolded within developmental psychology. The learning studies with children in the first few decades of this century were simply translations of paradigms used with animals and college students. The experiments differed from the earlier ones only in that the subjects happened to be children. Children underwent operant and classical conditioning, solved simple discrimination-learning problems, and even wandered through mazes seeking prizes rather than cheese at the end (Hicks & Carr, 1912). It should come as no surprise that children learned faster than rats but more slowly than college sophomores. In 1954, a review of children's learning concluded that the laws of learning are the same in children and other populations (Munn, 1954).

However, children soon showed that they were unlike rats in many ways. As learning theorists used slightly more complex tasks in the 1950s and 1960s, they came to view children as "rats with language." Children could label attributes of objects, such as their color or size, and use the labels to guide their learning which attribute always led to reinforcement. Learning seemed to be under cognitive control in other ways as well. Attending to relevant information, forming hypotheses about the correct answer, and generating strategies for gathering information increased their speed of learning. In fact, learning per se—choosing the stimulus that always leads to reinforcement—is rather trivial and anticlimactic. As Flavell and Hill noted, the learned response, such as choosing the black stimulus, is "correct for today only in this specific situation. The 'organismic change' thus amounts to a temporary pairing of two items which are already in the cognitive repertoire rather than any genuine and substantive modification of the repertoire itself" (1969, p. 44). Such "learning" comes after all the developmentally interesting processes described above have occurred. Furthermore, abstract, meaningless stimuli were used, usually colored, geometric shapes. Psychologists used these simple, meaningless tasks because they wanted to measure "pure" basic processes of learning, uncontaminated by previous learning. It is ironic, then, that the most interesting information from learning research has to do with children's use of their previously acquired cognitive, linguistic, and social abilities as they attempt to make sense of the simple, meaningless task put before them. The "contamination" was interesting indeed.

By the late 1960s, the attitude of many developmentalists toward learning research was that it is probably more fruitful to study the development of attention, language, or thinking directly, rather than indirectly through learning tasks. There was also dissatisfaction with the simplistic characterization of thinking as an internal response or at most a new chain of associations. Piaget's more complex description of thought was attracting the attention of developmentalists. Also, the active, strategic, hypothesis-forming child seen in learning tasks looked very much like a Piagetian child. Piaget's approach provided an attractive theoretical alternative at a critical point in the history of developmental psychology.

Another line of research on children's learning came from Skinner's work. Skinner was one of the most well-known psychologists in the world. In a survey conducted by a popular magazine, he was ranked fortieth in a list of the 100 most important people who ever lived, with Jesus Christ in the number-one spot. Skinner considered thoughts and feelings inappropriate for empirical study and therefore examined only observable behavior. His work concerned the way rats' behavior could be shaped and controlled by schedules of reinforcement. In operant conditioning, a particular behavior becomes more frequent if it is reinforced. This work led psychologists to wonder if children's behavior could be similarly influenced. In fact, in a novel, *Walden Two* (1948), Skinner proposed that children in his utopian society would be raised by behavioral engineers, specialists in operant conditioning. Such desirable behaviors as self-control and independence would be fostered by reinforcement, whereas such undesirable behaviors as jealousy and poor work habits would be extinguished because of lack of reinforcement from the environment.

In the 1960s, there were demonstrations that a wide variety of behaviors in infants and children could become more frequent if they were reinforced. There was particular interest in the fact that social reinforcers, such as attention, smiles, and praise from other people, were especially potent. There also were many studies of *behavior modification*, the application of principles of operant conditioning to naturally occurring undesirable behaviors, such as temper tantrums, avoidance of social interaction, and autistic children's lack of spoken language. The approach assumes that a common set of learning principles underlies both normal and abnormal behavior. The essence of the approach is to change the reinforcement contingencies so that desirable behavior is reinforced and thereby maintained, while undesirable behavior is ignored and thereby weakened. That is, in operant conditioning you try to catch the child doing something right and reinforce it. The area of behavior modification is still quite active today.

SOCIAL LEARNING

The history of general learning theory helps us understand early social learning theory. Social learning theory was born in the 1930s at Yale University, perhaps when Clark Hull offered a graduate seminar on relating learning theory to psychoanalysis. Many of those who would become the pioneers in social learning theory—O. H. Mowrer, Neal Miller, John Dollard, Robert Sears, Leonard Doob, and John Whiting— attended this seminar. One of the seminar topics led to the group's first major publication, *Frustration and Aggression* (Dollard et al., 1939), which explored the causes of aggression.

The young group of scholars, trained in learning theory by Hull but also inspired by Freud, combined these two traditions. In fact, one of their publications, *Personality and Psychotherapy* (Dollard & Miller, 1950), was dedicated to both Freud and Pavlov. Psychoanalysts did not welcome this reworking of Freudian concepts into learning terms. They protested that social learning theory distorted Freudian theory by ignoring important concepts such as the unconscious, psychosexual development, and ego controls. In general, social learning theorists took interesting and important content from Freudian theory, such as the concepts of dependency, aggression, identification, conscience formation, and defense mechanisms, but sought explanations for behavior in principles of S-R learning, which could be observed, rather than hydraulic models, which could not. In Dollard and Miller's words, "The ultimate goal is to combine the vitality of psychoanalysis, the rigor of the natural-science laboratory, and the facts of culture" (1950, p. 3). The guiding belief of social learning theorists was that personality is learned. They brought the parts of Freudian theory that were testable into the laboratory and ignored the rest. Thus, social learning theorists extended learning theory and changed its focus. By extending learning principles to important real-life social behaviors, they increased the plausibility of the theory.

Social learning theorists explored much territory in the 1940s and 1950s: imitation, neuroses, cross-cultural influences on personality, identification, and parental attitudes toward child rearing. Dollard and Miller were interested in developing psychotherapy based on social learning theory:

> If neurotic behavior is learned, it should be unlearned by some combination of the same principles by which it is taught. . . . we view the therapist as a kind of teacher and the patient as a learner. In the same way and by the same

principles that bad tennis habits can be corrected by a good coach, so bad mental and emotional habits can be corrected by a psychotherapist. There is this difference, however. Whereas only a few people want to play tennis, all the world wants a clear, free, efficient mind.

[1950, pp. 7–8]

A major focus of early social learning theory was socialization, the process by which society attempts to teach children to behave like the ideal adults of that society. As Dollard and Miller observed, "A system of child training built on the laws of learning might have the same powerful effect on the neurotic misery of our time as Pasteur's work had on infectious diseases" (1950, p. 8). Research examined correlations between characteristics of parents (for example, authoritarianism) or their child-rearing practices (early toilet training) and the child's personality at a later time. The interest in socialization, cross-cultural comparisons, Freudian concepts, and learning processes can be seen in a study by Whiting and Child (1953). Much of socialization involves giving up pleasurable activities. For example, during weaning, children learn to inhibit their desire to nurse. Cultures differ in whether their socialization practices are harsh or gentle, gradual or abrupt. Whiting and Child reasoned that socialization practices ought to be related to the culture's belief system, such as beliefs concerning illness. In cultures in which infantile behaviors, such as nursing, behaving dependently, and expressing aggression directly, are considered highly pleasurable and are given up reluctantly, behavior similar to these in adults, such as eating, should be considered therapeutic for illness. In contrast, cultures in which children are harshly and quickly forced to give up these infant behaviors should associate them with anxiety and consider them causes of illness. The results only partially supported these hypotheses, but the work greatly influenced developmental psychologists.

Another prototypic study examined dependency, identification, guilt, and conscience formation (Sears, Rau, & Alpert, 1965). A child, placed in a roomful of attractive toys, was asked to watch a hamster, which was in a box with no lid. The experimenter left the room to finish making the lid for the box. When the temptation to take a closer look at the toys became too great and the child took her eyes off the hamster for a moment, the hamster silently disappeared through a false floor in the box. Measures of conscience, specifically guilt, in the study included the length of time before deviating, the child's emotional reaction to the deviation, whether the child confessed, and on what the child blamed the disappearance.

Social learning theorists proposed that there are important learned drives, such as aggression and dependency. Learned drives are derived from primary biological drives. Thus, the need for food leads to a dependency drive, a need to be near the mother and nurtured by her. The presence of the mother is reinforcing, and the withdrawal of her love, even temporarily in response to a misdeed, is a form of punishment. In addition, the possibility of a general social drive was suggested by the fact that children are more receptive to social reinforcement after a period of social deprivation (Gewirtz & Baer, 1958). There was also evidence that children learn in order to receive social reinforcement (a reply of "Good girl!" from the experimenter).

A major theoretical change in social learning theory involved imitation. Miller and Dollard (1941) set out to show that one of the most powerful socialization forces is imitation. They proposed that a general tendency to imitate is learned because various imitative behaviors are reinforced, a process of operant conditioning. This reinforcement of imitation may start very early, as illustrated in the following episode involving an 11-month-old:

> Shamini (11 months) noticing great-grandmother snoring with open mouth, makes a face with jaws open wide but mouth pulled down to form a small 'o' as an imitation of what was an extreme facial gesture. This causes enormous though slightly embarrassed hilarity in (the) rest of (the) family. Shamini responds directly to the laughing others, looking at their faces, laughing, and repeats her "face" with great amusement several times.
>
> *[Reddy, 1991, p. 145]*

Later in development, a boy may be praised for being "just like his father." Models, such as parents or siblings, who have been rewarding to the child in the past are most likely to be imitated.

Bandura and Walters (1963) then carried the concept of imitation one step further by demonstrating that relatively new behaviors can be acquired by simply watching a model. (This cannot have been a stunning discovery to any parent!) The observer need not make an overt response or be reinforced. The punishment or reinforcement of the model's behavior has the same effect on the observer as it does on the model. Children who see a hard-working classmate praised by the teacher learn to try that behavior. And, on the side of evil, children who get away with a naughty behavior are quickly imitated as well. Bandura and Walters called this process *vicarious reinforcement*. They argued that social learning theory based on S–R notions could not account for learning that occurs without overt behavior—"no-trial learning," in Bandura's words.

Bandura and Walters's theory became influential in developmental psychology in the 1960s and early 1970s. It guided the majority of laboratory and observational studies of aggression, sex typing, and resistance to temptation. There was great interest in discovering which characteristics of models, such as warmth, power, and similarity to the observer, encouraged imitation. In addition, the list of social reinforcers was expanded to include peers.

In recent years, Bandura has moved even further from a traditional S–R account of imitation. His theory, as presented in *Social Learning Theory* (1977), *Social Foundations of Thought and Action* (1986), and a recent chapter (1989), has become increasingly cognitive. Bandura now calls his theory "social cognitive theory" and defines learning as "knowledge acquisition through cognitive processing of information" (1986, p. xii). He rejects what he calls the radical behaviorist "cognitive bypass operation" (Evans, 1989, p. 83) approach, which argues that cognitions can be ignored because they are simply products of external stimuli and therefore redundant with the stimuli in any explanation of behavior. He is less concerned with the literal duplication of behavior (imitation) than with observational learning as a more general process of acquiring information from another person, verbally or visually. In 1980, Bandura's contributions were recognized by a Distinguished Scientific Contribution award from the American Psychological Association "for masterful modeling as researcher, teacher, and theoretician" (*American Psychologist*, 1981, p. 27). His current account of social learning, along with contributions by Rosenthal and Zimmerman and others, is the focus of the rest of the chapter.

LEARNING THEORY TODAY

Since the late 1960s, research on children's "learning" has been guided by Piagetian and information-processing models much more than by learning theory. Currently, there is very little research on what traditionally has been considered children's learning. Because learning now is viewed as the acquisition of new knowledge, it is virtually indistinguishable from cognitive change over short periods of time. When current developmental psychologists refer to learning, they usually have in mind topics such as instruction in math or reading, the training and transfer of general study strategies such as monitoring and planning, error-correction strategies, and the novice-to-expert shift in knowledge or motor skills.

Regarding social learning, Bandura's current theoretical position is becoming increasingly difficult to distinguish from a currently more influential body of current research labeled "social cognition." This approach was stimulated by Piaget, Kohlberg, and social-attribution theory based on adult social psychology. This approach, even more than Bandura's, emphasizes the role of cognitive development in social development. The two approaches certainly are compatible. For example, television's effects on children depend on both cognitive and imitative processes. Whether children can comprehend the story (infer the protagonist's motives, relate the outcome to the earlier conflict) affects children's perceptions of the model and their tendency to imitate it.

The hope that studies of children's learning would lead to an adequate account of developmental changes in learning was not fulfilled. Research produced a complex literature, and investigators sometimes became so involved in examining parameters of a small set of tasks that they lost sight of the developmental issues that caused them to choose these tasks in the first place. Finally, one limitation, not unique to learning theory, was that much of the research was conducted with bright, upper-middle-class children in university towns. (Some 4-year-olds greeted experimenters with "What reinforcement do I get this time?") Despite the problems, this phase in the history of developmental psychology was an exciting and fruitful time. The discipline was becoming a laboratory science, and "facts" were accumulating rapidly. A number of astonishingly productive and enthusiastic researchers conducted programmatic research using cleverly designed experimental tasks. Studies built on previous research in an organized way. Variables were varied, and hypotheses were modified. There was confidence that developmental psychology was progressing.

GENERAL ORIENTATION TO THE THEORY

Fashioning a general orientation is difficult because learning theory is actually many theories, including some approaches, particularly Skinner's, that claim not to be theories at all. It is outside the scope of this chapter to explore the differences among these theories. Fortunately, despite their differences, they share important assumptions or characteristics that create a common orientation to psychology. Although the focus is on social learning theory (designated as "SLT" in the headings below), its conceptual connection to traditional learning theory (TLT) is noted below and reflected in the heading. Within each section, discussion centers first on traditional learning theory, then on modern social learning theory, especially Bandura's position. Although social learning theory shares the overall assumptions of traditional learning theory, there are important modifications that should be highlighted. The topics are the emphasis on learning (TLT and SLT), especially observational learning (SLT), a causal model that includes the environment (TLT) or an environment–person–behavior system (SLT), the views that acquired behaviors can be simple (TLT) or complex (SLT), the focus on both observable behaviors (TLT and SLT) and underlying cognitive processes (SLT), and the use of experimental methods (TLT and SLT).

EMPHASIS ON LEARNING (TLT AND SLT), ESPECIALLY OBSERVATIONAL LEARNING (SLT)

Traditional Learning Theory

Only a straw-man learning theorist would claim that all behavior is completely learned. Biology clearly sets limits on what each species can learn, when it can learn the behavior, and how quickly it can learn it. Species-specific behaviors sometimes intrude on learned behaviors. This influence of biology on learning was demonstrated dramatically by two of Skinner's former students, Breland and Breland (1961), who trained animals commercially. While trying to train raccoons to drop tokens into a slot, the Brelands found that the animals stopped to "wash" the tokens, as if they were food, even though there was no water around.

Although learning theorists acknowledge biological contributions, they always have chosen to study the environmental, nonbiological influences on behavior. This focus contrasts with that of Piaget and Freud, who incorporated both innate and experiential influences into their theories and considered how they interact.

Although there are many definitions of learning, a common one is "a more or less permanent change in behavior which occurs as a result of practice" (Kimble, 1961, p. 2). At its simplest, learning consists of some sort of association or connection between a stimulus and a response. At its most complex, learning involves acquiring abstract rules or a chain of reasoning.

Traditionally, learning has been divided into two types: *operant conditioning* (also called instrumental conditioning) and *classical conditioning*. Operant conditioning has been most thoroughly explored by Skinner. This type of learning begins with a behavior that the child spontaneously produces. He "operates" upon the environment. This behavior becomes conditioned when it comes under the control of a particular stimulus. Some stimulus leads the child to produce a certain behavior in order to receive a reinforcement. A baby learns that when a parent appears, if he smiles at the parent (the operant behavior) he will be picked up and played with (the reinforcement). If this sequence occurs a number of times, smiling can be said to be operantly conditioned as it increases in frequency. As this example illustrates, the role of the reinforcer is to increase the frequency of smiling by occurring immediately after that behavior.

Thousands of behaviors can be operantly conditioned in the same way as smiling or bar pressing. These behaviors range from children drooling (Johnston, Sloane, & Bijou, 1966) to pigeons guiding missiles to their targets in Skinner's Project Pigeon during World War II. Even problem behaviors can be modified operantly. Harris, Wolf, and Baer (1967) observed an extremely withdrawn child who spent 80 percent of the time at nursery school in solitary activities. Their observations revealed that the teachers had unintentionally reinforced this behavior by talking to him and comforting him when he was alone. The child was ignored by the teachers when he played with others. The program of operant conditioning reversed the above contingencies. The boy received the teachers' attention when he joined a group and was ignored when he withdrew. He soon spent 60 percent of his time playing with other children.

In contrast to operant conditioning, classical conditioning begins with a reflex—an innate connection between a stimulus and a response. Behaviors that can be classically conditioned include salivating when food is placed in the mouth, sucking when a nipple is placed in the infant's mouth, and constricting the pupil when a light is shone into the eye. The response is elicited, rather than spontaneously emitted, as is the case in operant conditioning. An unconditioned stimulus (nipple placed in the mouth) elicits the unconditioned response (sucking). A conditioned stimulus (sight of the bottle) occurs just before the bottle is given. After repeated pairing of the bottle and sucking, simply showing a bottle produces sucking. A new stimulus substitutes for an old one. Sucking has become a conditioned response. More exotic examples of classical conditioning are patients who experience asthmatic attacks triggered by stimuli such as elevators, children's choirs, bicycle races, political speeches, and the national anthem (Dekker & Groen, 1956).

The most famous case of classical conditioning in children is the "Little Albert" experiment. Watson and Rayner (1920) conditioned a fear response in 11-month-old Albert. A white rat was placed in front of the toddler. As he reached for it, a steel bar behind him was struck with a hammer, producing a noxious, painful sound. Albert started violently and cried. After several repetitions of this pairing of the rat and the sound, Albert cried and crawled away when the rat alone was presented. Albert's fear was a conditioned response to the conditioned stimulus, the white rat. The initial reflex was that the noxious sound (unconditioned stimulus) produced pain (unconditioned response). The conditioned response generalized to objects such as a rabbit, a fur coat, and a Santa Claus mask. Unfortunately for Albert, his mother removed him from the experiment before Watson had a chance to decondition him.*

At a later time, one of Watson's students, Mary Cover Jones (1924), found that a naturally acquired fear of animals in a 2-year-old child, Peter, could be eliminated by extinguishing this response, which presumably was a conditioned response. Peter was seated in a highchair and given a snack, which produced a positive response. As he ate, a white rabbit in a cage was brought closer and closer. The conditioned stimulus (the white rabbit) was not allowed to become powerful enough to evoke the response of fear, for example, by suddenly bringing the animal near. As the stimulus occurred without the related fear response, this association was weakened. At the same time, the negative fear response to the rabbit was being replaced by the positive response, eating. The procedure was quite successful. By the end of the study, Peter was stroking the rabbit and letting it nibble his fingers. This treatment obviously requires a skillful experimenter who does not inadvertently teach the child to associate eating with fear.

There is an interesting footnote to this research. Peter had to enter a hospital for treatment of scarlet fever. As Peter was leaving the hospital, an unfortunate incident occurred. A large dog lunged at him, frightening him terribly. When Jones then retested Peter, he had reacquired his fear response to animals and had to be deconditioned again.

This deconditioning technique for overcoming fears contrasts with Freud's psychoanalytic study of Little Hans's fear of horses. Whereas Freud was concerned with deep-seated, underlying anxieties, learning

---

* Harris (1979) pointed out that although the Little Albert experiment is one of psychology's most famous, it apparently was not as successful at establishing a conditioned fear response as is commonly believed. Over the years, textbook writers have "improved" the results of this now-famous case. In addition, there were methodological problems that muddy any interpretation of the results.

theorists try to change behavior. By very gradually approaching horses and at the same time establishing some positive response to horses, Hans's conditioned fear response should be weakened. Freud's view would be that these procedures treat only the symptoms, not the cause of the problem. If one symptom is removed, another may appear in its place.

Phobias are not easy to extinguish without intervention because they are self-perpetuating. By avoiding the feared situation, the person reduces the rising anxiety. Thus, the phobia is reinforced. In addition, he has no opportunity to extinguish the fear because he does not allow the feared stimulus to be present. There is an old joke about a man who is asked why he always holds a banana in his ear. His answer is that it keeps the lions away. When told there are no lions around, he replies, "See? It works!" Behaviors that are perceived to bring reinforcement are difficult to unlearn.

For learning theorists, development involves the accumulation of operantly and classically conditioned responses. In Bijou and Baer's words, "The developing child may be adequately regarded, in conceptual terms, as a cluster of interrelated responses interacting with stimuli" (1961, p. 15). Both operant and classical conditioning can be established within the first few days of birth, although with classical conditioning this learning is accomplished only after a large number of trials. Thus, learning changes behavior and thereby causes development from birth.

Modern Social Learning Theory

Social learning theorists retained the focus on learning but broadened the notion of learning in two main ways. First, they were especially interested in social behavior and the social context of behavior. They argued that learning theories based on animal research are inadequate to account for human behavior, which occurs in a social milieu. Children act aggressively, share, play with peers, learn sex-typed behaviors, and develop independence. Much of the socialization of children involves the shaping of behaviors directed toward other people. Thus, social learning theorists broadened the *content* of learning theory by proposing that even social behaviors could be explained by principles of learning.

Even behaviors that are not social in nature are influenced by the social *context* in which they occur. A boy's attempts to learn to play the piano may be reinforced by his parents but actively discouraged by his baseball teammates. As children grow older, others' expectations of them become greater. A 4-year-old who cannot add is not a cause for alarm to adults, but a 7-year-old who cannot add faces a social environment in school directed toward learning this concept.

Second, social learning theorists broadened the *types of learning* to be explained. They saw the importance of observational learning: acquiring new skills or information or altering old behaviors simply by watching other children and adults. In fact, Bandura (1986) claims that most learning comes from observational learning and instruction rather than from overt, trial-and-error behavior. Years ago Aristotle commented, "Imitation is natural to man from childhood, one of his advantages over the lower animals being this, that he is the most imitative creature in the world, and learns at first by imitation."

Imitation of the model's behavior when the model is no longer present is an especially important learning skill. The behavior acquired may be an interpersonal behavior, a perceptual-motor skill, or a conceptual rule. The critical features are that the child need not produce the behavior right away and the model need not be reinforced in order for the observer to learn. Thus, observational learning is particularly important for explaining how novel, complex behaviors are acquired during development. Operant conditioning can gradually produce relatively new behaviors by shaping, but it cannot explain how complex new behaviors emerge suddenly after watching peers play a new game or watching the antics of superheroes on television. Observational learning is especially important for acquiring behaviors in areas where mistakes are costly or life-threatening. There cannot be much trial-and-error learning in studying brain surgery or learning to drive a car.

How observational learning occurs is now illustrated by a real-life example and a laboratory study. One skill many boys and girls acquire today is playing soccer. This skill includes a complex set of conceptual and perceptual-motor skills. It is doubtful that this skill could be taught simply by telling the child how to play the game, though this type of instruction is important. Much of the learning comes from observing models playing—older children, parents, coaches, and professional soccer players on television. These models are particularly likely to be modeled because they are perceived as having high status, competence, and power—characteristics that encourage modeling (Bandura, 1986). Books on how to play soccer provide symbolic models. The various types of models demonstrate how to travel with the ball, pass, attempt goals, make corner kicks, and express elation appropriately after scoring a goal.

To a great extent, an understanding of the game is acquired through what Bandura calls *abstract modeling*: abstracting a general rule from observing specific behaviors. The child gradually extracts general concepts of group action in the game: team defensive strategy, the prediction of where one's teammates will be at a particular moment, strategies concerning how to play one's position, and so on.

During the course of observational learning, children try to reproduce the behaviors they have seen and receive feedback regarding how closely their behavior matches that of the model. A skillful pass meets with success when it reaches another player. Also, this behavior may be praised by the coach. An attempt to score that misses the goal gives immediate feedback, and players may adjust the angle of their kick next time or seek further verbal instruction or demonstration from others. Note that this reinforcement or nonreinforcement serves primarily as a source of information to children concerning their behavior. This feedback also serves as an incentive, encouraging children to seek future self-satisfaction, achievement, competence, or attention from others by participating in soccer. Unlike operant conditioning and classical conditioning, there is not an automatic "stamping in" of an association via reinforcement. Furthermore, there is much more than trial-and-error learning. Learning comes more from observing, listening to instruction, and remembering.

Social learning theory contributed the notion of *vicarious reinforcement*. Observing that others are reinforced for a particular behavior may impart to children the information that the behavior is desirable in that situation and may encourage them to imitate that behavior. Seeing others punished has the opposite effect. It should be noted, however, that Bandura found that reinforcement or punishment to the model or the child is not necessary for observational learning to occur: "After the capacity for observational learning has fully developed, one cannot keep people from learning what they have seen" (Bandura, 1977, p. 38).

Of the numerous laboratory studies that illustrate observational learning, an early influential one by Bandura, Ross, and Ross (1961) is described at the beginning of this chapter. Preschool children saw an aggressive adult model punch a large, inflated Bobo doll and hit it on the head with a hammer, saying "Sock him in the nose" and "Pow." In a comparison group, the model played nonaggressively with Tinkertoys, and in a control group there was no model. Later, the children were taken to a room that contained a variety of aggressive toys (Bobo doll, dart guns, tetherball with a face painted on it) and non-aggressive toys (tea set, teddy bears, trucks), including the toys the adult model had used aggressively. The children who had observed the aggressive model were more aggressive than the children who had seen a nonaggressive model or no model.

It is clear that Bandura and Freud give us opposite predictions concerning the effects of watching aggression in other people. Freud would see such an activity as a way of reducing aggressive tensions, thus lessening subsequent aggression. In contrast, Bandura would predict that viewing aggression, especially if the aggression is not punished, is likely to cause imitation, thereby increasing aggression.

We can conclude that children may become more aggressive as a result of observing an aggressive model. But how, exactly, does the model cause aggression? A model can cause imitative behaviors in several ways.

1. Teaching new behaviors. Perhaps the children in the 1961 study learned new forms of aggression, such as hitting a Bobo doll over the head with a hammer.

2. Strengthening or weakening children's inhibitions. Although the children presumably had been taught by their parents not to be aggressive (and the comparison groups were not aggressive), the aggressive model may have disinhibited the children's aggression. Disinhibition is especially likely because the model was not punished. Evidence for a general disinhibition of aggression comes from the fact that some of the aggressive behaviors differed from those presented by the model, for example, firing imaginary shots at objects in the room and saying "Stupid ball" and "Knock over people."

3. Drawing attention to particular objects and thereby increasing their use in various ways.

4. Increasing emotional arousal, which typically increases responsiveness.

A further result in this study is noteworthy. Boys were physically more aggressive than girls—thus, characteristics of the child influence imitation. However, other studies (for example, Bandura, 1965) revealed that one must make a distinction between learning and performance. We know that girls learn as much aggression from the model as do boys, because they can produce the aggressive behaviors when asked to or rewarded for doing so. However, they typically do not produce as much physical aggression, perhaps because there are stricter inhibitions of this behavior in girls than boys. The finding that children learn and remember what they observe even if it is not reproduced immediately is of interest to those concerned with violent models on television shows watched by children. Even if children do not immediately reproduce the aggression, they may store it for future use.

The basic paradigm of Bandura's study has been used to examine a variety of models (filmed, symbolic, real) and a variety of behaviors (prosocial behavior, styles of information processing, conservation of number). It is clear that observational learning is widespread during childhood. Much of the enculturation of children involves exhibiting desirable social behaviors and strategies of problem solving. Many of the behaviors pervasive within a culture reflect the fact that children in the culture are exposed to the same or similar models. Thus, considering observational learning greatly extends traditional learning theory's narrower portrayal of learning.

Observational learning also accounts in part for differences in personality among cultures. For example, cultures vary in how much effort they put into teaching aggression. The Dugum Dani, a warrior society in the New Guinea highlands, have a training program that brings boys closer and closer to real warfare (Gardner & Heider, 1969). War games include skewering the enemy (berry seeds) on a sharp stick, spearing a hoop tossed by the opposition, battling with grass "spears," and watching real battles from a distance. In contrast, the Polynesians of the Society Islands actively discourage aggression and rarely provide aggressive models (Levy, 1969). They teach their children that spirits punish aggression with illness and injury.

Observational learning not only is a process of normal socialization, it also can be a therapy for problem behaviors. For example, observational learning can help children overcome fears. In another study by Bandura (1967), nursery-school children who were afraid of dogs watched a child happily approach a dog gradually and play with it. After the therapy and even a month later, most of the previously fearful children would hand-feed a dog and even climb into a playpen with it. Showing the modeling sequence on film also proved effective in reducing fears.

CAUSAL MODEL INCLUDES ENVIRONMENT (TLT) OR ENVIRONMENT–PERSON–BEHAVIOR SYSTEM (SLT)

I imagine the mind of children as easily turned, this or that way as water itself.

[John Locke]

Traditional Learning Theory

The belief that changes in behavior are largely brought about by experience is closely linked with the interest in environmental influences on behavior. Skinner claimed that "a person does not act upon the world, the world acts upon him" (1971, p. 211). The environment is viewed as a set of stimuli. Stimuli can play several roles. They can serve as signals for the onset of reinforcement if the proper response is emitted; become linked with unconditioned stimuli and eventually elicit conditioned responses; become associated with responses, as in the verbal learning of pairs of nonsense stimuli; or serve as punishment or reinforcement. Thus, stimuli control behavior by determining which behavior occurs, when and where it occurs, and how frequently it occurs. In this way, a child's development takes a particular course.

It is interesting that learning theory's emphasis on the role of the environment fits so well with American democratic ideals. If the environment offers equal opportunity for all, then all humans can achieve their potential. A strong version of this belief in the influence of the environment is expressed in a famous quote from Watson:

> Give me a dozen healthy infants, well-formed, and my own specified world to bring them up in and I'll guarantee to take any one at random and train him to become any type of specialist I might select—doctor, lawyer, artist, merchant, chief, and yes, even beggar-man and thief, regardless of his talents, penchants, tendencies, abilities, vocations, and race of his ancestors.
>
> *[Watson, 1924, p. 104]*

It should be noted that Watson goes on to say: "I am going beyond my facts, and I admit it, but so have the advocates of the contrary and they have been doing it for many thousands of years."

The importance of reinforcement in controlling behavior is a central concept in learning theory. As already mentioned, the occurrence of reinforcement increases the frequency of the behavior it follows. Conversely, of course, a behavior not followed by reinforcement decreases in frequency. It undergoes extinction. Skinner even kept a cumulative record of his writing output as a way of providing self-reinforcement (Skinner, 1967).

Another way that reinforcement controls behavior is by *shaping* behavior. Pigeons do not naturally play table tennis. However, by beginning with the table-tennis-related behaviors they do have, it is possible to slowly modify these behaviors into a chain of movements appropriate to table tennis. The experimenter "ups the ante" (raises the requirement for obtaining reinforcement) as the behavior gradually comes to approximate the desired behavior. Early in training, moving toward the ball might be sufficient to receive reinforcement, but later on it may be necessary to make the ball drop onto the opponent's side in order to receive reinforcement.

Skinner has described his first attempt to use shaping on a human subject:

> I soon tried the procedure on a human subject—our 9-month-old daughter. I was holding her on my lap one evening when I turned on a table lamp beside the chair. She looked up and smiled, and I decided to see whether I could use the light as a reinforcer. I waited for a slight movement of her left hand and turned on the light for a moment. Almost immediately, she moved her hand again, and again I reinforced. I began to wait for bigger movements, and within a short time, she was lifting her arm in a wide arc—"to turn on the light."
>
> *[Skinner, 1980, p. 196]*

In natural settings, shaping may occur unintentionally. If their mothers do not immediately attend to them, preschoolers rapidly become noisier and more insistent until their mothers reinforce them with attention. Thus, the child's rapidly escalating negative behavior is shaped. Patterson notes that "rapid escalation is thought to be an important component in the repertoire of the trained fighter and well practiced coercive children" (1980, p. 7).

Modern Social Learning Theory

Although social learning theorists agree that the environment exerts a great deal of influence on behavior, they consider it only one of many forces operating in any situation. The entire learning context includes biological and psychological characteristics of the person (P), the person's behavior (B), and the environment (E). These three factors are highly interdependent, and each factor influences and is influenced by each of the others. The factors interact via a process that Bandura calls *reciprocal determinism.* Consider a situation in which a child observes another child giving some of her pennies to help poor children. Several characteristics of the observer influence whether she will imitate this behavior (P→B). Is she cognitively and socially developed enough to understand what it means to be poor? What are her standards of fairness or social justice? Is she even attending to the model's behavior at all? Has she observed her parents contributing to charities in the past? The environmental factors might include the social attractiveness of the model, whether the model was praised after she gave, and the salience of the model in that situation (E→P, E→B). If the girl feels pleased with herself after sharing, the behavioral act of sharing affects the child psychologically (B→P).

Although many theories acknowledge that personal and environmental factors such as these interact, the main contribution of Bandura's reciprocal determinism is that it recognizes that the child's behavior affects and in a sense "creates" her environment (B→E, P→E). In the sharing situation just described, the child who has habitually shared in the past and thereby elicited warmth and gratitude from others has created a positive, supportive milieu for herself. In contrast, an aggressive child may create a hostile world for herself wherever she goes, causing others to react negatively toward her. Another example of how behavior creates an environment is that children who watch television a great deal expose themselves to a different set of models from that of children who usually play with friends instead. Or the child may perfect a skill, such as drawing or ballet dancing, that creates an environment of social reinforcement in the form of praise from others. Thus, children act on the environment through their behavior and often change the environment in significant ways. Unlike earlier conceptions of learning, which viewed people as passive, social theory views people as active agents in their environments.

Evidence that children's behavior can change their social environment comes from a study by Brunk and Henngeler (1984). Two 10-year-old child actors exhibited either anxious-withdrawn or aggressively noncompliant behavior in a setting in which mothers attempted to engage each boy in a game of checkers. The mothers used more helping and rewards with the anxious-withdrawn child and more ignoring, commands and discipline with the aggressively noncompliant boy. Thus, the boys "created" two different social environments.

It should be noted that, in reciprocal determinism, behavior can affect thinking as well as the environment. Behavior causes certain experiences, which in turn affect how the child thinks and what he expects, which in turn affects behavior. The child may become skilled at playing board games and discover that this accomplishment earns the respect and admiration of others. He then begins to view himself as a good game player and comes to expect success and social reinforcement from this pastime.

In Bandura's theory, the influence of the environment becomes cognitive as children symbolically represent the relationship among the situation, their behavior, and the outcome. The essence of reinforcement is that it provides information about what effect their behavior has in the environment. Children may learn that physical aggression leads to favorable outcomes in certain situations—when playing football or getting an attractive toy from another child—but not when parents or teachers are nearby. Children develop a set of expectations concerning which events lead to which other events. These correlations among events are learned by direct experience, by instruction from others, and by observing others.

Social learning theorists consider the entire system of reinforcement in which a particular event is embedded. This systematic approach is nicely illustrated by research on coercive systems in families (Patterson & Bank, 1989; Patterson & Reid, 1984). Patterson and his colleagues analyzed the network of behaviors among members of the family during hostile interchanges, essentially providing a description of which behaviors lead to which other behaviors. Various "reinforcement traps" are typically found in family interaction. For example, a mother asks her son to clean his room, the child whines, the mother intensifies her command, the child resists, and the conflict rapidly escalates. When the behavior of the child becomes unbearably aversive for the mother, as when the child throws a temper tantrum, the mother gives up and the child stops his aversive behavior. Each person has ended the aversive behavior of the other. The mother has increased the chances that the child will act aversively in the future to obtain negative reinforcement (removing an aversive stimulus). The mother also has been negatively reinforced (the temper tantrum stopped), which increases the likelihood that she will give in on future occasions. This pattern of reinforcement should also increase the likelihood that a rapid escalation of conflict will occur in their future interactions. More generally, parents in normal and problem families differ in their discipline skills. In normal families the parents set up specific consequences for the child's misbehavior and consistently apply them. In contrast, in coercive dysfunctional families the child learns that parents may react explosively to misbehavior and make vague punishment threats but do not follow through on the threats.

Another example of a complex set of contingencies occurs when a young sister's teasing of her older brother leads to his hitting her, which in turn leads to punishment from the parents, which finally may even escalate the boy's aggression. The family can become a coercive system, in which each family member learns to cope with aversive behavior from others, such as hitting, teasing, ignoring, verbal abuse, and requests to do work, by counterattacking, which often ends the aversive behavior. Thus, aggressive behavior works. Each family member is periodically reinforced for behaving aggressively and coercively when overpowering another family member through negative behaviors. The difference between normal and problem families lies in how intense and frequent these interchanges are. After the problem family is made aware of these correlated events, an attempt is made to reduce the amount of aversive behavior with which the child must cope and lower the "payoff" for the child's coercive behaviors. If the child is old enough, the family—including the child—may write a contract specifying what behaviors will be punished by withdrawal of rewards. Thus, the expectations for behavior and the consequences of disobeying are presented in a clear and consistent way that can be easily grasped and represented symbolically by the aggressive child.

Acquired Behavior Can Be Simple (TLT) or Complex (SLT)

Traditional Learning Theory

Behavior is complex. People learn to play chess, write computer programs, organize governments, and create soufflés. Learning theorists' strategy is to break down complex behavior into simple units, study these units, then put the behavior back together again. They believe that in this way complex behavior can eventually be understood. The simplest units are associations—the atoms of psychology. The research strategy, then, is to study simple associations, then chains of S–R associations, and perhaps even hierarchies of chains. Metaphorically, many simple units of Tinkertoy sticks and joiners are combined to form a larger structure. During development, S–R associations can be strengthened, weakened, or chained with other associations.

The breakdown of complex concepts into simpler parts and the sequencing of units to be learned also characterize programmed instruction. In this technique, inspired by Skinner's analysis of operant learning, children read a short passage, answer a question, then are told whether they are correct. The child of today follows similar procedures with computers.

In contrast to learning psychologists, Freud and Piaget claimed that a simple behavior has meaning and can be understood only in its structural context. If complex behavior is reduced into simpler elements, the structure is destroyed and consequently the behavior is destroyed, in a sense. For example, a toddler's relationship with his parents involves a complex, organized set of behaviors, attitudes, expectations, and beliefs. A learning theorist would claim that this complex phenomenon can best be studied by first examining simple behaviors one at a time. The investigator might begin by finding out what stimuli cause smiling or crying. In contrast, structural theorists would claim that smiling and crying can be understood only by understanding the overall structure of the parent-child relationship and the child's organized perception of this relationship.

Modern Social Learning Theory

After children acquire new behaviors by observing various models, they can combine these behaviors to form more complex behaviors. A girl may become sex-typed by imitating specific behaviors of her mother, older sister, female teachers, and females on television. A child may at various times observe other children drawing houses and creatively synthesize these different styles into a unique style of drawing houses. Learning to play basketball requires integrating a number of simpler subskills, such as dribbling, guarding, and shooting baskets. This integration of simpler behavior into more complex units differs from traditional learning in important ways, however. For social learning theory, the integration has more cognitive involvement. Rather than a simple chaining of responses, there is an active reorganization of behaviors learned earlier. By mentally manipulating symbols, children can form unique combinations of these behaviors.

In addition to forming complex behaviors by drawing on various previously observed behaviors, it is possible to learn whole complex behaviors all at once. A young child may learn to play Monopoly after watching peers play one game. Acquiring large chunks of behavior by observation is a very efficient way to learn.

FOCUS ON OBSERVABLE BEHAVIOR (TLT AND SLT) AND UNDERLYING COGNITIVE PROCESSING (SLT)

> What is Matter?—Never mind.
>
> What is Mind?—No matter.
>
> [Punch, 1855]

Traditional Learning Theory

When the behaviorists revolted against the introspectionist psychologies of the early 1900s, they carved out what they believed to be the proper object of study: observable behavior rather than mental structures or conscious experience. Just as physical scientists could observe physical events, psychologists could now point to physical events (behaviors) as the content of their science. Rats press bars, children push buttons, and adults say words. Observable behavior is available to public inspection and can be objectively measured. Of course, there have always been some unobservable entities in learning theory. For example, no one has ever directly observed an "association" between a stimulus and a response. And over the years, learning theorists have added more and more hypothetical constructs to their explanations of behavior. The observable stimuli and responses went underground and became mental S–R associations. Mental S–R chains, expectations, concepts, and rules were added to the vocabulary of learning theory. Even today, however, an investigator with a learning-theory orientation includes as few cognitive processes as possible.

Modern Social Learning Theory

Bandura's social learning theory is a synthesis of earlier versions of social learning, which focused on overt, imitative behaviors and cognitive theory, particularly information-processing theory (see Chapter 4). According to Bandura, models mainly influence us by providing information rather than by eliciting matching behavior. Thus, in observational learning there can be learning without performing the model's behavior even once. There is even evidence that observational learning can sometimes be more effective than learning by direct participation (Kessler, White, Rosenthal, & Phibbs, 1973). Watching another person solve a problem may provide a better overall idea of the nature of the problem than being thoroughly immersed in it oneself.

The accompanying illustration presents Bandura's (1986) outline of the cognitive processes underlying observational learning and, to provide a context, the other component processes involved in observational learning. Much like a computer, the child selects and processes information, applies general rules or principles, weighs information, and makes a decision.

Information-processing theory stresses both attention and retention processes. Models must be attended to in order to have an in-

ATTENTIONAL PROCESSES	RETENTION PROCESSES	PRODUCTION PROCESSES	MOTIVATIONAL PROCESSES
Modeled events Salience Affective valence Complexity Prevalence Functional value	Symbolic coding Cognitive organization Cognitive rehearsal Enactive rehearsal	Cognitive representation Observation of enactments Feedback information Conception matching	External incentives Sensory Tangible Social Control Vicarious incentives Self-incentives Tangible Self-evaluative
Observer attributes Perceptual capabilities Perceptual set Cognitive capabilities Arousal level Acquired preferences	*Observer attributes* Cognitive skills Cognitive structures	*Observer attributes* Physical capabilities Component subskills	*Observer attributes* Incentive preferences Social comparative biases Internal standards

MODELED EVENTS → ... → MATCHING PATTERN

Subprocesses underlie observational learning, according to Bandura. [From Albert Bandura, *Social Foundations of Thought and Action*, © 1986, p. 52. Reprinted by permission of Prentice-Hall, Inc., Englewood Cliffs, NJ.]

fluence, and the important features of their behavior must be attended to, while unimportant features are ignored. Characteristics of both the model and the observer control attention. Certain models command attention because of their attractiveness, based on their high status or power. Certain behaviors of models, such as aggression, are more salient than others. Models appearing on television in adventure-filled programs are particularly effective at capturing attention. Even the consequences to the model affect attention. Children are more likely to attend to behavior that leads to either reward or punishment (Yussen, 1974), presumably because both highlight the model's behavior. As summarized in the illustration on page 203, attention to a model and its behavior is most likely if the model is salient and regarded favorably (affective valence), if the model's behavior is not too complex, if there are many opportunities to see the behavior (prevalence), and if the model's behavior has proven to be effective (functional value).

Children's ability to attend selectively and their past experiences influence which models they attend to and how effectively they attend. Mature perceptual capacities and an optimal level of arousal encourage attention to important aspects of the model's behavior. Children's perceptual set (what they expect to see), their cognitive ability to comprehend the event, and their preferences (interests) also influence which features are selected for processing.

Even if the model's behavior is attended to, it has little influence unless it is retained for future use when the model no longer is present. The event must be translated into symbols, integrated into the child's cognitive organization, and rehearsed. Cognitive rehearsal, or visualizing oneself successfully carrying out the desired sequence of activities, is a skill developed to a high degree in outstanding athletes as they mentally prepare for competition. Enactive rehearsal refers to activities such as actually practicing the modeled activity or verbally rehearsing it. Symbols are either visual images or verbal codes, depending on the behavior modeled and the child's developmental level. Bandura emphasizes that the representation of the model need not be structurally similar to the model's behavior. It may be a conception, rule, or set of propositions that abstracts the underlying conceptual structure rather than the concrete event itself.

The two remaining component processes, production processes and motivational processes, refer to the performance of behaviors once they are learned by observation. Both components have been topics of interest for learning theory throughout its history. Social learning theory, however, gives them a cognitive interpretation. During production, children mentally select and organize responses to serve as a representational model with which to compare the performed behavior. As a result of receiving feedback while monitoring this performance, children may modify their initial response. Finally, motivational processes refer to the fact that children tend to reproduce behavior they see resulting in desirable outcomes. In contrast to Piaget, who examines only the cognitive development underlying imitation, Bandura is interested also in why a child is motivated to imitate only certain actions of certain models at certain times and places.

Bandura's notion of abstract modeling, described earlier, is a radical departure from traditional learning theory. Bandura proposes that children can formulate an abstract rule by pulling out the relevant elements from a number of specific episodes of observational learning. Abstract modeling is the main mechanism for explaining language learning. As children observe that the past tense is usually formed by adding -ed, they abstract this as a general rule and correctly say "walked" and "talked" and incorrectly say "hitted" and "doed." They may even make very complex incorrect utterances such as "He was disingappeared."

To summarize this discussion of Bandura's theory, two points can be made. First, the traditional focus on observable behavior has been supplemented by a concern with the cognitive components underlying observational learning. However, compared with Piaget's theory of cognition, thinking stays near the surface. That is, external events are translated into a symbolic form and combined with other symbolically represented events or used as information to develop a more general rule; however, the theory does not specify a complex reworking of the information into broad cognitive structures of the type described by Piaget. Second, a child's failure to imitate a model's behavior is due to one or more of the four component processes: inadequately attending to the behavioral events, inadequately encoding and retaining these events, failing to perform because of physical limitations, or possessing low motivation. Stated differently, cognitive factors influence what is observed, how the person or event is perceived, how this new information is organized for the future, whether the observational learning has a lasting effect, and what the effect is.

A final important way in which Bandura sees cognition as mediating behavior is that self-perceptions influence which available behaviors a person will produce. He emphasizes *self-efficacy*: people's perception of their competence in dealing with their environment. All types of behavior—academic, social, or recreational—are affected by self-efficacy. Children may have the necessary skills for mastering a task, but if they do not perceive themselves as capable of actually using their skills to master the task, they may fail or may not even attempt the task.

For example, Collins (1982) gave difficult math problems to children with high or low math self-efficacy within each of two groups differing in levels of math ability. Although math ability obviously influenced their performance, significant effects of self-efficacy were found as well. Within each ability level, children who perceived themselves as efficacious solved more problems, more quickly rejected strategies that did not work, more willingly reworked failed problems, and displayed more positive attitudes toward mathematics. This positive reaction to failure among highly efficacious children reflects their attributions of their failure to insufficient effort. In contrast, low-efficacy children attribute their failure to low ability, an attribution that does not encourage them to try again.

The work on self-efficacy has two particularly important implications for development. First, in Bandura's view, the efficacy judgments most conducive to development are slight overestimations, because these help motivate children to try moderately challenging tasks that could hone their present skills. The second implication concerns children's motivation to become self-directed learners. Adults can enhance children's intrinsic (self-generated) interest in an activity by rewarding them wisely. As Zimmerman concludes, "It is not so much what one gives as rewards that determines children's intrinsic motivation, it's how the reward is given that matters" (1985, p. 152). When rewards are given to children because they have achieved a certain level of competence on a task, they will feel efficacious, value the activity, and choose it on further occasions. Rewards given for simply engaging in the activity are less likely to have this positive effect. In fact they can even destroy intrinsic interest (Lepper, Greene, & Nisbett, 1973).

During development, children gradually construct their self-knowledge about their efficacy in various situations from four main types of information. The most authentic and direct source of information is the success or failure of previous similar attempts. A second source is vicarious experiences of observing others fail or succeed on similar tasks. If children perceive themselves as similar to a model who succeeds, their self-efficacy is enhanced. In addition, children can acquire new coping strategies by observing successful others. A third source of information is verbal persuasion: others talk children into believing that they have the ability to achieve their goal. An example is a coach's locker room halftime pep talk. Finally, information comes from one's physiological state: arousal, anxiety, fatigue, and physical pain.

For all four sources of information, developmental changes influence how accurately children can process the information. The acquisition of language, the broadening of social awareness, increased differentiation of internal states, and the development of self-appraisal skills all play a role. Another relevant developmental change is that the family is the main contribution to the young child's self-efficacy, whereas the peer group and school context become increasingly important thereafter. Bandura notes that throughout the lifespan there are changes in which aspects of self-efficacy are most important. For example, adolescence and young adulthood bring new challenges to self-efficacy regarding heterosexual relationships, physical appearance, and occupational competence. During middle age, people may reevaluate their lives, doubt their efficacy concerning physical performance, and seek to achieve efficacy in new areas. A divorce or retooling for a new occupation may be the outcome. The elderly may face damaged self-efficacy as a result of perceived memory loss, slowed reactions, and lessened self-esteem because they no longer hold a job. A self-fulfilling prophecy can occur: if the elderly are insecure about their efficacy and expect to fail, they may limit their range of activities and invest little effort in any activity, thus ensuring their failure. Bandura argues that true declines as a result of aging can be offset to a great extent by real-world knowledge and coping strategies acquired throughout one's lifetime.

Self-efficacy is related to the processing of information outlined in the illustration on page 203. Interesting processing biases may be at work. People who tend to attend to and recall the negative features of their performance may underestimate their efficacy. Thus, parents and teachers can enhance children's self-efficacy by drawing attention to the positive as-pects of their performance and thereby increasing the salience of those aspects.

METHODOLOGY (TLT AND SLT)

Traditional Learning Theory

Learning theory took the physical sciences as its model, an emphasis that has been called "physics envy." The preferred method of study, therefore, was the tightly controlled, small-scale laboratory experiment. This precision was an important step, historically. Researchers adopted William James's attitude: "I wished, by treating psychology like a natural science, to help her become one." The experiments focused on changes in simple, observable behaviors brought about by certain features of the stimulus environment. The stimuli and responses were described in an objective and precise way so that the experiment could be replicated in other laboratories. Learning was measured by the number of trials needed to solve the problem or to establish the conditioned response or by the number of responses per unit of time.

The investigator's need to define and control the environment led to the development of certain apparatuses and paradigms suited to this purpose. One such apparatus is the Skinner box, a cage-box containing a lever that the animal presses, which delivers a food pellet to the tray below. The animal's responses are automatically recorded on a cumulative record, so the experimenter need not be present. This apparatus has become so well known to the general public that "Skinner box" appears in Webster's Third New International Dictionary. Skinner's concern with controlling the environment can be seen in another invention: a completely enclosed, temperature-controlled, soundproof "baby tender" constructed for one of his own infants. This device has been called a "baby box" and even an "heir conditioner" (Bradley, 1989). It was not, as many people believed, a Skinner box for conditioning babies.

Most laboratory studies of learning include a number of subjects in each experimental condition and compare conditions by looking at group characteristics, such as the average number of trials required to learn a problem. However, studies of operant conditioning sometimes examine changes over time in single subjects. In behavior modification, a common design is the A - B - A design. After determining the child's usual frequency of hitting behavior (A), the experimenter causes a decline in hitting as that behavior is ignored and prosocial behaviors are rewarded (B). Then, to prove that the changed contingencies are responsible for the change in behavior, the new contingencies are discontinued (A) and hitting increases. Afterward, of course, the desirable behavior is reinstated by further behavior modification.

One way investigators often ensure control over the environment of human subjects is to establish new associations or create new responses. In early experiments on associating two verbal units, researchers used nonsense syllables (for example, WIC - GAF) rather than words, so that previous associations were less likely to influence learning. Similarly, in the early social learning studies of imitation, by showing children an adult wearing a funny hat and marching around, it could be concluded that imitation actually reflects learning acquired in that setting rather than in the child's previous learning history.

Modern Social Learning Theory

Social learning theory retains the methodological spirit of traditional learning theory—rigorous, well-controlled laboratory experiments that determine which variables affect learning. The content has broadened to include social behaviors, social reinforcers, and abstract concepts, such as conservation or moral reasoning, but the methodology has changed little. Although most studies with a social learning orientation take place in the laboratory, there has been some research on social learning in natural settings. An early study by Bandura and Walters (1959) examined the puzzling fact that adolescent boys who exhibited antisocial aggression often came from "privileged," middle-class families in neighborhoods where law-abiding behavior was supported. Bandura and Walters discovered that the parents of the boys discouraged their sons' aggression toward them. However, the parents encouraged the boys to use aggression to solve their problems with their peers and with adults outside the home. The nature of this encouragement of aggression is illustrated in the following interchange between the interviewer (I) and a mother (M):

I: Have you ever encouraged Earl to stand up for himself?

M: Yes, I've taught young Earl, and his Dad has. I feel he should stand up for his rights, so you can get along in this world.

I: How have you encouraged him?

M: I've told him to look after himself and don't let anybody shove him around or anything like that, but not to look for trouble. I don't want him to be a sissy.

I: Have you ever encouraged Earl to use his fists to defend himself?

M: Oh yes. Oh yes. He knows how to fight.

[1959, p. 115]

These lessons were learned well. One of the boys interviewed mentioned his pride in his prowess at "stomping"—fighting with his feet: "Like my Dad, he said, 'If you know how to fight with your feet, then it's in your hands, you've got it made,' or something like that. 'You never need to be afraid of anybody'" (1959, p. 122). This information is consistent with laboratory studies of reinforcement and modeling, but it provides insights into real-life aggression that could not emerge in a controlled laboratory setting.

MECHANISMS OF DEVELOPMENT

There is controversy as to whether social learning theory or any current learning theory is truly a developmental theory. Is developmental change simply short-term change accumulating over a longer period of time? Are the central laws of learning the same, regardless of the child's cognitive level? If development is merely accumulated learning, then it should be possible to speed up development by providing appropriate experiences.

Learning and social learning theorists focus on *processes* of change, in contrast to Piaget and Freud who were also interested in *structural* change as the child goes through the stages. Social learning research has examined the situational variables that encourage or discourage observational learning more than it has studied how age and cognitive level affect observational learning. Bandura's current model of observational learning, described in the previous section, identifies a number of developmental variables. Development occurs because of three main factors: physical maturation, experience with the social world, and cognitive development. The first, *physical maturation*, holds little interest for social learning theorists. Its main relevance is that young children may not have the physical maturity to reproduce certain motor patterns they observe. The other two factors are much more important.

Experience with the social world causes development in two main ways. First, children acquire a repertoire of behaviors, learn the appropriate situations for these behaviors, and, because these behaviors are reinforced by others, become motivated to perform them. Thus, with increasing age, children have a larger and increasingly differentiated set of behaviors. Much of this increased exposure to social behaviors comes from the growing number and types of models children encounter from television, movies, books, school, and the neighborhood.

Second, as children become older, their social environment changes simply because society, ranging from their parents to the legal system, changes its expectations of them. This fact of life has received little attention from developmental theorists, with the exception of Erik Erikson in his account of cogwheeling. By observing a model, older children are expected to learn complex new skills quickly, with a minimum of verbal instruction. A teacher provides much more help when showing a first-grader how to write out addition problems than when showing a third-grader how to write out division problems. In short, children of different ages face different social environments.

Although the importance of experience has long been recognized by learning theorists, Bandura's concern with the third factor, *cognitive development*, provides new possibilities for explaining developmental changes in learning. Children's conceptions of the world and of themselves are developed through four processes: direct experience of the effects produced by their actions, vicarious experience of the effects produced by others' actions, judgments articulated by others, and inference of new knowledge from their preexisting knowledge.

All four component processes in Bandura's model in the illustration on page 203 undergo changes as the child's thinking develops. As described in the next chapter, on information processing, the child's attention, memory, and cognitive organization undergo dramatic changes during development. For example, older children have much better comprehension and recall of characters, behaviors, motivations, and outcomes of the behaviors in a television story (Newcomb & Collins, 1979). Young children often do not even make a connection between the model's behavior and the consequences of that behavior later on. Another relevant developmental change is that older children are more likely to rehearse verbally what they have observed than are younger children. Motor reproduction and motivational processes also become more complex, differentiated, and efficient as children become more able to integrate several pieces of information, accurately interpret feedback, develop standards for their own performance, and so forth.

Bandura points out one particularly critical developmental change in thinking—the growing ability to translate observations into symbols and to recombine these symbols. Very young children must rely heavily on visual images to represent past observations. Once children can use symbols, their observational learning is much more flexible and enduring. Symbols can be rehearsed and thereby stored in memory more efficiently than can visual images. Hypotheses about physical or social events can be formulated and tested. An increasingly sophisticated symbolic ability also makes it possible to model behavior by reading a description of it or listening to instruction rather than by having to see the behavior and try to reproduce it. The modeling can be symbolic rather than behavioral. Even the effect of vicarious reinforcement is influenced by the observer's symbolic ability. The young child may be most influenced to imitate by seeing another child rewarded with candy or toys, whereas the older child can infer more subtle consequences, such as the model's feelings of self-worth and achievement. The important role of using symbols in incentive processes can be seen when children represent future consequences of their imitative behavior and relate those consequences to their personal standards and goals. If they are compatible, a child is likely to perform the observed behaviors.

The experimental study of symbolic functioning is illustrated in an experiment by Bandura, Grusec, and Menlove (1966). A group of 7-year-olds recalled more of the behavior they observed on film if they were required to verbally describe the model's actions rather than simply to watch the film carefully. There was even lower recall if the children were told to count while viewing the film—an activity that interferes with symbolization. Thus, verbal encoding facilitates observational learning. However, in interpreting this study, we should note that the adults' or children's verbalizations may have increased attention to the model as well as encouraged symbolic representation.

MORAL REASONING AND BEHAVIOR

Social learning theory's mechanisms of development can be clarified by contrasting them with those of the structuralists, such as Piaget, in the area of moral reasoning and behavior. Learning, for Piaget, is a sort of "applied cognition" as one's cognitive structure is used to interpret new situations. What children can learn depends on their cognitive level. Piaget posits changes in the organization of thought. The child moves from an objective perspective, in which the amount of damage and degree of punishment are considered, to a subjective perspective, in which intentions and extenuating circumstances (such as fatigue or life-or-death factors) are taken into account. Change occurs because of the equilibration process, which brings into harmony social experience, experience with physical objects, and physical maturation.

Rosenthal and Zimmerman (1978) argue that structuralists are primarily concerned with underlying cognitive structures and thus do not have a robust theory of performance. That is, they do poorly at explaining how the child's knowledge is expressed in behavior and establishing which situational variables determine whether the knowledge is expressed in a particular situation. Social learning theorists carefully consider how the particular situation, the child's previous history of observational learning, and the particular content area determine the child's moral judgments.

More specifically, social learning theorists account for developmental changes in moral judgments by changes in a child's criteria for judgments, such as intentions, clumsiness, amount of damage, and long-range consequences. Also important are the child's personal standards, adults' prohibitions, expected punishment or reward, and peer influence. The particular factors the child thinks are important vary from situation to situation, depending on variables such as which situational factors are operating, which causes are most salient, and what the child's perceptual set is. Moral judgments involve a complex process of considering and weighing various criteria in a given social situation. Thus, moral judgments are expected to be much more variable from time to time and from situation to situation within a social learning framework than within a Piagetian framework. In some situations the child makes subjective judgments (based on intentions) and in other situations makes objective judgments (based on amount of damage). This is true from preschool age through adulthood. Rosenthal and Zimmerman argue that there are not dichotomous, mutually exclusive types of moral reasoning. Rather, the frequency of using various criteria changes from situation to situation and from age to age.

The increase in making subjective judgments as a function of age reflects the increasing exposure to models making subjective judgments, adults' heightened expectations of older children, older children's ease of inferring internal states from situational cues, the lessening effect of the salience of consequences, and the more refined analysis of moral criteria by older children. For example, parents are more likely to explain their reasons for disciplining to an 8-year-old than to a 3-year-old. The younger child is not impressed with arguments about fairness and equality and may respond better to physical controls. Similarly, parents' presentation of legal codes and societal punishment may be reserved for preadolescents and adolescents. An example of evidence for the role of parents is that young boys use moral-judgment rules that are similar in form and complexity to those of their mothers (Leon, 1984). Some mothers use a simple unidimensional rule based on damage alone, whereas others use a more complex integration that combines both intent and damage or even weighs damage differently, depending on the person's intent.

Piaget acknowledged the influence of parents and peers in providing experiences with authority figures and decision making that present conflicting ideas concerning morality, but he argued that the critical event is that these experiences spur a cognitive reorganization. Rosenthal and Zimmerman do not see the need to posit cognitive disequilibrium and a reorganization of logical structures during development as long as social experiences, particularly observational learning, provide a more parsimonious explanation. Even so, social learning theorists recognize that children must attain a certain level of cognition before they can comprehend certain types of moral reasoning.

The main evidence bolstering the social learning account is that children's moral judgments can be altered by a brief social experience in the laboratory. In a prototypic study (Bandura & McDonald, 1963), 5- to 11-year-old children were first assessed as having either an objective or a subjective moral orientation, based on Piaget's stories depicting moral dilemmas. One actor has good intentions but produces great material damage, the other actor has bad intentions but produces minimal material damage. The most extremely subjective or objective children were assigned to one of three conditions in the second phase.

1. In one group, first the model and then the child made judgments about stories. The model's judgment was always opposite that of the child's from the first phase. The experimenter praised the model's judgments and also praised the child's if she changed her decision after hearing the model.

2. A second condition was the same except that the child was not reinforced for changing her judgment.

3. In a third group, there was no model. The child was praised if her judgment changed from the first session.

A third phase tested for generalization. In another room, a different adult presented new stories that the child judged. There was no feedback. As predicted by social learning theory, the children adopted the model's moral standards, and this new moral perspective generalized to the new stories in the third phase. This generalization suggests that the children abstracted a general rule rather than imitated specific responses. These results occurred with or without verbal praise to the child. Thus, even without being reinforced, children observe and accept the moral judgments of others. There was no change in the group with no model. In a later study (Dorr & Fey, 1974), the same changes were maintained for at least one month.

The Piagetian rebuttal to such studies is that showing that a concept *can* be acquired in this way does not necessarily mean that children naturally acquire the concept in this way. It is even possible that a concept can be developed in different ways by different children. Thus, it is not yet clear if studies of observational learning are damaging to, complementary to, or irrelevant to Piaget's theory.

According to social learning theorists, observational learning can both transmit new moral rules and influence which of the rules already in the child's repertoire are considered appropriate for the particular situation. With respect to the selection of appropriate rules, models can make certain morally relevant dimensions more salient, change the child's weighting of the various morally relevant dimensions, and encourage the child to express his moral beliefs.

One developmental acquisition central to social learning theory's account of moral development is setting standards of conduct concerning one's own behavior. These are rules, goals, and expectations for one's own conduct abstracted from experiences such as observing others' standards of self-reinforcement or punishment and observing which behaviors of others occur in each situation. For example, after seeing a model criticize his own behavior as undeserving of a reward, children are less likely to reward themselves for similar behavior (Bandura, 1971). If the child's models are older, such as older siblings and parents, he may set impossibly high standards of conduct for himself. It is noteworthy, however, that when models require little of themselves but much of others, their attractiveness and influence decrease (Ormiston, 1972). The hypocrisy is detected. There are clear implications for parents who do not practice what they preach.

Reinforcement can play a role in children's adopting the standards of conduct observed in others. Imitating statements of self-criticism is encouraged by reinforcement. When a child tells her mother that she was wrong to raid the cookie jar, she is less likely to be punished. A general set of standards is abstracted from the standards of conduct observed or expressed and rewarded in specific situations. These standards, retained in memory in the form of symbols, guide behavior via anticipatory self-pride and self-criticism. The child may be moved to share her cookies with another child if she expects to feel good about herself afterward.

These internal standards constitute what Freud called the superego. However, social learning theorists stress that the parent of the same sex serves as only one of many models from which the child learns. Internal standards, along with self-reward and self-punishment, are especially effective because they can be applied to many situations; an external authority need not be present.

One critical difference between the Piagetian and social learning accounts of moral reasoning highlights a more general difference in the way the two theories explain changes in behavior as a function of age. As described earlier, Bandura proposes that at all ages children can use different features of the setting and the person to evaluate the morality of the person's behavior. As children get older, they become more proficient at weighing the various features in each situation. Piaget, however, proposed that the tendency to take these circumstances into account is itself an ability that is acquired as a result of cognitive development. The young child is unable to take extenuating circumstances into account.

Thus, Piaget saw widespread cognitive changes underlying the effect of situational factors on moral judgments. Or, more generally, Piaget believed that stimuli have an influence only if they can be assimilated into the child's current cognitive structure.

POSITION ON DEVELOPMENTAL ISSUES

HUMAN NATURE

For years, learning theory has served as textbook writers' favorite example of a theory with a mechanistic view of human behavior. The infant—"a lively squirming bit of flesh," in Watson's words—is material to be fashioned by parents and society. The learner is viewed as passive, nudged by the whim of the environment, influenced in a machinelike way by a chain of events. In this "mechanical mirror" model "the child is born empty of content into a world of coherently organized content. Like a mirror, however, the child comes to reflect his environment" (Langer, 1969, p. 51).

The mechanistic model, however, does not accurately represent the views of modern social learning theory. The main difference is that modern learning theory sees humans as active in many ways. The person actively operates on the environment, just as the environment acts on the person. People filter their experience through their current knowledge and expectations about the world, create their own environment as their own behavior influences the environment, and generate new behavior by reorganizing previously learned behaviors. People are also active in their self-regulation. They set their own standards, reinforce themselves when they act in accord with these standards, and use feedback to judge their success at observational learning.

Bandura certainly considers people more actively involved in their own development and learning than did Freud. Piaget, however, posited an even stronger role for activity than does Bandura. Although both Bandura and Piaget describe symbolic activity, this mental activity has a greater role in Piaget's theory. According to Piaget, children do not simply learn more or less automatically by watching or listening to others. As they assimilate and accommodate to new information, there is distortion of the information and a slight reorganization of their present cognitive structure. Although Bandura occasionally refers to these processes, he does not stress them.

There is a more basic difference in the role of interaction in Piaget's and Bandura's theories. For Piaget, the interaction or exchange between the child and the environment forms a structure that later becomes an internalized cognitive structure. The actions of sucking, hitting, and manipulating become mental schemes that serve as concepts. In contrast, for Bandura the structure of the interchange between the child and the environment is not important. What is important is the new information acquired as a result of this interchange. The child observes a new behavior in the model or learns that certain behaviors in others lead to reinforcement.

Although, in Bandura's view, people are active rather than passive and are often internally motivated, his theory still falls more into the mechanistic camp than the organismic camp. He stresses antecedent causes more than inherent properties and goals, quantitative rather than qualitative change, and component behaviors more than holistic structures. In addition, he is concerned with external as much as internal motivation. Social learning theory has elements of the contextualist world view in that it emphasizes the influence of social contexts on children. However, it gives little attention to historical–cultural influences.

A final point of comparison among social learning, Piagetian, and Freudian theories is the view of humans as rational or irrational. For Piaget, the essence of development is that children become more logical as their mental structures gradually come to reflect reality. Adults, having achieved formal operations, possess equilibrated, logical thinking. Although all three theorists consider logical thinking important, both Freud and Bandura see a larger role for illogical, irrational thought than does Piaget. This may be due to their focus on social and emotion-laden events. Adults often ignore critical information when making judgments, believe what they want to believe about themselves, make snap judgments about others, follow their intuitions about whether to invest in a business venture, and so on. For Bandura, children may think logically or illogically, depending on the types of models in problem-solving situations they have encountered. They acquire styles of processing information from others. Thus, children and even adults may show great variability in how logical they are.

QUALITATIVE VERSUS QUANTITATIVE DEVELOPMENT

Both traditional and modern learning theories view development as a process of quantitative change, in which learning episodes gradually accumulate over time. Development simply involves a multitude of short-term changes. Observational learning may change somewhat from toddlerhood, when symbolic functioning is severely limited, to middle childhood, when thinking is more advanced. However, we do not find either rapid qualitative changes in movement from one stage to another or massive cognitive reorganization. Bandura considers the search for stages counterproductive because stages draw attention away from indivdual differences and differences in the way a given child functions in different environments. Furthermore, a failure to learn may be dismissed as a lack of cognitive readiness when it actually reflects a poor learning environment. He thinks that an analysis of what subskills are needed to produce a certain behavior or knowledge is much more promising.

If smaller, more limited qualitative changes are considered, there are several candidates within social learning theory. Acquiring a new rule or adopting a new strategy of gathering information is more than a change in amount or strength.

NATURE VERSUS NURTURE

A young branch takes on all the bends one gives it.

[Chinese proverb]

The early militant environmentalism of traditional learning theory viewed the young mind in the way British empiricist John Locke viewed it: a blank slate on which experience writes. This extreme position has evolved into a more moderate position, which recognizes constraints on the effect of the environment. Bandura sums up the view of social learning theory:

> From a social learning perspective, human nature is characterized as a vast potentiality that can be fashioned by direct and vicarious experience into a variety of forms within biological limits. The level of psychological and physiological development, of course, restricts what can be acquired at any given time.
>
> *[1977, p. 13]*

Thus, children are malleable—but within limits. Within the constraints of children's biological makeup, experience provides data for forming rules through models and instruction and helps them polish the component skills needed for observational learning. The types of behaviors children encounter in their models and the reactions of others to these behaviors influence the particular set of behaviors they develop. With increasing age, children usually encounter an increasing variety of models, many of them contradictory. An important developmental achievement, learning to read, further broadens children's exposure to models by introducing them to symbolic models.

Bandura's view of the roles of biology and experience is captured in his notion of *reciprocal determinism*. The environment, the person (including physical maturation), and the person's behavior are interdependent forces operating in any event. Freud and Piaget were centrally concerned with the interaction of biological maturation and experience with the physical world (especially Piaget) and the social world (especially Freud). To these concerns, Bandura adds the idea that one's behavior can change one's environment.

Biology not only constrains learning but also makes learning possible. An organism's learning ability is innate. It has evolved as a way of surviving in a changing environment. The ability to learn from experience, especially the sensitivity to reinforcement, allows an organism to adapt to whatever demands the environment makes. The ability to process and store information, abstract general rules, and translate this information into behavior is obviously adaptive for humans.

WHAT DEVELOPS

Because what is learned depends greatly on what the environment has to offer, learning theorists propose few universal behaviors, those that we would be certain to find developing in every culture. Whereas Piaget, with certainty, predicted that all physically normal children in the world would develop concepts of object permanence, causality, and conservation, and whereas Freud predicted universal concern with sexuality and aggression, social learning theory appears to be almost content-free. Investigators have directed their energy toward process rather than content. One culture may encourage aggressive behavior, whereas another may discourage it. Superstitious behavior may be valued and nurtured in one culture, whereas scientific, analytic thinking may be fostered in another. In other words, there is no universal goal or endpoint to development. Piaget, in contrast, saw development moving toward a particular way of thinking: formal operations. And Freud saw mature sexuality and freedom from excessive anxiety as the goal of development.

What is universally developed is a skilled ability to learn by observing or listening to other people or by attending to symbolic characters—

in television and books in some societies. This learning allows the child to acquire large chunks of behavior. In essence, we see development of the four component abilities: attention, retention, production, and motivation. By symbolically representing models' behaviors, children can predict which behaviors will be punished or rewarded and can acquire a standard against which to evaluate their own behavior. A representational system also allows children to combine symbols in novel ways to form and test new rules, hypotheses, and behaviors. Although social learning theorists have researched many kinds of behavior, they have been especially interested in aggression, altruism, sex roles, and the ability to regulate the self. Regarding the latter, children develop some control over their actions, feelings, and thoughts by their internal standards for themselves and their self-reinforcements and punishments.

THEORETICAL NATURE OF THE THEORY

Most recent work in social learning theory falls into the category of functional theory. There is interchange between modest, limited hypotheses and empirical data. Questions are closely tied to a particular experimental problem, such as the observational learning of aggression. Bandura's theory is not a formal set of postulates in a deductive system. Rather, it is a loosely organized set of hypotheses that have been modified as a result of experimental evidence.

Although functional-theory construction dominates current learning theory, the other modes of theory construction (see the Introduction) arise from time to time. Clark Hull's learning theory is a common example of a deductive theory in psychology. The operant-conditioning movement, led by Skinner, is an inductive approach. Research leads to summary statements of the empirical relationships observed. For example, some statements describe the rat's behavior under a particular reinforcement schedule. In its extreme form, there is a one-way relationship between data and these summary statements. These statements do not contain hypothetical constructs that would lead to new theoretical questions. Finally, there is use of an implicit model in the notion of S–R associations. It is an analog to the reflex arc described by nineteenth-century neurologists. The reflex arc is a connection between a stimulus and a response in the central nervous system. The model implies that learning is linear (straight in and out) and automatic. This model created a scientific aura for research on learning.

EVALUATION OF THE THEORY

This evaluation does not rehash the now-familiar list of strengths and weaknesses of traditional learning theory, for which there are several excellent sources (Bowers, 1973; White, 1970). Because most of learning theory's current influence on developmental psychology lies within Bandura's modern social learning theory, the evaluation centers on this version. As in Chapter 2 on psychoanalytic theory, the focus is on what the theory can contribute to present and future research and theory building in developmental psychology. Learning theory, including Bandura's work, has been criticized and eclipsed by the Piagetian and information-processing approaches. Still, it has several strengths that developmentalists should not ignore: its focus on situational influences on behavior; its focus on the interface of cognition, social-emotional behavior, and motivation; and its testability. At the same time, two main weaknesses limit the theory: an inadequate account of cognitive development and an inadequate description of behavior in natural settings.

STRENGTHS

Focus on Situational Influences on Behavior

One characteristic of structural, trait, and organismic theories is that they locate the causes of behavior primarily in the person and therefore predict that a person will act similarly in different situations. Thus, Freud expected a child with a strong superego to be overly controlled in most situations. Similarly, Piaget was relatively uninterested in the fact that conservation is acquired for certain content areas (substance) before others (weight) or that a newly acquired piece of knowledge might be exhibited in one situation but not in another. Learning theory, in contrast, has taken the stance that a person's behavior in fact typically varies from situation to situation, depending on which eliciting stimuli and reinforcers are found in each situation and on what the person's previous experiences in these situations have been. In Bandura's version, the person, her behavior, and the situation all exert an influence, but much of his research has analyzed situational variables, such as the type of model present or the consequences to the model. More generally, social learning theorists today are part of a movement toward a contextualist (see Chapter 7) account of cognitive functioning that emphasizes connections between the person and the environment.

This attention to situational variables is sorely needed in current work on children's thinking, remembering, and learning. It is now common to find that the child applies a given concept to some materials but not others, that a concept is acquired earlier in one culture than another, and that teaching the child a concept or strategy does not ensure that it will be transferred to another task. There is, however, no generally accepted explanation of these results. As described in Chapter 1, neo-Piagetians tried to address this problem. Following social learning theory's analysis of situations, investigators could determine in which situations a behavior is most likely to occur and identify the social or physical features that affect the occurrence of the behavior. More specifically, it is necessary to analyze what demands on information processing each task makes, what style of information processing is modeled in the child's social environment, what instruction (if any) has been offered the child, whether reinforcement is given for performing the behavior, and so on.

As noted in Chapter 1, one limitation of Piaget's theory is that it deals more with describing the child's knowledge and how it develops than with explaining how knowledge is actually applied in a specific situation. Considering situational factors would be one step toward filling this gap. For example, Rosenthal and Zimmerman (1978) suggest that Piagetians have underestimated the role of observational learning in the acquisition of conservation. Some conservations are more frequently modeled and reinforced than are others. Children observe others comparing quantities by counting in many settings from very early in life. Learning to count to 10 before kindergarten is a heavily valued and reinforced skill in Western middle-class societies. Comparing the weights of objects is considered a less critical skill. It is used less in a child's day-to-day living and thus is less salient. Thus, décalages would be expected. A related reason for décalage, according to Rosenthal and Zimmerman, is that it is much easier to keep track of the number of objects than the amount of a continuous substance, because counting can be used to verify the former. Information concerning the number of objects is readily available. Children count pennies, keep track of the number of days until their birthday, and make sure that they are given the same number of cookies as their siblings receive. By analyzing these experiences, we can acquire a fuller understanding of develop-mental changes in how children think.

Focus on the Interface of Cognition, Social–Emotional Behavior, and Motivation

Although most theorists recognize that thinking develops in a social context, they do not provide a comprehensive account. This limitation is a serious problem. There are two central questions here. First, how does social experience affect cognitive development? Second, how does cognitive development influence children's understanding of social events? With respect to the first question, social learning theory describes how modeling, instruction from others and vicarious learning about reinforcement and punishment impart information to the child. Much new information comes from others rather than from direct trial-and-error experience with the physical world. Even styles of processing information, such as impulsive decision making, can be imitated. With respect to the second question, Bandura's answer is that cognitive development influences social comprehension in the following way: as children become increasingly skilled at attending selectively, representing events symbolically, using memory strategies, and reorganizing previous knowledge, they become more efficient at understanding the behavior they observe.

Although Piaget listed social experience as one of several factors underlying cognitive development, he gave much more attention to experience with physical objects, equilibration, and maturation. He did cite disagreements among peers as a source of conflict that might help overcome egocentrism. Also, adults verbally convey information about the world that may or may not be understood, depending on whether the child can assimilate it to his present level of cognitive development. Still, Piaget's handling of social experience was limited because he did not consider observational learning, expectations concerning punishment, and other phenomena described by social learning theory. In addition, Piaget did not consider social influences on how children verify their beliefs. In his theory, children test their beliefs by performing experiments on the environment, much as a scientist would, or by examining the logic of an argument. Bandura includes these forms of verification but also believes that children verify their ideas by observing the effects produced by the behavior of concrete or symbolic models or by comparing their own ideas with those of others.

Freud emphasized social influence, in that the prohibitions of society force children to develop structures of thought that can bring ultimate satisfaction and help them deal with anxiety. This view stresses the negative more than the positive influence of society—learning new behavior by observing others. Two of Freud's key concepts are given a new perspective by social learning theory. First, identification with the same-sex parent involves a great deal of observational learning. Freud's notion that children "incorporate" the parent and acquire a superego actually may involve children's observing or inferring from observation the parent's values, beliefs, and behaviors. Children also control their own behavior by repeating to themselves the parent's approving or disapproving statements. Second, defense mechanisms, such as displaced aggression, projection, or regression, can be acquired by observing others use these defenses, especially if these behaviors appear to ward off punishment or unhappiness. Freud did not seriously consider how cognitive development affects the comprehension of social behavior, except that the development of ego functions, such as memory and logical thought, brings the child closer to perceiving social reality.

Bandura's social learning theory has one distinct advantage over Piagetian and information-processing theories of cognition. It considers what has been called "hot" cognition (Zajonc, 1980), as opposed to "cold." Hot cognition refers to the emotional, motivational aspect of thinking; cold cognition includes the nature of thinking but not its emotional aspects. Examples of hot cognition include children's thinking about how to please their parents, experiencing sadness when they fail at a task, and feeling disappointed in themselves when they do not meet their own standards of conduct. Also, children are much more interested in some activities than others and thus apply their knowledge inconsistently. Motivation is a critical part of learning in real life, but it has been virtually ignored by Piagetian and information-processing theories. For Freud and Erikson, of course, motivation was a central concern.

Bandura has applied his work to a wide range of social concerns. Examples are terrorist tactics, sexual and racial stereotypes, transcultural modeling through satellite telecasting, pornography, deterrents to crime, and encouragement of healthy behavior.

In summary, social learning theory broadens other accounts of cognitive development by considering its social–emotional–motivational aspects. It specifies how, through observational learning and symbolic representation, thought interfaces with society.

Testability

Even those who have attacked learning theory admit that it is probably the most testable theory in psychology. Throughout the theory's history, learning researchers have defined terms clearly, stated hypotheses precisely, and kept unobservable, intervening variables to a minimum. Parsimony is highly valued. As mentioned earlier, learning theory was largely responsible for making developmental psychology an experimental science. Testability has led to disconfirmations that have caused the theory to change over the years. In response to disconfirming evidence, learning theorists added fruitful modifications. For example, when there was evidence that children learned and performed behaviors they had observed, even with no practice and even when the model was not reinforced, it was clearly necessary to modify the original social learning theories.

There is a greater proportion of difficult-to-test concepts in Bandura's theory than in earlier learning theories, but fewer than in Piaget's or Freud's theories. Symbolic representation, abstract modeling, and expectations are not unambiguously related to observable behavior. Given the cognitive zeitgeist of the field of developmental psychology, Bandura's theory will probably acquire even more cognitive terms. Although an increasing emphasis on cognition would enhance the theory (as noted in the next section), it is desirable to have a theory that reminds us that we are interested in behavior as well as in thinking. Thus, social learning theorists can serve as watchdogs on cognitive psychologists, who sometimes seem to have forgotten about behavior. We must remember that representations, mental operations, and concepts of other people ultimately are related to behavior.

WEAKNESSES

Inadequate Account of Cognitive Development

Bandura's theory is more complete than earlier learning theories because it emphasizes that the environment and a person's behavior are connected through the person's cognitive system. However, the nature of this cognitive system, how it develops, and how this development affects observational learning remain to be worked out. Although the theory has loosely adopted information-processing theory's (Chapter 4) account of thinking, only the general features are included, such as symbolic representation, attention, storage, rule construction, and verification. A sequence of events in the world is integrated with other similar sequences and more general concepts are abstracted. Knowledge seems to consist of a storehouse of observed empirical regularities. Perry (1989) calls these representations "summary cognitions" because they are summaries of a history of social experiences. Cognition still remains quite close to behavior. Bandura has not yet developed a detailed account of exactly how these cognitive processes—especially abstraction and integration—work, how the cognitive system changes during development, and how changes in cognitive development change observational learning.

One such problem to be worked out is how children's thinking is organized and how thought organization changes during development. Bandura clearly does not endorse complex cognitive organizations that characterize a particular stage and that change in a qualitative way as the child moves from one stage to another. However, he does not take the opposite view, from traditional learning theory, that specific associations, chains of associations, or specific facts are acquired piecemeal and joined together in very simple ways during development. He allows for domain-specific knowledge and skills for operating on this knowledge. He also sees an integration of various knowledge; abstract modeling, as common features are abstracted from several related events; creative modeling, as previous knowledge is reorganized to produce a novel behavior; and the construction of schemes, such as gender schemes. Thus, Bandura seems to allow for simple cognitive organization and restructuring, but stops far short of Piaget's equilibrated, highly organized structures. The exact nature of these developmental changes, however, is not yet described.

This description of cognitive changes is important because the way the child's knowledge is organized surely influences how an observed behavior is interpreted at each point in development. For example, watching another child share a toy with a friend may be regarded as an isolated behavior by a 4-year-old but may imply a set of meanings concerning fairness and reciprocity to an 8-year-old. What is learned from this observation differs for the two children. Furthermore, children's cognitive level limits their observational learning. A 4-year-old does not learn the rules of division after watching a 10-year-old do division problems. Social learning theorists recognize that one's developmental level influences what is learned during observation, but they do not have a detailed account of this process.

A specific portrayal of developmental changes in cognitive reorganization is also necessary for evaluating the criticism that, for social learning theory, development is simply learning accumulated over a long period of time. If children organize their thoughts differently over the course of development, then the theory is more clearly a developmental theory.

Finally, an account of a developing cognitive organization would indicate whether the process of observational learning itself changes during development. Bandura proposes that the ability to imitate develops very early in life. There is, in fact, evidence that even very young infants can imitate responses, at least responses already in their repertoire (Meltzoff & Moore, 1983). Bandura proposes that with further cognitive, perceptual, and motor development, this ability becomes more efficient and abstract. However, there is little experimental evidence concerning these changes. Which cognitive ability must be developed before children can form a cognitive representation of what they have observed or read about? What differences underlie infants' ability to copy mother when she sticks out her tongue and 10-year-olds' ability to operate a computer after reading the instruction manual? Investigators other than Bandura have begun to study this important developmental issue (Parton, 1976; Yando, Seitz, & Zigler, 1978).

Another issue concerning cognition is whether the processes of acquiring social and physical concepts are actually as similar as Bandura seems to believe. Observational learning may underlie both conservation and aggression but play a different role in the two cases. Most nonsocial events have either logical or empirical necessity. If stick A is taller than stick B and if stick B is taller than stick C, then it is logically necessary that stick A is taller than stick C. It could not be otherwise. An example of empirical necessity is that in our world a rock, when released, falls downward rather than upward. Logically and empirically necessary concepts are not violated in our experience. Most social events, however, are another matter. Children learn that hitting a peer usually, but not always, leads to disapproval. They learn that one should say "thank you" when given a gift, but that people do not always say this. Most social concepts involve conventions—social customs or rules of social interaction agreed upon by one's culture—rather than logically necessary rules. Even within the social realm, there may be important distinctions. School-age children distinguish between social conventions, such as wearing clothes in public, and logic-based moral judgments (Weston & Turiel, 1980).

These differences between physical and social concepts surely influence exactly how these concepts are acquired during observational learning. For example, expectations about physical events may be easier to develop than expectations concerning social events because the former are more consistent in the real world. Another difference between these concepts may be that children rely on different ways of verifying physical and social rules. It may be that children check the truth of physical rules primarily by logical tests or physical experiments but check their developing rules of social behavior by observing other people.

Inadequate Description of Behavior in Natural Settings

We know much more about the variables that *can* affect the learning of social behaviors than about what variables *actually* operate in the lives of children or what behaviors actually occur at various ages. We know how variables operate to produce short-term changes in the laboratory but not how they operate in natural environments. We do not know the ecology of aggression, sex typing, or dependency. For example, laboratory studies stimulated by social learning theory have identified many processes, such as imitation, abstract modeling, reinforcement, and concept formation, that mold sex-typed behaviors. Which processes, in fact, are most important in particular natural settings at each age? We need a taxonomy of the various situations in which children typically find themselves in each developmental period. The theory's contribution would be much greater if investigators would examine the models and reinforcement contingencies usually found in the typical environments of each phase of development. Our culture presumably rewards different behaviors at different developmental levels. It appears, for instance, that the elderly, in order to obtain reinforcements, often must learn "old, sick, helpless" behaviors and unlearn independent behaviors (Baltes & Barton, 1979).

Moreover, observational learning and patterns of reinforcement need to be tied systematically to social–ecological variables, such as mothers working outside the home, an increasing divorce rate, urbanization, racial unrest, and changing sex roles. A complete account of social learning must also take into account demographic variables, such as socio-economic level, race, sex, and geographic location. For instance, we need a description of developmental changes in aggression that takes into account the type of television programming seen by children in various subgroups of the population, the type of day care the child has, and the father's role in child rearing.

In summary, it is proposed here that the processes of observational learning and the variables affecting modeling, such as characteristics of the model, should be related to each point in development, taking demographic and other contextual variables into account.

A study of interpersonal coercive behaviors demonstrates that the approach recommended above is feasible. Patterson (1980) observed interactions between mothers and their children in their homes and in laboratory settings. These observations led him to label mothers of pre-schoolers as "unacknowledged victims" in our society. They are exposed to high densities of aversive events, such as crying, yelling, whining, noncompliance, and hitting. The younger the preschooler, the higher the density of these events. Families differ in how well they cope with these aversive events. In distressed families, the mother and siblings, though not the father, have an unusually large number of extended aversive interchanges with the problem child. In these families, the mother must take on the additional role of crisis manager. The mother adopts be-haviors that remove the aversive events (giving in to the child's demands, punishing the child, leaving the situation). Thus, it is possible to study principles of social learning as they are embedded in a particular set of circumstances, such as the child's level of maturation, the roles of mother and father, and the relative frequency of aversive and pleasant stimuli in the environment.

The point is that we have much data about processes of social learning but lack an accompanying ecologically based description of developmental change. In addition, in some instances, we have the des-cription but not the data; that is, we have rich descriptions of develop-mental changes tied to a social context, but the processes underlying these changes have not been analyzed from a social learning point of view. For example, there is much recent interest in interaction between toddlers and their mothers and fathers. The nature of this interaction appears to be influenced by such variables as the parent's sex, socio-economic class, and race. If this descriptive information were combined with social learning theory's principles of learning, we would have a powerful descriptive and explanatory account of development. The types of models available for verbal and nonverbal behavior, the vicarious reinforcement and punishment, and the degree of encouragement for abstract modeling certainly influence the nature of the parent–child interaction.

SUMMARY

Social learning theory is a natural outgrowth of the S–R learning tra-dition. It retains the spirit of the behaviorist movement: the experi-mentally rigorous study of how basic learning occurs as a result of environmental forces. The spotlight, however, has switched from a hungry rat pressing a bar to a child interacting with other people. The evidence mounted that children learn new behaviors by imitating others and that the effect of environmental influences is cognitively mediated, as seen in children's use of language and strategies during problem solving. This evidence converged to form the most influential current version of social learning theory—Albert Bandura's.

Bandura broke away from early social learning's interest in psychoanalytic concepts and its preoccupation with how imitation is maintained by reinforcement. He made social learning theory a more convincing explanation of learning by contributing three key concepts:

1. Observational learning can be much broader than mimicking another person's behavior. The child can symbolically construct a new behavior by listening to another person or simply by reading. Complex new behaviors as well as simple modifications of previously acquired behaviors can be learned in this way. Furthermore, overt behavior is not even necessary in order for learning to occur. As Bandura summarizes the influences of models, they "can serve as instructors, motivators, inhibitors, disinhibitors, social facilitators, and emotion arousers" (1989, p. 17).

2. Children are self-regulatory. Although reinforcement is not necessary for learning, it is helpful for self-regulation. Children observe which behaviors occurring around them lead to reinforcement and punishment and use these observations as sources of information to help them abstract rules, evaluate their performance, develop standards of conduct, set goals, and decide in which situations to use the observed behavior.

3. Reciprocal determinism provides a model of behavior change. Three sources of influence—the person, his behavior, and the environment—interact. The environment does not always exert the greatest control. The most novel feature of this three-pronged model is that children's behavior helps shape their environment, which in turn acts on them.

Children develop five skills that are very important for social learning—symbolization, vicarious learning, self-regulation, self-efficacy, and the ability to see the future consequences of present behaviors (Perry, 1989). During development, children become more skilled at the four component processes of observational learning: attention, retention, production, and motivation. In particular, the growing ability to use visual and verbal symbols boosts the child's observational learning. Much of social development results from the accumulation and integration of episodes of observational learning. Social learning theory has examined a wide variety of developmentally important behaviors, such as aggression, concept formation, language, and moral development (especially moral judgments and self-regulating standards of conduct). Rosenthal and Zimmerman's work in social learning theory has challenged Piaget's structural theory of development.

Bandura's theory is testable, flexible, and integrative. It is flexible in that it continues to change in light of research outcomes. It is integrative in that it brings together several areas that, by themselves, are somewhat limited. These areas include operant conditioning, information processing, reinforcement processes (direct and vicarious), and socialization processes. Social learning theory holds great promise for correcting several shortcomings of Piagetian and information-processing theory, currently the most influential cognitive approaches. First, the theory provides a way to conceptualize why the child's behavior or demonstrated knowledge might vary from situation to situation. Second, it shows that focusing on physical concepts and ignoring the social context in which they are acquired has resulted in an incomplete view of how concepts are learned.

There are two needed directions for further developing social learning theory. First, the interface between cognitive development and observational learning must be worked out in greater detail before the theory can be considered a truly developmental theory. Second, the theory could become much more powerful in predicting and exploring behavior if it acquired a broader ecological base. The theory has shown us that processes of social learning can guide development; the next step is to discover how the processes are tied to the environments typically found at various points in development, in various types of families, and in various socioeconomic niches.

Suggested Readings

Bandura systematically presents his theory in the following volumes.

Bandura, A. (1986). *Social foundations of thought and action.* Englewood Cliffs, NJ: Prentice-Hall.

Bandura, A. (1989). Social cognitive theory. In R. Vasta (Ed.), *Annals of child development* (Vol. 6). Greenwich, CT: JAI Press.

The following long interview with Bandura provides some interesting insights into his thinking.

Evans, R. I. (1989). *Albert Bandura: The man and his ideas—A dialogue*. New York: Praeger.

The following chapter applies a social learning–social interaction perspective to family functioning.

Patterson, A., & Bank, C. L. (1989). Some amplifying mechanisms for pathologic processes in families. In M. R. Gunnar & E. Thelen (Eds.), *Minnesota symposia on child psychology: Vol. 23. Self-processes and development*. Hillsdale, NJ: Erlbaum.

A present-day account of children's learning, now called the "experimental analysis of behavior," can be found in the following chapter.

Bijou, S. W. (1989). Behavior analysis. In R. Vasta (Ed.), *Annals of child development* (Vol. 6). Greenwich, CT: JAI Press.

4

INFORMATION-PROCESSING THEORY

1PDV1   ((*GOAL GETREL BLUE RED)
(HEARD (BIGGER)) (VALUE RED)
(VALUE BLUE) (HEARD BLUE) (HEARD RED)
NIL NIL NIL NIL NIL)
2P4   ((*GOAL COMPARE BLUE RED)
(*GOAL GETREL BLUE RED) (HEARD (BIG-
GER)) (VALUE RED) (VALUE BLUE) (HEARD
BLUE) (HEARD RED) NIL NIL NIL NIL)
[PERFORMANCE ON A CONSERVATION TASK,
KLAHR & WALLACE, 1976, p. 137]

E: How much is 6 + 3?
L: (Long pause) Nine.
E: OK, how did you know that?
L: I think I said . . . I think I said . . . oops,
um . . . I think he said . . . 8 was 1 and . . .
um . . . I mean 7 was 1, 8 was 2, 9 was 3.
E: OK.
L: Six and three are nine.
E: How did you know to do that? Why didn't
you count "1, 2, 3, 4, 5, 6, 7, 8, 9"?
How come you did "6, 7, 8, 9"?
L: Cause then you have to count all those numbers.
E: OK, well how did you know you didn't have
to count all of those numbers?
L: Why didn't . . . well I don't have to if
I don't want to.
[SIEGLER & JENKINS, 1989, p. 66]

I n the last two decades, the information-processing approach has spread quietly through the field of cognitive development. It is said that the approach "was never born; it gradually coalesced" (Kendler, 1987, p. 364). Information processing arrived with little fanfare and, surprisingly, with only moderate clashes with Piagetian theory. Both approaches currently stimulate research, but the information-processing viewpoint is more dominant.

Piagetian, Freudian, and learning theories are easily recognized as theories, and most psychologists who adhere to these theories are aware of their allegiance. In contrast, many developmental psychologists who study memory, attention, and problem solving are not aware that they have accepted certain assumptions and methods of the information-processing approach. They feel they are simply performing empirical, atheoretical studies of various aspects of thinking. This chapter makes explicit this implicit agreement about what thinking involves, what aspects of thought change during development, what questions are worth asking, and how these questions should be studied. We begin with a brief description of the information-processing approach, then continue with a historical sketch, a general orientation, descriptions of major developmental approaches, and an account of mechanisms of development. Later sections describe the position of information processing on developmental issues and the theoretical nature of the theory. The chapter ends with an evaluation pointing out strengths and weaknesses.

Information processing is not a single theory, but rather a framework characterizing a large number of research programs. Information-processing investigators study the flow of information through the cognitive system. This flow begins with an *input*, usually a stimulus, into the human information-processing system. The flow ends with an *output*, which could be information stored in long-term memory, physical behavior, speech, or a decision. Mental operations occur between input and output during real time. For example, the information may be attended to, transformed into some type of mental representation, compared with information already in long-term memory, assigned meaning, and used to formulate a response. These mental processes are similar in some ways to the workings of a computer as it registers information, performs certain operations on it, and stores it. More generally, both humans and computers manipulate symbols and transform input into output. The correspondence is, of course, only partial. The circuitry of a computer is quite unlike the anatomy of the brain. However, as we shall see later, the computer metaphor served as a valuable heuristic for developing the field of information processing.

To illustrate this description of the information-processing approach, consider what happens when a young boy first encounters the Dr. Dolittle story with the pushmi-pullyu, a horselike creature with a head at each end. The delighted child attends to the picture of the creature while ignoring other objects on the page and encodes it visually, as an image, or verbally, as a "pushmi-pullyu" or "two-headed horse." He processes this visual or verbal representation further as he compares it with previously stored information about horses or fantastic creatures such as unicorns. Furthermore, the child may derive certain implications about having two heads ("How does it know if it's coming or going?"), store the new information in a way that allows him to recognize pushmi-pullyus on future occasions, and finally laugh, ask his father to reread the page, or look ahead in the book for more pictures of the pushmi-pullyu.

Thus, the child transforms information over a period of time. An information-processing psychologist (who specializes in pushmi-pullyus?) might ask the following questions: Did the child process the input superficially, noting only its physical characteristics, or deeply, relating it to a system of meaning? How fast did he process the information? Did he process the pushmi-pullyu's features simultaneously or successively or in both ways? Were there limits to how much information he could analyze during the time he could see the picture? Did he "rehearse" the label "pushmi-pullyu" by repeating it several times aloud or to himself? How is the pushmi-pullyu as it is finally stored in long-term memory different from the input, the physical stimulus? If he is shown another picture of a pushmi-pullyu, how does he retrieve the relevant information from memory and "recognize" the picture? If investigators can answer these questions, they can write a set of rules describing how the child processes information.

As this example illustrates, information-processing psychologists look at what mental processes children apply to the information and, as a result, how they transform, manipulate, and use that information. In other words, they are primarily interested in how the processing system actually operates in real time in a particular situation—how the system changes external objects or events into a cognitively useful form according to certain rules.

Although the pushmi-pullyu example illustrates the "style" of information-processing psychologists, it masks the diversity of approaches within the field. The main division is that the approaches vary in the type of role that computer programs play in research and theorizing. At one extreme, we have *computer simulation*, in which the goal is to develop computer programs that model human thought. "Cognitive scientists" adopt the formal language used by computers and in fact see both computer programs and humans as examples of physical symbol systems. A sample of this formal language in an early simulation appears at the beginning of this chapter.

At the other extreme, the computer program serves as a loose metaphor to help researchers think about the processes the subject uses to represent, store, and solve problems about words, pictures, objects, or events. This "soft-core" (Klahr, 1989) information-processing approach is much more common than the "hard-core" simulation model among developmental information-processing psychologists. The soft-core researchers adopt the informal but not the formal language of computer science. That is, they talk about "information," "capacity," and "rules" but do not translate cognitive processes into a formal language in a computer program. They accept many of the assumptions and concepts of computer science. However, they tend to study cognition using the experimental method, much as experimental psychologists have for years in the study of processes of learning (see Chapter 3). A simple example of soft-core information processing would be a study in which some children see a group of pictures and some children see a list of words for those pictures. Psychologists compare the children's memory in the picture-only and word-only conditions. By looking at the relationship between different inputs (visual–pictorial or visual–verbal) and their outputs (types of errors, order in which the objects were recalled), they try to infer what mental processes the children in the two groups applied over time to the input. These processes might include verbal rehearsal, organizing the objects into categories, or constructing visual representations.

In between computer-simulation approaches and approaches that use computer processing as a loose metaphor, we find other information-processing psychologists. Some investigators develop flow diagrams (see the accompanying figure, which is described later), diagrams that depict a series of processing steps. Such flow diagrams can be used, at least in principle, to develop computer simulations of thought. (We look more carefully at such simulations later.)

HISTORY OF THE THEORY

ADULT INFORMATION PROCESSING

Once developmentalists entered the domain of experimental psychology en masse in the early 1960s, they felt reverberations from every significant event in adult experimental psychology. Information proces-

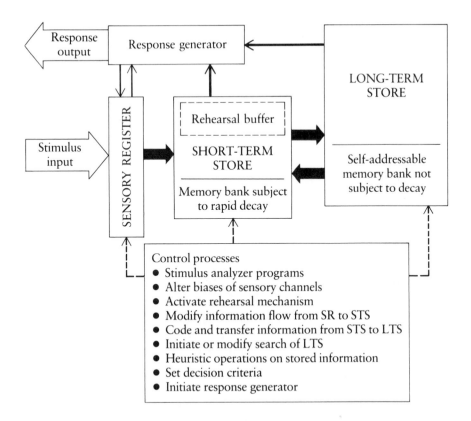

A flow diagram of the memory system. SR = sensory register. STS = short-term store. LTS = long-term store. [From "Storage and Retrieval Processes in Long-Term Memory," by Richard M. Shiffrin and Richard C. Atkinson, in *Psychological Review*, 1969, 76, 179–193. Reproduced by permission of the authors.]

sing is the first major theory of adult cognition to arise since developmental psychology became an experimental science. This minirevolution within adult experimental psychology gradually changed the prevailing view of thinking in children. The attraction of information-processing theory for developmentalists can be understood only by tracing the chain of events within adult experimental psychology that led from neobehaviorism to the information-processing approach. After this historical account comes a look at the much briefer history of the information-processing approach within developmental psychology.

Two general developments in the 1940s and 1950s eventually transformed adult experimental psychology. First, a crisis occurred within neobehaviorism. Second, technological advances in society changed the lives of psychologists forever. The first development, the crisis in neobehaviorism, is described in Chapter 3. This crisis arose partly because many psychologists lost confidence that verbal-learning research, the hallmark of neobehaviorism, was actually advancing our understanding of adult learning (Lachman, Lachman, & Butterfield, 1979). Studying how people remember nonsense syllables, such as GAV-HIG, and systematically varying parameters in learning tasks, such as the length of the list to be remembered and the degree of prior association between words, led to many experiments. The approach did not, however, lead to promising theories and an understanding of human thought in day-to-day living outside the laboratory.

At about the same time, the feeling of crisis was increased by a serious challenge to the theory from outside psychology. A young linguist named Noam Chomsky attacked the learning account of language acquisition, particularly in his now famous review (1959) of Skinner's book *Verbal Learning*. Chomsky argued that learning theory's account of language is wrong because it focuses on language output and a simple set of specific conditioned associations between words. Chomsky proposed that the essence of language is the underlying abstract rules that generate sentences. These rules are unobservable and must be inferred from the relations between language input and output.

The second influential development was the exposure of psychologists to conceptions of the human implicit in much of society's new technology. Lachman, Lachman, and Butterfield (1979) described several of these influences. First, World War II drew psychologists out of the laboratory because they were needed to improve the human operation of wartime equipment and weapons. Psychologists began to think of humans as information transmitters and decision makers when they examined how military personnel divided their attention between a plane's controls and instructions from a radio, detected blips on a radar screen, interpreted a plane's instrument readings, and made decisions about when to open fire on the enemy. A human and a machine (plane or weapon) operate together as a unit. It is desirable that this unit operate efficiently to avoid unfortunate errors, such as plunging into the ocean.

Another technological influence came from communication engineering and information theory. Engineers working on communication systems, such as the telephone, telegraph, radio, and television, developed the notion of "communication channels," which came to serve as a metaphor for human thought. Psychologists began to speak of "limited-capacity channels," "serial" (successive) and "parallel" (simultaneous) processes, "coding information" into large units, "uncertainty" (ambiguous information), and "structures."

Computer science formed yet another technological influence on psychology. Digital computers, robots, and other symbol-manipulating systems suggested to psychologists that people might also be considered symbol-manipulating systems. Newell and Simon (1961), in particular, argued convincingly that the logical capabilities of people could be simulated by appropriate computer programs.

The crisis of confidence within psychology and the technological advances outside psychology produced a generation of psychologists who, unlike the behaviorists, were willing to talk about the mind. They began to develop models of human information processing. In *stages-of-processing* models, information moves through several distinct stages involving attention and memory. These models were later challenged by Craik and Lockhart (1972), who claimed that memory should be characterized by many *levels of processing* rather than separate stages. The more deeply material is processed, the more likely it is to be placed in long-term memory and recalled at a later time. Thus, thinking about how the pushmi-pullyu resembles and differs from the horse is deeper processing than simply noticing its color and shape. Processing the meaning of the stimulus more deeply requires more attention and effort. More recently, the field of *cognitive science* has emerged. It is an amalgamation of cognitive psychology, computer science, philosophy, neuroscience, and linguistics. Also, the field of *artificial intelligence* develops robots, computer programs, or other devices that can play chess or other games, translate texts, serve drinks, perform mathematical calculations, keep track of a store's inventory, and move documents from one office to another. The goal is to produce maximally efficient and intelligent systems. Such devices typically do not model human intelligence and in some cases they surpass average mental skills, as anyone who has been humiliated by a computer in a chess game can attest. For example, the current computer chess champion, "Deep Thought," has beaten nearly all of its human opponents (Lindsay, 1991).

Since the days of neobehavioristic studies of verbal learning, investigators have moved from the use of nonsense syllables to meaningful material (sentences and stories) for studying memory. They have also moved from a focus on behavior to a focus on thinking and from the notion of a passive learner to the notion of an active learner. Whereas investigators used to believe that previous knowledge and strategies contaminated any "pure" measure of memory or association, they now consider these nuisance variables objects of interest. Psychologists changed their minds about what is worth studying. More important, they dared to be mentalistic, to consider behavior as merely an indicator of the more interesting underlying mental events. After causing an initial tremor in the field of psychology, the information-processing approach has quietly matured into a well-developed field. The 1970s and 1980s truly were the era of the mind.

CHILD INFORMATION PROCESSING

Although most developmental psychologists at first merely served as spectators to these dramatic changes in adult experimental psychology, many soon recognized the possibilities of information processing for studying children's thinking. In the late 1960s, many developmentalists had misgivings about the ultimate value of studies based on learning theory, along with uncertainty that Piagetian theory had a viable account of cognitive change. The information-processing approach was appealing because it permitted controlled experimental studies, as had learning theory, but it also supplied a fruitful new methodology, language, and metaphor for studying the development of thought. In addition, there already was interest in some of the topics studied by information-processing psychologists. Developmentalists had studied attention in discrimination learning and were becoming increasingly interested in language acquisition because of Chomsky's work. Also, a growing number of young Ph.D.s trained in adult cognition were beginning to study children.

As a result of all of these factors, information processing entered the field of developmental psychology. The number of studies of children's memory and, to a lesser extent, attention, comprehension, and problem solving has increased exponentially in the last 25 years, and no waning is in sight. Most of the early studies were simply direct translations of the adult research, using children as subjects. For example, children were given simpler versions of the memory and attention tasks given to adults. Eventually, as happened in learning theory years earlier (see Chapter 3), developmental research began to go beyond these simple translations and look at specifically developmental issues.

GENERAL ORIENTATION TO THE THEORY

How do we recognize an "information-processing cognitive developmental psychologist" when we see one? This species has distinctive markings that help "psychologist watchers" identify it. The following field guide describes several characteristics: viewing humans as information-processing devices, conceptualizing development as self-modification, conducting task analyses, and using information-processing methodology.

HUMANS AS INFORMATION-PROCESSING DEVICES

It is inevitable in this machine age that psychologists would ponder what people and machines have in common. Computers, hand calculators, electronic games, and people all deal with information in some form. More specifically, all manipulate symbols according to certain rules and store the results of these operations. Furthermore, we find striking correspondences in how people and machines process this input. We can compare perceiving with "input," thinking with a "computer program," storage capacity with number of "K," memory with a "memory bank," a decision with "output," and mental operations with "subroutines." In essence, the information-processing psychologist is asking, "How is the human organism programmed to make sense out of the complicated world around it?" and "What would an information-processing system require in order to exhibit the same behavior as the child?" (Klahr & Wallace, 1976, p. 5). Using the computer analogy, information-processing psychologists try to track detailed changes in the flow of information over time. They make a step-by-step analysis of what the person does to the information. How this new orientation breaks with the past is illustrated in its language. For example, "input–output" connotes a different sort of being than does "stimulus–response" or "assimilation–accommodation."

The input to the information-processing device is information, which can come in many forms. It might be a word, a paragraph, a mathematical or logical symbol, a blip on a radar screen, or a mental image. The device performs certain operations on this information, such as comparing it with previously stored information or transforming it into a representation *(encoding)*, for example, by transforming a written word into a mental image.

The adult mind can efficiently organize millions of pieces of information. How is such a remarkable device developed? Information-processing psychologists view children at various ages or cognitive levels as being in different states. Psychologists infer each knowledge state from the relationship between the input and output. Thus, each developmental level is characterized by a particular input–output relationship.

To illustrate, let us consider what happens when we show children a two-pan balance scale and ask them to order a set of blocks according to weight. How do they gather information about the weights (input) and use this information to make a set of decisions as to how to order the objects (output)? Baylor and Gascon (1974) used this situation to examine how children process information. They carefully analyzed the sequences of behavior of individual children: which block was placed on which pan, how many blocks were weighed at the same time, whether the heavier or lighter block was removed from the pan after weighing, and so on. Suppose we provide the same input, a set of seven blocks, to a 5-year-old and an 11-year-old. The differences in their output would lead us to infer how their states differ, that is, how they operate on the input. The 5-year-old may weigh one pair of blocks at a time but weigh each pair only once. After the child completes the weighing, he knows which block of each pair is heavier, but does not know how the blocks from different pairs compare in weight. In contrast, the 11-year-old might compare one block with each of the other blocks and always leave the heavier block on the pan. After she identifies the heaviest block, she carries out the same process with the remaining blocks until no blocks are left. The child has seriated the seven blocks. From the behaviors and perhaps from the children's descriptions of what they were doing, we can infer the rules used in each state, or age. As we change the input in various ways and observe how the output changes at the different ages, we can more confidently describe the nature of the information-processing system at each state.

At a finer level of analysis, we must look at developmental changes at each step from input to output. As we will see later, developmental changes are apparent in nearly every phase of processing—from attention through encoding to recall and decision making. Any or all of these changes could be responsible for the differences in the strategies used by the younger and the older child on the weight-seriation task.

The way that information-processing psychologists study the weight-seriation task contrasts with Piaget's approach to the same task. Although both are concerned with how children reach their answer, Piaget used the task to diagnose whether children have underlying mental operations, such as reversibility and transitivity. (If A is heavier than B and if B is heavier than C, then A must be heavier than C.) Baylor and Gascon, in contrast, inferred what specific rules the child used for that task. They made a more detailed analysis of the child's actions and related them to the stimulus characteristics of the task, such as how the blocks are arranged and how many blocks there are. Finally, they wrote a computer program based on the inferred rules to see if they could generate the child's sequence of actions.

Now that we have noted the general nature of the human information-processing device and its development, let us look more specifically at the flow of information through this device. Information processing has been called the "psychology of boxes and arrows." A well-known example is the influential Atkinson and Shiffrin (1969) flow diagram shown earlier. These flow diagrams are called "models." They communicate the theorist's claims about how humans process information. In this way, information-processing psychologists express their theories. A model outlines the temporal and functional relations among the stages of processing in the information-processing system. As far as we know, these stages do not correspond to different areas of the brain.

The Atkinson and Shiffrin model is typical of information-processing models in positing sensory registers, a short-term store (short-term memory), and a long-term store (long-term memory). *Sensory registers* in each modality retain all information reaching the sense organs, but only for perhaps a fraction of a second or several seconds, depending on the sense organ. Children's sensory registers appear to have as great a capacity as those of adults. However, children form sensory representations more slowly than do adults.

Any information selected for further processing continues to a short-term store. The *short-term store* can maintain a limited amount of information (perhaps 5 to 9 units in an adult) for up to approximately 15 to 30 seconds, or longer if the person verbally rehearses (repeats) or otherwise acts upon this information. Material that is not attended to further in short-term store and transferred to long-term store is quickly lost forever. Thus, we must either immediately dial the phone number we have looked up or keep repeating it. Information from the sensory register and the long-term store can be brought together to perform calculations or other activities in the short-term store. Thus, the short-term store is sometimes aptly called the "working memory." Finally, the *long-term store* has a large capacity and retains information indefinitely within a complex mental organization. During retrieval, information is summoned out of the long-term store and once again enters the short-term store.

The cognitive system performs various kinds of work. For example, when first-graders read, they filter out irrelevant information, such as the color of the letters, and perform preliminary analyses on information as they break the stimuli into letters or words and "recognize" these letters and words. They also transform the visual stimuli into a verbal code ("see Spot run") or a visual image (of Spot running) and search their long-term store for related information about Spot. Anywhere along the way the information may be lost, thus precluding further analysis. Thus, in assembly-line fashion, a sequence of operations is applied to the input. Metaphorically, information follows the arrows and "goes" in and out of boxes.

A crucial set of processes listed in the flow diagram, called *control processes,* consists of the "executives of the company." Like computer software, they direct the activities in each stage of processing, keep track of what is going on in all parts of the system, and make sure the entire system is working in harmony. Control processes help humans overcome structural limitations on how much information can be handled. Some of the most impressive developmental changes in information processing occur in these control processes.

With respect to development, both description and explanation (see the introductory chapter) questions could be raised about the stages of processing outlined in the flow diagram. First, in what way, if any, do the stages of processing differ at various ages? Do they differ quantitatively or qualitatively? Second, what causes the child to progress from one state to the next? Are changes in how the child compares the weights of blocks due to an increase in the capacity of short-term store or the more efficient retrieval of a relevant rule from long-term store or both?

Developmental psychologists have used levels-of-processing models as well as stages-of-processing models. Levels models describe memory as a set of actions that may process information at any of several levels, ranging from a superficial analysis of perceptual features to a deep analysis of meaning. As Brown (1979) points out, the levels-of-processing approach is very congenial to developmental approaches because children more and more actively relate the material to be remembered to their conceptual system and their goals.

Development as Self-Modification

For developmental psychology, an important breakthrough in computer simulation of cognitive development was the development of self-correcting, self-modifying programs (for example, Wallace, Klahr, & Bluff, 1987, and Simon, Newell, & Klahr, in press). Suppose a computer program simulates the cognitive state of a child at one point in time. Because a computer program can act on itself as a source of information, in principle it can change itself. Some computer simulations now consist of programs that ruthlessly reject procedures that turn out not to be useful, reorganize units already available, and increase or decrease the number of situations in which a particular operation will be used. These self-modifications, then, propel the program from state to state, or from one developmental level to another.

Many information-processing psychologists who use computers only metaphorically also posit self-correction through feedback. Children try out various rules or strategies in their attempts to attend to, comprehend, and remember the events of daily life. They learn how to select the most promising routes to solving a problem. By rejecting useless methods and retaining helpful ones, children gradually become more efficient information processors.

We encountered the notion of modification through feedback earlier, in social learning theory and Piaget's theory. All three theories view feedback as information to be evaluated and used to change behavior. However, information-processing theory and Piagetian theory essentially ignore learning theory's account of how this feedback can serve as reinforcement or punishment to increase or decrease the frequency of a response. Instead, they focus on how feedback aids the acquisition of new skills.

TASK ANALYSIS

One hallmark of the information-processing approach is the careful, almost compulsive analysis of the experimental or real-life task facing the child or adult. The investigator analyzes the task according to the various necessary and sufficient cognitive skills for performing it. This concern with the specific features of a particular task follows naturally from the approach's focus on the information available in the stimulus, the limits to the person's processing capacity, the goals of the task, and the person's processing skills. The unique demands of each particular task elicit a different set of processing activities. For example, conceptually unrelated objects may be rehearsed verbally, but related objects may be categorized into "kitchen objects" and "living-room objects" and then only briefly rehearsed. By analyzing task demands, the investigator can distinguish between the behaviors that children produce because they are necessary for adapting to the task and those they produce because of their inadequate information-processing abilities (Siegler, 1991).

This issue of task demands is of particular concern to developmentalists. Is there so much information that it exceeds the child's capacity and therefore cannot be comprehended, even though the child has the appropriate rule? If so, the child's knowledge may be underestimated. The child may be able to seriate weight if there are four blocks but not if there are seven. Is there salient but irrelevant information that draws the child's attention away from the important information? For example, the child may attend to differences in the sizes of the blocks, thereby ignoring their weights. Are there developmental changes in what behaviors the child has available to apply toward the goal of the particular task? Weighing the blocks, comparing them, and placing them in a line are performed differently at various ages.

The concern with task analysis is related to a central issue among the neo-Piagetians: domain-specific versus domain-general knowledge. Information-processing investigators tend to propose that the child acquires a set of rules that is specific to a particular domain, that is, limited to a certain task or set of tasks. A careful analysis of various tasks clarifies why a child may apply a rule (for example, a counting rule) or set of rules to certain tasks (adding) but not other relevant ones (class inclusion).

There is a common spirit in the information-processing and learning approaches. Both often break down tasks or behavior into their simple components. In addition, both are very concerned with the nature of the task stimuli. The information-processing approach, however, allows for more complexity in how people operate upon stimulus information. People can, for example, relate this new information to an organized set of knowledge about objects, people, and events.

METHODOLOGY

Information-processing psychologists investigate topics traditionally studied by experimental psychologists: memory, attention, text processing, language, and problem solving. However, the experiments sometimes are microscopic, in that they often look at very brief events, such as detecting whether a particular design flashed briefly on a screen is a spatial rotation of an earlier design. The studies often examine such temporal variables as the amount of time, in milliseconds, the stimulus is exposed and take temporal measures, such as reaction time (how long it takes the subject to decide whether the design was rotated). It is assumed that any mental activity takes a certain amount of time. There may, however, be differences in speed of processing between different ages, between normal and mentally retarded children, and between good and poor readers (Kail, 1991; Stanovich, 1978). Such a concern with time is not surprising, given the focus on the flow of information over time. Under certain conditions, it can be assumed that the longer the time between input and output, the greater the cognitive activity that is taking place. Consequently, it can be assumed that if two tasks are identical, except that one additional cognitive operation is required for one of the tasks, the difference in the time required to perform the two tasks provides a measure of the time needed to perform the additional operation.

Another powerful method is the *rule assessment* approach based on error analysis. The pattern of correct and incorrect answers over various types of trials reveals the rule or rules the child is using to solve the problem. A classic example is Siegler's (1978) work with the balance-scale task, to be described later. Although Piaget also made considerable use of children's errors, he did not analyze them in the elegant, systematic way sometimes found in information-processing work. Still another assessment is eye-movement analysis. What children look at, how long they look at stimuli, and the order in which they examine stimuli provide clues to their processes of attention and encoding.

Recently, Siegler, an information-processing psychologist, has adopted the *microgenetic method* advocated by Vygotsky (see Chapter 7). In this method, children are given a large number of trials on the same general type of problem (Siegler & Crowley, 1991). There can be multiple sessions spread over weeks or months. This design reveals changes in the child's cognitive performance during the session or across sessions. For example, children typically switch among several strategies over the trials on adding problems, memory problems, or reading tasks (Siegler, 1991; Siegler & Crowley, 1991). Several strategies seem to compete for a period of time, with the more efficient strategies gradually becoming more frequent. However, even after children discover a superior strategy they typically continue to use their less mature ones as well. The microgenetic method permits the investigator to focus on moments of sudden change, or cognitive insight. For instance, children sometimes show "hemming and hawing" behaviors on the trial just before the one on which they use a new strategy (Siegler & Jenkins, 1989). They take a long time to answer or they become inarticulate. Sometimes they even contradict their own behavior, as when one child swore he never counted, even though he had counted audibly. These odd behaviors may indicate increased cognitive activity associated with the discovery of a new strategy.

In addition to these traditional experimental methods, information-processing psychologists have developed two tools: models and computer simulation. The use of models in the form of flow diagrams is not, of course, unique to the information-processing approach. As we saw in an earlier chapter, even Freud occasionally tried to express his theoretical notions through diagrams. However, no other approach has relied as heavily as the information-processing approach on schematic models for theory building. We briefly discussed the simple flow-diagram model in the earlier figure. It is a typical information-processing model in that it is a schematic representation describing temporal and functional relationships among several stages of processing. Some models, however, are expressed in other forms, such as mathematical symbols, propositional logic, and formal grammars.

The advent of the computer gave psychologists and other scientists not only an efficient way to analyze their data but also a way to test theories of human thought. Computer simulation is an attempt to write a program that is specific enough, accurate enough, and complete enough to generate an output similar to that of humans. As information-processing psychologists pose the question: What would an information–processing system have to be like in order to behave as the child does? Psychologists develop a computer program that is intended to generate the child's performance on the task. Given the same input, do the computer program and the child produce the same output? Do they make the same errors and succeed on the same problems? The closer the correspondence, the better the simulation.

The development of a successful simulation can be a long and arduous task. Usually psychologists begin by gathering descriptions of how people solve a particular problem. For example, they might describe the order in which the child weighs blocks on a scale. They might also have the child describe what she is thinking and doing as she solves this weight-seriation problem. These data make up the "protocol." The problem-solving session may be videotaped so that it can be viewed many times. Researchers then try to write a set of rules or procedures that the child or a group of children used to order the weights. They then write a computer program that gives instructions based on this set of rules. The program must make specific statements about the capacity of the system, the representation of information, and the nature of the cognitive processes. If psychologists have left out some steps in the rules they wrote into the program, if their instructions are logically inconsistent, or if they have incorrectly inferred a rule from the child's behavior, the program either will not run or will give an output that does not correspond to the child's. Psychologists then try to correct the program and run it again. Often, this cycle must be repeated many times. With each repetition, the number of unexplained behaviors of the child becomes smaller and smaller. Eventually a satisfactory correspondence between the outputs may be achieved. In other words, the program essentially reproduces the protocol from which it was generated.

At this point, researchers apply more stringent tests. Can the program predict what other children of the same age or a different age would do? Can it predict what the child would do if there were 15 blocks instead of 7 or if the blocks were a different set of sizes? Can it predict what the child would do on a length-seriation task? Further modification of the program may be necessary to achieve this generalization. For example, for arithmetic skills it may be necessary to add information about the level of difficulty of back-up strategies—such as adding by counting your fingers—the frequency of problem presentation, and the effects of related knowledge (Siegler & Jenkins, 1989). The final simulation should match the children in terms of which problems are most difficult and which strategy is chosen on these problems (Siegler & Jenkins, 1989).

At some point, psychologists find that they have a satisfactory model of how humans behave in a particular type of task, such as seriating weight or playing chess. Ideally, they then develop a more general model that explains behavior on a wider set of tasks, for example, a model of memory during problem solving. Thus, as further changes are made in the program, it may become both more specific and more general. A good model will generalize to more behaviors than the small set of protocols on which it was based but be specific enough to be supported or refuted by empirical findings. By the preceding process, a model becomes less limited and more convincing as a theory of thinking.

One unexpected bonus of computer simulation is that it can suggest new hypotheses to psychologists. There may be implications of the simulation of which psychologists were unaware. Unexpected output from the program may suggest that a new variable should be examined. For example, if researchers found that the program predicted the same level of recall with 5 and with 10 items, they might look for a "chunking" mechanism that operates when there is a large number of items.

The information-processing approach may illustrate that researchers' methods sometimes encourage certain metaphors. It has been argued, for example, that the early learning theorist Tolman's use of the rat maze as an experimental apparatus led to his spatial view of cognition, particularly cognitive maps (Gigerenzer, 1991). Similarly, present-day cognitive researchers, who typically use computers heavily for data gathering and data analysis, may find computer-program metaphors particularly appealing. Their tool becomes their metaphor.

MAJOR DEVELOPMENTAL APPROACHES

The study of information processing in children is a diverse, multifaceted enterprise. Some information-processing psychologists use letters flashed briefly on a screen, while others make the stimuli available for half an hour. Some look at reaction time, while others look at children's own explanations of how they solved a problem. The common orientation presented earlier should not mask this diversity. The following smorgasbord offers a sampling of current information-processing research programs or influential earlier studies. We look at the development of memory, representation, problem solving, and intelligence. This division into four areas is strictly for convenience of presentation. In actuality, all four make up an indivisible psychological system. The programs are described in some detail in order to illustrate which problems have been considered worthy of study, which theoretical concepts have been advanced, and how developmentalists have actually studied cognitive development from the information-processing point of view.

MEMORY

Memory is a net; one finds it full of fish when he takes it from the brook; but a dozen miles of water have run through it without sticking.

[Oliver Wendell Holmes]

Children's memory is a fascinating phenomenon, but the area of study is fraught with contradictions. On the one hand, it is widely believed that young children have poor memories. On memory subscales of IQ tests or on laboratory memory tasks, they perform poorly compared with adults, and in more natural settings they find it difficult to memorize their phone numbers and street addresses. Yet parents or teachers who read stories to preschoolers know that children often memorize a story word for word after only a few readings. In fact, children become quite indignant if the reader inadvertently (or because it is past bedtime) leaves out a word or two.

A typical developmental information-processing psychologist conducts laboratory studies of memory in children. This recognition of the important role of memory in all phases of thought is shared with information-processing psychologists who study adults. Hundreds of these studies fill the developmental research journals of the last 25 years. This investment of psychologists' time and energy has paid off handsomely in knowledge not only about children's memory but also, as a bonus, about the development of language, attention, and complex cognitive structures such as the organization of the knowledge base. Although psychologists do not yet have the whole picture, some generalizations have emerged. Four main factors that cause developmental changes in memory are now presented, along with several studies that convey the flavor of the research. The factors are strategies, knowledge, metamemory, and capacity.

Strategies

Some memory activities are effortless and seemingly automatic: a baby recognizes her father's face, a boy relates to his friend the plot of his favorite television show seen the night before, an adult hums "White Christmas" while Christmas shopping. The person is not conscious of trying to remember and does not make an effort to remember. These acts of memory "just happen." They involve simple recognition rather than active recall; they involve recall as a by-product of a meaningful activity. There is little change in these types of memory during development. Simple recognition memory (indicating that an object or a picture has been seen before) is very good even in infants. It shows little improvement from infancy to maturity when possible differences in the efficiency of encoding are ruled out. By the end of the preschool years, coherent, comprehensible stories or past experiences that were of interest to the child are recalled fairly well.

When the material to be recalled is *not* part of a context that is meaningful to the child and memory itself must become the primary goal, then there *is* striking improvement in memory during development. Phone numbers, a group of unrelated objects, and the order in which pictures of toys were presented all fall into this category. Involuntary memory and deliberate memory have very different characteristics and require different theoretical explanations.

It is clear that there are developmental changes in what children do when they are trying to remember. In order to store unrelated information, the person must do something special to the material. This "something special" is a strategy. Defined more formally, strategies are "subject-controlled activities that are employed in the service of a memory goal" (Ornstein & Naus, 1985, p. 118). For example, if people want to remember what to buy at the store, they could say the items over and over again to themselves or put the items into categories such as "dairy products" and "vegetables." Or they could make up a silly story about the items ("The carrot swam through the sea of milk on the back of a tuna . . ."), mark the location of the items on their mental image of the supermarket, or simply write a list. These strategies are tools that humans have devised in their constant struggle to overcome their processing limitations.

In an early influential study of children's strategies, Flavell, Beach, and Chinsky (1966) asked young children to remember the order in which the experimenter pointed to several pictures of objects. During the delay between the presentation and the recall tests, a visor on a space helmet was lowered over the child's eyes so that he could not see the pictures. A trained lip reader noted any overt verbal rehearsal. Few 5-year-olds, over half of the 7-year-olds, and most of the 10-year-olds rehearsed. In a later experiment, Keeney, Cannizzo, and Flavell (1967) found evidence for a direct link between rehearsal and memory. First, those children who spontaneously rehearsed recalled more items than those who did not. Second, when the experimenter directed nonrehearsers to say the names of the objects during the delay between the presentation and the recall test, they successfully rehearsed. Consequently, they remembered the order of the objects. Thus, young children are capable of using rehearsal to aid memory if they are told to rehearse, but they are deficient at spontaneously producing the strategy. Flavell dubbed this a *production deficiency.* Young children have appropriate strategies but are deficient in knowing when, where, and how to use (produce) them effectively. Since the Flavell studies, a production deficiency has been rediscovered with many other memory tasks and many other strategies, such as leaving clues that will help in retrieval or classifying the items into categories (animals, furniture, and food). This research shows that older children are more likely than younger children to use the higher-order relations among stimuli, such as categories.

Even after children develop and use strategies, they continue to refine them. Ornstein, Naus, and Liberty (1975) found that verbal rehearsal becomes more systematic and organized during development. During the memory task, the children were to say the words aloud as they were presented. Third-graders tended to say each word alone as it was presented or perhaps with the previous word. In contrast, eighth-graders rehearsed cumulatively, including previously presented words as well as the new word.

By the preteen years, children typically can pick a strategy that fits the particular task and carry out the strategy spontaneously, quickly, and efficiently. Certain strategies, however, continue to develop during adolescence. An example is "elaboration," or constructing an image out of the materials to be remembered (Pressley, 1982).

A major developmental change during the grade-school and adolescent years involves learning to make maximal use of one's limited capacity. For example, during the grade-school years, children become more efficient in their use of study time. Older grade-school children are more likely than young children to select relevant material and ignore irrelevant material (Miller, 1990). For example, older children focus more on the important elements of the text, as reflected in their underlining and note taking (Brown & Smiley, 1978). Brown (1978) stresses the increase in the child's control of strategies and other cognitive processes. As if learning to conduct a great orchestra, children eventually bring the parts into perfect harmony and increase their control over the whole. These control processes eventually mature into those found in adults, as in the model shown on page 237.

Three recent lines of research illustrate some of the current questions asked in studies of memory strategies. First, investigators recently have identified rudimentary strategies in toddlers and preschoolers. For example, in one study (DeLoache, Cassidy, & Brown, 1985), 18- to 24-month-olds watched the experimenter hide a Big Bird stuffed animal. They were told to remember Big Bird's location so they could find him later. Even though the experimenter then distracted them with attractive toys for several minutes, they frequently stopped playing to talk about Big Bird or his hiding place ("Big Bird chair"), look at or point to the hiding place, hover near it, or try to get Big Bird. These strategylike behaviors were much less frequent in control conditions, such as when the experimenter rather than the child was to remember the location.

In a second line of research, the study of memory strategies has broadened to become the study of strategies as a developmental phenomenon of interest in itself, independent of its facilitation of memory (Bjorklund, 1990). The interview with L, which began this chapter, is an example of information-processing oriented work on mathematical strategies. Employing strategies is an important function of the control processes described earlier. One example is the finding that it is more effortful for younger children than for older ones to use a strategy (Guttentag, 1984). Thus, they have less remaining capacity to devote to memorizing per se than does an older child for whom the strategy itself requires less capacity-draining effort.

A third current issue is what causes strategies to develop. Strategies may be taught directly, and cultures may vary in the extent to which they emphasize such experiences. For instance, German teachers and parents spend more time teaching and explaining memory strategies to children then do American ones (Carr, Kurtz, Schneider, Turner, & Borkowski, 1989). Strategy development may also benefit from the development of knowledge, metamemory, and capacity, to be described next.

Knowledge

Memory is not a mental process separate from the rest of cognition. It is intermeshed in a broad system of thought. In fact, memory has been called "applied cognition" (Flavell, 1971a) because the cognitive system is simply directed to a particular set of problems, namely, storage and retrieval. There are two implications for development. First, children are more likely to remember material that is meaningful to them. When there is a match between what the child knows and what is to be remembered, there is what Brown (1975) calls "headfitting." The task fits the child's mental abilities. Second, as children become "world-wise" and acquire a growing store of knowledge about objects, events, and people in the world, they should be able to remember better.

There are numerous experimental demonstrations of the first phenomenon, remembering meaningful materials. For example, children who are skilled chess players have better recall of the locations of chess pieces on a chessboard, positioned as if in the middle of a game, than do adults who know less about chess (Chi, 1978). Similar results are found for knowledge about soccer (Schneider, Korkel, & Weinert, 1989) and baseball (Recht & Leslie, 1988).

Such cases of knowledge facilitating recall can be explained in several ways. First, a rich knowledge base may allow children to automatically access items to be recalled because these items have a rich network of associations with other items and with category labels (Bjorklund, 1987). Thus, items can be retrieved by many different cues; items are very accessible. In Piaget's terminology, memory is facilitated because children can easily assimilate the material to their cognitive structures.

A second explanation is that the knowledge base may increase the likelihood that an appropriate strategy is used, which in turn facilitates recall. Thus, a strategy mediates the effect of the knowledge base. According to one version of this argument, because of the ability to quickly process the information by relating it to previous knowledge, capacity is freed and can be applied to deliberately using a strategy (Bjorklund, 1987). Siegler concludes that "familiar content may serve as a kind of practice field upon which children exercise emerging cognitive skills, such as new memory strategies" (1991, p. 200). Six-year-olds, who typically do not group similar items together during recall, can, when asked to remember the names of classmates, show a great deal of grouping according to seating arrangement, reading groups, and sex of the children (Bjorklund & Zeman, 1982). In addition to these two main explanations is the suggestion that a rich knowledge base may facilitate recall by enhancing motivation or increasing children's understanding of the goal of the task.

One problem with examining the relationship between the knowledge base and recall is that a researcher needs to be able to describe the child's knowledge base accurately and in great detail. A rare attempt at such description was a study of a 4-year-old obsessed with dinosaur lore (Chi & Koeske, 1983). He knew the names of 40 different dinosaurs, understood the differences between a pachycephalosaur and a rhamphorhyncus, and persuaded his patient mother to spend an average of three hours a week reading his dinosaur books to him. His semantic network concerning a subset of dinosaurs well known to him is shown in the accompanying illustration. The diagram was generated by two procedures. First, Chi and Koeske observed which dinosaurs the child named in succession when asked to recall all the dinosaurs he could. Second, they assessed his knowledge and organization of dinosaur properties in a game: one person named two or three properties, and the other person guessed which dinosaur it was. As the figure shows, the links or associations within a category are strong, numerous, and conceptually close (for example, armored species are grouped in the left-side shaded area, A, and giant plant eaters in the right-side shaded area, P). This structure was not found for less familiar dinosaurs; in other words, knowledge of seven familiar dinosaurs (in the areas A and P) was more organized than the knowledge about less familiar dinosaurs. For example, the boy could say that diplodocus and brachiosaur both eat plants but not that two relatively unknown dinosaurs do. The patterns of linkages, or semantic network, are the essence of the structuring of the knowledge base. The boy's knowledge of the properties was useful for forming subsets on the basis of diet, appearance, and other characteristics. As expected, the boy could remember more of the better-known than of the lesser-known dinosaurs, perhaps because the former had many links to other dinosaurs and the items were more structured conceptually.

The increase in amount of knowledge during development is important for memory development. But perhaps even more critical is how knowledge is represented, specifically, how it is organized, as illustrated in Chi and Koeske's study of dinosaur knowledge. Young children may tend to form categories on the basis of perceptual features of objects, whereas older children may be more likely to use conceptual features. If

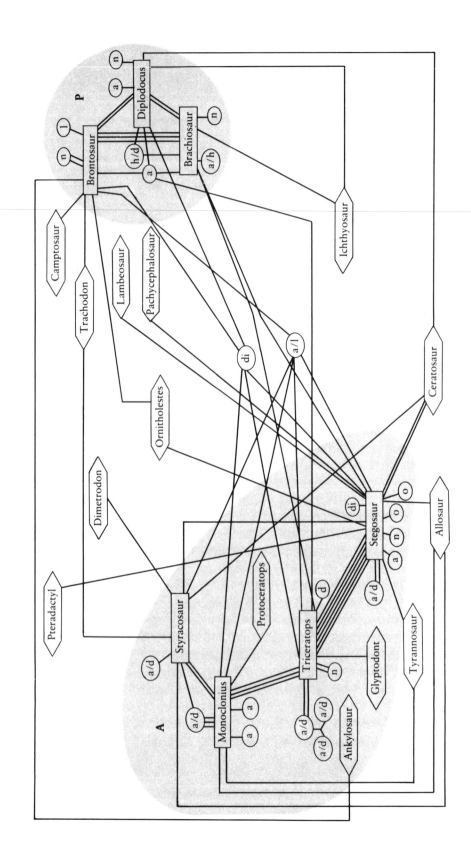

(Left) Semantic network representation of a child's knowledge concerning well-known dinosaurs (the seven enclosed in rectangles). The child's two categories are indicated by the two shaded areas: armored dinosaurs (A) and giant plant-eating dinosaurs (P). The characteristics include appearance (a), defense mechanism (d), diet (di), habitat (h), locomotion (l), nickname (n), and other (o). Other dinosaurs associated with the seven target dinosaurs are enclosed in hexagons. [Adapted from "Network Representation of a Child's Dinosaur Knowledge," by Michelene T. H. Chi and Randi D. Koeske, in Developmental Psychology, 1983, 19, 29-39. Reproduced by permission of the authors; © 1983 by the American Psychological Association, Inc.]

a memory task is not represented in a way that taps the child's knowledge base, then his considerable knowledge about the materials may not be beneficial. For example, for Chi and Koeske's subject, presenting categories of large plant eaters and armored dinosaurs, which are congruent with his own categories, should lead to greater recall than categories formed on some other basis, such as their aggressiveness or time of emergence during evolution.

A final observation about the relationship between knowledge and recall is that since children's interests and knowledge differ from those of adults, their most salient memories may differ from those of adults. One 5-year-old, when asked if he remembered the home he had moved from 2 years earlier, answered: "I remember lots about Michigan. I remember you left a piece of cheese at the back of the refrigerator and it got green stuff all over it."

The second claim made about the knowledge base was that developmental progress in knowledge should bring about progress in memory. Piaget's studies of memory described in Chapter 1 provide vivid examples of this progress. Children's memory of seriated (size-ordered) sticks improved (became more seriated) after their understanding of seriation improved.

As children increase their store of knowledge, they tend to make inferences that go beyond the information given. Hebb (1949) likens this feature of remembering to the way a paleontologist reconstructs a prehistoric creature. Just as a paleontologist generates a complete dinosaur from lone fragments and his general knowledge about the anatomy of dinosaurs, so does a person reconstruct an event by filling in among remembered fragments. For example, in one study (Paris & Carter, 1973) children were told, "The bird is inside the cage" and "The cage is under the table." Then the children were presented with sentences, some new and some heard earlier. Children as young as 7 often recalled, erroneously, that the sentence "The bird is under the table" had been presented earlier. They had spontaneously made a reasonable inference from the information they had been given.

Children's constructive memory also reflects their social beliefs, attitudes, and expectations. For example, school-age children with the most stereotyped views of gender-appropriate behavior recalled more pictures of traditional (for example, female secretary) than nontraditional (for example, male secretary) activities (Signorella & Liben, 1984). In addition, they sometimes even reconstructed the pictures, for example, recalling that a secretary was female when in fact the person was a male. In another study (Ceci, Caves, & Howe, 1981), 7- and 10-year-olds "remembered" that a character known to them to be powerful, such as "The Six Million Dollar Man," had been strong in a story heard three weeks earlier. In fact, the character had been weak in the story. This distortion of memory did not occur with unfamiliar characters.

Memory does not simply copy the world. Children "construct" a memory from inferences based on their knowledge. Younger children are less likely to make these inferences (Liben & Posnansky, 1977). In short, "creative memory" is a by-product of cognitive development.

These illustrations of how memory is tied to knowledge should further clarify how involuntary memory differs from the deliberate, voluntary memory discussed in an earlier section. If children have the knowledge necessary to understand the material, then they are likely to remember it without further ado.

Metamemory

"The horror of that moment," the King went on, "I shall never, *never* forget!"

"You will, though," the Queen said, "if you don't make a memorandum of it."

[Lewis Carroll]

Taking notes while listening to a lecture, underlining key points in a textbook on developmental theories, writing a shopping list before leaving for the supermarket, leaving one's completed homework by the front door the night before school, and mentally walking through the previous day in order to recall where a jacket might have been left all reflect *metamemory*. Metamemory is knowledge about memory and is a special case of *metacognition*, which is knowledge about any aspect of human thought. During development, we acquire an understanding that sometimes it is necessary to make an extra effort or do something special in order to remember and that certain factors facilitate or hinder memory. These factors can include person, task, or strategy variables (Flavell & Wellman, 1977). Examples are knowing that there are limits to how much can be remembered (person variable), that recognition is easier than recall (task variable), and that verbal rehearsal aids recall (strategy variable). Thus, children become amateur psychologists.

Preschoolers have limited knowledge about memory. For instance, they claim superhuman memory abilities, such as when they predict that they can remember ten items though they can remember only three or four (Flavell, Friedrichs, & Hoyt, 1970). With simple testing procedures, however, they do reveal some competence at metamemory. For example, 4-year-olds who view two strategies on videotape can choose the more helpful one. They know that they can better help themselves remember where Cookie Monster is hidden by marking his hiding place with a colored chip rather than by looking away when the stimulus array is rotated (Justice, 1989).

The more sophisticated facets of metamemory develop later. In a study by Kreutzer, Leonard, and Flavell (1975), children were asked whether it mattered if, after being told a phone number, they made the call immediately or got a drink of water first. Approximately 40 percent of the kindergartners, but more than 75 percent of the fifth-graders, thought it would be better to phone first. Presumably, children become increasingly aware that short-term memory fades rapidly. That strategies are helpful becomes common knowledge during the grade-school years. For example, Kreutzer and her colleagues posed a retrieval problem in which a child is trying to remember which Christmas he received his dog. Nearly half of the kindergartners were unable to suggest a way to recall the correct Christmas, but all of the fifth-graders could. The fifth-graders thought of aids such as taking a trip through the mind back to each Christmas and recalling the gifts received or trying to recall other things that happened when the dog was received in the hope that would provide a cue.

Kreutzer, Leonard, and Flavell found that children's thinking about strategies can become rather complex, as the following exchange with a third-grader demonstrates:

> Say the number is 633-8854. Then what I'd do is—say that my number is 633, so I won't have to remember that, really. And then I would think, now I've got to remember 88. Now I'm 8 years old, so I can remember, say, my age two times. And then I say how old my brother is, and how old he was last year. And that's how I'd usually remember that phone number. (Is that how you would most often remember a phone number?) Well, usually I write it down.

[1975, p. 11]

An important theoretical question concerns the relationship between knowledge about memory and memory behavior. Intuitively, it seems that there should be a close relationship. If children think that memory is automatic and do not realize that they need to do anything special to remember, they are not likely to bother to rehearse the material, look for similarities among the objects, and so on. Thus, the aforementioned production deficiency with respect to strategies may be caused by poorly developed metamemory. In addition, even after children initiate a strategy, surely they must be sensitive to whether their chosen strategy is working before they can decide to continue or drop that strategy. It appears, however, that the relationship between knowledge about memory and memory performance is not so simple. Knowledge does not necessarily lead to its use. Children are, however, more likely to continue to use a strategy if they attribute their success on the task to using the strategy (Fabricius & Hagen, 1984).

Capacity

A commonsense explanation of developmental improvement in memory would be that the memory span (the capacity of short-term memory) increases. For example, with increasing age children can repeat, in order, a longer string of numbers (for example, 3281734). Evidence suggests that the maturation of the nervous system throughout childhood causes increases in mental capacity (Case, 1985). This view connotes a container metaphor in which children have small boxes in their heads and adults have larger boxes (Schneider & Weinert, 1989) or a weightlifter metaphor in which older children have greater "raw mental muscle power" (Flavell, Miller, & Miller, 1993). The full story is more complicated, however. As mentioned earlier, when cognitive skills are practiced they become more automatic and thus less capacity demanding. Consequently, some of the developmental increase in capacity reflects the efficiency with which a constant amount of capacity is used rather than a neurological–structural increase in capacity. For example, as children become more skilled readers they can recognize words more quickly; as a result, a given amount of capacity goes much further. Thus, thanks to both maturation and experience, older children have a larger memory span than do younger.

It is interesting that this developmental increase in capacity appears to be domain general. Studies of reaction time (latency between presentation of a stimulus and the child's response) show that across a number of tasks the ratio between the capacity of adults and children of a particular age is the same (Hale, 1990; Kail, 1991). For example, Hale found that across four rather different tasks 10-year-olds were approximately 1.8 times slower than college students and 12-year-olds were 1.6 times slower. This supports neo-Piagetian Case's argument for certain capacity-based across-the-board changes during development.

Regardless of whether increased capacity proves to involve mainly maturation-based, "hard-wired" structural changes or experience-based changes in efficiency, the effects on memory are clear. As described in earlier sections, older children use this greater capacity to keep more items alive in short-term memory and invest it in memory strategies and metamemory activities—a wise investment, as we have seen.

REPRESENTATION

The research on memory we have described makes it clear that representational processes are closely tied to memory processes. *Representation* refers to the mental form in which information is cast. The child stores representations of external objects and events and then retrieves them when necessary. Knowledge can be represented in several ways, namely, words or sentences, actions, images, and abstract propositions (general "ideas" underlying statements). For the developmentalist, the issue is whether there are age-related changes in the ability and tendency to use these various types of representations. It is likely that 2-, 5-, and 10-year-olds differ in whether they represent a bicycle with the word "bicycle," a visual image of a bicycle, a nonverbal image of how it feels when riding a bicycle, or a set of propositions about the nature of bicycles.

Perhaps because adults rely heavily on language to represent knowledge, psychologists egocentrically have focused on how objects or events are verbally encoded and interpreted within a semantic network—the meaning system of language. (Because this research typically has used memory tasks, the results with children were summarized in the previous section.) With increasing age, children are more likely to rehearse verbally and make inferences about sentences based on an analysis of their meaning. However, people of any age, but especially infants and young children, may use nonverbal representations, such as visual images. Evidence is mounting that even young infants may construct simple mental representations (Mandler, 1988).

One type of representation of special interest to developmentalists is scripts, which were conceived of by information-processing psychologists studying adults (Schank & Abelson, 1977). Scripts are generalized, coherent mental representations of a series of events that occur in a consistent temporal order in everyday life. These scripts describe "what's supposed to happen" in certain situations, and they lead children to expect that certain events will occur in a particular order. If this order is violated, children may become confused. For example, a 2-year-old who once was given a bath before dinner rather than after, became very upset because she thought she would not be fed that evening (Hudson, 1990). Scripts also allow children to understand and interpret both old and new objects and events. As Nelson defines it, a script "(1) contains certain basic and obligatory events in sequence, (2) predicts open slots for options, objects and events and what they may contain, and (3) designates appropriate roles and actors" (1978, pp. 256–257). Nelson found that even young children develop scripts for familiar situations. To illustrate, a child might have a script for eating at a fast-food hamburger restaurant:

> I walk in there and I, I, I ask my daddy and then the daddy ask the lady and the lady gets it. One small coke, one cheeseburger. . . . They want to eat here so they don't need a tray. Then we go find a table. I eat it all up. All. And throw the . . . paper . . . the cheeseburgers in the garbage can. . . . Goodbye. Goodbye. Jump in the car. . . . Vroom! Vroom! Goodbye.
>
> *[1978, p. 260]*

Three features of scripts are noteworthy. First, both linguistic representation and nonverbal imagery of objects and events are likely to form scripts. Scripts are less verbal and less static than representations in semantic networks, which emphasize information about the meanings of words and concepts. Second, the script approach seems to correspond more closely than many of the other approaches we have considered to the way children represent complex events of their day-to-day lives. Third, the approach is immediately applicable to the social world of people and events. For these reasons, it is an important alternative to the approaches based more strictly on the computer metaphor.

This chapter describes several different types of representation: verbal or nonverbal representations of single objects or events, networks of representations such as semantic networks of words or propositions, scripted representations of a sequence of events in time and space, and (in the next section) representations of rules used for problem solving. A distinction that cuts across these types of representations is whether we represent differently information that permits us to *know how* to do something (procedural knowledge) and information that allows us to *know that* something is true (declarative knowledge). For example, knowing how to subtract may be represented differently than knowing that first-grade teachers smile when children subtract correctly.

PROBLEM SOLVING

Information-processing psychologists have long been interested in how people solve problems. We now look at two main approaches to these questions.

Siegler (1978) has used the rule assessment approach described in the section on methods to examine the rules children use to solve problems about many physical phenomena studied by Piaget. A good example is Inhelder and Piaget's balance-scale (teeter-totter) problem. On each arm of Siegler's scale are four equally spaced pegs on which weights can be placed. The child is to predict which side, if either, will go down. Two pieces of information are relevant: the number of weights (all of equal weight) on each side and their distance from the midpoint (fulcrum). Siegler identified four rules.

1. Children consider only the number of weights, so they predict that the side with the most weights will go down.

2. Children consider only the number of weights, unless they are equal on the two sides; then they also take the distance into account.

3. Children examine both weight and distance but do not know what to predict when one side has greater distance and the other side has more weights.

4. Children can assess the exact contribution of both weight and distance by multiplying the number of weights on each peg by that peg's ordinal distance from the fulcrum. (The ordinal position can be used because the pegs are an equal distance apart. The fourth peg from the midpoint is four times as far away as the first one.) By comparing the outcome of this computation for the two sides, children can predict which side will go down.

Siegler could determine which rule a child was using by systematically varying the number of weights and their distance in a series of problems. Each rule would lead to a characteristic pattern of correct and incorrect predictions over the series of problems. This study is an example of the error-analysis method mentioned earlier. Consider, for example, a "conflict-weight problem," in which there is more weight on one side, but the weights are more distant on the other side. The configuration is such that the side with more weights goes down. Children using rule 1 or 2 always correctly predict that the side with more weights will go down because they consider only the number of weights. Children using rule 3, however, are correct only about one third of the time, because they simply guess. They know that both distance and number of weights are important but cannot determine the exact contribution of each. Children using rule 4 are correct. Notice that the children's errors are as informative as their correct answers. The results were that the four rule models accurately described the pattern of predictions over the various types of trials of 89 percent of the children aged 5, 9, 13, and 17. Furthermore, as expected, the older children used more sophisticated rules than did the younger children. Siegler has conducted similar analyses on many other tasks, including conservation, projection of shadows, probability, speed, and mathematical calculations.

The simple set of rules revealed by Siegler is an appealing model of development, yet this simplicity has been a focus of criticism. It has been suggested (Strauss & Levin, 1981) that these simple rules emerge because Siegler's methodology restricts children to these rules. Presenting the same task in an open-ended rather than forced-choice manner may reveal other, perhaps more complex, rules. For other problems and limitations in the rule-assessment approach, see Ferretti and Butterfield (1986), Kerkman and Wright (1988) and Siegler (1983).

A second program of research on children's problem solving is by Klahr, sometimes in collaboration with Wallace, Siegler, Simon, Newell, or other colleagues. Klahr has been developing computer programs to simulate problem solving in children. He has examined class inclusion, conservation, transitivity, counting, balancing weights, as well as other concepts. Klahr has sought the "programmable Piaget" (Quillian, Wortman, & Baylor, 1964). He and his colleagues recently (Simon, Newell, & Klahr, in press), for example, formulated a computer model of how children can acquire number conservation as a result of training. The flavor of Klahr's approach can be conveyed by tracing the way that Siegler's four rules used to solve the balance-scale problem are translated into a computer program. A first step is to translate the four rules into the flow diagram in "Decision tree diagrams for models I–IV." This diagram shows the steps involved in applying each rule. "Yes" and "No" answers lead to different events. Constructing a flow diagram is an intermediary step between rules stated in everyday language and rules stated in a production system in a language that can be fed into

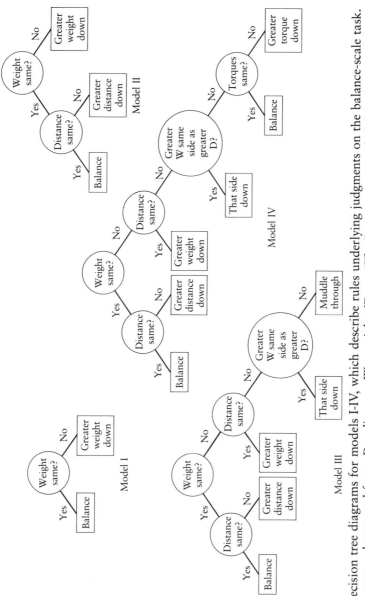

Decision tree diagrams for models I-IV, which describe rules underlying judgments on the balance-scale task. Torque = downward force. D = distance. W = weight. [From "The Representation of Children's Knowledge," by David Klahr and Robert S. Siegler, in *Advances in Child Development and Behavior*, vol. 12, edited by H. W. Reese and L. P. Lipsitt. Copyright © 1978. Reproduced by permission of Academic Press, Inc., and the authors.]

```
Model I
        P1:((Same W) --> (Say "balance"))
        P2:((Side X more W) --> (Say "X down"))

Model II
        P1:((Same W) --> (Say "balance"))
        P2:((Side X more W) --> (Say "X down"))
        P3:((Same W) (Side X more D) --> (Say "X down"))

Model III
        P1:((Same W) --> (Say "balance"))
        P2:((Side X more W) --> (Say "X down"))
        P3:((Same W) (Side X more D) --> (Say "X down"))
        P4:((Side X more W) (Side X less D) --> muddle through)
        P5:((Side X more W) (Side X more D) --> (Say "X down"))

Model IV
        P1:((Same W) --> (Say "balance"))
        P2:((Side X more W) --> (Say "X down"))
        P3:((Same W) (Side X more D) --> (Say "X down"))
        P4':((Side X more W) (Side X less D) --> (get Torques))
        P5:((Side X more W) (Side X more D) --> (Say "X down"))
        P6:((Same Torque) --> (Say "balance"))
        P7:((Side X more Torque) --> (Say "X down"))
```

	Productions	Transitional requirements Operators
I -> II	add P3	add distance encoding and comparison
II -> III	add P4, P5	
III -> IV	modify P4; add P6, P7	add torque computation and comparison

Production-system (P) representations for models I-IV, which describe rules underlying judgments on the balance-scale task. Written in a special language called PSG. Torque = downward force. D = distance. W = weight. [From "The Representation of Children's Knowledge," by David Klahr and Robert S. Siegler, in *Advances in Child Development and Behavior*, vol. 12, edited by H. W. Reese and L. P. Lipsitt. Copyright © 1978. Reproduced by permission of Academic Press, Inc., and the authors.]

a computer. The illustration "Production-system representations for models I–IV" describes, in computer language, the production system for the four rules. Several terms must be explained at this point. Models I to IV correspond to the four rules described. A *production system* is a set of productions stored in long-term memory. *Productions* are condition–action rules for changing the set of information currently activated in the cognitive system. Productions take the following form: "If X is present, Y occurs." For example, in production 1 (P1), if the number of weights is the same, the child says that they balance. Thus, there is recognition (X is present) and then action (Y occurs). Recognition occurs if the conditions are satisfied, that is, if there is a match. If the conditions are not satisfied, the production does not "fire." If two productions are satisfied, then some conflict-resolution principle must decide which production should fire. As condition–action rules are applied for several cycles, they transform the initial knowledge state regarding the task into its final state by adding, deleting, or changing the elements of the state. As the production system goes through these cycles, it leaves a record, or "trace," of what it knew and did at each step.

Let us look more closely at one of the models shown on the facing page. Recall that in model II the distance is considered only if the weights are equal. Model II is a production system containing three productions (condition–action rules). The "condition" part of the condition–action rule refers to tests for the sameness or difference in weight or distance. The "action" part after the arrow refers to a response. Thus, in P1 if the number of weights is the same on both sides (condition), the child says they will balance (action). P2 says that if side X has more weights than side W, then side X will go down. Finally, in P3 if the number of weights on each side is the same but there is more distance on side X than the other sid᷄, then the child predicts that X will go down. At the bottom of the illustration is a list of what changes in the set of productions occur when the child moves from one model to the next during development.

The formal representation of production systems may make its greatest contribution by describing the behavior of individual children. The illustration "Trace of 7-year-old Jan's production system" shows how the production system runs for a 7-year-old child, Jan. For our purposes, we need not be concerned with most of the notations; the interested reader is referred to Klahr and Siegler (1978) for a detailed account. The important sections are the descriptions of the state of "working memory" (currently available information) after each cycle of applying the production system. For example, as cycle 2 begins, working memory (WM) has four elements: more distance on the right arm, more weights on the left arm, task is to predict, and criterion is weight. During recognition tests, P2 and P4 (productions 2 and 4 in the particular model Jan uses) match (recognize) these elements, and since P4 happens to be a special case of P2, P4 fires. The output directs the system to find what is big (FIND BIG). After doing so, the production system moves on to cycle 3. The result of cycle 2 appears at the beginning of cycle 3, and the process continues. Notice that on some cycles the system recognizes conflict between two productions and attempts to resolve the conflict.

As if this model were not already complicated enough, there is additional information written into the model, such as the general problem-solving abilities and semantic knowledge the child brings to the task at each developmental level. Also, the model becomes more complex as

```
        (0003|0020)
Cycle 1
  WM: ((PREDICT) (CRITERION WEIGHT))

  Fire P8: ((PREDICT) (<DIMENSION.1>) ABS --> ATTEND)
      Output from ATTEND (input to WM) ::> (weight more left)(distance more right)

Cycle 2
  WM: ((DISTANCE MORE RIGHT) (WEIGHT MORE LEFT) (PREDICT) (CRITERION WEIGHT) )
      CONFLICT.SET: (P2 P4)
  Fire P4: ((PREDICT) (WEIGHT MORE) (DISTANCE MORE) --> FIND.BIG)
      Output from FIND.BIG (input to WM) ::> (distance big right)(weight big left)

Cycle 3
  WM: ((WEIGHT BIG LEFT) (DISTANCE BIG RIGHT) (PREDICT) (WEIGHT MORE LEFT)
      (DISTANCE MORE RIGHT) (CRITERION WEIGHT))
      CONFLICT.SET: (P2 P4 P5 P6 P7)
      CONFLICT.SET: (P4 P5) AFTER SPECIAL.CASE.ORDER
      CONFLICT.SET: (P5) AFTER WM.ORDER
  Fire P5: ((PREDICT) (CRITERION <DIMENSION.1>)(<DIMENSION.1> BIG <SIDE.1>)
      (<DIMENSION.2> BIG <SIDE.2.) --> (MADE **) (EXPECT <SIDE.1> DOWN) SAY.D)

********** LEFT down

Cycle 4
  WM: ((EXPECT LEFT DOWN) (MADE (PREDICT)) (CRITERION WEIGHT) (WEIGHT BIG LEFT)
      (DISTANCE BIG RIGHT) (WEIGHT MORE LEFT) (DISTANCE MORE RIGHT))
  Fire E1: ((EXPECT) --> LOOK)
      Output from LOOK (input to WM) ::> (see right down)

Cycle 5
  WM: ((SEE RIGHT DOWN) (EXPECT LEFT DOWN) (MADE (PREDICT)) (CRITERION WEIGHT)
      (WEIGHT BIG LEFT) (DISTANCE BIG RIGHT) (WEIGHT MORE LEFT) (DISTANCE MORE RIGHT))
      CONFLICT.SET: (E1,E3)
  Fire E3: ((EXPECT <SIDE.1> <DIRECTION>)
              (SEE <SIDE.1> <DIRECTION>) ABS (SEE) --> (DID **) (SEE ===> SAW)
(RESULT WRONG))

Cycle 6
  WM: ((RESULT WRONG) (DID (EXPECT LEFT DOWN)) (SAW RIGHT DOWN) (MADE (PREDICT))
      (CRITERION WEIGHT) (WEIGHT BIG LEFT) (DISTANCE BIG RIGHT) (WEIGHT MORE LEFT)
      (DISTANCE MORE RIGHT))
  Fire SW2: ((RESULT WRONG) (CRITERION WEIGHT) --> (OLD **) (WEIGHT ===> DISTANCE))

Cycle 7
  WM: ((OLD (RESULT WRONG)) (CRITERION DISTANCE) (DID (EXPECT LEFT DOWN))
      (SAW RIGHT DOWN) (MADE (PREDICT)) (WEIGHT BIG LEFT) (DISTANCE BIG RIGHT)
      (WEIGHT MORE LEFT) (DISTANCE MORE RIGHT))
```

Trace of 7-year-old Jan's production system (P) running on a conflict-distance problem in the balance-scale task. ABS = absent. WM = working memory. E = problem number. [From "The Representation of Children's Knowledge," by David Klahr and Robert S. Siegler, in *Advances in Child Development and Behavior*, vol 12, edited by H. W. Reese and L. P. Lipsitt. Copyright © 1978. Reproduced by permission of Academic Press, Inc., and the authors.]

the child changes her strategies during the task as a result of training. Psychologists who do computer simulation have learned to live with this complexity for the sake of a complete and specific theory.

A formal model produces a detailed, explicit, moment-by-moment description of how the child solves the problem. Ideally, it contains all relevant information about the child and the task. The Klahr and Siegler work is perhaps the best example of the task-analysis approach described in the general orientation section. Note that one strength of this description is that it includes not only the formal structure of the way the child solves the problem, but also the demands of the experimental situation, for example, the nature of the feedback and the way the scale is presented. Since both the cognitive state and the situation affect performance, especially in children, it is important that they both be specified in any theory of problem solving.

Other researched areas of problem solving include planning, causal inference, analogy, tool use, and logical deduction (Siegler, 1991, Chapter 8). There are computer simulations of skills such as children's mathematical thinking (Siegler, 1987, 1988) and language acquisition (MacWhinney, 1987). Some work extends down to preschoolers. For example, a "dog–cat–mouse" problem presented to preschoolers requires moving each animal to its favorite food (Klahr, 1985). Only certain types of moves are permissible. Children's series of moves to place the dog with the bone, the cat with the fish, and the mouse with the cheese reveal their strategies of problem solving. Finally, much of Klahr's recent work examines the development of scientific reasoning strategies (e.g., Dunbar & Klahr, 1989). Children are presented with a programmable robot, taught how to operate it, and then asked to generate and test hypotheses about an additional feature of the robot.

INTELLIGENCE

Robert Sternberg's theory is an attempt to combine the best aspects of three frameworks. His focus on cognitive processes, capacity, and the time course of thinking, along with his careful task analyses, are in the tradition of the information-processing approach. The concern with individual differences reflects the psychometric (IQ testing, for example) approach. Finally, his interest in cognitive development and logical operations shows the influence of Piaget.

Sternberg (1985) characterizes intelligence as a set of components —elementary processes that operate on internal representations of objects, events, or symbols. There are three types of components: *knowledge-acquisition components* (described later), *performance components,* and *metacomponents.* When the child does not have the knowledge needed to solve the problem, knowledge-acquisition components obtain relevant information. The metacomponents, which are used in planning and decision making in task performance, then combine the new information with previous knowledge to construct an appropriate problem-solving strategy from among the performance components. The performance components then actually solve the problem. Thus, the metacomponents, much like the control processes and metacognitive processes described earlier, orchestrate the other two components into goal-directed behavior. Metacomponents perform duties such as deciding how best to allocate mental capacity to the other components during the limited time for problem solving, keeping track of what one has done, and deciding how to respond to feedback. If the child already has the understanding required for solving the problem, then only the metacomponents and performance components come into play.

As an example of the performance components, consider the following analogy problem used by Sternberg (1979): N.J.:N.Y.::N.H.: (a.R.I., b.N.D.). The better answer is R.I. The seven performance components for these types of problems include the following. The first involves *encoding,* identifying various attributes of the first two terms. For example, N.J. might be encoded as New Jersey and N.Y. as New York. Second, *inferring* specifies the relations between the first and second term; for example, both are abbreviations, are states near each other, and begin with N. Third, in *mapping* the person compares the encoded attributes of the first and third terms; for example, both are states and begin with N. Fourth, *application* carries the relations identified earlier to the third term and each of the possible answers. R.I. has the proximity relation; N.D. starts with N, but N stands for "North" rather than "New." Fifth, *comparison* involves comparing and contrasting the possible answers. Sixth, *justification* entails comparing the better answer (based on proximity) with one's notion of the ideal answer to decide whether the chosen option is good enough. And seventh is *responding.*

Although school-age children and adults use the same performance components to solve analogy problems, they differ in their allocation of cognitive resources to the various performance components (Sternberg & Rifkin, 1979). For example, adults spend more time encoding the terms than they spend in the subsequent steps. Seven-year-olds do the opposite. High-IQ children are more like adults in this respect.

The knowledge-acquisition components appear to provide a striking difference between average and intellectually gifted children. Gifted children are particularly adept at *selective encoding* (differentiating relevant and irrelevant information), *selective combination* (integrating information in a meaningful way), and *selective comparison* (relating newly encoded information to knowledge the child already has). More than average individuals, gifted persons are able to use these skills to deal with novel situations in insightful, original ways. Sternberg supported this claim in a study with insight problems such as this one:

> You have black socks and blue socks in a drawer, mixed in a ratio of 4 to 5. Because it is dark, you are unable to see the colors of the socks that you take out of the drawer. How many socks do you have to take out of the drawer to be assured of having a pair of socks of the same color?

> *[1986, p. 213]*

Selective encoding is necessary for detecting that the ratio of the socks is irrelevant. Regardless of the ratio, taking out three socks would insure that a pair of socks was obtained.

The other two knowledge-acquisition components can be illustrated by examples of insight among famous scientists. Selective combination was crucial to Darwin's ability to combine facts, known to him for years, into a coherent framework that became his theory of evolution. Insight based on selective comparison can be seen in the chemist Kekulé's dream about a snake curling back on itself and catching its tail. Upon awakening he realized that this image was a metaphor for the structure of the benzene ring.

With respect to development, all three types of components become more available, accessible, and easily executed. In an older child or an expert, the increasing automaticity of the components in a particular domain frees capacity for other tasks. Sternberg proposes that retarded children have poor automaticity. If they are not able to automatize subskills such as recognizing letters or words, the higher-order skills needed for smooth reading will be very slow to develop. Probably the most important developmental change lies in the metacomponents, particularly in the acquisition of strategies for using one's information-processing skills. For example, inadequate metacomponents can be seen when young children or retarded children choose the wrong performance and knowledge-acquisition components for their strategies or do not shift to an alternate strategy if the chosen one is not successful.

Sternberg calls his theory a "triarchic theory of intelligence" because it includes three subtheories. The *componential* subtheory refers to the components of intelligence described earlier. The *experiential* subtheory involves the abilities, discussed earlier, to deal with novel demands and to automatize information processing. The *contextual* subtheory emphasizes the cultural context of thinking. That is, intelligent behavior is social and practical behavior; it is adaptive in particular real-world environments and is influenced by social–cultural forces. For example, intelligent people actively select an environment that draws on their strengths or helps them compensate for their weaknesses. Examples of Sternberg's tests for everyday intelligence are asking subjects to identify real couples and fake couples in photographs or assessing their knowledge about career management. This broad, complex theory of intelligence has developed far from its start in Sternberg's seventh-grade science project in which he constructed an IQ test that has been referred to as the "less-than-widely-used Sternberg Test of Mental Abilities" (*American Psychologist*, 1982, p. 74).

COMMENT

It is time to summarize these sections on memory, representation, problem solving and intelligence. Although model building in developmental psychology is far behind that in adult psychology, progress has been made. An adequate developmental model must do the following:

1. Account for both verbal and nonverbal representations

2. Express, through depth-of-processing, "stage" (sensory register, short-term store, long-term store), or some other type of model the operation of both involuntary and deliberate memory

3. Specify the workings of the control processes, including strategies

4. Describe the interplay between memory, capacity constraints, strategies, metamemory, and the knowledge system with its rules and organization

5. Identify and describe the organization of rules or mental components that underlie problem solving and intelligence

6. Account for the development of all these aspects of the information-processing system by specifiying self-modification processes and their links to biological and environmental influences

The information-processing approach has contributed several new languages for representing the thinking of adults and children. As Siegler (1986) notes, although any type of information can be described by any of the four languages, each language is most appropriate for certain types of information. Semantic networks are most useful for modeling declarative knowledge (general world knowledge and basic concepts). Production systems and flow diagrams usually model procedural knowledge (how to play tennis, solve balance-scale problems, or do math problems). Finally, scripts are most useful for representing abstract event sequences such as everyday social events.

MECHANISMS OF DEVELOPMENT

Klahr and Wallace have voiced the research priorities of the field of information processing in children: "A theory of transition can be no better than the associated theory of what it is that is undergoing that transition" (1976, p. 14). Stated differently, "One never sees transitions, only by-products of transitions; so the empirical snapshots provide a major source of support for theories of transition" (Klahr, 1984, p. 106). Thus, the first task is to describe carefully each step in the acquisition of a concept, such as each of the four models shown on page 266. Only then is it possible to identify the sorts of mechanisms that might cause the change. Most of the research programs outlined in the previous section have followed this sequence. At first, researchers compared processing at different ages. Some research programs are still at this descriptive level, while others have begun to look at mechanisms of development.

Investigators have identified both general and specific sources of changes in processing. Two general sources of change are the acquisition of particular cognitive skills and increases in capacity or rate of processing. Cognitive skills that may bring about changes in the way information is processed include the child's growing knowledge about various aspects of the physical and social world, knowledge about memory and other mental phenomena, representational abilities, and higher-order cognitive operations such as those suggested by Piaget. Eight-year-olds faced with memorizing the multiplication tables—the ultimate terror of the third grade—have certain aids unavailable to 5-year-olds. They possess the underlying mental operations, such as the necessary "groupings" in Piaget's theory, that provide a meaningful framework in which to fit the rote memorizing. Also they have more experience with abstract concepts, quantities of objects, addition, and so forth, in their daily lives. Finally, as they study the tables, they can rehearse the items, look for relationships in the materials ($6 \times 8 = 8 \times 6$), perhaps monitor their own progress through self-testing, and so on.

The other proposed general mechanism of development, increases in capacity or rate of processing, is much more ambiguous. It is difficult to differentiate, experimentally, increases in absolute capacity or rate of processing from increases in the efficiency of processing through the skillful use of strategies or the automatizing of mental processes. The more automatic (less effortful) a process, the less capacity it requires. Consequently, capacity is made available for other processes. Increase in either total capacity or in the efficiency of a constant capacity may provide new possibilities for the developing organism (Case, 1985; Pascual-Leone, 1970).

A satisfactory account of developmental change must go beyond these general mechanisms and identify specific mechanisms of change. Investigators have used two main techniques to study specific mechanisms of development: training studies and self-modifying computer programs. Training studies that have brought about changes in processing suggest that changes in development may come about through certain kinds of experiences. The experiences include encountering conflict between different predictions, becoming more familiar with the task materials, trying out a strategy that works, and acquiring more knowledge about the physical and social world. These experiences lead to new rules or strategies, which in turn lead to better (or at least different) memory, representation, and problem solving. For example, Siegler (1978) found that teaching children what information to encode (both distance and number of weights) enabled them to learn from feedback regarding their predictions on the balance scale and subsequently to adopt new rules for problem solving.

A much smaller group of psychologists has used computer simulation to look at mechanisms of development. Although most computer simulations have simply (or not so simply!) described the behavior of children of various ages, recently there have been attempts to describe how changes in thinking occur. Most of these models have come from studies in which subjects learn during a short period of time, the experimental session. However, in principle, similar models could describe developmental changes over longer periods of time (Klahr, 1982).

Klahr (1984) has proposed that learning occurs when children analyze their stored record of previous behavior and its results. This analysis involves such principles as detection of regularity, elimination of redundancy, organization of subsystems according to their similarity and relatedness, and global rather than refined processing in the initial stages of processing. These principles could lead the child to develop new rules for solving the problem, strengthen certain old rules, generalize old rules, and restrict the situations in which an old rule is used

(Klahr, 1989, in press). More specifically, the child compares several related experiences (sequences of events), extracts a common feature from these events, and generalizes this feature to other related situations (Klahr, 1984). A very simple example is that on many occasions a child might count objects, move them, count them again, and compare the results of the two countings. The type of objects and the type of transformation would vary, but the constancy of the number before and after the transformation would be common to the situation. This rule gradually becomes more general to include, for example, larger numbers. Finally, redundancy is eliminated, for example, by removing the second counting because it is not needed if the objects are only moved. For more complex examples and a fuller account of these and other principles of change, the reader is referred to Klahr (1984, in press). The essence of these principles is that they reflect the operation of a self-modifying system. The system works on itself to produce change.

Klahr argues that it is crucial to develop specific, explicit, formal accounts of mechanisms of transition, in contrast to vague verbal statements: "For 40 years now, we have had *assimilation* and *accommodation,* the mysterious and shadowy forces of equilibration, the 'Batman and Robin' of the developmental processes. . . . Why is it that after all this time, we know no more about them than when they first sprang upon the scene?" (1982, p. 80). The information-processing approach probably has better theoretical equipment for achieving this goal of *specific* accounts of cognitive change than do other theories.

POSITION ON DEVELOPMENTAL ISSUES

HUMAN NATURE

In an update of Newton's view that humans are machines, humans are now computers. (Presumably, children are microcomputers.) In this mechanistic view, we have input followed by a series of events and finally output. Although the information-processing approach is mechanistic in that it posits input–output machinelike devices, it is organismic in its emphasis on overall organization and on an active organism. The ultimate goal of information-processing models is to characterize the organization of cognitive processing into a system, not just an aggregate of parts. Information-processing theorists believe that this holism is achieved by control processes that organize and direct the varied cognitive components. Most adherents to the information-processing point of view do not, however, posit the tightly knit, organized set of underlying logical mental operations proposed by Piaget.

Like social learning theory, the information-processing approach has been criticized for positing a passive organism (Shaw & Bransford, 1977). However, this criticism is probably unfair to most investigators. This undeserved reputation for positing passivity may come from the models and metaphors of information processing. Flow diagrams seem to portray static structures nudged into activity by intruding arrows, and a computer must wait for environmental input. And, robots aside, computers and flow charts typically do not move themselves and never ask questions of adults, call a friend, or select a good book to read. There certainly is nothing inherent in the information-processing approach that would call for a passive organism. It is true that people react to input in what has been called "bottom-up processing"—from the stimulus "up" to the higher levels of the cognitive system. And when processing is automatic, the organism can be characterized as passive. However, there is also "top-down processing" as long-term memory interprets the input, applies rules and strategies, searches for further information in the environment, or even "constructs" information as it makes inferences based on the input and on previous knowledge. Humans are also active in that they are self-modifying cognitive systems (but, as described earlier, some computer programs have this feature). People bring about their own learning and development, with help from experience with the environment, of course. In addition, children become more active cognitively with increasing age as they develop control processes to enhance their memory by rehearsing, making written reminders, and relating new information to old.

Finally, the theory is contextual only in its careful attention to the nature of the task situation in which the child is operating. There is little interest in the social content of information processing.

QUALITATIVE VERSUS QUANTITATIVE DEVELOPMENT

Information-processing theories allow for both qualitative and quantitative development. Most do not have the emphasis on the qualitative, stagelike development found in Piagetian and psychoanalytic theory, but they do identify more qualitative change than does social learning theory. Examples of qualitative development are the emergence of new strategies for storage or retrieval, rules for problem solving, or modes of representation (for example, verbal representation after language is developed). Quantitative development appears in increases in the number of items remembered, in the amount of information in semantic memory, in the number of strategies in one's repertoire, and in the increasingly efficient application of strategies. There is often interplay between quantitative and qualitative development, as when experience with weights leads to a new rule about balance scales, which then becomes more efficiently and consistently applied to a variety of situations.

NATURE VERSUS NURTURE

Unlike most developmental theories, information-processing theories focusing on children have had little to say about this issue. There has been more interest in specifying the exact interplay between information from the environment and the state of the processing system at one or several points in time than in unraveling the nature and nurture influences. However, the implicit view seems to be that the two influences interact to produce change. The impact of the environment is obvious as it continually brings input to the cognitive system. On the nature side, examples of important influences are that neurological development increases the efficiency of the transmission of neuronal impulses and that the visual system limits how long information can stay in the visual sensory register. Although there has been little interest in studying the role of biology in information processing, Klahr and Wallace (1976) suggest that the tendency toward economical, nonredundant, efficient processing is innate. Also, modularity theories (see the introductory chapter) propose that the processing system also may be pretuned to process certain types of stimuli, such as linguistic input. Promising recent work on neuropsychological aspects of adult cognition is beginning to influence developmental views of information processing (e.g., Diamond, 1990).

WHAT DEVELOPS

Stated most generally, cognitive processing develops. It becomes more efficient and organized in its operation and acquires more and more content as the child explores the world. More specifically, children acquire strategies, rules, scripts, representations, deeper levels of processing, or a broader knowledge base, depending on the particular approach. Another way to describe what develops comes from Brown (1975): "knowing" (development of knowledge about the world), "knowing about knowing" (metacognition), and "knowing how to know" (development of strategies). A major goal of current research is to map out the developmental relationships among these three areas.

THEORETICAL NATURE OF THE THEORY

Information-processing theories are characterized by the use of models. The computer model as a formal theoretical model or as a loose metaphor has formed the main theme of this chapter. The various information-processing approaches discussed share this computer model but vary in whether they use flow diagrams, tree diagrams, and computer programs or merely use computer language metaphorically to describe laboratory studies of memory, representation, and problem solving. For the first time in this book, we must consider the possibility that models can be used for inductive, deductive, and functional theory building.

Most information-processing psychologists find the computer metaphor useful for conceptualizing laboratory research on basic cognitive processes. Following the traditional role of empirical psychologists, they either collect data from related studies and stay close to the facts (inductive theory building) or, more commonly, go back and forth between data and hypothetical constructs, such as short-term memory (functional theory building). The much smaller group of information-processing psychologists that develops detailed flow diagrams or computer programs follows the functional or deductive mode of theory building. The approach is functional when flow diagrams, tree diagrams, or computer programs are developed, tested in light of the data, corrected, and tested again through many cycles. On the other hand, the approach can become deductive but in a new and curious way. Once all the psychological assumptions are stated in a formal language—a mathematical, logical, or computer language—the program can be "run" and thereby can generate the implications of or make deductions from these assumptions. Thus, a computer program can serve as a deductive theory. The possibilities of this approach are exciting because the computer can make the deductions much faster and more accurately than can humans.

EVALUATION OF THE THEORY

The information-processing approach to development not only dominates current laboratory research on cognition but also has spread to other areas. In social development, information-processing notions appear in Bandura's social learning theory and in accounts of the development of moral judgments (Leon, 1980), peer interaction (Dodge, 1986), and social scripts (Nelson, 1986). The study of the comprehension of stories or other texts, often called "discourse processing," also has a distinct information-processing flavor. Finally, some information-processing psychologists study reading and instructional techniques, with obvious relevance for the education of children.

Despite the growing influence of the information-processing approach to development, the theory is not often scrutinized with respect to its strengths and weaknesses as a *developmental* theory. The following evaluation considers the information-processing approach both as a developmental model or metaphor and as a method of research on development. The theory's strengths lie in its ability to express the complexity of thought, its specificity concerning performance, and its rigorous methodology. Its weaknesses include the shortcomings of the computer model, problems with addressing certain developmental issues, and a lack of concern with the context of behavior.

STRENGTHS

Ability to Express the Complexity of Thought

In Chapter 3, social learning theory was criticized for its overly simple account of thinking and learning. In contrast, the information-processing approach tries to specify a variety of cognitive processes, ranging from the simple detection of a stimulus to the development of complex rules. Furthermore, it attempts to characterize how perception, attention, memory, language, and abstract mental operations might be interrelated. The approach posits an intricate organization of thought in which control processes direct and supervise. For example, children learn to handle large amounts of information by "chunking" it or by relating it to what they already know.

Because both production systems and rules used to solve problems are often written for individual subjects, they can highlight subtle differences in how people of the same age process information. Thus, it is possible to study individual differences in problem solving and tailor instructional materials to fit the individual needs of students.

Specificity Concerning Performance

Perhaps the greatest strength of information-processing theories is that they make specific predictions about the child's behavior from moment to moment, based on a fine-grained analysis of the task and the current state of the child's cognitive system. This statement is especially true for computer-simulation programs, which attempt to specify all assumptions and relevant variables. Psychologists are forced to clear up any muddled theoretical thinking.

The Piagetian and the information-processing approaches have much in common. Both attempt to explain how more advanced concepts grow out of earlier, simpler ones—specifically, how a child's current cognitive system both constrains and permits the emergence of new knowledge. However, information-processing investigators attempt to be more explicit about *how* children use their cognitive skills in a given situation. This is a theory of performance, which, as mentioned in Chapter 1, is lacking in Piaget's theory. Information-processing theories describe how attention, memory, strategies, representational processes, and logical operations "connect" with tasks. For example, if the task requires a decision about relative weights, the information-processing approach would specify how the child selects certain information about the objects or the scale, encodes it, and applies rules from long-term memory. Piaget's décalages (asynchronies in applying a concept to different but related tasks or content areas) become less mysterious when investigators analyze the information-processing demands of each task (Baylor & Lemoyne, 1975). It is not surprising that tasks with different information-processing requirements elicit different behaviors. More generally, the information-processing approach emphasizes, more than does Piaget, processing limitations, strategies for overcoming these limitations, domain-specific knowledge about the task at hand, and specific behaviors involved in the process of change on a particular task (Siegler, 1991).

Rigorous Methodology

One outcome of the theory's specificity is that hypotheses generated by the theory are testable—a trait shared with social learning theory. Researchers use stringent and precise experimental methods. As one psychologist comments, "Many of us have become methodological behaviorists in order to become good cognitive psychologists" (Mandler, 1979, p. 281). Laboratory research on basic processing often makes precise measurements of processing time. More molar behavior and larger units of time are also examined under controlled conditions. Computer simulation requires that all relevant information about the task or child be stated in the programs. Gaps, contradictions, and vague statements are not permitted. The strict requirements demanded by computers are not easy to meet.

For developmental research, error analysis has proved to be a particularly powerful assessment procedure. By cleverly designing different types of problems, researchers have discovered two kinds of limitations in young children. One, illustrated by Siegler's balance-scale experiments, is that young children are using simpler, less complete rules, procedures, or strategies than are older children. The other limitation is different. Children basically are using the correct rule, but they have various "bugs" in the application of the rules, which lead to errors. For instance, after Brown and Burton (1978) used error analysis to detect bugs in students' application of the subtraction procedure, they wrote a computer program appropriately dubbed "Buggy," which taught prospective teachers to detect various bugs in their students' math work. One subtraction bug, for example, involves knowing how to borrow but not borrowing when the top number is zero.

WEAKNESSES

The preceding short section on strengths is followed by a much longer section on weaknesses. This imbalance does not necessarily reflect an abundance of weaknesses in the theory. Rather, most of the strengths were mentioned earlier in the chapter, whereas few weaknesses have been mentioned and must now draw our attention.

Shortcomings of the Computer Model

A basic problem with flow diagrams or computer program simulations is that these models may adequately describe human output (behavior), given knowledge of the input, but still differ in important respects from the way people think. For example, a computer program might process the information sequentially, while a child might process all the information simultaneously, and both could arrive at the same decision (output) in the task. Similarly, it is possible for different programs to predict performance equally well. This is one limitation to the generally good testability mentioned earlier. To help avoid the problem, Simon (1972) has proposed that models meet certain criteria. They should be consistent with what we know about the physiology of the nervous system and about behavior in tasks other than the one examined. They should also be sufficient to produce the behavior of interest, and they should be definite and concrete. Still, it can be difficult to judge the psychological validity of a model that meets these requirements.

Information-processing models have been very productive but, like all models, are subject to abuse. Information-processing psychologists have perhaps been overenthusiastic in adopting models. In particular, memory metaphors, which are much less formal and complete than flow diagrams and computer models, abound in the literature. Roediger (1979) points out that memory metaphors usually are spatial metaphors, implying that we "search" our mental space for objects stored in physical space. There almost seems to be a "homunculus" (little person) who rifles through the files of memory until he finds the necessary paper. In these files or in semantic networks, concepts are stored at different "distances" from each other. Even the levels-of-processing approach has us wandering deeper and deeper into the dark recesses of the mind. Examples of cognitive metaphors in Roediger's list include a workbench, a pushdown stack (of clean plates in a restaurant), an acid bath, a dictionary, and a subway map. In a spoof of memory models, Hintzman (1974) likened memory to a "cow's belly." Information (like food) is transferred from the "short-term stomach" to the "long-term stomach." In this way, we "ruminate" over ideas and "digest" information.

Memory metaphors are suggested by the technology of the times, beginning with Plato's notion that memory is like the impression of a seal on a wax tablet, which in his time was a method of storing information. Much later we find the gramophone, switchboard, tape recorder, computer, and holograph used as metaphors. It has even been suggested (Langlois, Cooper, & Woodson, 1985) that a bank automatic teller machine might be an appropriate metaphor for a child. It processes information, is somewhat interactive, and usually follows instructions but sometimes has a mind of its own! What metaphors will future technology bring? Today's computer metaphor may eventually seem as naive as Plato's wax tablet.

The use of such metaphors is not necessarily bad. They explain abstract cognitive structures and processes in terms of concrete objects already familiar to people. Furthermore, they have helped psychologists view cognition from a new perspective and have suggested new research. However, we should use them with caution because they are a potentially dangerous tool. As George Eliot cautioned: "We all of us, grave or light, get our thoughts entangled in metaphors, and act fatally on the strength of them." First, these metaphors, and even the more formal models, usually have excess meaning that was not intended. Thus, flow diagrams may make us erroneously think of memory as passive, spatially organized, unaffected by emotion, and unrelated to other cognitive processes. Moreover, because flow diagrams are necessarily spatial representations, they may be interpreted in spatial terms. It must be kept in mind that a model is similar only *in certain ways* to the phenomenon to which it is applied.

A second caution is that adopting a particular model may seriously limit our thinking. Once psychologists began to express memory as a series of discrete steps (boxes in a flow diagram), it took several years before the less discrete, more gradual levels-of-processing approach could be seriously proposed.

One problem specific to the computer-simulation models has to do with computer techniques. Undoubtedly the greatest impediment to the acceptance of this approach is the "language barrier." Although most psychologists use computers, few are truly bilingual, speaking both their native language and one of the computer languages used in simulations. It can take hours for the neophyte to wade through the detailed description in computer language of a 30-minute experimental session with one child. Part of the problem is that in order to be complete and to run successfully, the program must contain much that is psychologically trivial, such as which block is picked up first. Although the underlying explanation of the behavior may be elegantly simple, the superficial complexity may alienate many psychologists potentially sympathetic to the computer-simulation approach. As psychologists become even more familiar with computers, this problem may lessen.

Aside from the problem of comprehending computer programs, however, is the problem of writing them. Even people skilled in writing simulations are faced with a time-consuming, often tedious, task. One problem is that the obvious must be included in the program. An example (cited by Kendler, 1987) is a college campus computer dating program that contained much information about the students' interests and attitudes. The results were not considered successful by a brother and sister who were paired together. No one thought to instruct the computer that siblings should not be paired.

Another problem with computer models is that they tend to be highly specific, precise models of very limited, specific behaviors. Because they must consider all relevant variables, it is difficult to develop more general models that can run successfully.

Problems with Addressing Certain Developmental Issues

The information-processing approach has advanced our understanding of adult cognitive systems. How successfully has it addressed developmental issues? The introductory chapter proposed three tasks for a developmental theory: (1) to *describe* changes *within* one or several areas of behavior, (2) to *describe* changes in the relations *among* several areas of behavior, and (3) to *explain* the course of development that has been described. With respect to the first task, the information-processing approach rates high marks for its careful, refined descriptions of the memory system at various cognitive levels. An exception is that there is relatively little work on information processing in adolescents or infants and toddlers. Recent methodological advances in studying infants are beginning to show unexpected representational competence early in life. This neglect of infancy is unfortunate because, to be a viable developmental theory, the information-processing approach must describe preverbal, cognitively immature humans. It is important, for example, to know what kinds of nonverbal representations infants are capable of and why their recognition memory is so advanced. An important question for developmentalists is how these nonverbal representational systems and the later verbal representational systems are related developmentally.

With respect to the second task—describing relations among simultaneous changes in various areas—the information-processing approach has sketched out some of the relations among memory, language, higher cognitive processes, and perception in a limited way. These broad outlines require much filling in over the next few years. The most progress has come in the area of language and thought, for example, story comprehension, verbal rehearsal, and semantic memory.

The largest gap in fulfilling these first two tasks is the paucity of knowledge about the links between cognition and emotions, motivation, and social development. In principle, there is no reason why this should be so. Information about people, as well as objects, must be processed. Important questions about the relation between cognitive and socioemotional variables include the following: How do children's emotional states affect their learning at various ages? Are encoding and retrieval strategies applied to social as well as physical objects and events? Does acquiring social experience and developing social scripts provide a framework for attending to, encoding, interpreting, and storing social events? Freud observed rampant memory distortions and repressions of childhood experiences, but information-processing theorists have given little attention to these phenomena. Recent work on distortions in memory due to scripts and gender or racial stereotypes is promising in this respect. Focusing on physical concepts may be a reasonable initial strategy for a young theory, but this limitation should be recognized and eventually corrected. Fortunately, there is a growing interest in the intersect of information processing and social behavior (e.g., Dodge, 1986).

The third task—explaining development—poses difficulties for the information-processing approach, as it has for each of the theories already examined. Important forces of change have been identified, including broader encoding, strategy construction, an increasingly complex knowledge base, automatization of skills, detection of regularities, generalization, metacomponential processes, and elimination of redundancy. Still, developmental changes in these mechanisms themselves and accounts of exactly how the mechanisms operate to effect change are not well understood. For example, it is known that young children have strategy production deficiencies that disappear during the middle school years, but the causes of this production deficiency and its disappearance still elude investigators. Likewise, it is clear that strategies of problem solving become more sophisticated, but there is little information concerning the forces that propel this development. Although the developments of control processes and improved encoding appear to be important achievements for memory and problem solving, the information-processing approach has not yet explained how these developments come about.

Other problems also remain to be solved. Why are some dimensions, such as number of weights, easier for young children to encode than other dimensions, such as distance of the weights from the fulcrum? In natural settings, what causes children to encode previously ignored dimensions? Finally, it is not yet clear exactly how a complex, well-organized knowledge base enhances recall. The main problem is that the evidence is primarily correlational. An advanced knowledge base is associated with improved recall, but the causal relationship is not well supported (e.g., DeMarie-Dreblow, 1991). An advanced knowledge base may lead to a strategy such as chunking, to increased speed of access in semantic memory, to greater understanding of the goal of the task, or to improved attention to relevant information. Thus, the knowledge base is a global variable that needs to be specified further.

A central developmental issue is whether developmental change is the same as the novice-to-expert shift in adults. That is, is change in adults as they become more knowledgeable about an area equivalent to cognitive development in children? The theory's view of development is very closely tied to its view of change in adults. A child, in a sense, is a "universal novice" (Brown & DeLoache, 1978), lacking knowledge in more areas than adults do. One important difference is that when adults "learn" in an experimental session, they are simply learning to make efficient use of what they already know. For example, when learning to play chess, adults may grasp the rules by generalizing from other games they know and rearranging this previous knowledge to fit chess. Also, adults have more sophisticated strategies of learning that allow them to move from the novice to the expert stage more quickly and to generalize new knowledge to other situations. In contrast, much change in children is due to the acquisition of *new* rules, concepts, or cognitive skills, rather than the rearrangement of old ones. Before children can learn chess, they must develop the ability to mentally move the pieces according to certain rules, to form a cognitive map of the location of pieces on the board, and so on. It is not clear that studying change in adults elucidates these kinds of changes in children.

A related problem is that it is difficult to relate the short-term changes examined by information-processing psychologists to the long-term, stagelike qualitative changes postulated by Piaget. It may be that these seemingly revolutionary changes from stage to stage can be reduced to short-term quantitative changes if the level of analysis is refined enough. Or it may be that the information-processing approach will need to add some principles of functioning that cause major qualitative changes in cognitive organization.

A recent movement within the information-processing computer simulation framework addresses these issues of change. In the connectionist, or neural-network, approach (e.g., McClelland, 1989), models are computer simulations of cognitive procedures based on an analogy with the connections among neurons in the brain. These models depict learning, or development, as a process of strengthening some connections and weakening others as a result of experience. High-strength and low-strength connections exhibit "excitation" and "inhibition," respectively, analogous to characteristics of connections between neurons. A very large number of interconnected neurological processing units operate simultaneously—hence, parallel processing. A stimulus, such as a word, activates this network of strong and weak interconnections, producing a particular pattern of activated units. Consequently, the pattern of association strengths in the system is changed slightly. All of this may sound somewhat familiar because in a sense it is a more complex, "high-tech" version of learning theory's associationism (see Chapter 3).

Thus far few connectionist models have been constructed for developmental change in children. However, a recent model (McClelland & Jenkins, 1991) simulates rule acquisition on Siegler's balance-scale task, described earlier. It is too early to evaluate the contribution to developmental psychology of this new look in information processing. Certainly its concern with patterns of connections nicely supplements the concern with symbols in other information-processing approaches.

Lack of Concern with the Context of Behavior

Critics (for example, Neisser, 1985) have attacked information-processing psychologists' insensitivity to the natural context of behavior. The image of the child is of a "rational, decontextualized isolated mind with limited knowledge, without interests, without feelings, attitudes, or views of the world" (Sigel, 1986, p. 99). The information-processing approach has focused on the processing mechanisms the person brings to a task or setting and on the task parameters more than on the interplay between the demands or possibilities of the larger setting and the needs, goals, and abilities of the person. Moreover, information-processing-oriented cross-cultural work is rare. Shaw and Bransford point out that "we tend to forget that humans and animals are active, investigatory creatures driven by definite intents through a complex, changing environment replete with meaning at a variety of levels of analysis" (1977, pp. 3-4). They argue that the passive, purposeless computer provides a sterile model for human cognition. Similarly, several developmentalists (Brown, 1978; Meacham, 1977) have pointed out that memory is an activity applied to the child's goals in real-life settings. This ecological attitude toward knowledge can be expressed as follows: "Ask not what's inside your head, but what your head is inside of" (Mace, 1977).

The field appears to be belatedly moving into its natural-history phase. Whereas most theories begin with observations of people in natural settings, information processing began in the laboratory, with research in artificial situations. Only recently has it begun looking at context effects and more realistic and ecologically valid materials and tasks (e.g., Resnick, Levine, & Teasley, 1991). Information-processing psychologists can now be found studying reading, sign language, conversations, stories, social behavior in natural settings, and memory for events occurring years earlier. Sternberg's theory of intelligence, for instance, considers social influences and the fit between a person's intelligence and the demands of everyday life.

Many of the weaknesses of the information-processing approach can be summed up in James Anderson's conclusion about what a reader would conclude about the mind after reading a recent 904-page book surveying cognitive science: "Minds talk a lot . . . they move a little, they see a little, but they don't feel much else" (1991, p. 287).

SUMMARY

The information-processing approach studies how human symbol-manipulation systems, of limited capacity, work. Investigators take the computer program as a model—either as a metaphoric heuristic device or as a way of simulating and testing their views concerning the nature of human thought. There are developmental changes in how children attend to, represent, store, and combine information. These changes occur at various points in the system: the sensory store, short-term memory, and long-term memory. Much of this development occurs via self-modification, as children formulate rules of decision making and modify them as a result of feedback. Investigators often begin by performing a task analysis. They then either formulate a computer program simulating how the child solves a problem or stores information or test the efficiency of the child's processing by conducting experiments.

Humans are limited in how much information they can process at a given time and in how fast they can process this information. Much of development involves learning how to overcome these limitations by acquiring efficient control processes. Research on memory, the most-studied area of development in information processing, shows that much of memory development is caused by the acquisition of strategies, the growing store of domain-specific knowledge, increased meta-memory, and greater functional capacity.

Changes in the representation of information and the rules for problem solving also alter the processing of information. These highly dependent changes in memory, representation, and problem solving are closely connected to other aspects of cognitive change, such as the growing knowledge of the world and the acquisition of the Piagetian mental operations. Intelligence can be seen as the efficient and insightful application of information-processing components.

Mechanisms of development, such as encoding, generalization, strategy construction, and automatic processing, cause more efficient processing (Siegler, 1991). Information-processing theorists view humans as active, organized, self-modifying systems. Development involves both quantitative and qualitative change and both genetic and environmental influences. The essence of development is an increasingly efficient system for controlling the flow of information.

The strengths of the theory are its ability to express the complexity of thought, its specificity concerning performance, and its rigorous methodology. Weaknesses involve certain shortcomings of the computer model, problems with addressing certain developmental issues, and a lack of concern with the natural context of behavior.

SUGGESTED READINGS

The following books describe current research on specific topics in memory, attention, and problem solving.

Kail, R. (1990). *The development of memory in children* (3rd ed.). New York: W. H. Freeman.

Siegler, R. S. (1991). *Children's thinking* (2nd ed.). Englewood Cliffs, NJ: Prentice-Hall.

For a look at programs of research directed toward the computer simulation of children's thinking, the reader is referred to the following sources.

Klahr, D. (1992). Information processing approaches to cognitive development. In M. H. Bornstein & M. E. Lamb (Eds.), *Developmental psychology: An advanced textbook* (2nd. ed.). Hillsdale, NJ: Erlbaum.

Rabinowitz, F. M., Grant, M. J., & Dingley, H. L. (1987). Computer simulation, cognition, and development: An introduction. In J. Bisanz, C. J. Brainerd, & R. Kail (Eds.), *Formal methods in developmental psychology: Progress in cognitive development research*. New York: Springer-Verlag.

5

ETHOLOGICAL THEORY

*At the beginning of these experiments, I had sat myself
down in the grass amongst the ducklings and, in order
to make them follow me, had dragged myself, sitting,
away from them. . . . The ducklings,
in contrast to the greylag goslings, were most demanding and tiring charges, for, imagine a two-hour walk
with such children—all the time squatting low and
quacking without interruption! In the interests of
science I submitted myself literally for hours on
end to this ordeal.*
[LORENZ, 1952, p. 42]

*The initial phase, that of protest, may begin immedi-
ately or may be delayed; it lasts from a few hours to a
week or more. During it the young child appears acute-
ly distressed at having lost his mother and seeks to
recapture her by the full exercise of his limited resources. He will often cry loudly, shake his cot, throw himself about, and look eagerly towards any sight or
sound which might prove to be his missing mother. . . .
During the phase of despair, which succeeds protest,
the child's preoccupation with his missing mother is
still evident, though his behavior suggests increasing
hopelessness. The active physical movements diminish
or come to an end, and he may cry monotonously or
intermittently. He is withdrawn and inactive, makes no
demands on people in the environment, and appears to
be in a state of deep mourning.*
[BOWLBY, 1969, p. 27]

D
evelopmental psychologists have not taken Shakespeare's advice, "Neither a borrower, nor a lender be." Some of the most fruitful ideas about development have been borrowed from other areas of psychology and even other sciences. Ethology is one example of this. Ethology is the study of the evolutionarily significant behavior of a species in its natural surroundings. As a subdiscipline of biology, it looks at the biological and evolutionary blueprints for behavior.

The theory had its start years ago with European biologists and naturalists and eventually reached developmental psychologists in the last few decades via John Bowlby's studies of infant attachment. Ethological theory now provides the main theoretical foundation for the evolutionary perspective on development.

As Rousseau observed, "One needs to look near at hand in order to study men, but to study man, one must look from afar." Ethology places humans in a broad context, the animal world. It is humbling to contemplate the fact that there are more species of insects in a square kilometer of Brazilian forest than there are species of primates in the world (Wilson, 1975). The English geneticist Haldane, when asked about the nature of God, is said to have remarked that he displays "an inordinate fondness for beetles." The human species is just one small part of the huge, evolving animal kingdom. We are one of an estimated three to ten million species.

This chapter focuses on the implications of ethology for human development. It must be emphasized that most ethological research examines nonhuman species. How comfortably psychologists can apply concepts from animal research to human behavior is a controversial issue we return to later.

The chapter begins with a history followed by a general orientation. After that comes a section on main contributions of ethology to human developmental psychology and then sections on mechanisms of development, the theory's position on developmental issues, the theoretical nature of the theory, and evaluation.

HISTORY OF THE THEORY

Ethology is linked to the German zoologists of the 1700s and 1800s who studied innate behaviors scientifically. The concept of evolution was strengthened by Darwin's painstaking observations of fossils and variations in plant and animal life. He, along with Alfred Wallace, was forced to conclude that nature ruthlessly selects certain characteristics because they lead to survival: "What a book a devil's chaplain might write on the clumsy, wasteful, blundering, low, and horribly cruel works of nature" (Darwin, quoted in Shapley, Rapput, and Wright, 1965, p. 446). As a result of this selective force, species changed and sometimes were differentiated into subspecies. Thus, many animals, including humans, are related through common ancestors. Darwin proposed that intelligence and other behaviors, as well as physical structures, were products of evolution. If they increased the chances of survival, they were retained; if they did not, they disappeared. Darwin's claim of a common ancestry of humans and other primates was not received well in Victorian England: Montagu (1973) related an anecdote about a shocked wife of an English bishop. She said that she certainly hoped that the theory was false, but if it were true, that not many people would find out about it.

Darwin's careful observing and cataloguing of plants and animals were imitated by ethologists years later. Just as he carefully described animal and plant life, he also described his own infants' behavior, as in the following excerpt on fears:

> Before the present one was 4 1/2 months old I had been accustomed to make close to him many strange and loud noises, which were all taken as excellent jokes, but at this period I one day made a loud snoring noise which I had never done before; he instantly looked grave and then burst out crying. . . . May we not suspect that the vague but very real fears of children, which are quite independent of experience, are the inherited effects of real dangers and abject superstitions during ancient savage times?
>
> *[1877, p. 289]*

Ethology as a distinct discipline began in the 1930s with the European zoologists Konrad Lorenz and Niko Tinbergen. They developed, often in collaboration, many of the key concepts discussed in the next section. Tinbergen describes this new approach as having "started as a revolt by young zoologists against the dead animal" (Cohen, 1977, p. 316). Ethologists saw animals as active organisms living within a particular ecological niche, not as passive organisms prodded by stimuli, as in the tradition of learning theory. Their studies of species as diverse as ducklings, butterflies, and stickleback fish gave scientific meaning to the sometimes mystical term *instinct*. Many of Lorenz's observations were of wild animals that wandered freely in and around his home. Lorenz and Tinbergen's work was honored with the Nobel Prize in

Medicine or Physiology in 1973, which they shared with another ethologist, Karl von Frisch. For psychologists, Eibl-Eibesfeldt's work (1975, 1989), beginning in the 1950s and continuing in the present, is especially important, for he was one of the first to make a formal connection between psychology and ethology. This link with psychology fueled an interest in ethological accounts of human behavior.

Ethology has continued to influence studies of behavior in Europe and, more recently, has had an impact in the United States. The ethological perspective guides both observational and laboratory studies, including both neurobiological–physiological and behavioral studies. In recent years, ethology has become closely aligned with comparative psychology, which emphasizes laboratory research on various animal species, to form a new synthesis in North America. Work on such topics as how infant rats find the nest by odor, how monkeys interact with their peers, and how mammalian mothers treat their infants immediately after birth combines experimental and observational methods. This work is more empirical and experimental and less speculative and theoretical than the earlier European "classical" ethological studies. The focus now is on the immediate causes of the behavior—for example, scent or temperature—rather than the evolutionary origins of the behavior. Observation, however, continues to play an important role and has become scientifically respectable: "To have made 'inspired observation' respectable again in the behavioral sciences is, I believe, a positive achievement of ethology" (Tinbergen, quoted in Cohen, 1977, pp. 323–324).

Part of the broad appeal of ethology is due to popularized accounts accessible to the general public. *The Naked Ape* (Morris, 1967), *The Territorial Imperative* (Ardrey, 1966), and *On Aggression* (Lorenz, 1966) proposed exciting ideas about innate causes of human behavior but have been criticized for exaggerating the biological influence on human social behavior.

Today there are several closely related, even overlapping, biological approaches to studying behavior: psychobiology, physiological psychology, behavioral evolution, comparative psychology, behavioral neuroscience, behavioral ecology, sociobiology, and of course ethology. The word "developmental" could be placed in front of each label. Among the various approaches there is a tension between two viewpoints. Some approaches favor a reductionist approach and study cells, neural impulses, and hormones. Others focus on the behaviors of the whole organism and tend to consider the organism in its ecological niche (Dewsbury, 1991). Ethologists and comparative psychologists tend to fall in the latter category.

Sociobiology has become almost synonymous with ethology. *Sociobiology* is defined by its main spokesman, E. O. Wilson, as the "study of the biological basis of all social behavior" (1975, p. 4). Although these two fields overlap a great deal, sociobiology focuses on species and on social structures, such as customs, rituals, schools, and the legal system, rather than on the individual. Sociobiology considers how individuals' behavior affects not only their own chances for survival but also those of their kin. The field is a hybrid of ethology, ecology (the study of how organisms are related to their environment), genetics, and population biology. Sociobiologists' work on such topics as reproductive patterns, altruism, parenting, and social hierarchies is beginning to influence developmental research (MacDonald, 1988).

Developmental psychology was receptive to ethology because developmentalists have a tradition of observing children (e.g., Barker & Wright, 1955) and considering the biological basis of development (Gesell, 1945; G. S. Hall, 1904). Many developmentalists continued to observe children even through psychology's behaviorist years. The most important figure to bring ethology to the attention of developmental psychologists was John Bowlby. His turn from a Freudian to an ethological account of infant–caretaker social attachment in the 1950s in England laid the groundwork for subsequent research in this area in both Europe and North America. (His work is described later.) More recently, ethologically oriented psychologists have extended the approach to other areas of infant behavior, for instance, facial expressions and biases toward looking at certain objects, such as faces. With older children, the work focuses on peer interaction. It is interesting that one of the founding fathers of ethology, Tinbergen, has studied autistic children and interpreted their behavior as an extreme fear response to being looked at by other people (Tinbergen & Tinbergen, 1972).

Currently, developmental psychologists are quite interested in biological influences more generally. Recent books (e.g., Carey & Gelman, 1991; Gibson & Petersen, 1991) have addressed biologically based research on many areas of development, including language, infant cognition, and early social development.

It should be noted that much of the recent animal research by North American ethologists and comparative psychologists is developmental. This research on maternal and newborn behaviors in animals is beginning to influence human developmental research. The importance of human and animal developmental research has been expressed as follows: "The developmental point of view is basic to an understanding of how evolutionary and ecological parameters are achieved in individuals and groups. The gap between molecular biology and natural selection will be filled by developmental analysis of the nervous system, behavior, and psychology" (Gottlieb, 1979, p. 169). The study of the development of behavior is "the backbone of comparative psychology. Shortcomings in its study inevitably handicap other lines of investigation, from behavioral evolution and psychogenetics to the study of individual and group behavior" (Schneirla, 1966, p. 283).

GENERAL ORIENTATION TO THE THEORY

Ethology is characterized by four basic concepts: (1) species-specific innate behavior, (2) an evolutionary perspective, (3) learning predispositions, and (4) ethological methodology. The theoretical notions described here are based primarily on "classical" ethology, that is, on the contributions of European ethologists, particularly Lorenz, Tinbergen, and Eibl-Eibesfeldt. These contributions have influenced ethological accounts of human development more than have recent related approaches such as sociobiology or psychobiology. However, the latter approaches are likely to become increasingly influential on human developmental research.

SPECIES-SPECIFIC INNATE BEHAVIOR

An animal lacking "instincts" altogether would be a complete slave of conditioning.

[Ghiselin & Scudo (1986, p. 194)]

Innate behaviors are considered similar to organs of the body, in that both are essentially the same in all members of a species, are inherited, and are adaptive (Lorenz, 1937). Just as physical structures are under genetic control, so are certain behaviors. Although no physical structures or behaviors are completely innate, because they are always expressed in a particular environment, ethology emphasizes the biological contributions to behavior.

Ethologists generally agree that a behavior is innate if it has these four characteristics (Cairns, 1979):

1. It is stereotyped in its form (that is, has an unvarying sequence of actions) across individuals in a species.

2. It is present without relevant previous experience that could have allowed it to be learned.

3. It is universal for the species (that is, found in all members).

4. It is relatively unchanged as a result of experience and learning after it is established.

For example, in certain songbirds the same song appears in all members of the species at sexual maturity, even if they have never heard the song sung by other members of the species. As this example illustrates, some innate behaviors are not present at birth and appear later as a result of physical maturation. In contrast to innate behaviors, learned behaviors, such as chimpanzees' use of sticks as "tools," vary in form from individual to individual, require relevant previous experience, usually vary in their occurrence among members of the species, and change as a result of subsequent experience.

Innate behaviors are termed *species-specific,* which means that they occur among all members of the species or at least a particular subgroup, such as all the males or all the young. If other species also have the behavior, two inferences are possible. One is that the two species are related, perhaps having split into separate lines at some point in their evolution. That is, they have common ancestors. The other possible inference is that the behavior has evolved independently in the two species, perhaps because they had similar physical environments and needs. For example, in many species the young cling to the mother's fur—a necessity for survival if the infant must travel with its mother as she moves throughout an area in search of food or flees from predators. Conclusions about similar behaviors in different species must be drawn cautiously, not only because they may have evolved independently, but also because the behaviors may have different meanings or functions in the two species. An example is tail wagging in dogs and cats.

Two types of innate behaviors, reflexes and fixed action patterns, have particular relevance for humans. *Reflexes,* simple responses to stimuli, have long been familiar to psychologists. Examples from the human infant are grasping a finger placed in the hand, spreading the toes when the bottom of the foot is stroked, and turning toward a nipple when it brushes the cheek. Any long-haired parent would agree with ethologists' interesting observation that infants are particularly likely to grasp hair, especially during feeding. Ethologists speculate that this reflex originally served to facilitate clinging to the mother's fur. Many of these reflexes are quite strong. A premature baby can grasp a clothesline and support its own weight, for instance. This ability is later lost. More complex reflexes in newborns or young infants are coordinated swimming, crawling, and walking movements when the body's weight is supported.

Classical ethology (Lorenz and Tinbergen) emphasized fixed action patterns. A *fixed action pattern* is a complex innate behavior that promotes the survival of the species. It is a "genetically programmed sequence of coordinated motor actions" (Hess, 1970, p. 7) that arises from specific inherited mechanisms in the central nervous system. Examples are squirrels burying nuts, birds performing courtship "dances," spiders spinning webs, and stickleback fish fighting to protect their territory. Fixed action patterns can become very elaborate, as when the male bowerbird spends hours building a love nest decorated with flowers, fruit, shells, and colorful beetles to attract a mate. He adjusts a twig here, adds a flower there, and seemingly stops to admire his work from time to time. The adaptive value of these fixed action patterns is that they often end in eating, mating, or protecting the species from harm.

A fixed action pattern is elicited by a *sign stimulus*—a particular stimulus whose presence automatically releases the fixed action pattern. Lorenz (1966) likens this process to a key opening a lock. An example is when the red belly of a male stickleback fish venturing into another stickleback's territory triggers fighting behavior. A decoy that only vaguely resembles the stickleback in shape but is red on its lower half elicits this fixed action pattern, whereas an accurate decoy without the red area usually does not (Tinbergen, 1951). Thus, the sign stimulus is specific and sometimes must be in a particular orientation or position. Tinbergen (1958) discovered this particular sign stimulus when he noticed that his sticklebacks in an aquarium near a window facing a street would become agitated at a certain time of the day. He eventually realized that a red mail truck passed by at that time, a stimulus that approximated the natural sign stimulus. A further example of the specificity of the sign stimulus is that a hen will not rescue a distressed, flailing chick she can see under a glass bell but cannot hear. However, she will rescue the chick immediately if she can hear the distress cries even if she cannot see it (Brückner, 1933).

When the sign stimulus is an appropriate exaggeration of the normal sign stimulus, it encourages the fixed action pattern. Fishermen take advantage of this fact by using lures that exaggerate the natural prey (the sign stimuli) of the larger fish.

The ease with which a sign stimulus elicits the fixed action pattern depends on a second facilitating factor—*action-specific energy*. According to Lorenz, energy for each of several drives gradually builds up in the central nervous system. This energy creates a readiness to act or a certain "mood." The need to discharge this energy periodically is met when the fixed action pattern occurs and thereby releases the energy. The longer the period of time since the behavior last occurred, the greater the buildup of energy and the more likely the sign stimulus will release the behavior. If the pressure becomes very great, the behavior can occur even without the sign stimulus. This is sometimes seen in animals kept in captivity, as when a hand-fed starling with no experience at hunting prey attacks invisible insects and appears to kill and swallow them (Lorenz, 1937). Another example is that the female rat is in such a state of readiness to retrieve her young shortly after birth that if no young are present, she will repeatedly grasp her own tail or one of her hind legs and carry it back to the nest (Eibl-Eibesfeldt, 1975). A human example is that infants who do not get enough opportunity to suck during feeding because the hole in the nipple is too large will cry and make sucking movements even when no object is in the mouth (Spitz, 1957).

When drives operate simultaneously, ambivalent behavior results. For instance, the male stickleback fish's zigzag courtship dance is actually a result of two conflicting drives. The "zig" toward the female is due to the aggressive drive, whereas the "zag" away from her is motivated by a desire to lead her to the nest in order to mate. According to Lorenz (1966), this behavior has become ritualized into the innate courtship behavior of the species.

This buildup and release of biologically based energy is similar to Freud's conception of drives. In addition, in both theories this energy can be displaced toward an object other than the intended target, as in displaced aggression. Whereas Freud is concerned with sexual and aggressive drives, Lorenz (1966) refers to the "big four" drives: hunger, reproduction, aggression, and flight. These drives are expressed through a number of specific fixed action patterns, such as sucking, nest building, attacking, and running. More recently, many ethologists have dropped the notion of drive completely. They argue that the concept is not a useful one because it is not easily tested, is confusing, and leads to simplistic explanations of behavior.

The concept of fixed action pattern has also been modified in several ways (Beer, 1973; Dewsbury, 1978). For instance, research has found that many fixed action patterns are more variable than originally thought. They are now sometimes called "modal action patterns." Furthermore, part of the requirement that the sign stimulus must be specific actually reflected the nature of the sensory system rather than innate mechanisms in the central nervous system. Finally, displacement activities may have alternative explanations, such as the removal of inhibitions from common behavior.

Innate reflexes and fixed action patterns have developmental significance. These behaviors permit young infants' survival, either by allowing them to seek food and hide from predators on their own or by binding them to an adult caretaker through behaviors such as crying, grasping, sucking, or smiling. For example, the infant greylag gosling calls "wi-wi," especially when alone, and elicits a reassuring reply from its mother. Furthermore, with physical maturation come new behaviors such as nest building, which allow even further adaptation to the environment. This fit between the organism's needs and the innate behaviors it possesses is not accidental but the product of the long evolutionary history of its species.

The emphasis on innate behavior directed by drives should not leave the impression that ethologists think learning is unimportant. Rather, most ethologists simply argue that it is necessary to describe and understand innate behavior before studying how it is modified by the environment. Most behavior is viewed as an interweaving of innate and learned components. A raven innately knows how to build a nest, but through trial and error learns that broken glass and pieces of ice are less suitable than twigs for this purpose (Eibl-Eibesfeldt, 1975). An innate skill can easily be adapted to new situations, as when English titmice quickly learned how to use innate gnawing behaviors to open milk bottles. The survival value of this interweaving of innate and learned behaviors is clear.

Even a primarily learned behavior can contribute to survival. An example comes from Lorenz's description of how a learned act, "shaking hands," becomes an appeasement gesture:

> Who does not know the dog who has done some mischief and now approaches his master on its belly, sits up in front of him, ears back, and with a most convincing "don't-hit-me" face attempts to shake hands? I once saw a poodle perform this movement before another dog of whom he was afraid.
>
> *[1950, p. 178]*

EVOLUTIONARY PERSPECTIVE

> A chicken is just the egg's way of making another egg.
>
> *[Anonymous]*

> A simple day of one's life, nay even any individual life as a whole, is but a minute blow of the chisel at the ever unfinished statue [of evolution].
>
> *[Schrödinger, 1958, p. 11]*

Evolution involves phylogenetic change, or change in a species over generations, in contrast to ontogenetic change, or developmental change in a single lifetime. Darwin's evolutionary theory is as follows: given that there is variation among members of a species and given the nature of the environment of the species, certain variations are more likely to survive than others. Because characteristics have a genetic basis and surviving animals are those who reproduce, the most adaptive characteristics are passed on to offspring. There have been changes in the specifics of the theory, particularly in light of modern molecular genetics, and also disagreements such as whether evolution can involve sudden changes. However, the basic notions have not changed since Darwin's time.

From an evolutionary perspective, humans are an experiment in nature. A person is viewed "as though seen through the front end of a telescope, at a greater than usual distance and temporarily diminished in size, in order to view him simultaneously with an array of other social experiments" (Wilson, 1978, p. 17). Each species, including humans, is a solution to a problem posed by the environment. These problems include how to avoid predators, how to obtain food, and how to reproduce.

The course of development within an individual follows a pattern that was acquired by the species because it facilitated survival. Just as certain physical characteristics, such as the upright stance and the hand with opposable fingers and thumb, facilitated making and using tools, so did certain behaviors—reflexes and fixed action patterns—facilitate survival through mating, food gathering, caretaking, and so forth. Social behaviors, such as interindividual communication and cooperation, encourage group cohesion and thereby increase the chances of survival. Darwin saw the "struggle for existence" and the "survival of the fittest" operating at the level of observable behavior as well as in bodily structures. New behaviors arose through natural genetic variations or mutations and, if they allowed the organism to survive long enough to reproduce, were genetically transmitted to the next generation. These successful behaviors gradually became more common in the whole population over many generations.

Inferring the course of evolution is not as simple as it seems, however. It is not always obvious what the survival value of an innate behavior is. For example, a behavior may lead to the death of individuals but increase the survival of relatives or other members of the species. When an individual bird spots a predator, it gives a warning call to the flock, thus attracting the predator's attention and endangering the bird's life. The flock, however, survives. A further complication is that many existing behaviors, such as many of the reflexes in the human infant, are no longer necessary for survival; they are relics. Many of the early arguments about evolution illustrate the dangers of armchair speculation in this area. It was once claimed that flamingos are pink because that makes it difficult for predators to see them against the sunset (Thayer, 1909).

We cannot overemphasize the importance of evolutionary theory in ethological thought. When ethologists ask why a particular behavior occurs, they are mainly asking how that behavior facilitates adaptation to the environment, and therefore survival, for that species. This type of explanation is not seriously sought by any other major theory of development (but see Gibson's theory in Chapter 6). Most theories seek explanations for development in the learning experiences or the physical maturation of individuals during their lifetimes. Thus, ethology provides a broader context for viewing development.

LEARNING PREDISPOSITIONS

The biological control of behavior can be seen not only in innate behaviors acquired during evolution but also in predispositions toward certain kinds of learning. To a great extent the brain is "like an exposed negative, waiting to be dipped into developer fluid" (Wilson, 1975, p. 156). Species differ in which aspects of their behavior are modifiable, in what kinds of learning occur most easily, and in the mechanisms of learning. Learning predispositions include sensitive periods and general or specific learning abilities. *Sensitive,* or *critical, periods* are specific periods when the animal is biologically ready to acquire a new behavior. During those times, the animal is especially responsive to particular stimuli and has certain behaviors that are particularly susceptible to modification.

The most popular ethological example of a sensitive period comes from Lorenz. Shortly after birth, usually in the first day or two, certain birds (for example, geese) are most able to learn the distinctive characteristics of their mother and therefore their species. During this sensitive period, the young learn to follow a stimulus and come to prefer that stimulus—a phenomenon called *imprinting.* Imprinting increases the survival of the young because it ensures that they stay close to the parent and therefore near food and shelter and far from predators and other dangerous situations. The stimulus to be followed must meet certain criteria, for example, it must make a certain call note or type of movement. The particular criteria vary from species to species, but the mother always meets the criteria. In the wild, a row of ducklings scurrying after their mother is a common sight. However, as Lorenz discovered, certain "unnatural" objects also meet the criteria. Young birds have become imprinted on flashing lights, electric trains, moving milk bottles, and a squatting, quacking Konrad Lorenz (see the excerpt at the beginning of this chapter). Horses and sheep have also become imprinted on humans. Lorenz considered imprinting critical because he thought it was irreversible; a duckling imprinted on a flashing light does not become imprinted on its real mother if she appears for the first time after the end of the sensitive period.

In many species, imprinting has a long-term effect on sexual behavior. Lorenz (1931) discovered that jackdaws raised by humans will join a flock of jackdaws but return to their first love, a human, during the reproductive season. They try to attract the human with their species' courting patterns.

Sensitive periods have also been identified for behaviors such as learning bird songs, learning to distinguish males and females of the species, developing a social relationship with humans, and forming a bond between the newborn and the mother. In the last case, for example, mother goats form a bond with their young in the first five minutes after birth. If the young are removed right after birth for two hours, the mother attacks them upon their return. Waiting five minutes after birth before removal, however, leads to their acceptance later (Klopfer, 1971).

The notion of a sensitive period has evolved somewhat in recent years. The statement that can be made with most confidence is that how experience affects the organism depends on the stage of development at which the experience occurs (Bateson, 1978). More specific sensitive periods, such as a clearly demarcated time for imprinting, seem to exist only in certain species, and sensitive periods can differ greatly even among closely related species. Moreover, there is disagreement whether the length of the sensitive period is determined solely by a genetic mechanism or is affected somewhat by the animal's experiences as well (Hess, 1973). For example, it may be possible to produce imprinting even after the sensitive period has ended if the appropriate stimulus is exposed for a long enough time (Bateson, 1973). Thus, it is clear that sensitive periods are much more complex than was originally thought. For a recent discussion of sensitive periods in human developmental psychology, see Bornstein (1989).

Sensitive periods involve learning predispositions: in the case of imprinting, the young bird is biologically pretuned to notice certain types of objects, sounds, or movements, yet it links up a response to this stimulus as a result of experience, that is, of seeing the object and following it. Thus, biology prepares the bird to learn from experience. The learning involved in imprinting or other behavior acquired during sensitive periods should not be confused with operant conditioning (discussed in Chapter 3). Imprinting is acquired with no reinforcement; it even increases when punishment in the form of an electric shock occurs, and it resists extinction.

The concept of a sensitive period, in a general sense, has been applied widely in developmental psychology. Its implications for human infant attachment are discussed later. Most generally, the sensitive period supports the argument that early experience is particularly important for adult behavior, as suggested by Freud and many researchers of early development. Furthermore, all stage theories claim that at each stage the child is particularly sensitive to certain experiences, such as motor exploration in the sensorimotor period (Piaget), the meeting of one's needs by other people in the stage of trust versus mistrust (Erikson), and the satisfaction or deprivation of anal drives during the anal stage (Freud). Most nonstage theories also use the concept of readiness—the idea that a child is most likely to learn from an experience if it comes at the optimal time. A child may not profit from being shown how to put objects to be remembered into categories when she is 3 years old but may have increased recall as a result of this experience at age 6. Finally, it should be noted that sensitive periods are a central notion in embryological development. A particular drug taken by a pregnant woman will have no effect or a devastating effect on the fetus, depending on its stage of development.

In addition to sensitive periods, a second way in which biology indirectly controls behavior is found in *general and specific learning skills*. Particularly in humans, the genetic endowment includes a tremendous general ability to learn from experience. As Lorenz (1959) noted, humans are "specialists in nonspecialization." We have evolved a central nervous system that is capable of flexible thinking, hands that can perform many different actions, and a language system that permits symbolic thought and verbal communication. The advantage of this flexibility is that the organism can adjust to a changing environment. There is less reliance on fixed action patterns for survival, especially during adulthood. Another way in which a general learning ability is tied to innate factors is the ability to learn via reinforcement and punishment. This ability to be affected by the consequences of one's behavior must be built into the nervous system.

As a result of humans' biologically based general ability to learn, we have developed cultures to help us adapt. The culture is picked up by the next generation by imitation and other forms of learning. Thus, even cultural adaptation has its biological origins.

General learning abilities are complemented by specific learning skills, each applied to a particular domain, such as the representation of spatial locations. Specific learning skills reflect the fact that an organism does not learn everything equally easily. Each species has its own bias toward certain kinds of learning. Contrary to the claims of classical learning theory, it is not the case that all responses are equally easily conditioned to all stimuli. Specific learning skills are easily identified when various species are compared. The digger wasp, during its morning inspection of up to 15 nests, decides how much food is needed by each nest and retains the information for the entire day. A well-known example of an amazing specific memory skill is the ability of salmon to return to their spawning ground by remembering the odor of the waters in which they were born. Rats, which normally live in burrows, learn to make their way through a psychologist's maze faster than herons and frogs (Eibl-Eibesfeldt, 1975). Wild rats quickly learn, after an unfortunate experience, to avoid poisonous bait (Barnett, 1963). When new bait is presented, rats will eat very small quantities and, if they fall ill, avoid the bait. Even within a particular type of learning—for example, visual discrimination and recognition—learning may be specialized. For instance, herring gulls learn to recognize their own chicks but not their own eggs, even though the eggs have distinctive markings that could easily be recognized (Tinbergen, 1951). Humans also have specialized learning skills. Chomsky (1965) and others have claimed that human infants are pretuned to process and acquire language. The rapid acquisition of language early in life, the culturally universal forms of early utterances, and the occurrence of babbling in infants born deaf all point to this conclusion.

An interesting footnote to animal learning comes from Lorenz, who suggests that once a behavior is learned, deviating from it often causes great fear. He offers the following anecdote to illustrate this point. A greylag goose that lived in Lorenz's room had developed a routine for entering the house every evening. At first she had always walked past the staircase to a window before climbing the stairs. This detour was shortened until she merely turned toward the window at the foot of the stairs instead of going over to it. One evening Lorenz forgot to let the goose into the house. When he finally remembered as darkness approached, the goose ran in and immediately ascended the stairs:

> Upon this something shattering happened: Arrived at the fifth step, she suddenly stopped, made a long neck, in geese a sign of fear, and spread her wings as for flight. Then she uttered a warning cry and very nearly took off. Now she hesitated a moment, turned around, ran hurriedly down the five steps and

set forth resolutely, like someone on a very important mission, on her original path to the window and back. This time she mounted the steps according to her former custom from the left side. On the fifth step she stopped again, looked around, shook herself, and performed a greeting display behavior regularly seen in greylags when anxious tension has given place to relief. I hardly believed my eyes. To me there is no doubt about the interpretation of this occurrence: The habit had become a custom which the goose could not break without being stricken by fear.

[1963, p. 112]

Methodology

Ethologists rely on two general methods for studying behavior: naturalistic observation and laboratory experimentation. Their particular version of naturalistic observation ranks as one of their main contributions to psychology. On the other hand, laboratory experimentation is probably used in the majority of present-day ethological studies. Both are necessary to the theory.

Naturalistic Observation

Methods influence theories. Rather than observe animal learning in the wild, learning theorists observed bar pressing in rats and table tennis in pigeons in the lab. These could hardly be considered typical species-specific behaviors. It is unlikely that interesting natural behaviors, such as defending a territory or building a nest, would occur often in barren laboratory cages. In contrast, ethologists emphasize naturalistic observation and thus are more likely to attend to such behaviors.

Naturalistic observation is closely tied to the three characteristics of the theory mentioned earlier. If one wants to describe species-specific innate behaviors or learning predispositions that evolved because they led to survival in that species' natural habitat, there is no substitute for observing animals in their typical environments. In particular, the function of a behavior can be understood only if one sees how it fits into the species' natural environment in order to satisfy the animal's needs. Giraffes' long necks make sense when they are observed eating leaves from tall trees; young gulls' innate "freezing" rather than fleeing in the face of danger is understandable when one notes that their nests are built on narrow ledges or steep cliffs (Eibl-Eibesfeldt, 1975).

Observations of animals in captivity are inadequate because their behavior may be abnormal. One cause of abnormal behavior in this setting is that animals are usually healthier in their natural environments and therefore are more likely to behave in ways typical of their species. Another cause is the absence of sign stimuli that would release fixed action patterns. Thus, behavior is often redirected. Particularly in the older zoos, where most animals are in cages, we see restless pacing back and forth, constant rocking, and killing of the young by the mother. These abnormal behaviors can often be avoided by a simple change in the environment. For example, an armadillo in the Amsterdam zoo made various abnormal, stereotyped movements until a layer of dirt was placed on the floor of its bare cage. The animal could then bury itself at night when it slept (Eibl-Eibesfeldt, 1975). Ironically, giving too much care to the animal may cause problems. Titmice in a zoo threw their young out of the nest soon after birth. The problem was that food was too readily available. The young quickly became full, stopped gaping, and consequently were taken for dead by the parents. Young titmice in the wild never stop gaping unless they are sick or dead because the parents must hunt for food and the infants are never full (Koenig, 1951). In the human, abnormal behavior— for example, rocking—has been observed in children in unnatural environments such as orphanages and hospitals.

Ideally, ethologists follow a particular sequence of steps when studying an organism.

1. They develop an *ethogram,* an extensive, detailed description of the behavior of a species in its natural environment. An ethogram is like an inventory or a catalog. It includes the animal's behaviors, the characteristics of the environment, and the events immediately preceding and following each behavior. Of interest are not only the types of behaviors—for example, nesting and food gathering—but also their frequency, stimulus context, function, and ontogenetic development. Psychologists have been particularly oblivious to the frequency of a behavior in natural settings. The problem of not having scientific data about frequency was noted long ago by Thorndike: "Dogs get lost hundreds of times and no one notices it or sends a scientific account of it to a magazine. But let one find its way from Brooklyn to Yonkers and the fact immediately becomes a circulating anecdote" (1898, p. 4).

It is as important to describe the environment as it is to describe the organism's behavior. In fact, a complete description of the setting essentially defines the animal that inhabits it: "If we specify in detail the niche of a fish (its medium, its predators and prey, its nest, etc.), we have in a way described the fish" (Michaels & Carello, 1981, p. 14).

The descriptive labels must be refined until two or more observers can agree, in nearly every case, regarding what behavior occurred and when it began and ended. Did the child smile or grimace, and for how long? When a behavior is described, a main concern is with the structure of that behavior: what elicits it, what the components are, in what order these components appear, and what ends the behavior. Note that these "raw data" in the ethogram are not totally unbiased observations. The observations typically focus on fixed action patterns that have evolved as an aid to survival. Furthermore, ethologists historically have been particularly interested in observing fixed action patterns that involve social behavior.

2. They classify these behaviors according to their function, that is, which drives they serve or how they encourage survival. These categories—such as caretaking, mating, and defending territory—serve as working hypotheses rather than immutable facts. As one investigator has observed, "The investigator of behavior is faced with a potential paradox in that categories of behavior must be formed . . . but these categories are unlikely to be either homogeneous (i.e., indivisible) or mutually exclusive (i.e., functionally independent) on refined analysis. Stated briefly, and without much exaggeration, categories of behavior *must be formed,* but the investigator *must not believe them*" (Fentress, 1973, p. 163).

3. They compare how a given fixed action pattern functions in various species and how a given need is met by various fixed action patterns in different species. Of special interest are similar fixed action patterns in closely related species. If several closely related species of birds have a similar courtship dance, they may have a common ancestor. Such species comparisons, along with changes in behavior inferred from fossils (for example, an increase in brain size), provide evidence about the evolutionary course of a behavior.

4. They use laboratory experiments to determine the immediate causes of the behavior described in the first three steps. From the viewpoint of ethologists, psychology has worked backward historically by performing laboratory research before obtaining a sufficient data base of naturalistic observations.

Ethologists increase the power of the observational method by filming or videotaping their observations. There are two advantages. First, filming permits repeated viewing of the same behavioral sample. Thus, it is possible to compare how various observers describe the behavior. Do they agree that a particular facial expression in an infant is a smile? Do they agree that the courtship of a particular species of bird always begins by hanging upside down? Interobserver agreement increases our confidence in the observations. Multiple viewing also allows a single observer to return to an earlier observation to check a hypothesis formed after observations of many individuals. After observing many human babies, an investigator may notice that they seem to be less fearful of strangers when strangers kneel down than when they stand. By viewing all of the observations again, this hypothesis can be checked.

The second advantage of filmed observations is that the action can be sped up or slowed down. When this is done, previously unnoticed patterns of behavior sometimes emerge. For example, a flirting look often involves raising the eyebrows for only one-sixth of a second—a movement that becomes a noticeable invariant part of the flirting sequence only when the film is slowed down (Eibl-Eibesfeldt, 1975). By speeding up films, investigators have noted that people who eat alone look up and around after every few bites, as if scanning the horizon for enemies, as baboons and chimps do (Eibl-Eibesfeldt, 1975). This is much less obvious at a normal camera speed.

Filming humans poses special problems because their awareness that they are being filmed is likely to change their behavior. The one-way mirror, which makes unobtrusive filming possible in the laboratory, is obviously of little use in field settings. Eibl-Eibesfeldt has made use of one clever solution to this problem. A mirror prism inserted in his camera allows camera operators to point the camera at a right angle to the target. Subjects know the camera is present but do not think they are being filmed.

Laboratory Studies

For an ethologist, a behavior has both a phylogenetic cause and an immediate cause. A spider spins a web "because" that innate food-gathering behavior has allowed the species to survive. In addition to this phylogenetic cause, various types of immediate causes can be identified. Spinning a web may be caused by specific physiological events, particular inborn neurological pathways, the presence of a sign stimulus, certain aspects of motor experience, and so on. These various causes of behavior suggested by the observational studies can be clarified by controlled experiments.

The classical ethological experiment is the *deprivation study,* which determines whether a behavior is innate or learned. In this method, the animal is deprived of specific experiences that could be relevant to the behavior of interest. Obviously, the organism is not deprived of broad aspects of experience—a procedure that would cause widespread disruption of behavior or even physical deterioration. As an illustration of the deprivation study, an ethologist interested in the origin of nut-burying behavior raised squirrels in isolation in a cage with a bare floor and provided a diet of only liquid food. The squirrels had no exposure to other squirrels (who could serve as models), nuts, or earth (which could provide digging practice). Under these conditions, squirrels demonstrated a stereotyped sequence of nut-burying behaviors at the same age as do squirrels in the wild. When presented with a nut at this time, they ate until satiated, then dug an imaginary hole in the concrete floor, pushed the nut into the hole with their snouts, covered it with invisible soil, and carefully patted down the "soil" to finish the job (Eibl-Eibesfeldt, 1975). Thus, since there was no opportunity to learn this behavior, it must be an innate fixed action pattern of the species.

Other ethological laboratory experiments are not different in method from those of comparative psychology or physiological psychology. They clarify which variables influence behavior and what the underlying physiological mechanisms are. For example, by systematically varying stimuli, researchers can determine which attributes of a stimulus are critical for eliciting the response. The experiments examine a variety of responses, ranging from pupil dilation (which indicates interest or attraction) to the amount of time spent near the stimulus. Although the laboratory experimental method is shared with the mainstream of experimental psychology, ethology maintains its distinctiveness by the content it chooses to study: behaviors tailored to the survival of the species.

CONTRIBUTIONS TO HUMAN DEVELOPMENTAL PSYCHOLOGY

Ethologists are interested in the same categories of adaptive behaviors in humans as in other animals: for example, feeding, communication, parent-child interaction, and reproduction. However, there is no unified ethological view of development. Instead, particular topics have been selected by ethologically oriented psychologists. The study of children has focused primarily on infant attachment but has examined the organization of peer interaction, facial expressions, bodily movements, and problem solving. A look at representative research in each of these areas will show ethology's imprint on both the content and the methodology of developmental research.

INFANT–CARETAKER ATTACHMENT

Bowlby's Theory

John Bowlby, a London psychoanalyst, is credited with bringing ethology to the attention of developmental psychologists. His observations of infants separated for a long time from their mothers led him to conclude that an early social "attachment" between infant and caretaker is crucial for normal development. A disrupted relationship between mother and infant often leads to the infant's protest, then despair, characterized by grief and mourning, then detachment, and finally, in some cases, psychopathology (see the excerpt at the beginning of this chapter). Evidence for the attachment bond in normal situations includes protest when the parent leaves and greeting behaviors, such as smiling and babbling, when the parent returns. Children also seek their attachment figure when under stress.

Drawing on observations of mother–infant bonding in nonhuman primates, Bowlby (1969) proposed that attachment to a caretaker has evolved because it promotes the survival of helpless infants by protecting them from predators or exposure to the elements. Separation of the infant from its mother can be a fatal error in many animals. At birth and throughout early development, infants have a biological predisposition to maintain proximity to adults of the species. In animals other than humans, the young often use the mother's odor or the warmth of the nest to keep in contact with her (Moltz & Leon, 1983; Rosenblatt, 1976). Many of the human newborn's reflexes served this function during human evolution. One of these reflexes is grasping an object such as a finger or the hair when it contacts the infant's palm, just as many mammalian infants stay with the mother by clinging to her hair. Another reflex is an embracing movement in response to a sudden loud sound or a loss of support. This reflex may have prevented many ancestral infants from falling when the mother suddenly ran upon seeing a predator.

Of course, these reflexes have little value for attachment in human infants, who need not physically attach themselves to the parent in order to survive. Of more importance to human newborns are signaling mechanisms such as crying, babbling, and smiling—both the spontaneous "gas" smile present in newborns and the true "social" or "answering" smile that emerges several weeks later. These behaviors communicate the infants' needs and encourage the adult to come to them. The infants' immature motor system is compensated for by these signaling abilities. Just as following the imprinted object in ducklings maintains proximity, so do signaling behaviors serve this purpose in humans. The result is the same. The infant is protected and nurtured. These signaling behaviors are more complex than the simple reflexes and are often considered to be fixed action patterns. As the infant matures, other behaviors, such as crawling, walking, and talking, facilitate contact between parent and child.

There is support for Bowlby's notion that signaling behaviors are innate. Even infants born blind or blind and deaf acquire a social smile at approximately 6 weeks, as do normal infants. In fact, children blind and deaf since birth reveal a wide range of normal behaviors, including laughing, crying, babbling, and pouting, and typical facial expressions of fear, anger, and sadness (Eibl-Eibesfeldt, 1975, 1989). For example, they throw back their heads when laughing and stamp their feet when angry. Thus, these naturally occurring "deprivation experiments" show that visual and auditory experiences that would allow imitative learning are not necessary for these signaling or expressive behaviors to develop. Further evidence for the universality of the human smile and other expressions comes from observations of these behaviors in infants in many cultures (see Eibl-Eibesfeldt, 1975, for a review). Darwin long ago observed smiling in infants of every culture with which he had contact.

It is highly unlikely that these expressive behaviors could be taught to these normal infants or to blind and deaf children. Smiling and laughing involve a complex sequence of coordinated movements or sounds. Eibl-Eibesfeldt (1975) describes a deaf and blind 12-year-old with severe brain damage who was unable to learn simple actions such as bringing a spoon to her mouth, in spite of an intense training program. Yet she was able to smile, laugh, and cry. Even the possibility that blind and deaf children might learn facial expressions by touching the mother's face and imitating those movements was ruled out by a child deaf and blind since birth, who was born with no arms. Despite these handicaps, he showed normal facial expressions.

Bowlby proposed four principles, quoted below, which account for the development of the infant's bias toward humans in general and attachment to a particular adult, the caretaker:

1. An in-built bias toward looking at certain patterns in preference to others and at things that move

2. Exposure learning, by which the familiar comes to be distinguished from the strange

3. An in-built bias to approach the familiar (and later to withdraw from the strange)

4. Feedback of results, by which a behavioral sequence is augmented when it is followed by certain results and diminished when it is followed by others (1969, p. 273)

As a result of these principles of development, the attachment to adults in general evolves, usually around 6 to 9 months of age, into attachment to one or a few specific adults. This specific attachment can be seen in the infant's protest when separated from a particular adult, as opposed to all adults. This separation is an innate "cue to danger" that elicits signaling behavior intended to restore proximity.

The infant and adult behaviors eventually become synchronized into an "attachment behavioral system," according to Bowlby. The appearance and behavior of each member serve as sign stimuli for the fixed action pattern in the other. Each member of the system comes to expect that the other will respond to its own behavior in certain ways. Children's expectations are part of their "internal working models"—mental representations of the attachment figures, the self, and the relationship (Bretherton, 1991). These models help children to interpret and evaluate new situations, then choose a behavior such as playing or seeking the attachment figure for comfort. When infants' expectation that the parent will respond to their cries or calls (their basic trust, in Erikson's theory) is shattered by weeks or months of absence of the parent, anxiety arises. Infants' distress, angry protest, and rejection of others eventually turns into grieving for the lost parent and general detachment from humans. After a period of grieving, infants may develop new specific attachments.

Between the ages of about 9 and 18 months, an infant's various individual behaviors, especially sucking, clinging, crying, smiling, and following, become incorporated into more complex, self-correcting "control systems." These systems have the goal of maintaining an acceptable proximity to the mother. Control systems are described later in the chapter.

Bowlby's theory of attachment includes many of the characteristics of the general theory of ethology. Species-specific reflexes and fixed action patterns, which are the products of evolution, ensure the proximity of the mother to the child. Lorenz's drives, however, are not used in the theory. Sensitive periods and general and specific learning abilities biologically predispose infants and caretakers to develop a system of synchronized interactions. Bowlby goes beyond general ethological theory by suggesting that a control system regulates the distance between the child and the caretaker. In keeping with ethological theory, Bowlby relies heavily on observations of children and animals. However, much of the observational research on attachment stimulated by his theory was conducted in laboratory settings. Mary Ainsworth developed methods for assessing attachment and conducted much Bowlby-inspired resarch in this area.

The ethological account of attachment, with its focus on innate behaviors, obviously contrasts with learning theory's focus on the reinforcement value of food (or, in later versions, other stimuli, such as warmth and physical contact), which establishes the mother as a secondary reinforcer. Although it seems likely that pleasant interactions have a positive effect on the bond between child and adult, ethologists point out that attachment occurs even when the attachment object physically abuses the infant. Ethology also differs from Freudian theory in accounting for attachment. Although some ethologists think that drives are involved in attachment, these drives are not primarily sexual in nature. Finally, ethology differs from both traditional learning and Freudian theory in stressing the infant's effect on the parent as much as the parent's effect on the child.

Bowlby (1980) has incorporated into his theory some of the notions of information-processing theory. Unsatisfactory early social relationships, abnormally strong repression, and thinking disorders can be explained in part by general principles of selective attention and selective forgetting. For example, if young children's attachment behavior is continually aroused but not responded to, they eventually exclude from awareness the sights, thoughts, or feelings that normally would activate attachment behavior.

Bowlby continually applied his ideas about attachment to his clinical work. Interestingly, his final book (1991), a biography of Darwin, traces Darwin's chronically poor health back to his failure to fully mourn his mother's death when he was 8 years old.

Adults' Responsiveness to Infants

One of the most important contributions of the ethological account of attachment is that adults, as well as infants, are biologically predisposed to develop attachment. In species in which infants depend on parents for survival, innate caretaking responses in adults should be retained over the course of evolution. Adult attachment behavior can be elicited by signaling behaviors or by the infant's babyish appearance. Many infants emit calls to which the parent responds. For example, ultrasonic sounds from a young mouse elicit nest-building behavior in the adult female mouse (Noirot, 1974). Human signaling behaviors, such as smiling, visually fixating the face, and babbling, elicit the parent's attention and interest.

The idea that the infant's babyish appearance also elicits caretaking was proposed by Lorenz (1943). He noted that the infants of many species, especially mammals, share certain physical characteristics, which are depicted in the illustration below. These characteristics include a head that is large in relation to the body, a forehead that is large in relation to the rest of the face, limbs that are relatively short and

Characteristics of babyishness or cuteness common to several species. [From "Die angeborenen Formen möglicher Erfahrung," by Konrad Lorenz, in Zeitschrift für Tierpsychologie, 1943, 5, 235-409. Reproduced by permission of Verlag Paul Parey.]

heavy, large eyes at or below the midline of the head, and round, prominent cheeks. This description is simply an objective description of what is better known as cuteness. This babyishness is exaggerated in baby dolls for children and in young animals in the Disney cartoon films. Interestingly, Gould (1980) has observed that as Mickey Mouse became more lovable and well behaved over the years, his physical appearance became more babyish—a larger head with softer, more rounded features and larger eyes.

Studies of adults' and children's responses to pictures of infants or to live infants have included physiological measures (pupil enlargement or changes in heart rate), behavioral measures (amount of interaction with the infant), or self-reports (rating the attractiveness of faces). This research shows that people respond positively to infant faces. For example, 12- and 13-year-old girls who had begun menstruation rated pictures of infants more positively than did boys of the same age. In contrast, girls who had not begun menstruation did not differ from boys in their ratings (Goldberg, Blumberg, & Kriger, 1982). However, the responsiveness to the infants is not always greatest among females or during the childbearing years. The pattern of results depends on the type of response measure used, the physical and social nature of the testing situation, the person's experience with young children, and the person's cultural background (Berman, 1980). Thus, social factors, such as cultural expectations, appear to play at least some role in responsiveness to infants. Interpretation is also clouded by the fact that infants as young as 4 months also prefer looking at babies to looking at children or adults (McCall & Kennedy, 1980).

Research Stimulated by Bowlby

Now that Bowlby's and Lorenz's accounts of human attachment have been described, we turn to recent empirical work on human attachment. Bowlby's portrayal of attachment stimulated novel and important research. Psychologists studied attachment from Uganda to Scotland to university laboratories in Baltimore.

The caretaker forms an emotional bond to the child in the first few hours or days of life. This *bonding* encourages caretaking and thus enhances survival. One of the most exciting discoveries from attachment research is that there may be a sensitive period for bonding during the first few hours after birth. It is tempting to draw an analogy with the sensitive period for imprinting in birds. Klaus and Kennell (1976) compared two groups of mothers and newborns. A control group followed usual hospital procedures, that is, a look at their babies at birth, brief contact at 6 to 8 hours, and 20 to 30 minutes of contact every 4 hours when they fed their infants. An "extra-contact group" was given their nude babies for 1 hour of contact in the first 2 hours after birth and for 5 extra hours, compared with the control group, on each of the following 3 days. At the babies' examination 1 month later, the mothers from the extra-contact group held and soothed the infants more, showed more eye contact and fondling when they fed the infants, and reported that they were less likely to leave the infants with another caretaker, in comparison to the control group. The differences were still present at 1 year. By 5 years of age, children in the extra-contact group had higher IQ and language-test scores. Although there is disagreement about the replicability, methodological adequacy, and proper interpretation of this research (Myers, 1984), the research does point to the importance of events occurring shortly after birth.

A different body of research points out the infant's bias toward attending to people early in life. Newborns prefer to look at human faces rather than inanimate objects. By the third week, the infant gurgles and makes various "pleasure sounds" in response to the sound of the human voice. Interpretations of this early predisposition toward social stimuli must be made very cautiously, however. On the one hand, social stimuli may constitute sign stimuli that elicit the infant's innate responses. On the other hand, the responses may be mediated by the infant's preference for stimuli that are complex or involve movement and high black-white contrast (with respect to the eyes, hairline, and the like). Of course, this preference may be due to the nature of the nervous system and ultimately may be as biological as the first explanation (see Cohen & Salapatek, 1975, for a discussion of these issues). Another type of facial preference is infants' preference for female faces that have been rated by adults as attractive rather than unattractive (Langlois et al., 1987).

Infants also appear to be predisposed to learn to discriminate their mother's odor from that of others. Two-week-old breast-fed infants turned toward a pad that had been worn in their mother's underarm area rather than a pad worn by some other lactating female (Cernoch & Porter, 1985). Just as infants can recognize their mother's odor, so do mothers quickly recognize their infant's distinctive smell. Six hours after giving birth, and after only a single exposure to their babies, blindfolded mothers could pick out, by smell alone, their own baby from a set of three babies (Russell, Mendelson, & Peeke, 1983).

One of Bowlby's colleagues, Ainsworth (1973), focused on the role of the attached parent as a "secure base" for exploration. The parent is a secure home port from which children venture to explore the next room or the next block and to which they return from time to time for "emotional refueling" (Mahler, 1968). If, however, the responses to children's signaling behaviors are inappropriate (unpredictable, slow, abusive, or not matched to the child's needs), children feel insecure and are less likely to use the mother as a base for exploring a strange environment (Ainsworth, 1973). Lamb (1978) also stresses the appropriateness of the adult's responses rather than the total amount of interaction. Thus, infants become attached to fathers who respond appropriately to the child's signals, even when the total amount of time spent with the father is small.

Ainsworth (e.g., Ainsworth, Blehar, Waters, & Wall, 1978) devised a "strange situation" to assess toddlers' patterns of attachment to their mothers. The child, a parent, and a stranger in a laboratory setting proceed through a sequence of episodes, gradually moving from low stress (child with parent) to high stress (child with stranger in parent's absence). Based on their reactions to these events, children are classified as securely attached, avoidantly attached, or ambivantly attached to their parent. The dyad's type of attachment depends on many factors, including the parent's sensitivity to the child's needs and stresses in the family (e.g., Ainsworth et al., 1978; Sroufe, 1985). The pattern of attachment predicts later child behaviors, such as social functioning in preschool (Sroufe, 1983).

A further controversy surrounds the issue of how parental physical abuse of the infant affects the attachment bond. After reviewing the effects of maltreatment of infants of various nonhuman species, Rajecki, Lamb, and Obmascher (1978) concluded that there is no evidence that maltreatment interferes with the development or maintenance of the social bond. Although this result seems to be counter to common sense, it makes some sense within an ethological framework. Physical assault causes distress in infants, which leads them to seek proximity to their attachment figure, even when that figure is the source of the abuse. On the other hand, as Rajecki and colleagues point out, child abuse would not seem to be the "ordinarily expectable environment" for which evolution prepares the child. Perhaps abusive parents have other behaviors, such as feeding, clothing, and stimulating the child, that promote survival.

The work on attachment spearheaded by Bowlby has grown to include not only the above issues, which are closely tied to ethology, but also much broader questions about early social relations. These topics include fear of strangers, individual differences in the course of attachment, the role of cognitive development in attachment, sex differences in parent–child attachment, temperament and attachment, and multiple attachments (day care, a kibbutz, peers, and fathers). In addition, attachment now is viewed as a lifelong process of forming affectional bonds with various people (Ainsworth, in press; Parkes, Stevenson-Hinde, & Marris, 1991). For the most recent work on attachment and early social development more generally, see Bretherton (1991) and Gewirtz and Kurtines (1991).

PEER INTERACTION

Ethologists argue that children are innately predisposed towards interacting with other people in adaptive ways (Eibl-Eibesfeldt, 1989). Children's social interactions involve not only the family, especially the parents, but also the peer group. Ethological studies of animals' dominance hierarchies, aggression, play, altruistic behavior, and nonverbal communication led naturally to observations of these behaviors in groups of children in natural settings (Blurton-Jones, 1972; McGrew, 1972).

A basic feature of the organization of nonhuman primate groups is the *dominance hierarchy:* a pattern of social relationships related to the resolution of social conflict. It involves the distribution of power, especially access to resources such as food or mates, among group members by setting implicit "rules" as to who can control whom (Hinde, 1974). To illustrate ethologically oriented research on children's dominance hierarchies, we turn to a study by Strayer and Strayer (1976). They videotaped the free play of a group of preschool children toward the end of the school year, when the group had stabilized. The dominance relations could be inferred from the outcomes of three categories of naturally occurring social conflict between two children. These conflicts included physical attacks, threat gestures, and object or position struggles (physical or nonphysical struggles over a toy, standing at the front of the line, and the like). In response to these conflicts, a child could submit, seek help, counterattack, give up the object or position, or make no response. The child who wins in these encounters is considered to be the more dominant. These categories of initiated conflict and response to the conflict are quite similar to those used to study relations in nonhuman primate groups. The analysis of the videotapes revealed a relatively rigid and stable dominance hierarchy in the group. Although boys initiated more conflict than did girls, boys were not higher in the hierarchy than girls overall. It is interesting that there was a low frequency of counterattacks. Strayer and Strayer suggest that this indicates that the stable dominance hierarchy minimizes group aggression, just as it does in nonhuman primate groups. Other research, in agreement with this argument, shows that conflicts are high among humans when groups first form, then drop drastically (Savin-Williams, 1976).

The Strayer and Strayer study reflects the ethological approach in its content (dominance hierarchies observed in animals), method (observation of behavior in its natural context and subsequent categorization of this behavior), and theory (emphasis on behaviors adaptive for the species). The following sampling of research illustrates other areas of peer interaction of interest to ethologists: patterns of play in preschool children (Smith & Connolly, 1972), maintaining a preferred physical distance from other people (Peery & Crane, 1980), and children's appeasement behaviors, such as slumping the shoulders and bowing the head, which cause aggression to cease (Ginsburg, Pollman, & Wauson, 1977). The ethological approach clearly contrasts with social learning theory's focus on how a behavior (for example, aggression) in individual children is affected by reinforcement, punishment, and imitation.

It may seem strange that negative, aggressive, power-oriented social relationships have been of much greater interest than have positive, cohesive relationships. Indeed, Strayer (1980) reports that during a period of observation at a nursery school, there were fewer than 200 competitive or aggressive episodes in contrast to more than 1000 affiliative episodes. Strayer and his associates have recently tried to correct this bias toward examining negative behaviors by studying naturally occurring friendship groups in preschool children, stable patterns of proximity and contact behaviors among children, sharing, and helping. It is interesting that they found that the children's social preferences did not appear to be strongly related to the dominance hierarchy. That is, the more dominant children were not necessarily preferred for play and other contact. Finally, it should be noted that sociobiologists have been interested in developing genetic models to outline a biological basis of altruistic behavior.

Another aspect of peer interaction is the maintenance of a preferred distance between the self and another person, just as birds on a wire keep a certain distance from one another. The desire to prevent another person from coming too close has been observed in many cultures, but the preferred distance may vary from culture to culture. One experiment (Barash, 1973) examined the response to violation of one's territory. A person sat down close to another person in a library with many empty seats. The subject frequently turned away and sometimes built a barrier of books or other objects between the intruder and himself. This preferred distance may be related to the establishment of group territories. These territories are common in many animal species and serve to spread out the population to avoid starvation and over-crowding.

One important aspect of social interaction at any phase in the life span involves obtaining resources from the environment. As Charles-worth expresses it:

> Whether it is an infant crying for attention, a preschooler struggling with a sibling over a toy, an adolescent trying to impress a peer, a graduate seeking a job, a scientist writing a grant proposal, or an octogenarian looking for someone to shovel snow, the possibility is always present of failing to acquire what one needs because of the competing needs of someone else. While all needs obviously do not have to be satisfied, a certain proportion of them must be if the individual is to carry out normal life functions.
>
> *[1988, p. 24]*

Charlesworth (1988) has proposed a model for identifying which resources children seek, how they try to acquire these resources, and how successful they are in these attempts. A child often must compete with others in order to obtain and keep resources. Competitive be-haviors can range from aggression and intimidation to manipulation, deception, and even cooperation. Cooperation can be a form of com-petition in at least two ways. First, two children may work together to obtain a resource sought by other children. Second, the contribution of one person may be greater than but result in fewer resources than that of the person with whom she is cooperating. Charlesworth refers to such "cheating" in lions. Male lions drive the prey downwind to an area where the females are waiting to kill the prey. Although the females have the more dangerous and demanding task, the males take the greater share of the kill (Trivers, 1985).

The task of obtaining resources changes developmentally. In most families infants need only signal their needs through crying or fussing in order to obtain resources. Later, during socialization, children acquire a variety of skills for obtaining resources—aggressing, lying, threatening, frightening, flattering, helping, sharing, and working together. Through experience, children learn which strategy is most effective in various situations. The types of resources that are most important also change developmentally. Charlesworth suggests that Erikson's eight developmen-tal crises, or tasks, can be seen as changes in which resources are needed most critically—such as access to food and attention in infancy, materials and tools during grade school, and a mate during late adolescence.

Charlesworth (1988) has examined preschoolers' resource-obtain-ing behaviors in a situation in which four children attempt to obtain a resource—viewing a cartoon movie. One child can view the cartoon only if a second child turns on the movie light and a third turns a crank to start the movie. A fourth child must simply be a bystander. The most successful strategy is to somehow get into the viewing position and then get others to turn on the light and crank the switch. Thus, a mixture of assertive, selfish, and cooperative behaviors is required. The tendency to adopt this strategy can be predicted from such factors as dominance rank in the classroom, gender, age, and friendship. An analysis of the videotapes of the children's interaction has led to an observational scheme that categorizes various types of preschool resources, resource-acquisition behaviors, reactions to such behaviors, and outcomes of the interaction. Resource-acquisition behaviors include several types of verbal behaviors, such as requests, appeals to take turns, and threats, and several types of physical behaviors, such as touches, blocks, and attacks.

More generally, Charlesworth has attempted to describe (1) the nature of children's behavior and their resource environments and (2) how the interaction between the two changes developmentally and underlies individual differences in how well children adapt to their environments. Some children have fewer resources available than others, and some are more skilled at obtaining them. Children who have mental or physical handicaps or who come from physically or psychologically impoverished environments may be at a disadvantage in obtaining resources necessary for satisfactory development.

Ethologists have studied a variety of other aspects of peer interaction, as described by Eibl-Eibesfeldt (1989). Examples include play, sibling ambivalence, and altruism.

Hinde (1989, in press) recently has developed an ethological model of social relationships. In this model, the developing organism, with its own propensities, functions within a network of social relationships of various levels of complexity. These levels range from a dyadic relationship to the family to the community to the larger society. A child's interactions with others can be understood only within the context of these interactions, particularly the social relationships in that context. A child behaves differently in different contexts in part because of these differing relationships in the various contexts. Moreover, each social relationship is related to other social relationships. For example, the nature of the parent–child relationship carries over into children's relationships with their peers. Thus, Hinde emphasizes the dynamic relations between levels of society. His model provides a bridge between ethology and the contextual approaches described in Chapter 7.

Hinde applies ethology's descriptive approach in that a first step is to describe the child's social relationships: What do a child and his friend do together? How diverse are these interactions? What kinds of affect do they involve? Are interactions reciprocal or dominant-submissive? How do the children perceive each other? How much intimacy and commitment is there? Does the interaction change from one context to another?

FACIAL EXPRESSIONS AND BODILY MOVEMENTS

Certain facial expressions or bodily movements communicate emotions or intentions. Earlier we saw evidence from deaf and blind children that some of these expressions are innate. In addition, cross-cultural studies reveal certain universal behaviors. For example, Darwin and generations of explorers and anthropologists have observed that smiling indicates pleasure or appeasement. It has been suggested that the adaptive significance of an infant's smile is to make the tired, busy mother of the young infant feel that those difficult first months are worthwhile (Robson, 1967). Another expression, anger, is expressed by a forward stance (threatening attack), clenched fists, and a facial expression of rage in the bared teeth and the turning downward of the corners of the mouth (Eibl-Eibesfeldt, 1975). Eibl-Eibesfeldt reports "agreement in the smallest detail" in the flirting behavior of girls in nine different cultural groups studied. The flirting sequences include smiling, then lifting the eyebrows in a quick, jerky movement in such a way that the eye slit briefly enlarges, then a turning away, a lowering of the gaze, and a dropping of the eyelids. These universal expressions and movements should not, however, mask the many emotions and meanings that are expressed in different ways in different cultures. For example, "No" may be expressed by shaking the head, sticking out the tongue, or pointing the lips and pushing them outward.

Human nonverbal expressions have been compared with those of other animals. Certain monkeys have a "silent bared-teeth display," which indicates submission. This expression may be related to the human smile, which turns away aggression (Eibl-Eibesfeldt, 1975). A slightly different baring of the teeth, however, indicates aggressive intent. Bowing the head, shaking the fist (waving a claw in crabs), and kissing and embracing upon meeting in chimpanzees all have their human counterparts. Like other primates, children sometimes display lowered-brow expressions when being assertive during free play (Brannigan & Humphries, 1972). As zoo visitors know, chimpanzees even seem to laugh (at the human animals staring at them). Ethologists have argued that these social signals communicate intent and thus enhance social interaction and stabilize the social group.

PROBLEM SOLVING

Cognitive ethology, or comparative developmental evolutionary psychology, is a rapidly growing area (Antinucci, 1989; Byrne & Whiten, 1991). The ethological viewpoint is that intelligence increases adaptation to the environment and therefore survival. As a result of evolution, the human brain is prepared for what is called an "evolutionarily expected environment." A child's cognitive system is designed to deal with a certain general type of environment, the type in which the species has evolved. A biological approach to cognitive development suggests a biological basis for concepts such as a theory of mind (Baron-Cohen, 1991) and object permanence (Diamond, 1991). Work on cognition in primates other than humans has revealed surprising skills such as deception, pretense, communication, counting, self-recognition in mirrors, and the concept of object permanence. Consider deception and pretense, for example. Chimpanzees have been seen to pretend in the presence of other chimps that there is no food present, thus saving it for themselves (Byrne & Whiten, 1988). They also will pretend to pull an imaginary pull toy, and even carefully disentangle the imaginary string (Hayes, 1951).

Although most ethological research on children reflects the theory's long-standing interest in social interaction, there are a few recent attempts to clarify the nature of cognitive development by observing naturally occurring problem-solving episodes. Charlesworth (1983) observed toddlers' responses to barriers (or "blocks") encountered in their everyday lives at home. Examples of these problems include being unable to reach a glass of juice (a physical block), being told by their mother to stop an activity (a social block), and being asked by someone to identify something (an informational block). In each case, the problem refers to a relationship between the children and their environment. A block can come from outside individuals or from individuals themselves—their need or desire for something unavailable. Charlesworth recorded all blocks to children's behavior and their response to each block, for example, compliance, ignoring, or hitting. The 3 1/2- to 4 1/2-year-olds, for example, encountered approximately 18 problems per hour and solved the problems 33 percent of the time. Social blocks occurred much more frequently than physical or informational blocks in these situations. It is striking that solving social problems is not assessed to any extent on standard intelligence tests or on Piagetian cognitive tasks. In addition, many of the problem-solving episodes lasted several minutes—much longer than the problems presented in intelligence tests.

Charlesworth (1988) also has examined problem solving in a Down's syndrome girl and among preschoolers at nursery school in free play or instructional settings. In addition, he has documented the greater frequency of blocks, particularly informational and physical ones, among physically handicapped than among normal children. The handicapped children interacted with the teachers more than did the normal children, who were involved in significantly more peer interaction. Finally, his ethological analysis included undergraduate honor students who faced blocks such as deciding what to wear in cold weather, running out of eggs for breakfast, facing difficulty in finding library materials, being asked for advice by a friend, and forgetting how to make garlic bread.

The Charlesworth research illustrates the kind of information about cognition that we do not have from current approaches to studying this topic. The intelligence-testing approach views intelligence as a trait or disposition that is revealed by certain tests administered by an adult, usually in a setting unfamiliar to the child. Laboratory studies of problem solving examine a narrow range of tasks, which typically involve physical, nonsocial events. In contrast, Charlesworth's ethological research studies the function and ecological significance of children's spontaneous use of their intelligence. The research tells us which features of everyday life pose problems, how they are usually handled, and how the children's reactions change developmentally. Intelligence in action helps the children adapt to the physical and social problems created by parents, peers, their own body, furniture, and toys in their environment.

Although Piaget's account of the sensorimotor period came from his observations of his own children, most of his information about children past infancy came from semistructured interviews. He had little concern with the frequency of occurrence of various categories of behavior because his concern was with the underlying knowledge structures. He also did not ask which kinds of everyday environmental circumstances require the use of such knowledge as conservation or transitive reasoning and whether these circumstances are more frequent at some developmental levels than others. The main similarity between the Piagetian and the ethological approach to intelligence is their mutual concern with how an organism adapts to its environment. Both identify biological predispositions toward learning, for example, the assimilation–accommodation process (Piaget) and specialized learning abilities (ethology).

Developmental psychologists are showing a renewed interest in biological predispositions toward acquiring certain specialized cognitive abilities. This interest was stimulated mainly by the recent findings of infant precocity referred to in earlier chapters. Examples are infant competencies in language, multimodal perception, and the perception of objects, causality, and animacy. These competencies appear so early and so easily that it is difficult to argue that they could be acquired primarily through experience. Infants seem to have an innate "set of guidelines that serves learners in the search for order in what would otherwise be a blooming, buzzing, confusion of sensory inputs" (Gelman, 1991, p. 312). Also compelling from a biological point of view is the fact that these competencies are the sorts that humans would be expected to have acquired during evolution.

MECHANISMS OF DEVELOPMENT

Because ethologists have chosen to focus on behaviors with a strong biological component, they stress biological processes as mechanisms of development. Physical maturation, including hormonal changes, locomotor development, and increased efficiency of the nervous system, underlies the emergence of sensitive periods or of fixed action patterns at appropriate times. For example, the reproductive drive and nest-building behavior surface when a bird matures to the point where reproduction is possible. All of these biological mechanisms of behavior interact with experience, of course.

In addition to the biological changes over the life span are the innate general and specific learning abilities discussed earlier. The learning abilities, built into the nervous system, allow the organism to profit from its experience.

Although ethologists emphasize biological mechanisms, they also study learned behaviors that lead to adaptation. For example, even if it turns out that dominance hierarchies and altruism in children are entirely learned, such behavior patterns are still of interest because they lead to a socially cohesive group, which is considered an adaptive system.

POSITION ON DEVELOPMENTAL ISSUES

HUMAN NATURE

Human nature is just one hodgepodge out of many conceivable.

[Wilson, 1978, p. 23]

Humans are social animals with certain species-specific characteristics. They are biological organisms that have evolved within a particular environmental niche. Human intelligence, language, social attachment, and perhaps even aggression and altruism are part of human nature because they serve or once served a purpose in the struggle of the species to survive. Children's developmental level, therefore, is defined mainly in terms of the biologically-based behaviors they possess.

Identifying the theory's world view highlights the differences among ethological theorists. As the later section on models indicates, Lorenz stressed the automatic, reflexlike nature of behavior, whereas Bowlby focused on systems of behavior. The former view is primarily mechanistic, the latter organismic. In the Lorenzian view, as in the Freudian view, humans are moved by biological drives to hunt for food, seek a mate, and run for safety. In addition, sign stimuli elicit fixed action patterns automatically. These notions are much less central in both Bowlby's theory and modern ethological theory, in which humans spontaneously act to meet the demands of their environment. They actively search for the parent, food, or a mate. Children explore, play, solve problems, and seek out playmates. In Bowlby's control-systems approach, the human seeks to maintain a certain state, for example, an acceptable degree of proximity to the caretaker. The child actively maintains that state by calling for the mother or crawling toward her. Thus, the child is self-regulating and active. This cybernetic system, in which humans interact with the environment and use feedback to maintain equilibrium, is reminiscent of Piaget's notion of the equilibration process. Finally, the theory is contextual in its focus on the links between the species' distant evolutionary history and the present and on the nature of the organism's immediate physical and social setting to which it must adapt.

QUALITATIVE VERSUS QUANTITATIVE DEVELOPMENT

Ethology allows for both qualitative and quantitative change. It is not a stage theory and therefore does not posit large-scale qualitative changes in development. In a sense, there is qualitative change when biological maturation proceeds to the point where a sign stimulus triggers a fixed action pattern that has never appeared before. In this way, a new behavior appears in a more or less discontinuous fashion. There is also qualitative change when a drive or system is expressed in different behaviors as the child develops. One such instance is attachment, which is expressed at first by crying or smiling and later by crawling toward the mother or talking to her. The underlying attachment, however, is changing quantitatively, usually toward increased organization, security, and efficiency. More generally, there is quantitative change in that the interweaving of innate and learned components becomes smoother and more efficient during development.

NATURE VERSUS NURTURE

Although ethologists focus on the biological basis of behavior, like most of the theorists in this volume they are interactionists with respect to the effects of heredity and environment. The genotype and the environment operate together to produce changes in children over their lifetime. One implication of this interaction is that a particular experience has more impact if it occurs during a relevant sensitive period rather than at another time.

Ethologists' view of how innate and environmental factors interact has changed over the years. Lorenz originally proposed an "instinct-training interlocking," or chaining of units of behavior that are either innate or learned. More recently, ethologists have rejected the distinction between innate and learned behaviors. Both heredity and environment contribute to all behavior, and there is a continual interweaving of these influences.

WHAT DEVELOPS

The most important behaviors to develop are species-specific behaviors that are important for survival. These include such behaviors as social attachment, dominance–submission, eating, mating, and infant care. In addition, what develops are drives (according to Lorenz), fixed action patterns, and control systems (according to Bowlby). The theory seeks to explain similarities in what behaviors are acquired and how they develop in all humans and in both humans and other animals. Although interspecies differences in development are of interest, little attention is given to individual differences within a species.

THEORETICAL NATURE OF THE THEORY

Classical ethology (Lorenz) draws loosely on the reflex model and the hydraulic or "flush toilet" model (Dewsbury, 1978). Sign stimuli, fixed action patterns, and reflexes are hallmarks of the reflex model. This model, as described in earlier chapters on Freudian and learning theory, is a mechanistic, stimulus–response model. It is based on early views of how the nervous system operates. The hydraulic energy model, also used by Freudian and learning theory, refers to the drive notion. As in physical systems, when pressure builds up, it must be released somehow. In Lorenz's account, this drive energy is released when the appropriate sign stimulus "opens the valve." When the pressure becomes too great, the behavior is displayed in the absence of an appropriate sign stimulus.

Bowlby used control-systems theory from engineering as a model of how attachment forms an organizational system. Control systems are goal-directed and use feedback to regulate the system in order to achieve this goal. A simple control system is a thermostat, which maintains a particular room temperature (the goal) by comparing the actual temperature (the feedback) with the desired temperature. With respect to behavioral systems, Bowlby proposes that genetic action causes the behavioral system to develop, but the developed system is flexible enough to adjust to changes in the environment, within prescribed limits. Just as the human respiratory system works within a particular range of oxygen, a behavioral system operates efficiently within a certain range of variation in relevant features of the environment. The particular acceptable range of social and physical stimuli relevant for attachment varies from species to species. In human attachment, infants have a goal: an acceptable degree of proximity to the adult. When infants detect that the adult is too far away (feedback), they correct this state by crying or crawling, which reestablishes contact and re-achieves equilibrium in the system. The limits of acceptable distance vary, depending on internal factors, such as hunger or illness, and external factors, such as the presence of an adult stranger or other cues of danger. The development of a secure attachment expands the distance acceptable by establishing the caretaker as a secure base from which the child can explore.

Ethologists have used various models of exactly how biological regulating mechanisms control the course of development while allowing for the modification of development by the environment. One model, proposed by Waddington (1957), represents development as a ball rolling down an "epigenetic landscape." As the ball descends, the landscape becomes increasingly furrowed by valleys that greatly restrict the sideways movement of the ball. Slight perturbations from the developmental pathway can be corrected later through a "self-righting tendency," and the ball returns to its earlier groove. Thus, the general course of development is set, but some variation is possible because of particular environmental events.

Other models of the interactions of biological controls and environmental forces are discussed by Bateson (1976). One model, for instance, analyzes the costs and benefits of a behavior to a species (McFarland, 1976). Although these models have developmental implications, they have had little impact on human developmental research thus far.

Because ethology seeks causes on many levels, the inductive, deductive, and functional modes of theory construction can also be seen. The development of the ethogram is primarily an inductive activity, in that the resulting description is little more than a listing of facts about the animal's behavior. The application of the theory of evolution is, on the other hand, a deductive process, in that hypotheses are generated from a set of propositions. Finally, as in most psychological and biological research, there is the functional mode of theory development in the close interplay between theory and data as hypotheses are formulated, tested, and modified.

EVALUATION OF THE THEORY

STRENGTHS

With respect to its utility for developmental psychology, ethology has already demonstrated several strengths. In addition, some of its potential contributions have not been fully exploited by developmental psychologists. Both realized and potential advantages are explored in three areas: theory, method, and content.

Theoretical Contributions

Ethology broadens our perspective on what constitutes an explanation of development. We can fully "understand" the child's behavior only if we expand our vision to include a larger space (the larger social context) and a larger time span (the history of the species). Tinbergen (1973) has identified four types of questions about the causes of behavior, based in part on the time span involved, which varies from seconds to centuries. The "four whys" refer to causes that are immediate, ontogenetic, functional, or phylogenetic.

1. Immediate causes are the antecedent external or internal events that come directly before the behavior. The infant smiles after viewing a human face or cries as a result of hunger pangs. Physiologically based motivation states are a common immediate cause.

2. Ontogenetic causation encompasses a longer time span and refers to how the genotype and the environment interact to produce changes in behavior over the child's lifetime. In this process, earlier events contribute to later events, as when a secure attachment may later on allow the child to explore new environments confidently and even later encourage various independent behaviors.

3. Functional causes refer to the immediate adaptive value of a behavior. An ethologist asks: "What is this behavior trying to achieve?" Children behave in certain ways in order to obtain food, protection, desired resources, and so on. For example, the infant's cry brings the parent.

4. In phylogenetic causation, the cause of a behavior lies in the earlier forms of the behavior as it was shaped over generations as a result of the food supply, types of predators, mating patterns, and so on. Thus, a developmental psychologist seeking a phylogenetic cause of sex differences in behavior would consider environmental pressures in the early history of the human species.

Most developmental research has examined immediate causes or ontogenetic causes. Much less attention has been given to phylogenetic causes or to the behavior's functions (immediate function or survival value). Development cannot be completely understood, however, until all these causes are identified and explored. With the exception of Vygotsky and the contextualists (see Chapter 7), most other theories either have ignored the larger context of behavior or have simply acknowledged its influence but have not studied it. Piaget and Gibson (see Chapter 6) were concerned with adaptation to the environment but developed few theoretical concepts to deal with the process. Erikson stressed the influence of society on the developing individual and made cross-cultural comparisons but did not seriously consider phylogenetic adaptation.

Related to the notion that there are various valid types of causes is the belief that there must be various levels of analysis of behavior. The organism, with its genetic, physiological, psychological, and behavioral aspects, is part of a system that includes the environment, with its physical, interpersonal, and cultural aspects (Hinde, 1989). Therefore, ethologists study each of these levels, with the ultimate aim of understanding the entire organism–environment system. Each level of analysis contributes to our understanding of behavior and has its own set of principles. Behavior can never be reduced to any single level, such as the physiological. Only a theory with multiple levels of analysis is likely to disentangle the complex interweaving of innate and environmental forces during development. Although human developmental research currently proceeds at all these levels, progress at relating the various levels has been very slow. Ethological principles, because they concern many levels and their interrelationships, are potentially a unifying force in developmental psychology.

Ethology's focus on the function of behavior helps the investigator relate the child's behavior to its natural context. The way investigators think about children's aggressive behavior changes if they discover that one of its functions is to increase the overall stability and cohesiveness of the group. The focus changes from a problem in the child to a feature of human groups. Thus, looking at function gives a broader context in which to embed a particular behavior.

Questions about function usually lead to questions about adaptation. Eibl-Eibesfeldt (1975) argues that ethology can fruitfully study cultural adaptation as well as the biologically based phylogenetic adaptation that is the theoretical core of ethology. Most human behaviors are not a matter of life and death. Few behaviors of the human child literally and directly avoid predators or avert starvation or exposure. Even the weak, ill, mentally retarded, and physically deformed are cared for and reproduce. In short, many of the evolutionary forces that operate on other species are less influential for human survival. Thus, the notion of adaptation in humans may be most fruitfully applied to the question of how behaviors taught by a society produce *optimal adaptation* (rather than biological survival). Optimal adaptation might include happiness, a feeling of competence at play, success at school, efficient use of tools (for example, eating utensils, scissors, and pencils), and so on. When Charlesworth studies how children solve problems, he does not see mistakes and inefficient problem solving leading to death, and success leading to survival. He does, however, see how infants, by applying their intelligence, increase their control over their physical and social environments. If ritualistic behaviors, such as greeting, giving gifts, and communicating dominance or submission to others, lead to a more stable group, they are of interest to ethologists even if they turn out to be culturally based rather than biologically controlled adaptations. As these examples illustrate, looking at phylogenetic adaptation in other species can suggest hypotheses about cultural adaptation in humans.

Another central theoretical notion is that behavior and its development can be understood best from a comparative point of view. Although ethology typically compares species, its concepts apply equally well to comparisons across cultures and among developmental levels. Ethologists have much in common with anthropologists. The basic logic of the comparative approach is that contrast brings understanding. We begin to understand a behavior by seeing where in today's human and nonhuman world or in previous times the behavior appears and does not appear. It is just as informative to know what an organism does not do as to know what it does do.

Comparative studies can identify universal, species-specific, and culture-specific characteristics. For example, one universal aspect of development is that the organism is "ready" for different experiences at different ages. The timing of experience is important. However, there may be specific critical periods only in certain species, and the particular culture may modify the outcome of the critical period. Also, comparative studies suggest certain universal tasks of development, at least among primates, for instance, establishing proximity to the mother, communication, play, parenting, and food gathering. All species have some mechanism of care for the embryo and newborn, but there are species differences and, within humans, cultural differences in the exact form these mechanisms take.

A final important theoretical contribution is ethology's interest in development throughout the life span. Different behaviors are required for adaptation at different developmental points: staying close to the mother in infancy, exploring and playing in childhood, and reproducing and finding a place in the social hierarchy in adulthood.

Methodological Contributions

What can we learn from scientists who spend hours staring at crabs and birds? The most timely contribution of ethology is its method of observing behavior in its natural context. Although it is not new for developmental psychologists to observe children at school or at home (for example, Barker & Wright, 1955), ethology provides theoretically based observational methods that supplement the more common empirical, atheoretical descriptions of ongoing behavior. Ethology suggests which behaviors are most important, stresses the need to note what environmental events precede and follow the behavior, and provides a detailed analysis of how the organism and environment interact. It also describes the structure of the behavior and suggests how behaviors can be classified and compared with other species, cultures, or ages. In particular, observing the two-way interaction between people is fruitful for developmental psychology. Developmental psychologists recognize that infants can affect parents as well as be influenced by them. It is even recognized that three-way interactions—among infant, mother, and father—must be considered. Ethologists have developed observational techniques to examine these interactions (Hutt & Hutt, 1970). For example, a sequence analysis of social interaction records that if person A does X, then person B does Y. This can show exactly how infants and their parents control and modify each other's behavior and can identify situations in which one person's behavior has multiple causes.

Ethological observations can fruitfully be combined with traditional developmental methods. Developmental psychologists, particularly those studying cognition during childhood, have relied too heavily on the questioning of children. As Charlesworth comments, "As soon as a research subject has the appropriate Piagetian operations and can talk, researchers stop observing and start asking. It's less strenuous that way" (1988, p. 298). Ethologically-based observations can supplement these verbal methods in important ways. Another possibility, largely untapped, is ethologically based longitudinal research, in which the same children are observed over a period of months or years. This method could identify continuities and discontinuities not only in the child's behavior—the usual focus of longitudinal studies—but also in the child's environment and the interaction between the child and the environment. Ethology includes a changing physical and social world as well as a changing child in its account of development. The social environment, in particular, changes its demands on the child during development.

The criticism in Chapter 4 that information processing is lacking in ecological validity points to the need for observational studies of cognitive and perceptual development. As an illustration, consider what ethologically oriented observational studies might contribute to the understanding of the development of attention. Developmental psychologists nearly always examine attention in the laboratory. They typically examine infants' preferences for attending to one of two stimuli placed in front of them or older children's attention to physical attributes, such as shape, color, or size. The experimenter presents a stimulus or a task, and the child responds to it in some way. The child looks preferentially at one object rather than another, sorts the objects, or tries to remember them. An ethologist, in contrast, would ask the following questions: What types of objects or events does the child look at or listen to at home and at school? What events elicit attention, maintain it, and end it? What events distract the child? How often do distractions occur? Does efficient attention lead to efficient problem solving or other adaptive behaviors? How does attentional behavior differ from setting to setting? Does playful, exploratory attention resemble that observed in other primates, humans of other ages, and other cultures? Can the dominance hierarchy be inferred by who looks at whom and for how long?

Such questions are seldom, if ever, raised in studies of attention. The questions about how attention actually operates cause a shift in focus that makes previous research appear narrow and inflexible. Paralleling Charlesworth's ethological studies of intelligence, it is likely that many distractions and other events controlling attention are social and dynamic, rather than nonsocial and static, as is assumed by laboratory researchers. Laboratory studies tell us what *can* happen during the attentional process. Ethological studies tell us what in fact usually *does* happen, and what function the behavior has. Such studies suggest new variables to be examined in depth in the laboratory. In a similar way, ethological methods could be applied fruitfully to the other theories examined in this volume. We know little about the natural context of the spontaneous occurrence of defense mechanisms, mathematical reasoning, ego-strengthening experiences, memory strategies, visual search for objects, and operant conditioning. A final example is the recent work on children's "theory of mind," described in Chapter 1. Although we now know a great deal about children's developing understanding of the mind, we know almost nothing about how they actually use this knowledge in their daily lives to function effectively in their social environment.

Ethologically based observational studies potentially could make a tremendous contribution to developmental research in the next few years because the field is moving toward an ecologically based approach (see Chapter 7). B. L. White (1969) described developmental psychology as "an edifice without a foundation" because the field has slighted its natural-history phase, which would have established a data base. It has been suggested that the field moved too quickly into its experimental phase. Bronfenbrenner characterized much of developmental psychology as the "science of the strange behavior of children in strange situations with strange adults for the briefest possible periods of time" (1977, p. 513). Ethology can play a heuristic role in this new interest in ecology. In addition, federal social policy relevant to children badly needs a description of the present environments of children and an understanding of how these environments enhance or disrupt development.

Content Contributions

Many of the theoretical and methodological contributions outlined here are potential rather than realized in developmental research. In terms of achieved contribution, ethology has had most of its influence on developmental psychology by bringing certain content areas to the attention of investigators. Although ethological methods and theory potentially cut across all content areas, the greatest influence has come through work on attachment. Bowlby's biologically based account of attachment challenged learning theory and stimulated hundreds of studies not only of attachment but also of such related topics as fear of strangers, parent–child interactions, the effects of early experience, and sensitive periods. Other behaviors considered to be universal and important for adaptation are peer interaction (for example, dominance hierarchies), nonverbal communication (facial expressions and bodily movements), and problem solving. Ethology brought new life to these areas, which previously had been limited mainly to the point of view of social learning theory and Piagetian theory. In addition, ethology pointed out certain behaviors that typically were overlooked. Examples of these are averting one's gaze, hunching one's shoulders, sticking out the tongue, and regulating the distance between the self and the mother.

Developmental psychologists have tended to assimilate biology's concern with immediate causes (Tinbergen's first type of cause, described earlier), such as neuropsychology. But, as Charlesworth commented, "the lab coat and microscope used to isolate biological variables to generate universal principles are no more important to acquiring understanding of the biological nature of human development than walking shoes and a clipboard to discover organism–environment connections to identify significant individual differenes in adaptation" (1992, p. 13). He identified topics from ethology involving more distant causes that developmental psychologists have begun to examine. Examples include the evolution of self-knowledge and deception, the link between stress in childhood and timing of puberty, child maltreatment and natural selection, and the development of reproductive strategies.

WEAKNESSES

It is important to point out critical shortcomings in theoretical, methodological, and substantive areas that must be addressed by ethological theory if it is to fulfill its promise as a theory of development. Some of these shortcomings merely reflect a lack of developmental research in certain areas; others are more serious because they reflect the incompleteness of the theory itself.

Theoretical Limitations

As is true of other theories, ethology describes more than it explains. Many of the ethological notions that are most useful to developmental psychology require further elaboration if they are to serve as specific explanations of development. These notions include sensitive periods, the development of innate behaviors in an attachment structure, and the two-way influence between children and their social and physical environments. The need for more specificity can be illustrated by considering the notion of a sensitive period. Concluding that children acquire a behavior "because" they are in a sensitive period is similar to concluding that they acquire conservation because they are in the stage of concrete operations. These general descriptive notions are only a first step. Invoking a sensitive period does not explain why the organism is pretuned to certain experiences at one time rather than another. A sensitive period must be understood not as a particular period of time, but as a particular developmental level. A developmental level is a specific organization of capabilities that allows the child to interact with the environment in certain ways but not other ways. We need to be able to specify in a detailed way the exact process by which sensitive periods operate. What causes them to begin, have their effect, and end? More generally, what moves development along? Are the effects of extra contact between mother and infant in the first few hours after birth due to biological, perceptual, or cognitive variables or all these variables in interaction? Although the many studies of sensitive periods in other animals are beginning to provide a specific explanation, theoretical and empirical work on sensitive periods in humans lags far behind.

This lack of detailed explanation also can be seen in an example drawn from a typical topic of ethological research: the dominance structure of peer groups. By what process do children detect and understand the existence of this hierarchy and their own place in it? How do they use feedback from their interactions with other children in order to adjust their subsequent behavior? For example, the development of transitive reasoning (A > B > C . . .) may be related to the perception of the dominance hierarchy in groups (Edelman & Omark, 1973). Since most human behavior is cognitively mediated, we need an account of the cognitive processes involved when social cues in the environment are interpreted and influence subsequent social behavior. In other words, how is information about the environment assimilated and linked up with behavior?

In addition to the problem of the lack of specific mechanisms of development involving immediate and ontogenetic causes, there is a problem with phylogenetic causes and how a behavior functions as an aid to survival. Questions about phylogenetic development and the origins of the behavior in biological adaptation are useful when we try to form hypotheses about a behavior, but in fact they are unanswerable with respect to human behavior. The phylogeny of anatomical structures can be gleaned from fossils, but we have no fossils of human behavior. At best we can speculate about how an upright stance, enlarged brain area, and increasingly sophisticated tools reflect changes in human behavior in our history. The other potential source of information about phylogeny— similar behaviors in closely related species—is also suspect. With respect to adaptation, Bowlby can speculate that the function of attachment is to keep the infant and caretaker close together, but what kind of evidence could be gathered in support of this? The function of attachment in humans may or may not be the same as in other primates. It is tempting to note superficial similarities in human and nonhuman primates, such as showing the teeth, and claim a phylogenetic relationship, but the claim may not be valid. The general problem remains of making inferences about human behavior on the basis of the behavior of other animals.

Methodological Limitations

One obvious limitation to applying ethological methods to humans is that the most critical experiments are unethical. We cannot perform deprivation experiments such as preventing an infant from seeing a human smile for the first few weeks of life in order to see if the social smile is innate. In an early misguided experiment, Frederick II (1194–1250) raised babies in silence and near isolation to find out if there is a "natural" human language. The babies, not surprisingly, died before the outcome was clear (Wallbank & Taylor, 1960). Instead of deprivation experiments, we must rely on naturally occurring deprivation, such as infants born blind or deaf. Even simply observing people raises ethical and legal questions about the invasion of privacy. The ethical issues are especially problematic because human social environments are very complex and therefore need to be manipulated experimentally in order to tease apart the influence of each variable. Bowlby's hypothesis concerning the effects of disrupting the early bond between mother and infant cannot be evaluated adequately because this event is confounded with changes in the organization of the entire family, economic changes within the family, changes in the father's behavior, the mother's detachment from the infant when she returns because she has changed during her long illness, and so on. For ethical reasons, however, the necessary experimental manipulations cannot be performed.

Another limitation to applying the methods of ethology lies in four basic problems inherent in observational research. First, it is difficult, often tedious, research to do. Large investments of time and effort are required for videotaping, making detailed descriptions of the behavior, classifying the behavior, and establishing adequate interobserver reliability as to when the behavior begins and ends and how it should be classified. An example of the last item is the difficulty of agreeing when an infant shows fear. Furthermore, it may be necessary to observe children in many different settings to obtain a description of typical behavior because it is not clear what constitutes a "natural environment" for children in a highly technological society. Should we study children running through a meadow, sitting in a classroom, or playing with electronic games? Finally, so many events may be occurring simultaneously that not all the behaviors can be attended to and recorded. Even taping may miss certain important behaviors, such as facial expressions. In short, a comprehensive, detailed ethogram of a species is a large undertaking. As Charlesworth notes, "Unlike most tests, which throw out a small net with a small mesh, the present method throws out a big net with a small mesh and thereby catches many small fish. Herein, of course, lies a big problem of effort and cost. The net gets awfully heavy very quickly" (1979, p. 522).

A second problem with the observational method is that with children beyond infancy there is a danger that the very presence of the observer changes the child's behavior. This is less of a problem when children are involved in group activities of interest to them and have become used to the observer's presence.

Third, there are conceptual problems in dividing the stream of behavior into units. The investigator must choose an appropriate level of analysis—not so large a unit of behavior that critical features of the behavior are lost, but not so small that the overall structure of the behavior is lost. Furthermore, it is not always clear what behaviors are relevant. If one is interested in dependency behaviors, the decision to record touching others, looking at others, or asking for help depends on the age of the child. A related problem is that many behaviors have multiple meanings. When one child hits another child, this behavior may function as a sign of aggression or affection or playfulness. It is almost inevitable that preconceived notions about what behaviors are relevant or irrelevant influence the choice of behaviors to describe and the language used to encode the behavior. An observer unfamiliar with Bowlby's work might well record that the infant crawled to the door of the adjoining room but would probably not record the distance between the mother and the infant.

Fourth, although a main reason for observing behavior in its natural context is to discover the function of the behavior, the function cannot always be inferred. For example, one function of attachment is to establish the mother as a secure base for the child's exploration later on. In this case, the behavior has a delayed function that could not be validated until much later.

Content Limitations

Certain developmental phenomena may not be easily studied from the ethological perspective. Many interesting psychological events are not consistently reflected in spontaneous behavior. Charlesworth found it necessary to limit his investigation of intelligence to overt behaviors, such as removing a physical barrier blocking a desired object. Many other aspects of intelligence, such as the mental manipulations of symbols, are not as easy to observe. Since behavior becomes more cognitively mediated and motivation becomes more complex with increasing age, observation of overt behavior may in general be more informative in infants and toddlers than in older children. Another implication of the mediated nature of behavior in humans is that fixed action patterns, drives, and sign stimuli, which guide observation of animals, may be much less useful for observing children.

Another limitation to the content of ethological research has been the search for behaviors found in all members of a species rather than a focus on individual differences within a species. Both types of information are important for developmental research. Actually, there is nothing inherent in ethological theory or methods that would prohibit a focus on individual variation. For example, Ainsworth (1973) observed that infants vary in whether they have a secure or an anxious attachment. In addition, she noted variations in the age at which an attachment to a specific person is acquired. Variations between children in the form of a behavior, its time of acquisition, and its frequency could be due to genetic variability or environmental variability or both in interaction. By observing individual differences in naturally occurring behavior, ethology is in a position to supplement traditional sources of information about individual differences: standardized tests that measure personality, intelligence, academic achievement, and aptitude. This potential contribution has not been exploited. However, developmental psychologists are beginning to look at the role of individual differences in natural selection (Charlesworth, 1992; Hinde, in press). Topics include the effect of child abuse and neglect, quality of education, poor nutrition, and temperament on health and psychological well-being during childhood and reproductive success during adulthood.

SUMMARY

Ethology is one of zoology's main contributions to developmental psychology. Thousands of hours spent observing animals have revealed important concepts concerning behavior. Each species, including humans, has a set of innate behaviors specific to the species. These behaviors have evolved phylogenetically because they have increased the species' chances of survival in its particular environment. Some of the most important behaviors are social, such as mating rituals, imprinting, dominance behaviors, and some forms of communication. Of particular interest are fixed action patterns elicited by sign stimuli. Even learned behaviors have a strong genetic component because each species has particular learning predispositions in the form of sensitive periods or general and specific learning abilities. Behaviors are studied by both observations in natural settings and experimental studies in laboratories.

The ethological point of view is most influential within developmental psychology in work on attachment. There is some evidence that the very young infant and the adult are pretuned to respond to each other. This work has expanded to include the effects of separation from the mother, the role of the father, the mother as a base for exploration, and bonding in the newborn. Observation of dominance hierarchies in mammals and other animals has led to studies of the human peer group, especially in preschool groups. Other work has revealed commonalities and differences in the facial expressions and bodily movements of humans and other animals. Most recently, a few investigators have asked what kinds of problems children attempt to solve and how they try to solve them in natural settings.

With respect to developmental issues, ethologists see humans as a species that has evolved in order to survive within a particular environmental niche. Theorists vary in whether this adaptation is primarily passive, in response to drives or sign stimuli, or active and self-regulating. Behavior changes both quantitatively and qualitatively as innate and environmental factors interact during development. The result is an organism that can operate efficiently within its environment. Ethologists sometimes draw on models such as control systems or hydraulic drive-reduction systems.

Ethology has several strengths to offer the current field of developmental psychology. With respect to theory, it provides a broad evolutionary perspective on behavior that has encouraged investigators to look at the function of children's behaviors. Ethologists advocate more observational studies of children in natural settings in order to determine the function of particular behaviors. A final contribution is the identification of several content areas as particularly important in development, such as dominance hierarchies, attachment, and nonverbal communication.

Ethology has certain weaknesses, however, that limit its usefulness for developmental psychology. Its theoretical notions, such as sensitive periods, have not yet reached an explanatory level. With respect to methodology, the observational method poses difficulties, and deprivation experiments are not possible with humans. Finally, certain aspects of development, such as language and abstract thought in older children, have not been given much attention by ethologists.

In conclusion, ethology is a fruitful source of working hypotheses about what behaviors are important and why they are acquired. An ethological attitude opens the investigator's eyes to a broad context that spans space and time and various levels of analysis. In particular, ethologically based observations in the early phases of a research project can give "the big picture" of the behavior that will later be studied in a controlled laboratory setting. Although the theory has certain limitations that probably can never be overcome, much of the potential of the theory has not yet been realized. Because of the renewed interest in the context of development, the time is right for drawing on ethology for inspiration.

SuGGESTED READINGS

The following readings survey ethological research on both humans and animals.

Eibl-Eibesfeldt, I. (1989). *Human ethology.* New York: Aldine de Gruyter. This 848-page book provides a comprehensive journey, with many photographs, through work on human ethology. Much research on children is included.

Smith, P. K. (1990). Ethology, sociobiology and developmental psychology: In memory of Niko Tinbergen and Konrad Lorenz. *British Journal of Developmental Psychology, 8,* 187–200. Smith presents an interesting historical account of the main leaders and ideas in ethology.

The following works focus on attachment.

Ainsworth, M. D. S., & Bowlby, J. (1991). An ethological approach to personality development. *American Psychologist, 46,* 333–341. In this interesting article the authors provide a historical account of their research and theorizing on attachment.

Bowlby, J. (1969). *Attachment and loss.* Vol. 1: *Attachment.* New York: Basic Books. This classic work is Bowlby's influential statement about attachment.

The notion of a sensitive period is one of the most important from ethology for developmental psychology.

Bornstein, M. H. (1989). Sensitive periods in development: Structural characteristics and causal interpretations. *Psychological Bulletin, 105,* 179–197.

Lorenz delights us with this account of his life with animals.

Lorenz, K. Z. (1952). *King Solomon's ring.* New York: Crowell.

6

GIBSON'S PERCEPTUAL-DEVELOPMENT THEORY

We tested 36 infants ranging in age from 6 months to 14 months on the visual cliff. Each child was placed upon the center board, and his mother called him to her from the cliff side and the shallow side successively. All of the 27 infants who moved off the board crawled out on the shallow side at least once; only three of them crept off the brink onto the glass suspended above the pattern on the floor. Many of the infants crawled away from the mother when she called to them from the cliff side; others cried when she stood there, because they could not come to her without crossing an apparent chasm. The experiment thus demonstrated that most human infants can discriminate depth as soon as they can crawl.

[GIBSON & WALK, 1960, p. 64]

Infants of 12 months were familiarized in the dark with an object of either a hard or an elastic (spongy) substance. Following 60 seconds of manipulation, a visual preference test was given with simultaneous presentation of two films of identical objects, one moving in a pattern characteristic of a rigid object and one moving in a pattern characteristic of an elastic object. Infants handled the two substances differently in an appropriate manner and looked preferentially with more and longer first looks to the type of substance familiarized. . . . The results . . . suggest that quite young infants detect intermodal invariants specifying some substances and perceive the affordance of the substance.

[GIBSON & WALKER, 1984, p. 453]

C hildhood is a time of perceptual discovery. Children learn to tell apart various faces, balls, juices, words, flowers, insects, seashells, and television heroes. They perceive and explore the wondrous objects and events in the environment occupied by their species. Although discovery about the world is exciting in itself, it is also necessary for adaptation to the environment. Humans must accurately perceive objects in order to learn to understand them and use them. Recognizing the importance of perception for adaptation, Eleanor Gibson has taken on a question largely ignored by other theorists we have met: How do we learn to perceive our world? Surely this is a basic question for psychology. Gibson's answer to this question is that children learn to detect information that specifies objects, events, and places in the world. As they perceive, they differentiate this information rather than add to it. Thus, this view is in sharp contrast to other views of perception, which see perceptual learning as a process of adding meaning to sparse, ambiguous stimuli. For Gibson, the perceptual array is already rich, complex, and valid.

Gibson's theory of perceptual development is not a grand, wide-ranging theory of development as is Piaget's or Freud's. It has the more modest goal of explaining one area of behavior: perceptual learning and development.

The organization of this chapter is as follows. First is a biographical sketch, followed by a general orientation to the theory, then a description of main developmental trends. Sections on the mechanisms of development, the theory's position on developmental issues, and the theoretical nature of the theory are followed by an evaluation.

BIOGRAPHICAL SKETCH

Eleanor J. Gibson's studies in psychology began at Smith College, from which she graduated in 1931. She then stayed on as a teaching assistant and married a young faculty member, James Gibson, who was to become an eminent psychologist. She earned her master's degree with a thesis on learning in 1933. Subsequently, she became an instructor at Smith and attended the Gestaltist Kurt Koffka's lectures regularly. Gibson moved on to Yale, hoping to study animal behavior, but instead studied people. In 1938, she obtained a Ph.D. under Clark Hull, the great learning theorist, at Yale. Gibson, however, did not feel intellectually comfortable in the S–R climate of Yale. Her career was interrupted by her husband's relocation for military service during World War II. The Gibsons returned to Smith and later went to Cornell, where Eleanor Gibson became a research associate.

Gibson's work in the 1950s and 1960s developed the new fields of perceptual learning and perceptual development. At Cornell she studied goats and sheep at the "Behavior Farm," babies on "visual cliffs," and children in reading-related situations in the laboratory. She became a professor at Cornell in 1966. Her research and theorizing culminated in 1969 in *Principles of Perceptual Learning and Development,* which won the Century psychology prize. The book was hailed as one of the most influential books on development in the recent history of the field (Hartup & Yonas, 1971). In the next decade, she continued her wide-ranging research but turned her attention more and more to how children learn to read. Some of this work is summarized in *The Psychology of Reading* (1975), written with Harry Levin. She then returned to infants to study early perceptual development. Cornell honored her with an appointment as the Susan Linn Sage Professor Emeritus of Psychology. *An Odyssey in Learning and Perception* (1991) is a recent collection of her major papers. More than a decade after her "retirement," she continues her research and writing.

Gibson has been awarded many honors, including the Gold Medal Award and the Distinguished Scientific Contribution Award of the American Psychological Association, the Howard Crosby Warren Medal of the Society of Experimental Psychologists, and the National Medal of Science. In addition, she was elected to the National Academy of Sciences, the American Academy of Arts and Sciences, and the National Academy of Education. She also has served as president of the Eastern Psychological Association.

GENERAL ORIENTATION TO THE THEORY

Five characteristics of Gibson's theory place it in the proper place in our growing cognitive map of developmental theories. These characteristics include the notions that humans are active perceivers, that information for perception is specified in stimulation, and that ecology is an important consideration in our understanding of human perception. Two more characteristics are the claims that much of perceptual development depends on perceptual learning and that experimental methods should include simulations of natural environments.

H*UMANS AS* A*CTIVE* P*ERCEIVERS*

Gibson often refers to "the perceiver as performer" (Gibson & Rader, 1979). In her view, children and adults discover, explore, attend, extract information, and differentiate objects. These are the behaviors of an active organism who does something in order to learn about the world. For example, consider how young children perceive balls. Although even infants can discriminate footballs, small rubber balls, basketballs, and other balls on the basis of obvious differences such as size or color, only after more experience with balls do young children detect more subtle differences in shape, texture, and so on. Young children not only detect differences among objects but also abstract more complex information: a football that looks different when it is seen from different angles and distances is actually a unitary object; rolling a ball across the room is an event in time and space. They also detect what kinds of behaviors are possible with different types of balls. By observing and playing with objects, children pull out more and more information about objects, events, and the spatial layout of the environment.

Both general and specific motivations underlie the perceptual activities of children. Humans, as a species, are inherently motivated to explore and learn about their world. There are, however, goals and needs specific to each task or situation. A girl putting together a puzzle attends to shape and color because these attributes are information she needs to achieve her goal of completing the puzzle. In contrast, a girl playing in a swing may be concerned with the pleasurable feeling of the wind blowing her hair and her body moving in space. In another setting, a baby learning to walk must be very attentive to the position of her body in space and the distance between furniture. Adults also have different goals relevant to perception in different situations. For example, Gibson points out that mountain climbers are more attentive to where they place each step than are people taking a leisurely walk (Gibson & Rader, 1979). In short, perception is always motivated by goals that are important to the person. These goals, which give direction to the person's perceptual activities, may be as diverse as problem solving, amusement, and locomotion.

I*NFORMATION* I*S* S*PECIFIED IN* S*TIMULATION*

Gibson's description of the active, self-motivated child exploring the world seems quite similar to Piaget's view of children. The theorists part, however, in their conceptions of how children "know" the world through activity. Piagetian children "construct" their knowledge by forming schemes based on their motor behaviors with objects. Because perception produces static images, it must be corrected by veridical, operational knowledge. Similarly, other approaches see perception as an act of enriching a sparse, ambiguous, uninformative retinal image. For instance, learning theorists propose that distinctive verbal labels added to objects make them more discriminable. The labels "beagle" and "foxhound" would increase the perceptual distinctiveness of these dogs. Information-processing approaches describe processes that add meaning to the stimulus by relating it to memories in the long-term store. They refer to going beyond the information given by making inferences based on knowledge of the world. The Piagetian, learning, and information-processing approaches consider perception and cognition to be an additive process. The child adds something—actions, words, meaning—to the stimulus.

In contrast, Gibson believes that stimulation is a rich source of information that extends over space and time. The developmental issue, then, is how children learn to extract more and more information from stimulation. The assumption that information is inherent in stimulation is the most controversial claim in the theory. It is important, therefore, that we consider this claim carefully.

There is a spatiotemporal array in stimulation. That is, stimulation is not static and frozen in space and time. As Gibson comments, "There is no shutter on the retina, no such thing as a static image" (1988, p. 5). Stimulation specifies events, places, and objects. Thus, if children can extract this information, they perceive events, places, and objects. They do not perceive a single, discrete "stimulus," such as an object. Rather, from the entire spatiotemporal array, they perceive the information that specifies particular objects. In other words, stimulation is a field of available information to be differentiated.

Stimulation carries many levels of information. At the simplest and most concrete level, the child discriminates objects by one or several *distinctive features,* or attributes that differentiate them. Suppose a child moves near an ocean and for the first time in his life encounters hundreds of shells. He begins a collection and attempts to identify the shells with the help of a guidebook with photographs. Although he is perceptually capable of telling all of the shells apart if he places them side by side, he actually notices only a few distinctive features at first, perhaps only salient differences in color, shape and size. Only after much playing with the shells and comparing them with the pictures in the book does he realize that the stimulus class of shells has a particular set of distinctive features that allows him to determine the appropriate label for each shell. Although size is a salient feature, it is seldom important. In contrast, slight differences in the shape of the "crown" at the top of the shell or subtle differences in the colored pattern on the shell are quite important. Although this information has always been in the light stimulating the eye, it was not really noticed or abstracted as a defining feature until the child had more perceptual experience with the shells.

At a more abstract level of analysis, we can perceive a higher-order structure to light or sound. A good example is the musical pattern we call a melody. We abstract a melody from a succession of notes on the piano. This melody is recognized as the same melody even if it is transposed to a different key or played at a different tempo or on a saxophone instead of a piano. The pattern is there in stimulation but may not be perceived at first. Thus, perceptual learning is a process of learning to perceive what has always been there. Gibson (1977, p. 157) has noted that her theory might be called a "seek and ye shall find" theory. Young children, having limited experience with objects and events in the world, often do not perceive subtle differences in the appearance of objects or patterns (organized light). They must search out these differences.

It is instructive to carry the musical example to perceptual learning in adults. When we hear a new orchestral work, we have a relatively undifferentiated perception of the work after the first hearing. Only after listening to the work several times are we able to extract melodies and their transformations, grasp the overall structure of the piece, and perhaps even differentiate the various instruments of the orchestra. For most Americans, this task is more difficult with Eastern music or modern compositions using the 12-tone scale, which are less familiar, than with the first hearing of yet another Haydn symphony. In this musical example, stimulation has remained the same throughout the repeated playing of the record. What has changed is what information we have extracted. In the beginning we listened, yet did not hear. We gradually perceived more and more of what had always been there. Our perception became both more specific, as we became aware of subtle musical qualities, and more abstract, as we perceived musical patterns. Thus, the information is in the stimulation, but sometimes we must learn to perceive it. Our perception improves not by filling in the raw auditory stimulus by adding words or applying schemes, not by cognitively gluing together the notes, but by listening to the music and directing our attention. We attend to relational information—distinctive features and patterns concerning relationships among the parts—not to bits and pieces of information. In Gibson's words,

There is structure in the array, relational information that does not have to be pieced together because, like truth, it is already there. This is the assumption I want to proceed with. I do not want a construction theory, with processors at every stage like an assembly line.

[1977, p. 157]

IMPORTANCE OF ECOLOGY

More than most theories of perception, Gibson's theory stresses the natural behavior of the perceiver in a particular environment. People need to perceive objects, spatial layouts, and temporal events in order to adapt to the world: to walk around in it, find things in it, play in it, and even survive in it. These stimuli are complex relational units, not simple sensations of light or sound.

In recent years, Gibson's research and theorizing has centered on the notion of *affordances,* a concept introduced by James Gibson. Affordances are what an environment offers or provides for an organism; they are opportunities for action. Humans' environments "afford" surfaces of support, objects to grasp, passageways allowing movement, and barriers preventing movement. Thus, the person and the environment form a whole, with a meshing of the person's activities and the environment's affordances. The utility of a property of the environment depends on the capacities of the organism. If an infant cannot yet stand, a solid surface does not afford "standing on." Gibson claims that affordances are perceived directly: "We do not perceive stimuli or retinal images or sensations or even just things; what we perceive are things that we can eat, or write with, or sit down on, or talk to" (1982, p. 60).

As new motor skills are acquired during development, new affordances are discovered. When children start to walk, they learn to perceive if a surface affords solid support for walking. This affordance is irrelevant for and unknown to a younger infant. In one experiment (Gibson et al., 1987), infants faced a walkway raised 4 feet from the floor. Their smiling mothers stood 6 feet away on the other side of the walkway. The walkway for one condition was a rigid surface (strong plywood covered with a patterned fabric), and the other was a patterned fabric on a waterbed, which affords locomotion for a crawler, but not a walker. The infants who could walk looked at and felt the water bed more than the rigid surface before they either walked on the rigid surface or crawled onto the water bed. The infants who could only crawl showed little, if any, differentiation of the two surfaces; they readily moved onto both of them.

We can look at ecological influences in two overlapping ways: by tracing our evolutionary heritage and by focusing on how specific environments mesh with the child's perception. Both are emphasized by ethologists as well. First, let us consider how the human species has evolved adaptive ways of perceiving the world. In Gibson's words, the search for information about complex relations among stimuli is

> so much a part of man's nature, evolved over millions of years, that it is as ingrained, strong, and unconscious as the functions of digestion and breathing and much more elaborately provided for. We have many windows on the world: systems for listening, looking, touching, tasting and accompanying patterns of exploration like scanning, palpating, and licking.

> *[1977, p. 157]*

Each species is specialized for perceiving critical information in its environment. For example, bats are pretuned to use acoustic information (interpreting feedback from sounds) to help them navigate in dark caves. Birds and primates rely heavily on their visual perception of spatial layout, prey, and predators, and hands permit humans and other primates to detect whether an object can be grasped and manipulated. Thus, what information is extracted from the environment depends on the species. Affordances are directly perceived because the species has evolved a perceptual system that detects or can learn to detect the affordances that increase the likelihood of survival. The environment affords food, mates, and places to hide from predators.

Let us now look at ecological influences in the second sense: the fit between children's immediate environment and their percepetual activities. Evolutionary heritage provides the perceptual equipment and the motivation to perceive—or learn to perceive—objects, events, and spatial arrays. By exploring and playing, children learn the affordances of objects, surfaces, and events. The particular information they attend to, however, depends on what the immediate environment provides and on what their goals are in that situation. Hungry 3-year-olds notice another child's ice-cream cone, perceive hunger pangs, listen for the music of the neighborhood ice-cream truck, and look for their mother. Young football players, however, attend to a different sort of information. They continually search for and track the ball, perceive the spatial relationship between other players and the ball, and use feedback concerning their attempts to kick the ball (falling down, kicking erratically, and so on). In these examples, there is a relation—ideally, a match—between the child's goals and the information extracted from the environment. According to Gibson, attempts to study perception in isolation from any consideration of the environment are misguided. Psychologists can understand perceptual development only by studying the correspondence between children's perceptual activities, their goals, and what information is available to them. Recall that in Chapter 4 the information-processing approach was criticized for focusing on the child's cognitive skills and giving little attention to how these skills "fit" with the child's goals in a particular environment. Gibson certainly would agree with this criticism.

PRIMACY OF PERCEPTUAL LEARNING IN PERCEPTUAL DEVELOPMENT

As the previous sections indicate, Gibson believes that much of perceptual development involves perceptual learning. Perception improves as the child explores, compares, searches, and abstracts information in a variety of settings. The process of perceptual learning is much the same in children and adults. An adult facing an unfamiliar task, such as reading the Russian alphabet or learning to play chess, must learn what to attend to, much as the child does in a larger number of situations. Overall, adults can pick up the needed information much more economically than can children, partly because they understand what the task involves and what type of information in stimulation is relevant; however, children are quite efficient at extracting information in very familiar situations, such as looking through a new friend's toy collection.

Gibson recently has focused on ecologically relevant perceptual learning in infants. One important type of learning involves recognizing faces, particularly the mother's moving face with its accompanying voice. A second is learning what sights and sounds and tactual sensations go together in the world. For example, infants learn that a tapping hand makes a particular sort of sound (Spelke, 1976) and that a sponge is squeezable (Gibson & Walker, 1984). Gibson believes that infants learn about multimodal events. Third, babies learn about what kinds of physical support different surfaces provide. And fourth, babies learn that their behavior can control (bring about) an environmental event. Looking, mouthing, and grasping lead to certain sensations and events as babies explore the world.

METHODOLOGY

Although Gibson's research, as well as other research stimulated by her theory, follows the experimental procedures of other areas of developmental psychology, it is unusual in one way. It tries to increase the ecological validity of the experimental setting. This does not mean that Gibsonians necessarily observe perceptual activities in their natural settings. It does mean that they attempt to simulate (mimic important features) in the experimental setting the stimulation, tasks, and goals of the child's natural environment. In an early experiment on depth, for instance, Gibson, along with Walk (1960), constructed a "visual cliff," which simulates a cliff or drop-off in the real world. Gibson was inspired to create this miniature Grand Canyon after visiting the real Grand Canyon with her young child and pondering, with some concern, the child's ability to perceive it as a drop-off. The visual cliff is a table with a glass top that gives the impression of a solid surface on one half of the table; on the other half of the table the floor is visible through the glass. Thus, the apparatus displays information specifying a drop-off. Some of the results were described at the beginning of the chapter. Infants crawl on the "cliff" half but refuse to crawl onto the half of the glass that hangs over the apparent "thin air." The visual-cliff experiments demonstrated that children perceive depth at an edge at least as early as 6 or 7 months, when they begin to crawl. Research using heart rate indicates that even younger infants differentiate the cliff and noncliff sides (Campos, Langer, & Krowitz, 1970). The visual cliff has been used widely to study depth perception in many species.

The close connection between theory and methods can be seen in the materials and procedures Gibson recently has selected for her experiments. Multimodal stimulation (e.g., faces that move and make sounds and objects that can be touched), various kinds of environmental supports for locomotion (e.g., solid or nonsolid surfaces), and opportunities for obtaining feedback from exploratory activities (and thus detecting contingencies) are found in the child's daily life and Gibson's laboratory.

DEVELOPMENTAL TRENDS

From the seemingly diverse perceptual changes during childhood, Gibson (1969) identifies three developmental trends: (1) increasing specificity of correspondence between the information in stimulation and what is perceived, (2) optimization of attention, and (3) increasing economy of information pickup. These trends refer to three overlapping and interrelated aspects of perceptual learning. The trends arise from the children's ever-widening range of experiences as they explore different situations. All lead to the detection of affordances.

INCREASING SPECIFICITY OF PERCEPTION

There is a growing correspondence between what the child perceives and what information is in stimulation. In other words, perception becomes more exact. The toddler may be insensitive to perceptual differences among members of the class "fish." The older child may discriminate among guppies, goldfish, and trout. Thus, perception has become more differentiated.

One well-known experiment demonstrates the increasing specificity of perceiving graphic patterns and nicely illustrates the type of research generated by the theory. Gibson, Gibson, Pick, and Osser (1962) presented letterlike forms—forms constructed on the same principles as printed capital letters in the English alphabet. On each trial the child's task was to select from a set of forms the two or three forms identical to the standard form. The nonidentical forms differed from the standard in several ways, for example, in orientation (reversed or rotated to an upside-down position, analogous to M versus W) or shape (a straight line changed to a curve or vice versa, analogous to D versus O). With increasing age, from 4 to 8, there is increased differentiation of the forms. Many of the forms younger children consider to be the same as the standard are, in fact, not the same. For example, a child might pick a reversal of the standard, analogous to confusing M and W in our alphabet. Older children's perception corresponds more closely to the forms. They usually pick forms that are exactly the same as the standard. Their superior performance is presumably due to their greater experience with letters of the alphabet.

OPTIMIZATION OF ATTENTION

For Gibson, perceptual development is nearly synonymous with attentional development. Attention refers to activities that gather information, especially information about the affordances of objects. Attentional activities include peripheral exploratory activities, such as looking back and forth between two faces, turning the head to facilitate locating a sound, and sniffing a rose. In addition, there are central, nonobservable attentional activities, for example, attending to an object's color rather than its shape. As a result of all these activities, the child extracts certain information and ignores other information. How efficiently children carry out attentional activities depends to a great extent on their developmental level. Although to some extent children perceive selectively from the beginning, during development they learn to tailor their perception to the requirements of each situation.

Gibson (1988, in press) posits a sequence of phases in the development of exploration (attention) during infancy. These phases are not strictly stages, because they overlap in time and vary across situations. In each phase infants make use of whatever motor abilities they possess at that point to explore their environment. In phase 1 (birth to about 4 months), infants have some control over their head and limb movements, so they can actively look, listen, and mouth objects, such as the fist, they can get into their mouths. They attend to (explore) *events,* particularly motions, in their immediate visual surround. By moving their head and eyes, they scan the visual layout and discover rudimentary properties of objects and layouts. From information in the motion within the optic array, they can perceive depth, the unity of an object, and causal relations between events. They also can discriminate their own movement from that of other objects or their surroundings. During event perception, looking is somewhat coordinated with other systems, such as listening or exploring tactually. For example, when given a choice of two faces, infants prefer to look at a face where mouth movements match the vowel sounds heard rather than at a face where there is a mismatch (Kuhl & Meltzoff, 1982). Similarly, infants tend to look at a filmed event matching a sound track (a hand playing a rhythm with percussion instruments) rather than a filmed event that does not match (Spelke, 1976). During this phase babies learn about social events, including communication. They hear adults speaking to them, and even neonates can discriminate messages in their native language from a foreign language (Mehler et al., 1988) and their mother's voice from others (Fifer & Moon, 1988).

In phase 2 (around 4 to 7 months) infants gain more control over their arms and hands. Reaching and grasping reveal new affordances and distinctive features of *objects.* Visual acuity has improved as well. Infants no longer have to depend on motion to provide information about objects, because their own actions with their hands reveal new affordances of objects. There are new opportunities for multimodal perceptual learning, as babies learn that objects can be not only seen and heard but also squeezed, hit, banged, and thrown. Infants can identify objects and even show tactual recognition of an object first examined visually (Streri & Pecheux, 1986). They also detect both similarities and differences among objects. Finally, they perceive a partly covered object as a unitary object. For example, infants perceive a long stick protruding on either side of a rectangular object as a single unbroken stick, but only if they see the stick move back and forth or in depth rather than remain stationary (Kellman & Spelke, 1983).

Babies have a new awareness of the self and can link proprioceptive information from their own body to a visual image of their body. Bahrick and Watson (1985) found that, remarkably, 5-month-olds could discriminate between a live videodisplay of their own moving legs and that of another identically dressed infant or their own legs taped at another time. In the latter two displays proprioceptive and visual information were not synchronized.

One of the most striking demonstrations of object perception is the perception of a living object in motion. For example, Fox and McDaniel (1982) presented a biological-motion light pattern—a videotape of 10 lights mounted on the joints of the arms, legs, and hips of a figure running in the dark. Another display included the same number of lights, but their movement was random. Infants of 4 and 6 months tended to look at the running pattern, which indicates both their ability to differentiate an object in biological motion from a random array and their preference for viewing a pattern of moving lights organized into a unitary object.

In phase 3 (around 8 to 12 months), attention expands to the larger *array* as infants become ambulatory. They explore behind obstacles and themselves, around corners, on top of furniture, and inside cabinets. Their perception of the layout guides their locomotion around obstacles, through openings, and onto safe, solid surfaces. A toddler crossing a room needs a great deal of affordance information in order to crawl under a table, over rather than around a blanket on the floor, and around rather than over the dog. Toddlers even make compensatory, or righting, responses when they have to walk around obstacles down a hallway that appears to move (Schmuckler, 1987). Objects' affordance of being carried seems to fascinate toddlers, who often carry objects from one place to another for the sheer joy of doing so. Gibson (1988) notes that this affordance may take a while to be learned, for there are reports that toddlers sometimes try to carry a toy or piece of furniture almost as large as themselves.

During development, attention becomes more efficient in several ways. It becomes more exploratory and less captive: children can actively scan an object rather than only passively react to a bright light or sudden movement that "catches" their attention. Attention also becomes more systematic and less random, more selective in the information picked up, and more exclusive, in that irrelevant information is ignored. For instance, older children use more efficient attentional strategies than do younger children to decide if two drawings of houses are the same or different (Vurpillot & Ball, 1979). Older children actively and systematically look back and forth between corresponding parts of the two houses, attending to relevant features (the windows) until they can reach a decision. Younger children settle for a few random glances before making their decision. Similarly, if children are asked to remember the locations of several pictures of objects, but distracting pictures are also present, young children attend to both the pictures they are to remember and the distractors. In contrast, older children ignore the distractors (Miller, Haynes, DeMarie-Dreblow, & Woody-Ramsey, 1986). As these examples suggest, older children extract a more useful set of information because of their more efficient selection of information.

As children learn more about themselves and the world, they learn what kind of attention each setting requires. For instance, they attend differently when crossing a street, looking for a particular brand of cereal in a store, playing basketball, and reading a book. Scanning from left to right, for example, would be efficient for reading but inefficient for shooting a basket. Much of the improvement in fitting attention to the setting comes from feedback that children themselves evaluate. Children probably will not learn to shoot baskets if they do not learn to look at the basket. It is likely, however, that some improvement comes from instruction, such as "Keep your eye on the ball" when batting and "Look both ways before crossing the street."

INCREASING ECONOMY OF INFORMATION PICKUP

Although the mechanisms for extracting information are the same throughout the life span, they become more efficient, or economical. Children achieve economy by detecting distinctive features in stimulation, extracting invariants over time, and processing larger units of structure.

1. *Detecting features* was introduced earlier in this chapter as a way to discriminate between objects. Imagine, for example, that a practical joker mixed up the container labels on the entire stock of ice cream in a 48-flavor ice-cream store. An efficient way to tell the flavors apart and group together identical flavors would be to pick out the minimal set of distinctive features that distinguish the types of ice cream. The set might include the following: color, nuts versus no nuts, sherbet versus nonsherbet, flavor (fruit-based, chocolate-based, or other), and smooth versus textured.

Faces are another group of objects that can be differentiated by distinctive features. Cartoonists take advantage of striking facial characteristics by exaggerating them in caricatures. Distinctive features of faces—a toothy grin or large nose—can bring instant recognition.

2. A second aid to economy of information pickup, the *extraction of invariants,* is the search for relations that remain constant over change. Children extract information for the constant size and shape of objects despite changes in their appearance as they move toward or away from them. It is clearly more economical to perceive a single, constant mother of a particular size and shape than a succession of different mothers who expand and shrink.

One invariant examined experimentally by Gibson, Owsley, and Johnston (1978) is the perception of the rigidity, or lack of malleability, of a moving object. They asked whether the property of rigidity could be extracted when the object underwent various kinds of movement. Infants 5 months of age watched a round, disklike piece of foam rubber move in three rigid ways—for example, rotation in the frontal plane, rotation around the vertical axis, and movement toward or away from them—in succession until they habituated, that is, stopped looking at the object. Then they saw, in succession, a fourth rigid motion, perhaps rotation around the horizontal axis, and a nonrigid, elastic motion: an experimenter continually squeezed and released the spongy disk. The infants showed little interest in the new rigid motion but much interest in the nonrigid motion. Thus, the infants discriminated rigid motions from nonrigid motions. The invariant property, rigidity, was extracted from the stimulus flux during the first three movements. The authors concluded that the nonrigid movement "was perceived as different, presumably because it offered information about a new property of the object, that object being otherwise unchanged" (p. 414).

3. A third route to economical perception is the *extraction of large units of perceptual structure.* A basic tenet of Gibson's theory is that the world is structured and that we gradually become more aware of this structure. We do not impose structure on an unstructured world; the structure is extracted by our perceptual systems. As mentioned earlier, music has a melodic structure that we may or may not detect immediately. Furthermore, much of learning to read is a process of detecting the structure in written discourse. Words and sentences have structure, or rule systems. The structure of words is apparent when we break words into letter clusters *(-ed, -ing, -ight)*. In addition, there are regularities in the spelling-to-sound correspondences, as in the letter unit *-ing* and the sound associated with that unit.

Children are perceiving economically if they pick the most useful level of analysis for the particular task: distinctive features, invariant relations, or higher-order structure. Once the appropriate level of analysis is chosen, children are economical if they extract the minimal number of properties necessary to accomplish their goal. If they need to discriminate the letters b and d, it is sufficient and therefore economical to note only their orientation, not their color or size.

Recently, Gibson (1988) has modified her views. She used to consider distinctive features, invariants, and higher-order structure the essence of perceptual learning, but she now sees them mainly as a source of information that leads to the discovery of the affordances of objects. In addition, she considers the detection of higher-order structure as only one aspect of the more general process of differentiating various levels of structure and discovering their relations. The parts are related to the whole; for example, infants eventually abstract both the overall intonation of a voice and the more subtle aspects within that pattern.

MECHANISMS OF DEVELOPMENT

We have seen that perceptual development brings specific perception, optimal attention, and economical information pickup. The next step is to identify the mechanisms causing these changes. Gibson proposed that the exploratory activities of the *peripheral mechanisms of attention* make perceptual development possible. Children move their eyes to the television, turn their heads toward the sound of a distant call, move their hands over sap dripping down a tree, sniff when they hear dinner being prepared, and cautiously roll a brussels sprout over the tongue. By exploring, the child exposes his receptors to selected stimulation. This exposure, in turn, may lead to the detection of features, relations, and higher-order structure. Also, observation of consequences of exploratory activity permits the detection of contingent relations, as when reaching for a rattle leads to an interesting noise. All these activities together lead to the discovery of affordances.

Earlier, Gibson (1969) had proposed two other mechanisms. One is the abstraction of distinctive features, invariant relations, and higher structures. The other is the filtering out of irrelevant information, as in the "cocktail-party phenomenon" (or "birthday-party phenomenon" in children), in which all background noise is filtered out in order to hear a single voice. However, she now gives little attention to these mechanisms.

The processes of perceptual development are closely related to cognitive development. Using the manipulation of objects as an example, Gibson proposes "a spiraling process, beginning with perception of the simplest affordances, such as separability and contractability, then moving on to chewability and graspability, then to reachability, to hideability, and eventually to all the refinements of transportability. With each new coil of the spiral, new properties of surfaces, objects, and events are perceived as consequences of perceptual activity, building an ever richer cognitive world" (1988, p. 34).

Although Gibson would include neurological change as an underlying mechanism of change, she gives little attention to it. She is more concerned with experience of a variety of objects and events, growing cognition that helps the child learn what perceptual information is relevant for accomplishing each goal, and intrinsic motivation that keeps the child actively exploring the environment in an attempt to understand it and adapt to it.

POSITION ON DEVELOPMENTAL ISSUES

HUMAN NATURE

Gibson's view of human nature is much like Piaget's. In their organismic view, people are inherently motivated creatures who actively explore and try to make sense out of their world. Ideally, this is an organized and efficient process in which the child's needs and goals mesh with the nature of the environment. In their view, the child has a tremendous capacity to learn from experience and adapt to the environment. Both Gibson and Piaget describe complex organisms who are sensitive to the complex structure of the environment. The theorists differ, however, in the source of this structure. Gibson believes that in stimulation there is structure, which specifies the information available to be perceived. The child learns to detect this structure. In contrast, Piaget believes that to a great extent the nature of the interaction between the child and the world provides the structure.

QUALITATIVE VERSUS QUANTITATIVE DEVELOPMENT

Gibson's three trends in perceptual development described earlier imply that development is gradual. Just as perception in adults can gradually improve with practice, so does perception in children gradually improve as a result of experience. Perceptual development is not stagelike. There may, however, be specific qualitative changes in the attentional strategies children use. For example, children's systematic visual comparison of two objects may replace their earlier random looking at the two objects.

NATURE VERSUS NURTURE

The species' genetic nature is influenced during evolution by the species' environment. There is a fit between the two. Thus, what information children extract from the environment depends on their species-specific genetic endowment, in addition to their developmental level, immediate goals, and unique set of learning experiences. Babies are innately equipped to find out what the world is like and what it means to them. As we have seen, Gibson has been primarily interested in describing and explaining how children learn from experience and what they learn, especially affordances.

In recent years Gibson, like other researchers of perceptual development, has increasingly focused on infant perceptual abilities. Researchers currently show little interest in identifying experiences contributing to perceptual development in older children.

WHAT DEVELOPS

Babies learn to detect information relevant for locomotion, grasping and handling objects, and basic communication skills (Gibson, 1992). They learn that the self is distinct from other objects and perceive the constancy of the layout and permanent features of the world. They learn about various features of objects, multimodal invariants, causal relations in events, and means–end relations. During development, by perceptual exploring we can detect the perceptual structure of the world, including affordances, and learn how to apply this knowledge to our goals.

THEORETICAL NATURE OF THE THEORY

Unlike the previous theories in this volume, Gibson's theory makes almost no use of models. In our taxonomy, it is best characterized as a functional theory. The approach is research oriented, and there is close interplay between research and theorizing. The theoretical notions, such as differentiation, distinctive features, and affordances, stay close enough to observations to be testable but are general enough to organize and give meaning to a wide variety of empirical observations.

EVALUATION OF THE THEORY

Gibson's theory is less ambitious than the others in this volume. She has limited her field of inquiry to one area: perceptual learning and development. Within that area, however, she has searched for unifying principles that tie together diverse phenomena. In her 1969 book, topics range from reading to controlled early experience in rats, from the perception of faces to the perception of causality.

Although Gibson's theory is the most well-known theory of perceptual development, it does not dominate research efforts in that area. In fact, no theory does. Most perceptual researchers appear to be on a fact-finding mission, gathering basic descriptive information about the perceptual capacities of children, especially infants. Given the empirical orientation of work on perception in children, the evaluation will focus on the potential of Gibson's theory to guide perceptual research and tie it to other areas of development.

The strengths of the theory are its focus on the ecological context of perception and the connections between knowledge and perception. The main weakness is the unclear relation between perception and cognition.

STRENGTHS

Focus on the Ecological Context of Perception

As Gibson comments: "Only a few hardy perception psychologists still study perception of the real world rather than small displays on computer screens" (1991, p. 607). For years, Gibson has been concerned with how perception serves us in our daily lives. She studies the perception of meaningful stimulation—patterns, objects, and events—rather than points of light or brief, static stimuli. In James Gibson's words, she works on "perception outdoors under the sky instead of perception of points in a darkroom" (1979, p. xii). The perception of the affordances of natural units is essential for adapting to the environment. This ecological orientation has relevance for the current state of cognitive developmental research. Her theory could enrich the information-processing approach by directing it towards (1) larger, more complex properties of the environment to be processed, (2) events rather than static stimuli, (3) and the function of perception for behavior.

First, Gibson criticizes the tendency of information-processing researchers to break down the world into objects and properties of objects. In Gibson's words, "Such a conception requires them to invent 'processing mechanisms' to put the world together" (1977, p. 156). In contrast, her view is that stimulation consists not of bits and pieces but of an entire array that changes over time. Because of her orientation, she showed that even young infants can detect complex and meaningful properties of the world such as pliability and traversability.

Second, information-processing approaches should take seriously her concern with the processing of events that occur over time: a rapidly approaching object, a ball rolling across the floor, one object striking another, liquid being poured out of a glass. This change in focus would broaden our understanding of processing based on the typically studied static stimuli, such as pictures, letters, objects, and written words. Most real-life events involve the movement of one or several objects or people—a complex set of information. Moreover, Gibson (1992) suggests that multimodal perceptual events, such as shaking a rattle or grasping a sponge, provide a natural organization for knowledge. Perceptual events may subsequently be reflected in conceptual categories or the organization of memory, much as scripted event knowledge (see Chapter 4) can lead to conceptual categories (Nelson, 1986).

Third, information-processing psychologists should, like Gibson, consider the function of children's perceptual and cognitive activities. Why do children try to memorize information or solve a problem? Why does an infant look carefully at a room before starting across it? How do these activities help them adapt to their environment? In particular, information-processing psychologists rarely consider how children process information concerning the affordance of properties of the environment for actions in the environment. More generally, current research on cognitive development usually ignores the implications of cognition for action. Gibson's work does not leave the baby wrapped in thought (Pick, in press). The close connection between perception, knowledge, and action is particularly important for infancy, because as physical maturation brings new motor abilities, such as walking, perceptual learning bring new knowledge about which aspects of the environment support these activities (e.g., solid surfaces).

Focus on the Connections Between Knowledge and Perception

Gibson's theory of perception is not the first to claim a close link between knowledge and perception, but it gives us a new way to think about their relation. Most theories have viewed knowledge as a way of correcting perception (Piaget) or enriching perception (Bruner). In contrast, in Gibson's view children discover a complex, structured world; they do not create that complexity and structure. Knowledge is a way of directing perceptual activities in a way that leads to the efficient and accurate extraction of meaningful information from the visual array. Information is meaningful if it indicates properties that are of use to a child, given her abilities in general and her needs at that moment. As children learn more about tasks and goals, they learn what information is relevant and how to gather this information efficiently. They know, for example, that size may be an important distinctive feature for differentiating balls for sports, but not for differentiating letters of the alphabet. In the other direction, perception helps cognitive development in that the detection of surfaces, events, and objects—and their affordances—is the foundation of knowledge about the world. Through exploratory behavior and perceptual learning we discover categories of events or objects (e.g., "things you can walk on"), abstract properties such as number, and causal relations among objects or events. And we develop cognitive maps of the extended environment.

WEAKNESSES

Unclear Relation Between Perception and Cognition

Although Gibson's focus on the interplay between perception and knowledge about tasks and goals was selected as a strength of the theory, in other respects this relationship remains both unclear and unconvincing. The basic problem is that Gibson proposes a theory of the *direct* perception of the environment, but then includes some behaviors that seem to involve indirect, interpretive cognition. For instance, Gibson's examples of perceptual learning include reading maps, interpreting x-ray and aerial photographs, and identifying material under a microscope. Others include detecting means–end relations, perceiving causality, learning that events in the world can be contingent on one's own actions, and perceiving conservation as an invariance over time and over an event sequence (1969, pp. 8–9, 388). Furthermore, children are said to perceive affordances such as swinging (on swings), warmth and light for reading (from a fire), and hiding (behind a screen). Many psychologists seem uncomfortable designating these psychological activities as "perceptual." For example, Horowitz (1983) argues that instead of proposing that a chair affords sitting, one could propose more parsimoniously that the perceiver, because of previous experience, associates a chair with sitting. Although perceptual processes certainly are heavily involved in these cases, much of the learning concerns the interpretation and categorization of the information. Gibson has jumped from the perceptual discrimination of objects to the relating of objects to a rich network of abstract concepts.

Even if we agree with Gibson that much of perception does not depend on cognitive processes, it is necessary to examine the relationship between perceiving and thinking in a detailed way. Of course, it must be admitted that "perceptual" and "conceptual" processes are arbitrary divisions that psychologists sometimes impose on an underlying continuum from sensory to higher-order cognitive processes. Still, it is confusing to treat discrimination, identification, and interpretation similarly and claim that they all involve the abstraction of information already in the stimulus array. Deciding whether a shadow seen on an x-ray should be diagnosed as tuberculosis (Gibson, 1969, p. 9) seems to go far beyond direct perception of the x-ray. The main point being made here is that the theory needs to specify more clearly the similarities and differences among these activities along the perceptual–cognitive continuum. Stated differently, it is not clear what is *not* perception. What are the limits to direct perception? Perhaps further developments within the theory will address this question.

SUMMARY

Gibson asks an old question: How do we perceive our world? Her answer, however, is new. We learn to perceive by extracting, from stimulation, information that specifies objects, events, and places and their affordances for the child's actions. Thus, humans are active perceivers who directly perceive distinctive features, invariant relations, and higher-order structure. Perceptual development is largely a process of increasing the efficiency of perception as a result of experience. This is perceptual learning. The ecological context of this learning is important because children learn to perceive information that helps them adapt to this environment. In each setting, children's goals—whether playing or reading or climbing over a fence—guide their pickup of information. In general, the fit between the goal and perception improves during development.

Gibson identifies three main developmental trends. First, perception becomes more specific as children learn to differentiate stimulation. Second, attention becomes more optimal as it becomes more active and selective. Children abstract information, filter out irrelevant information, and refine their peripheral mechanisms of attention. Third, there is an increasing economy of information pickup as perception becomes more efficient. Children learn to extract information at the most useful level of analysis: distinctive features, invariant relations, or higher-order structure.

On developmental issues, Gibson views humans as active, self-motivated creatures who develop primarily quantitatively but who also develop qualitatively. Nature and nurture interact to produce an efficient, adaptive perceptual system. The strengths of the theory are its focus on the ecological context of perception and its recognition of the connections between knowledge and perception. An area of the theory needing further development is the relation between perception and other psychological activities, particularly memory and decision making.

SUGGESTED READINGS

The best sources for Gibson's theory are her own publications.

Gibson, E. J. (1969). *Principles of perceptual learning and development.*

New York: Appleton-Century-Crofts. This book presents Gibson's theory just before she began emphasizing affordances and infancy.

Gibson, E. J. (1992). *How to think about perceptual learning: Twenty-five years later.* In H. L. Pick, Jr., P. Van den Broek, & D. C. Knill (Eds.), *Cognition: Conceptual and methodological issues.* Washington, DC: American Psychological Association. In this chapter Gibson presents an up-to-date version of her theory.

Gibson, E. J. (1991). *An odyssey in learning and perception.* Cambridge, MA: Bradford/MIT Press. This collection of Gibson's major papers over her career also includes new material by her in introductions to each section and an epilogue.

This article puts Gibson's career into a historical perspective and identifies her main contributions.

Pick, H. L., Jr. (1992). Eleanor J. Gibson: Learning to perceive and perceiving to learn. *Developmental Psychology, 28,* 787–794.

7

VYGOTSKY'S THEORY AND THE CONTEXTUALISTS

The experimenter has removed a crayon of a needed color before the child begins to draw. The child talks to himself: Where's the pencil? I need a blue pencil. Never mind, I'll draw with the red one and wet it with water; it will become dark and look like blue.

[VYGOTSKY, 1962, p. 16]

Mothers and their children construct a jigsaw puzzle together.
A 2 1/2-year-old:

C: Oh. *(glances at model, then looks at pieces pile)* Oh, now where's this one go? *(picks up black cargo square, looks at copy, then at pieces pile)*
M: Where does it go on this other one? Look at the other truck and then you can tell. *(child looks at model, then glances at pieces pile, then looks at model, then glances at pieces pile)*
C: Well ... *(looks at copy, then at model)*. . . I look at it. . . . Um, this other puzzle has a black one over there. *(child points to black cargo square in model)*
M: Um-hm. . . . So where do you want to put the black one on this puzzle? *(child picks up black cargo square from pieces pile, looks at copy)*
C: Well, where do you put it there? Over there? *(inserts back cargo square correctly in copy)*

[WERTSCH, 1979, p. 13]

A 4-year-old:
C: I'll tell you when I need help, Mom.
[WERTSCH & HICKMANN, 1987, p. 261]

Most of the theories that have influenced developmental research in the Western world have viewed individuals as separate from their social and physical environments. In these views, such as Piaget's, development is seen primarily as an individual activity and the environment as simply an "influence on" an individual's development. In North America in particular, a democratic political philosophy, a focus on the rights of individuals, and, historically, the romantic ideal of a lone explorer separated from family in search of new land have directed the attention of developmental psychologists to an isolated autonomous individual whose development is facilitated by or restricted by the environment. This view is challenged by a number of other social belief systems and their corresponding psychological theories, many of them Eastern (e.g., Markus & Kitayama, 1991). Of this group, the most influential for present-day developmental psychologists is the approach of the Soviet psychologist Lev Vygotsky and, more generally, the "contextualists." In the Vygotskian–contextualist view, humans are embedded in a social matrix (context) and human behavior cannot be understood independently of this matrix. As Bhaskar said, "To think of contexts as existing in addition to or apart from practices is like imagining smiles alongside or beside faces" (1983, p. 87). Although contextualism has existed for some time, it is presented last because, of the theories in this book, it has had the most recent widespread influence.

Several recent influences and events have made developmentalists more receptive to the contextualists. Ethological and Gibsonian theorists directed our attention to the purposes of behaviors for daily life and the fit between human abilities and our ecological niche. However, they do not focus on the social–cultural aspects of this niche as much as do the contextualists. In addition, the findings of domain-specific (context-specific) developments by the neo-Piagetians, as discussed in Chapter 1, also increased our interest in the contexts of development. However, the concern was with the nature of particular tasks or domains of knowledge rather than the socially embedded nature of all types of knowledge. Finally, trends in a discipline tend to "correct" the direction of previous trends. Thus, the contextual approach balances, or corrects, the Piagetian and information-processing focus on the individual.

Present-day contextualists differ widely in their interests and methods. Labels such as "cultural psychology" and "ecological psychology" connote some of these differences. However, all contextualists share the conviction that developmental psychology has slighted the social contexts of development. A main spokesperson, Barbara Rogoff, describes the contextual position:

The purpose of thinking is to act effectively; activities are goal directed (tacitly or explicitly), with social and cultural definition of goals and means of handling problems. The structure of problems that humans attempt to solve, the knowledge base that provides resources, and the strategies for solution that are considered more or less effective or sophisticated are situated in a social matrix of purposes and values. The problems that are posed, the tools that are available to solve them, and the tactics that are favored build on the sociocultural definitions and available technologies with which an individual functions.

[1990, p. 6]

The organization of this chapter is as follows. First is a biographical sketch of Vygotsky, to put the approach into historical perspective. Much of the material for this sketch came from Luria (1979), Cole and Scribner (1978), and Wertsch (1985b). Next is a general orientation to the theory, followed by examples of typical research that illustrate this orientation. The final sections address mechanisms of development, the theory's position on developmental issues, the theoretical nature of the theory, and, in an evaluation, strengths and weaknesses.

BIOGRAPHICAL SKETCH

Lev Semyonovich Vygotsky was born in 1896, the same year as Piaget, into an intellectual Russian Jewish family. His large family valued stimulating conversations around the samovar. By age 15 Vygotsky was called "the little professor" because of his reputation as a leader of student discussions (Wertsch, 1985b). He often organized debates and mock trials in which his friends took the roles of historical figures such as Aristotle and Napoleon (Wertsch, 1985b). He was well educated. He received a degree in law from Moscow University and also read widely in literature, linguistics, psychology, the arts, social science, and philosophy. He later wrote his dissertation on Shakespeare's *Hamlet*. This interest in language and literature was to be expressed in his later work on cognitive development. Vygotsky taught psychology at a teacher's college in a provincial town in western Russia. In his work he encountered children with congenital defects such as blindness, deafness, and mental retardation. His search for ways to help these children fulfill their potential brought him face to face with issues in cognitive development.

Vygotsky's systematic work in psychology began in 1924 when the Russian psychologist Alexander Luria, impressed by the brilliance of one of Vygotsky's lectures, obtained a position for him at the Institute of Psychology in Moscow. Luria described this event starring an unknown young teacher from the provinces:

> When Vygotsky got up to deliver his speech, he had no printed text from which to read, not even notes. Yet he spoke fluently, never seeming to stop and search his memory for the next idea. . . . Instead of choosing a minor theme, as might befit a young man of twenty-eight speaking for the first time to a gathering of the graybeards of his profession, Vygotsky chose the difficult theme of the relation between conditioned reflexes and man's conscious behavior. . . . It was clear that this man from a small provincial town in western Russia was an intellectual force who would have to be listened to.
>
> *[1979, pp. 38–39]*

Vygotsky's speeches continued to inspire his listeners in the following years. Students sometimes even listened to his lectures through open windows when the auditorium was overflowing.

Vygotsky, Luria, and Leontiev, the "troika" of the Vygotskian school (Luria, 1979), enthusiastically constructed a new psychology based on Marxism as part of the construction of a new socialist state following the Russian Revolution. As Luria described it, "Our aim, overambitious in the manner characteristic of the times, was to create a new, comprehensive approach to human psychological processes" (1979, p. 40). Vygotsky's lack of formal training was not a problem to such a radical group! Wertsch (1985b) argues that it was largely because of the great social upheaval that Vygotsky was able to develop his theory and influence the psychology and education of the times.

Vygotsky and his colleagues wanted to change citizens' thinking from a feudal (landlords and serfs) mentality of helplessness and alienation to a socialistic mentality of self-directed activity and commitment to a larger social unit based on sharing, cooperation, and support. The new Soviet view was that each person is responsible for the progress of the whole society. A main goal was to eliminate the massive illiteracy of Soviet society. In reaction to previous Russian psychologists, Vygotsky and his colleagues constructed a cultural-historical view of developmental psychology and emphasized higher mental activities such as thinking, memory, and reasoning. Vygotsky drew on Pavlov's work on "higher nervous activity" and was aware of European psychologists such as Piaget, Binet, and Freud. In fact, several of his publications included critiques of Piaget (e.g., Vygotsky, 1962).

Vygotsky extended Marx's and Engels' ideas about economics and politics to psychology in three main ways, all of which will be described more fully later. First, he extended to human development their argument that humans transform themselves, as well as nature, through labor and tool use. The mode of economic production—for example, socialist, capitalist, or feudal—determines people's working conditions and social interactions, which in turn influence their cognitions—cognitive styles, attitudes, perception of reality, and beliefs. As Vygotsky translated this to developmental psychology, children's interactions with others in social settings and the "psychological tools" such as language used in this interaction shape children's thinking. Action with tools creates thought. Second, Vygotsky argued that the economic collectivist principle of shared goods is paralleled by socially shared cognition. The adult collective is responsible for sharing its knowledge with children and other less advanced members of society in order to advance their cognitive development. Third, Vygotsky advanced the Marxist principle (from Hegel) of *dialectical* change—that all phenomena constantly undergo change and move toward a synthesis of conflicting, contradictory elements. For Vygotsky, this process constitutes "development." Human thought, like other phenomena, can be understood only by examining its history. There can be conflict between developing psychological structures, between a currently held concept and a new one, between the child and her environment, between nature and nurture, and so on. The idea that cognition can be fully understood only by studying how it develops hardly seems revolutionary today, but in Vygotsky's time this was not a widely accepted view.

Vygotsky remained interested in education, especially mental and physical handicaps, and medical problems such as blindness, aphasia, and severe mental retardation. In fact, he undertook medical training for several years. He established several research laboratories, some of them dedicated to the study of children with physical or mental problems. Vygotsky lectured widely, conducted research continually, and published approximately 180 works.

In the early 1930s Vygotsky fell victim to the political strife surrounding Stalin's rule. The government accused him of being a "bourgeois psychologist" of the ilk of Piaget and other Western psychologists. In fact, he was viewed suspiciously for often referring to these writers. He also was criticized for suggesting that illiterate minority people in the remote, nonindustrialized parts of Russia had not yet developed the intellectual prowess of those in more modern sections. Particularly suspect was his interest in intellectual testing—a "pedological perversion" denounced by the Communist Party. The party blacklisted him during the Stalinist purges, as it did many psychologists. From 1936 to 1956 his work was banned, though it continued to circulate underground. Vygotsky's influential book, *Thought and Language,* was published in Russia in 1934, the year of his death. He died of tuberculosis at age 37 after only 10 years of professional work in psychology—though those were 10 quite remarkable years. Vygotsky's early brilliance and premature death led him to be called "the Mozart of psychology" (Toulmin, 1978). His theory "was sketchily proposed by a young genius in a mortal race with tuberculosis, during an intellectual revolution on foreign soil, over a half-century ago" (Rogoff & Goncu, 1987, p. 23).

Vygotsky's ideas were continued through the work of Luria and others, particularly those in the Soviet Union involved in building a "theory of activity." His influence is felt there even today. Only a few short articles by Vygotsky were available in English until a translation of *Thought and Language* was published in 1962. The efforts of several scholars, including Michael Cole, James Wertsch, Jean Valsiner, and Ann Brown in the United States, made Vygotsky's ideas more accessible to the English-speaking world. An important event was the publication in 1987 of the first of six planned volumes of *The Collected Works of L. S. Vygotsky* (Rieber & Carton, 1987).

The last decade has seen a renewed interest in Vygotsky's work and, more generally, in approaches that emphasize the social-cultural context of human development. Important publications include those by Bronfenbrenner (1989a), Bruner (1990), Cohen and Siegel (1991), Cole (1992b), Cole and Scribner (1974), Ratner (1991), Rogoff (1990), Schweder (1991), Valsiner (1988, 1989), Van der Veer and Valsiner (1991), Wertsch (1985a, 1985b, 1991), Wertsch and Tulviste (1992), and Winegar and Valsiner (1992), and this chapter draws heavily from them. Vygotsky's ideas are also influencing education (e.g., Moll, 1990).

GENERAL ORIENTATION TO THE THEORY

Vygotsky and present-day contextualists share certain assumptions, which are described below. However, they have certain differences, mainly in emphases, which are pointed out. The main characteristics are the child-in-activity-in-context as the unit of study, the zone of proximal development, the sociocultural origins of mental functioning, the mediation of intellectual functioning by tools provided by culture, and the contextualist methodology.

CHILD-IN-ACTIVITY-IN-CONTEXT IS THE UNIT OF STUDY

The introductory chapter described the contextualist world view (a quick rereading of that section would be useful at this point). Its expression in Vygotskian and current contextualist approaches is described here. Rather than focus on the child, contextualists view a child-in-context participating in some event as the smallest meaningful unit of study. A child is not a constant, universal organism operating in a vacuum. Rather, the mind is inherently social: "The path from object to child and from child to object passes through another person" (Vygotsky, 1978, p. 30). The child, the other person, and the social context are fused in some activity. The social–cultural–historical context defines and shapes any particular child and his experience. At the same time children affect their contexts. Because of this interrelatedness, looking at a child while ignoring his context distorts our concept of the nature of children. Focusing on a child alone tends to encourage us to look for causes of behavior within the child rather than in the context. In actuality, the same developmental process can lead to different outcomes, depending on the circumstances.

This fusion of children and their contexts may not seem like a new concept, because several theories already discussed emphasize the interaction between children and their environments. The difference is that the previous accounts (except perhaps Gibson's) consider the person and the environment to be separate entities that enter into interactions. In contrast, contextualists view this perceived separation as artificial and distorting. Instead, a single unit or process exists, in that certain forms of social practice relate the child and her needs and goals to the environment and define what the environment means to the child. Children behave in certain ways because they have needs and goals that involve the environment. Goals are as diverse as planning a birthday party, trying to convince your parents to buy you a bicycle, attempting to remember which friend borrowed your baseball glove, and figuring out whether you have enough money to buy a candy bar. Social problem solving and communicating one's feelings and desires to others are not just "special cases" of predominantly "cold" cognition unrelated to personal needs; they are the fabric of everyday life.

To see how the mind is "socially distributed" (Hutchins, 1991), consider the following exchange between a mother and her 24-month-old:

M: Did you like the apartment at the beach?

C: Yeah. And I have fun in the, in the, in the water.

M: You had fun in the water?

C: Yeah. I come to the ocean.

M: You went to the ocean?

C: Yeah.

M: Did you play in the ocean?

C: And my sandals off.

M: You took your sandals off?

C: And my jamas off.

M: And your jamas off. And what did you wear to the beach?

C: I wear hot cocoa shirt.

M: Oh, your cocoa shirt, yeah. And your bathing suit?

C: Yeah. And my cocoa shirt.

M: Yeah. Did we walk to the beach?

C: Yeah.

[Hudson, 1990, pp. 181–182]

The dyad is carrying out the process of remembering. This child's mind extends beyond her skin. It seems to flow into her surroundings as her surroundings flow into her mind. It is hard to say where her mind ends and the external world begins.

What is a context? Contexts have many levels. Bronfenbrenner's (1989a, pp. 226–229) "ecological psychology" depicts the environment as a system of nested structures, ranging from the immediate face-to-face interaction with another person to general, all-encompassing cultural belief systems.

1. A *microsystem* is a "pattern of activities, roles, and interpersonal relations experienced by the developing person in a given face-to-face setting." The setting includes (a) particular physical and material features and (b) other people with particular temperaments, personalities, and systems of belief. A child's home, school, and peer group are important microsystems.

2. The *mesosystem* includes "the linkages and processes taking place between two or more settings containing the developing person."

For example, we might ask if the peer group and school system support or contradict the parents' value system. Thus, a mesosystem is a system of microsystems.

3. The *exosystem* "encompasses the linkage and processes taking place between two or more settings, at least one of which does not ordinarily contain the developing person." Events in this system "influence processes within the immediate setting that does contain that person." An example is the relation between the home and the parent's work place. A stressful work environment may increase a parent's irritability at home, which could lead to child abuse. This level includes the major institutions of society, such as the economic system, the transportation system, local government, and the mass media. As an example of the latter, watching television may interfere with family interaction.

4. The *macrosystem* "consists of the overarching pattern of micro-, meso- and exosystems characteristic of a given culture, subculture, or other broader social context." Of particular importance are the "belief systems, resources, hazards, life styles, opportunity structures, life course options, and patterns of social interchange that are embedded in each of these systems." This system is a general cultural "blueprint" that helps design the social structures and activities occurring at lower, more concrete levels. This blueprint influences how parents, teachers, and significant others in the child's life "consciously or unconsciously define the goals, risks, and ways of raising the next generation." There tends to be consistency among the important settings of a particular culture. Bronfenbrenner points out that within a given society, one elementary school classroom looks and operates much like every other. The nature of the prototypic classroom reflects unstated beliefs of the society.

Stated differently, culture consists of shared beliefs, values, knowledge, skills, structured relationships, ways of doing things (customs), and symbol systems (such as spoken and written language). Culture also includes physical settings (such as buildings and highways) and objects (such as tools, computers, television, and art). Within the overall culture, ethnic subcultures or pervasive different lifestyles present different contexts. For example, processes of child rearing differ among different races, social classes, dual-career versus one-career families, rural versus urban communities, single- versus two-parent families, and so on. Throughout this chapter are examples of how these aspects of culture influence (1) what children think about and acquire skills in (e.g., academics, sports, weaving), (2) how they acquire information and skills (e.g., from other children versus adults; verbally or nonverbally), (3) when in development children are allowed to participate in certain activities (e.g., adult work, sex, care of younger siblings), and (4) who is allowed to participate in certain activities (e.g., only one gender, certain social classes).

It is important to understand that all of these levels of social context also incorporate physical and historical influences. The climate, type of terrain, urban or rural setting, population density, health care, and physical risks are intertwined with social contexts. Culture is, to a great extent, a group's response to its physical ecology, which biases toward certain forms of economic activity, such as farming or hunting. These activities in turn dictate a particular social organization and division of labor, which in turn influence child-rearing practices. Vygotsky also emphasized that the history of a culture powerfully shapes all levels of contexts. Wars, natural disasters, revolutions, and civil rights movements reverberate at all contextual levels. At any one point in history a culture is both a product of its own history and a provider of contexts that shape children's development and, consequently, the future of the culture.

Vygotsky and his colleagues provide a striking illustration of how socioeconomic cultural change brings psychological change in a naturally occurring experiment involving illiterate peasants working on small farms under a feudal lord in a remote area of the Soviet Union (Luria, 1976). As part of the movement towards a modern socialist state, they became involved in collective farming practices that required meetings to plan production and make other decisions. They also learned to read and write. Among the illiterate peasants' without these new experiences, classification, concept formation, reasoning, and problem-solving skills were concrete and practical. For example, when told that all bears in the far north are white, the peasants would not predict what color a particular bear there would be. A typical reply was "I don't know what color the bears there are, I never saw them" (p. 108). After even minimal schooling the farm workers, in contrast, could consider this logical problem in the abstract and create logical groupings. It should be noted that Vygotsky may have overestimated the concreteness of the peasants' thinking (Cole, 1988). More recent research in traditional societies shows that such people do think in a logical abstract manner in certain contexts. The schooling and training may simply have taught the peasants to use their abstract thinking in contexts in which they previously did not use it.

These various levels of contexts form a system in which changes at one level affect the other levels. A recession may cause a father to lose his job. This may lead to tension at home, which in turn may cause the child to have problems at school. Such rippling effects can move in the opposite direction as well (from developing child to culture) and bring about social change.

In recent years psychologists typically have studied culture by comparing cultures and emphasizing differences in behavior. As Cole (1992b) points out, however, this *culture-as-difference* approach ignores the fact that the ability to construct and operate in a culturally organized environment is a *universal,* species-specific characteristic of humans. We need to understand these universal mechanisms of cultural influences as well as the diversity of content they produce. In the *culture-as-medium* approach, culture organizes the child's everyday experiences. As a culture develops over many generations it provides artifacts that mediate between people and between people and their physical environment. An example is the above conversation between mother and child, which guides the child's cognitive structuring of her experiences. Culture-as-difference studies can of course lead to culture-as-medium studies by spotlighting the critical events in the child's life that express a particular cultural attitude that pushes the child in a particular direction.

The more "distant" levels of context, such as cultural beliefs about what kinds of skills children should acquire, often reach a child through the immediate social situation in which a child engages in activities with a parent, sibling, or peer that encourage these skills. Vygotsky expressed this process in his most well-known concept—the *zone of proximal development.*

ZONE OF PROXIMAL DEVELOPMENT

Vygotsky defined the zone of proximal (nearby) development as the distance between a child's "actual developmental level as determined by independent problem solving" and the higher level of "potential development as determined through problem solving under adult guidance or in collaboration with more capable peers" (1978, p. 86). A more competent person collaborates with a child to help him move from where he is now to where he can be with help. This person accomplishes this feat by means of prompts, clues, modeling, explanation, leading questions, discussion, joint participation, encouragement, control of the child's attention, and so on. As Vygotsky explained, "learning awakens a variety of internal developmental processes that are able to operate only when the child is interacting with people in his environment and in cooperation with his peers" (1978, p. 90). The more skilled adult builds on the competencies the child already has and presents him with activities supporting a level of competence slightly beyond where the child is now.

The dyadic memory episode described earlier provides one example of the zone of proximal development. The mother's prompts and hints scaffold the child's attempts to recall and help her organize her memories. Because the mother and child have a shared understanding of the earlier event they are able to talk about it together. Another example is the protocol at the start of this chapter in which a mother, helping her child construct a puzzle identical to a completed model, directs his attention to particular puzzle pieces in the model, points to corresponding pieces in his puzzle, and says the names of parts of the puzzle. The mother engages in "building bridges" (Rogoff, 1990, p. 8) between the child's present abilities and new skills. She does this by arranging and structuring his behavior in the task. An example from infancy is that parents draw their infant's attention to important aspects of the environment by carrying her close to, or pointing to, certain objects and events. Finally, children in various cultures learn skills valued by the culture— weaving, hunting, sorcery, healing, reading, taking a bus, or operating computers—by observing others and responding to their informal instruction. For example, a nomadic tribe of magicians and other entertainers in Pakistan highly values the skills of careful observation, refined visual discrimination, sensitivity to the characteristics of other people, and selective attention to the important aspects of a task (Berland, 1982). When the adults were tested on a conservation task, if even a single grain of rice spilled out during the pouring or a few drops of water remained in the transfer container they would judge that there now was less. They sometimes remarked that "when there is little food and many stomachs, our eyes, ears, and noses are more sensitive than goldsmiths' scales" (p. 174). The adults engage in everyday activities with children that encourage these perceptual skills, which are relevant to their nomadic life (e.g., acute awareness of surroundings) and magic performances (e.g., control of the audience's attention). Thus, adults provide "user-friendly" contexts that help children perfect skills that are needed to survive or succeed in the culture. Each culture has its own "cultural curriculum" (Rogoff, 1990, p. 190).

Vygotsky described the relation between the actual and potential levels as follows:

> The zone of proximal development defines those functions that have not yet matured but are in the process of maturation, functions that will mature tomorrow but are currently in an embryonic state. These functions could be

termed the "buds" or "flowers" of development rather than the "fruits" of development. The actual developmental level characterizes mental development restrospectively, while the zone of proximal development characterizes mental development prospectively.

[1978, pp. 86–87]

Vygotsky and other contextualists believe that development can be understood only by looking directly at the process of change, not at a static child frozen in one developmental moment. Process is more important than product (e.g., correct or incorrect answers). They look directly at a child's series of actions and thoughts as she tries to solve a problem and, in the process, advance her own thinking. Rather than focus on what concepts a child "has," they examine what a child actually does over time when involved in an activity, typically with other people and objects. Vygotsky took this developmental stance not only for short-term learning when moving through the zone and long-term development throughout childhood, but also for the development of a species over many generations and for sociocultural history. He stated that to study a child's development means

to study it in the process of change. . . . To encompass in research the process of a given thing's development in all its phases and changes—from birth to death—fundamentally means to discover its nature, its essence, for "it is only in movement that a body shows what it is."

[1978, p. 65]

As we will see later, this view has important implications for how one assesses a child's ability. It also speaks to instruction. Instruction, whether formal schooling or informal apprenticeships, should be based on children's potential level (their "readiness") more than on their actual level: "The only 'good learning' is that which is in advance of development" (Vygotsky, 1978, p. 89).

Vygotsky was particularly interested in how the zone operates in explicitly instructional settings. Instruction is based on the assumption that it is mainly by changing social interaction that one can change a child's own functioning. Palincsar and Brown (1984, 1988) have incorporated this notion in their "reciprocal teaching" intervention program in which a child alternates between the roles of questioner and respondent during reading lessons. A main goal is a shift from teacher-regulated activity to child self-regulation (see also Moll, 1990). However, in Rogoff's (1990) extension of the notion of the zone, adults need not explicitly instruct children in face-to-face interaction; children can learn from skilled adults at a distance by observing everyday activities in which there is no intention to teach the child. Instruction can be implicit as well as explicit. Learning is a natural by-product of involvement in tasks with adults or more competent peers. Any verbal explanation occurs naturally while working together rather than as part of intentional instruction. Interactions in the zone do not have to be verbal, especially those involving infants and young children. Their behaviors resemble "those appropriate for anyone learning in an unfamiliar culture: stay near a trusted guide, watch the guide's activities and get involved in the activities when possible, and attend to any instruction the guide provides" (Rogoff, 1990, p. 17).

Rogoff expresses these ideas in her notion of *guided participation,* which

> involves collaboration and shared understanding in routine problem-solving activities. Interaction with other people assists children in their development by guiding their participation in relevant activities, helping them adapt their understanding to new situations, structuring their problem-solving attempts, and assisting them in assuming responsibility for managing problem solving. . . . Routine arrangements . . . guide children's increasingly skilled and appropriate participation in the daily activities valued in their culture.
>
> *[1990, p. 191]*

Children share in the views and values of the more expert partner, offer their own views, and engage "in the process of stretching their concepts to find a common ground" (p. 196). They are encouraged to try out their emerging skills in the task. Rogoff uses the metaphor of apprenticeship to capture the notion of children's active verbal or nonverbal participation in real-life settings with more skilled, supportive others. These cultural apprenticeships "provide the beginner with access to both the overt aspects of the skill and the more hidden inner processes of thought" (p. 40).

A cultural apprenticeship can be illustrated by the way in which Mayan girls learn how to weave on a loom—an important skill in that culture (Rogoff, 1990). Very young girls watch their mothers and other adult women weave. By age 5 they are plaiting long leaves on a play loom fashioned from pieces of thread they find. By age 7 they weave, with help, on real looms and by 9 weave simple items alone.

Learning within the zone is possible in part because of *intersubjectivity*—shared understanding, based on a common focus of attention and a common goal, between a child and a more competent person. For infants and young children, this person is most likely to be a parent because their frequent experience together builds shared understandings. For example, in a laboratory classification task, a mother related the task to the kitchen in the child's home: "We're going to organize things by categories. You know, just like we don't put the spoons in the pan drawer and all that stuff" (Rogoff & Gardner, 1984). It is important to note that intersubjectivity not only contributes to learning from social interactions but also results from these interactions. Each builds on and contributes to the other throughout development.

It must be emphasized that instruction within the zone is not unidirectional. The child's behavior affects the adult's behavior as much as the adult's behavior affects the child. The child actively constructs new knowledge and skills with the help of more skilled others. Children actively contribute in that, motivated to learn, they "invite" the adult to participate and gradually take on more responsibility for carrying out the activity. And the adult adjusts the level of guidance to the child's response. Current contextualist approaches, especially those of Rogoff (1990) and Bronfenbrenner (1989a), emphasize children's active role in their own development. The term "collaborate" is often used to reflect the child's equal contribution. Integrated with Vygotsky's framework, the notion is that a child is an active partner in the process of moving through the zone of proximal development. Children seek out certain social contexts, ask more skilled adults for help in these contexts, and gradually take on more responsibility in these settings.

Bronfenbrenner (1989a, 1989b) has identified four ways in which children's nature actively shapes their social contexts:

1. Personal attributes encourage or discourage reactions from other people that facilitate or damage psychological development (see also Bandura's "reciprocal determinism" in Chapter 3). A fussy baby, a physically unattractive preschooler, or a hyperactive school-age child may repel adults. A happy, smiling baby, a beautiful preschooler, or a good-natured, calm 8-year-old has the opposite effect and thus creates a different environment for herself. She is likely to respond in kind to warm social attention, setting in motion a chain of reciprocal exchanges that chart a course of development for her that is rather different from that of the other child.

2. From early in life, children display individual differences in their tendency to approach or avoid particular aspects of the social and physical world. Temperamental differences are expressed in social extroversion, shyness (avoiding social stimulation), resistance to changes in the environment, a high activity level, and so on. Consequently, different children seek out different types of contexts and thus engage in somewhat different developmentally relevant activities. One child may prefer to be a "child in structured, quiet, two-person context" whereas another may tend to be a "child in unpredictable, loud, multiperson context." In this way, different skills and learning styles may develop.

3. Children also differ in the "tendency to engage and persist in progressively more complex activities; for example, to elaborate, restructure . . . and even to create new features in one's environment" (Bronfenbrenner, 1989b, pp. 8–9). Differences in creativity and the need for change also affect children's choice of settings.

4. Age differences (and individual differences) arise in children's conceptions of their power to achieve their goals and to control their successes and failures (see Bandura's notion of self-efficacy in Chapter 3). For example, preschoolers tend to overpredict how well they perform, even in the face of negative feedback. This Pollyanna belief system actually may be quite adaptive, because it keeps young children with limited competencies trying new activities that in reality are well beyond their ability; this experience has the effect of helping them develop the needed skills (Bjorklund & Green, 1992).

Bronfenbrenner cautions that these contributions of an active individual "do not *determine* the course of development; rather, they may be thought of as 'putting the spin' on a body in motion. The effect of that spin depends on the other forces, and resources, in the total ecological system" (1989b, p. 12).

A final comment about the zone is that although it usually is used to refer to child–adult or child–skilled peer interactions, Vygotsky actually had a broader definition in mind. The zone can refer to any situation in which some activity is leading children beyond their current level of functioning. Thus the zone can operate during play, work, school studies, and other leading activities (Griffin & Cole, 1989). Regarding play, it is only within the mental support system provided by play that young children can begin to use objects in a symbolic way—substitute one object for another and thereby separate the object's meaning from the object itself. When children "ride" a stick they separate the stick from its usual meaning. In play, children are no longer captured by the way objects look. They can make an object mean Y even though they can see it is an X. Play creates a zone of proximal development for a child because he operates at a higher level than in nonplay activities: "In play it is as though he were a head taller than himself" (Vygotsky, 1978, p. 102).

THE SOCIOCULTURAL ORIGINS OF INDIVIDUAL MENTAL FUNCTIONING: THE INTERMENTAL CONSTRUCTS THE INTRAMENTAL

What happens to children cognitively when they interact with adults? Vygotsky's answer is that interaction between a child and an adult or older child on the intermental (between-minds) plane becomes internalized into the child's mind, the intramental (within-mind) plane. The external becomes internal. In this sense, thinking is always social and reflects the culture in which the dyad operates. Thinking, remembering, and attending are activities not only of an individual; they first were carried out between individuals. As Vygotsky expresses it, any higher intellectual function acquired during development

> appears twice, or on two planes. . . . It appears first between people as an intermental category, and then within the child as an intramental category. This is equally true with regard to voluntary attention, logical memory, the formation of concepts, and the development of will.

[1960, pp. 197–198]

This movement from the intermental to the intramental is related to the first two characteristics described in this section. First, it explains why a child-in-activity-in-context is the smallest possible unit to study. Intramental activity cannot be divorced from intermental activity between children and people in their social context. Second, the internalization of social processes can be seen during a child's movement through the zone of proximal development. Children eventually internalize the mode of problem solving that was first supported socially. As Vygotsky expressed it, "Children grow into the intellectual life of those around them" (1978, p. 88). Both social interaction and the language involved are internalized. In a sense, children mentally interact with themselves as they did earlier with other people. Children gradually take on more and more responsibility for problem solving and become more self-regulated rather than other-regulated.

The notions that social activity shapes the mind and that a collectivist society shares the knowledge and experience with less advanced members of society come from Marxist philosophy. This view that intermental (between-people) activity is primary and intramental (within a person) activity is secondary—derived from the primary one—is opposite the view of much of contemporary Western psychology, which locates cognition "inside" an autonomous individual.

Different types of settings offer different types of interpsychological activities. Teacher–student cognitive activities may be more formal, verbal, and objective than parent–child or older peer–younger peer activities. Scientific thinking may emerge from the first, whereas intuitive, concrete thought may be more prevalent in the latter two. Because children encounter a variety of settings they incorporate a variety of mental processes (Tulviste, 1991).

One particularly important aspect of society is language. Just as two people communicate with each other, so does a child communicate with herself as she thinks. In fact, internalization of interpersonal communication leads to intrapersonal communications during development. The dialoguelike, question-and-answer interaction between adult and child becomes an internal dialogue, as evidenced in the following child talking to himself as he looks for a word in a dictionary: "Now, where do I find this? I know, I know, under 'C'" (Berk & Garvin, 1984). We will describe the role of language in cognitive development in more detail later.

Both Vygotsky and Piaget emphasized the internalization of interaction between a child and the world. However, Vygotsky stressed social interaction whereas Piaget was more interested in motor actions on physical objects. For Piaget, for example, physical reversibility, such as crawling from A to B and back to A or pouring liquid from container A to B and back to A, later becomes the important concrete operation of mental reversibility. The process, but not the content, is similar for Vygotsky. For Vygotsky, the structure of conversations becomes the structure of thought. Collaboration and dialogue between two people leads to these sorts of mental activity during individual private thought. Although Piaget also recognized the influence of other people on a developing child, he emphasized internalization of regularities in the child's motoric interactions with physical objects. Also, he did not address the changing nature of society itself during the life of an individual or over generations.

Intramental processes and structures do not copy intermental ones perfectly. Rather, intermental processes are transformed during the internalization process. For example, inner speech, to be described later, is an abbreviated, personal version of external speech. Rogoff emphasizes that children actively constrain what they retain from social exchanges. She explains: "The individual's use of this shared understanding is not the same as what was constructed jointly; it is an appropriation of the shared activity by each individual that reflects the individual's understanding of and involvement in the activity" (1990, p. 195). She uses an analogy of the constant exchange of water and air between the body and the environment. Just as bodies filter and transform air and water to meet biological needs, so do our minds assimilate these social activities in our "social sea" to our current needs and abilities. In the process minds are changed. A child can now better handle another, similar situation.

A child's selective appropriation of a new idea from a social exchange can be seen in the following conversation between a mother (P. Miller) and her (then) 4-year-old daughter:

M: What do you think you'd like to be when you grow up?

C: A mommy!

M: That's nice . . . but if you want you can be a mommy and something else.

C: I just want to be a mommy.

M: You know, I'm a mommy and a teacher—two things. You could do that too.

C: I just want to be a mommy.

(This continues for a while until the child concedes—sort of.)

C: Okay . . . I'll be a mommy and a bird!

The child appropriated certain meanings from this conversation and ignored other aspects of the mother's meaning.

Rogoff (1990) favors the notion of appropriation over internalization because the latter connotes a barrier between the individual and interpersonal aspects of functioning—a barrier that does not in fact exist. She argues that because "internal" and "external" are naturally blended in the shared meaning of social exchanges, there are no barriers between self and other; "internal" and "external" are not separate. As Rogoff states, "It is impossible to say 'whose' an object of joint focus is, or 'whose' a collaborative idea is" (p. 195). In this view, children's changed understanding is a natural by-product of their participation in joint thinking, not an external idea gone underground.

INTELLECTUAL FUNCTIONING IS MEDIATED BY TOOLS PROVIDED BY A CULTURE

As mentioned earlier, Vygotsky and Soviet social theorists claimed that humans create themselves (that is, their intellectual functioning) through activity: "Humans master themselves from the outside—through psychological tools" (Vygotsky, 1981, p. 141). Peers and adults assist in this self-shaping process by helping children learn how to use their culture's psychological and technical tools. Psychological tools include language systems, counting systems, writing, diagrams, maps, conventional signs, and works of art. Other examples are various strategies for learning, attending, or memorizing, like those described by information-processing psychologists. Some tools that influence thinking are physical devices such as computers, calculators, and typewriters. People use psychological tools to control thought or behavior, just as they use technical tools such as axes and plows to control nature. Both kinds of tools mediate between the child and the environment. However, technical tools are externally oriented—towards changing objects—whereas psychological tools are internally oriented—towards changing ways of thinking and controlling and organizing behavior.

Psychological tools transform the *elementary mental functions*—mental abilities we have in common with other animals—into *higher mental functions* such as voluntary attention and logical and abstract thinking. Elementary mental functions are controlled by external stimuli, such as when perception and attention are elicited by a physical object. Higher mental functions use language and other symbol systems to voluntarily think about these objects and use them to solve problems.

Each tool involves a different cognitive skill or style. For a contemporary example, one might argue that people's style of thinking is transformed when they "write" with a computer with a word processing program rather than with a pen or typewriter. A computer permits users to continually and rapidly translate reorganizations of their thoughts into an external form that they can evaluate immediately. Will children who use computers during their cognitive formative years develop thinking that differs from that of previous generations? An older example is the invention of paper. Societies without paper made different demands on children's memory than do societies with paper. The rote memorization of oral texts was less important after the invention of paper.

These examples show that a culture's tools connect children, through their activities, with the physical and social world. A culture creates these tools to help people master the environment, the favored tools are passed on to children during social interchanges, and in turn the tools shape children's minds. Children use the tools to help themselves think; tools actually transform thought. For example, once language is used to help memory, the nature of remembering may change to a more verbal form. More generally, we learn to use artificial devices to organize and control our attempts to adapt to our social and physical surroundings. The Vygotskian phrase "historical construction of the mind" refers to how the invention of tools over the course of the history of a culture has brought changes in how people in that culture think. A particular culture at a particular moment in its history provides certain possibilities for children's development.

For Vygotsky, language is the most important psychological tool. It frees us from our immediate perceptual experience and allows us to represent the unseen, the past, and the future. Thinking and language are dynamically related; comprehending and producing language are processes that transform, not merely influence, the process of thinking. Language "alters the entire flow and structure of mental functions. It does this by determining the structure of a new instrumental act, just as a technical tool alters the process of a natural adaptation by determining the form of labor operations" (Vygotsky, 1981, p. 137). "Just as a mold gives shape to a substance, words can shape an activity into a structure" (Vygotsky, 1978, p. 28). Language is primarily a social device for social contact, communication, and interpersonal influence. This social tool goes into the mental underground to direct thinking, control one's own behavior during development, organize categories of reality, represent the past, and plan for the future. The intermental becomes intramental.

Language also transforms the way children use technical tools. It reorganizes and controls their behavior with these objects, thus permitting new forms of problem solving. For example, Vygotsky (1978) described Levina's observations of children trying to obtain a piece of candy out of reach in a cupboard. Preschoolers typically first try to get the candy silently, then begin to talk aloud to themselves about the problem. Eventually the speech becomes more planful and addresses, for example, the possible usefulness of a stool and a stick. Vygotsky concluded: "Children not only speak about what they are doing; their speech and action are part of one and the same complex psychological function, directed toward the solution of the problem at hand. . . . Children solve practical tasks with the help of their speech, as well as their eyes and hands" (pp. 25–26). There is a unity of perception, speech, and action. Language is a tool and works in conjunction with other tools.

Although language was a product of history, it then changed the course of history. Language changed the way adults interacted with each other and raised their children. Recently, contextualists have pointed out that cultures vary in how much parents use language in their interactions with children. For example, the Navajo tend to teach quietly by demonstration (Cazden & John, 1971). The direction of gaze and facial expression can be effective nonverbal teaching cues. Verbal communication may be more necessary in cultures in which children are separated from adults and have little opportunity to observe and participate in adult occupational and recreational activities (Rogoff, 1990). When infants are carried on cradleboards on the mother's back all day and children are in the setting where their parents work so that they can observe work activities, explicit verbalizations about how to do things may be less important.

Contemporary contextualists also point out that using verbal mediation to solve problems is more prevalent in the Western industrialized world. For example, Kearins (1981, 1986) compared Australian aboriginal children of desert origin and European Australian children on visual spatial memory tasks. She showed children aged 6 to 17 an array of items and asked them to recreate the array after she piled the items together. The aboriginal children performed better than the European Australian children. The latter tried to use verbal mediational strategies, such as rehearsing the names of the items, which were inefficient for this type of task. In contrast, the aboriginal children were more successful because they used relevant visual strategies developed to help them find their way around the desert.

Different cultures emphasize different kinds of tools (for example, verbal or nonverbal), skills (reading, mathematics, or spatial memory), and social interaction (formal schooling or informal or formal apprenticeships) because of different cultural needs and values. Many cultures use schooling to transmit important tools to children. A culture that emphasizes the memorization of religious texts instills different cognitive skills from a culture with schools stressing conceptual understanding and scientific reasoning. These are intellectual skills needed in a highly technological society relying heavily on communication through books and other symbolic media. We should not assume that these values are shared by all cultures, or even that they would be adaptive in other cultures. Rogoff (1990) notes that in 1744 a group of North American Indians politely declined an invitation from the commissioners from Virginia to send boys to William and Mary College. The Indian leaders explained that several of their youth who had been instructed in such institutions returned "ignorant of every means of living in the woods; unable to bear either cold or hunger; knew neither how to build a cabin, take a deer, or kill an enemy . . . neither fit for hunters, warriors, or counsellors; they were totally good for nothing" (Drake, 1834, p. 25). More generally, the definition of intelligence differs from one culture to another. For instance, adults in a Ugandan village describe an intelligent person as slow and careful, whereas Westernized groups emphasize speed of thinking (Wober, 1972). In contrast, Kenyans include the responsible participation in family and social life in their definition of intelligence (Super & Harkness, 1983).

In summary, the culture provides children with tools and other resources "that invite, afford, or motivate the particular form of development they require to live in such a world" (Shotter, 1989, p. 192). Tools help shape children's thinking and children use tools to express their thoughts to others.

METHODOLOGY

Vygotsky favored a *dynamic assessment* of children's potential developmental levels rather than only a static assessment of their actual levels. He felt that what children can do with the assistance of others is a better reflection of their intellectual ability than what they can do alone. A child "is" what he "can be." A dynamic assessment directly measures children's readiness or potential for learning, rather than the products of previous learning. Standardized intelligence tests assess the latter. Dynamic assessments often reveal performance gains that are undetected by standard assessments. This is especially true of "underachievers" who do not typically work up to their ability level.

To illustrate how dynamic and traditional assessments can lead to different conclusions, Vygotsky presented the following example:

> Imagine that we have examined two children and have determined that the mental age of both is seven years. This means that both children solve tasks accessible to seven-year-olds. However, when we attempt to push these children further in carrying out the tests, there turns out to be an essential difference between them. With the help of leading questions, examples, and demonstrations, one of them easily solves test items taken from two years above the child's level of (actual) development. The other solves test items that are only a half-year above his or her level of (actual) development. . . . With the help of this method, we can take stock not only of today's completed process of development, not only the cycles that are already concluded and done, not only the processes of maturation that are completed; we can also take stock of processes that are now in the state of coming into being, that are only ripening, or only developing.

[1956, pp. 446–448]

These two children obviously are not the same cognitively. One can proceed far with help and thus is said to have a "wide" zone; the other cannot and thus has a "narrow" zone.

The zone of proximal development can be assessed in several ways. One way is to provide a single clue and observe how much a child improves. Ferrara, Brown, and Campione (1986) favored providing an increasingly specific series of clues and determining how many are needed for a child to solve the problem. Children were to pretend they were a spy who wanted to send a message in a secret code. To figure out the code they had to find the pattern in a series of letters and add the next four letters, for example, NGOHPIQJ _ _ _ _. The first clue was "Is this problem like any other you've seen before?" A later clue was "Point to the N and O in the alphabet . . . and to the G and H. . . . Does that help at all?"

Another version of the gradation-of-cues approach involves presenting, during the adult assistance phase, only those aspects of the problem that the child did not understand initially. For instance, Soviet researcher Egorova (as reported in Wozniak, 1980) assessed children's visual analytic ability by counting the number of features mentioned when children described a cherry tree branch. Children then were shown pairs of pictures designed to teach only those features they had not mentioned on the initial assessment. Each pair differed on a single feature such as shape or number. Children described the pictures and, if they could not detect the differing feature, were given a series of prompts (cues) by the tester. Then the original assessment was repeated. This study showed a pattern of results typical of Soviet dynamic assessments: normal children progressed the most, learning-disabled children also benefited substantially, and mentally retarded children benefited minimally.

Another implication of the zone of proximal development for assessment is that a child will perform at a higher level in some settings than others. In earlier chapters this was attributed to characteristics of the task (salience, familiarity) or the child (degree of experience, mental modules). The contextualists would identify social support and motivated problem solving as other causes. The former is illustrated by the examples of zone research observed in this chapter. An example of the latter is that young children often reveal greater social cognition in family contexts than in the laboratory. At home they effectively use their social intelligence on what matters most to them emotionally—their own rights, needs, and interests. For example, Dunn (1988) describes a 24-month-old with an older sister who had three imaginary friends— Lilly, Allelujah, and Peepee. The younger child taunted her sibling by announcing that she was Allelujah! This rather advanced understanding of what would upset her sister and the ability to pretend to have a different identity are skills that are more advanced than those usually seen in the laboratory in children this young.

Vygotsky's studies of the zone illustrate his more general method of studying development by looking at change during one or several experimental sessions. This has been called the *microgenetic* method. The researcher tries to capture a "developmental moment." As we saw in the chapter on information processing, this method of observing change is used today by Robert Siegler and other investigators. One example of Vygotsky's use of this method is setting up obstacles that disrupt routine procedures of problem solving and observing attempts to cope with this change. Another example is providing various materials or tools that could be used for problem solving and observing how children of different ages select from and use these objects. Because the task typically exceeds a child's cognitive level she must construct a new skill. Some of these methods will be illustrated in the next section by specific studies using the "double-stimulation" method. It is obvious from the focus on the *process* of problem solving that careful observation of behavior and qualitative descriptions of types of behavior are essential Vygotskian methodology.

For contemporary research, the main methodological message of the contextualists is that in order to understand behavior we must study the child's context as well as the child. Better yet, we should study the phenomenon in several contexts. We must sample environments like we do subjects. Researchers cannot assume that they have observed a general developmental phenomenon if they have included only one context. In fact, universal developmental phenomena may be rare. Developmental processes themselves may vary from one context to another. For example, in different cultures or subcultures the process by which parents attempt to instill values in their children may vary. Cultures may vary in the use of verbal instruction, modeling, and punishment. One particularly compelling example concerns Baumrind's (e.g., 1973) often-cited research demonstrating the superiority of the authoritative pattern of child rearing (a combination of firmness and support) over highly controlling or permissive patterns for increasing achievement and independence in children. However, more recent research (Dornbusch, Ritter, Leiderman, Roberts, & Fraleigh, 1987) shows that this result is found mainly among whites, not African-Americans, Asians, or Hispanics. For example, the Asian parents were high on control, but their children generally received high grades in school. And controlling parents were associated with low grades among Hispanic girls but not Hispanic boys. Thus, the same parent–child behaviors may have different meaning in different cultures and for different social categories of children. Parental control may be interpreted as caring in one culture and a negative attitude in another.

Because of these considerations, contemporary contextualist research often is cross-cultural and includes samples from several countries, social classes, or ethnic groups. Similarly, multicontext research is necessary for assessing an individual, because a child may demonstrate a concept in one context but not another (see the discussion of domain-specific concepts in Chapter 1). Other characteristics of contextualist methodology include studying dyads or larger social groups rather than a child alone and observing them in everyday as well as laboratory settings. Ideally (though rarely in reality), contextual research examines each of Bronfenbrenner's four levels of context.

Researchers must be very careful when choosing the methods for assessing abilities in cultures other than their own. Consider how one might assess whether a person can classify objects in an abstract way, characteristic of adults in literate societies. Cole, Gay, Glick, and Sharp (1971) reported that African Kpelle farmers, when asked to put together the items that go together, sorted 20 objects into functional groups (e.g., knife with orange, potato with hoe) rather than into abstract categorical groups (e.g., foods, tools). Knife and orange go together, for example, because you cut an orange with a knife. (Such functional groupings are also typical of young children in literate societies.) At one point the experimenter happened to ask how a fool would do it. The farmers immediately put the foods together, the tools together, and so on! It should not be concluded that people do not possess a particular cognitive skill when they do not demonstrate it. They may be capable of abstract thinking but simply consider other ways of thinking to be more useful for certain everyday activities. This is an example of Wertsch's (1991, p. 93) "tool kit" metaphor for both cultural differences and age differences. Cultural groups differ in cognitive functioning not so much in what processes they possess as in which contexts they use them—in which psychological tool they select from their tool kit in a particular context.

EXAMPLES OF VYGOTSKIAN–CONTEXTUALIST RESEARCH

The following examples of research illustrate the characteristics of the theory, as described in the preceding section. Still other topics often addressed by Vygotsky include mental retardation, deafness, play, emotions, perception, and attention. He also studied schizophrenia, negativity in adolescents, the psychology of art, and even creativity in actors. Present-day contextualists study additional topics such as planning (e.g., Baker-Sennett, Matusov, & Rogoff, in press), schooling (e.g., Cole, 1990), intelligence (Ceci, 1990), collaborative interactions with peers (e.g., Ellis & Gauvain,1992; Tudge & Rogoff, 1989), and mother–infant interaction (e.g., Mosier & Rogoff, 1991).

EGOCENTRIC AND INNER SPEECH

Vygotsky was "forever intrigued with the inventive powers that language bestowed on mind—in ordinary speech, in the novels of Tolstoi and the plays of Chekov and the *Diary* of Doestoevski, in the stage directions of Stanislavskii, in the play of children" (Bruner, 1987, p. 2). Much of his research examined this powerful interplay between mind and language.

Vygotsky proposed that speech and thought are at first independent. Examples of nonconceptual speech are babbling and sounds produced in the presence of certain objects. There are numerous examples of nonverbal thought from Piaget's work with infants. Speech and thought begin to merge at around age 2. At that time "the knot is tied for the problem of thought and language" (Vygotsky, 1962, p. 43). Children learn that objects have names and thus use words as symbols. Next, at about age 3, speech between people splits into communicative speech to others and *egocentric speech*, which is audible speech for self. In egocentric speech, a child talks aloud to himself in a running dialogue, but uses his speech to guide his thinking, to think through a problem and plan his actions. Two examples appearing earlier in this chapter were the children talking to themselves while trying to obtain out-of-reach candy and while looking up a word in a dictionary. Later, at about age 7 or 8, egocentric speech becomes *inner speech*. Children now can silently "think in words," though inner speech is more abbreviated, idiosyncratic, and fragmented than spoken language. Just as children earlier used language only to influence others, they use it in egocentric and inner speech to influence themselves. In this way, language reflects its social origins: "When children find that they are unable to solve a problem . . . instead of appealing to the adult, children appeal to themselves" (Vygotsky, 1978, p. 27). The intermental becomes the intramental; interpersonal communication becomes intrapersonal communication.

Note that in form (auditory spoken), egocentric speech is like speech between people. However, in function it is like inner speech because both serve to direct thinking and behavior. Egocentric speech is spoken because children do not yet fully differentiate speech for others (communicative speech) and speech for self. As evidence, Vygotsky observed that children produced less egocentric speech in situations in which communication with others was impossible or difficult (a noisy room, a deaf or foreign-speaking peer, no one present) or undesirable (a stranger present). If egocentric speech were solely for oneself, then these conditions should have no effect. When children differentiate speech for others and the self, egocentric speech becomes inner speech.

Vygotsky found that egocentric speech increases when the task is made more difficult so that the child cannot solve it directly with other tools at his disposal. Some of Vygotsky's manipulations were to remove paper or a pencil of a needed color before a child began to draw, as seen in the protocol at the beginning of this chapter. With these impediments, egocentric speech nearly doubled among 5- to 7-year-olds (Luria, 1961). A recent example of research on egocentric speech is a longitudinal study in which children were observed while doing math work at their desks in their classroom (Bivens & Berk, 1990). As Vygotsky would have predicted, egocentric speech moved from external to more internal forms, such as lip movements and inaudible mutterings, from ages 7 to 10. Moreover, children with greater egocentric speech tended to have higher math achievement scores a year later, which suggests that egocentric speech facilitates learning. It should be noted, however, that egocentric speech never disappears entirely. Adults occasionally use egocentric speech to direct their activities for difficult tasks, as when they mutter to themselves while filling out income tax forms or assembling a bookshelf. For contemporary research on egocentric speech, now called "private speech," see Diaz and Berk (1991) and Zivin (1979).

We can compare Vygotsky's and Piaget's use of the term "egocentric speech" (see Piaget, 1962, for his response to Vygotsky's views on this topic). Piaget thought it simply reflects the child's inability to take another person's perspective. It has no use to children. In contrast, Vygotsky thought that egocentric speech helps children direct their problem-solving activities. Moreover, Piaget thought that egocentric speech just fades away, whereas Vygotsky thought it becomes inner speech. More generally, Piaget and Vygotsky have opposite views of the relationship between language and thought. Piaget thought that cognition is prior to, and broader than, language. Children develop through the sensorimotor period before acquiring language, and language is but one expression of the emerging symbolic ability around 18 to 24 months. Vygotsky thought that language and thought begin independently, then partially merge. As a result, language gives a tremendous boost to cognition, permitting forms of thinking that are not possible without the help of language.

Speech and thought never completely overlap, even in adults. There is always some nonverbal thought, such as tying one's shoes or playing the piano, and some nonconceptual speech—rote verbalizations such as saying a familiar address. Even when thoughts are expressed in words, they are never the same thing, according to Vygotsky. There is always a hidden subtext in our speech. As Vygotsky expressed it, "To understand another's speech, it is not sufficient to understand his words—we must understand his thought. But even that is not enough—we must also know its motivation" (1962, p. 151). For example, Vygotsky (1962) described a passage by Dostoevsky in which six drunken workmen conduct a brief but complex conversation, though the only speech is a single profane word. Depending on the way it was spoken, it indicated contempt, doubt, anger, delight, and so on. The developmental implication is that language acquisition is more than learning language structure and word meanings; it also requires the child to understand intonations of speech and the dynamics of social contexts, and to detect the thoughts and feelings of the speaker. Vygotsky was years ahead of his time in this very contemporary-sounding view of language pragmatics.

DEVELOPMENT OF CONCEPTS

One of Vygotsky's applications of the microgenetic method described earlier is the *double-stimulation method* developed by Sakharov, one of Vygotsky's collaborators. A child is given a task in which she can select certain materials to serve as a new means to solve a problem. The term "double stimulation" refers to the presence of two stimulus sources—typically, a stimulus with symbolic qualities, such as a word, and a nonsymbolic stimulus, often with perceptual qualities, such as a colored block. An older child is more likely than a younger child to use symbolic as well as nonsymbolic stimulus sources to solve a problem. By observing the child's choice of objects, actions on those objects, and remarks while thinking about the problem, the experimenter can infer the small cognitive advances emerging during the session.

To examine the development of concepts using this method, Vygotsky designed a set of 22 wooden blocks of different colors, shapes, heights, and sizes (horizontal area), now cleverly called the "Vygotsky blocks." No two blocks are identical. On the bottom of each block is one of four nonsense words: bik, cev, mur, or lag. "Bik" appears on all short, large blocks, regardless of color or shape, "cev" on all short, small ones, "mur" on all tall, small ones, and "lag" on all tall, large ones. The experimenter first spreads the blocks randomly in front of the child, then turns over one block to expose its name. The child is asked to select all the blocks she thinks are the same kind. After the child does this, the experimenter turns over one of the selected blocks that he knows is wrong and shows the child that it does not have the correct word. He asks the child to try again. This sequence is repeated until the child discovers which characteristics define the word. For example, a child's first collection for "bik" might consist of all short blocks, thus including some "cev" blocks as well. Eventually she would eliminate the latter blocks. Not only the child's initial collection but also her response to correction and efficiency in finding a solution indicate her cognitive level. In this use of the double-stimulation method, the physical characteristics of the objects are one source of stimulation and the nonsense words—the means of solving the problem—are another source. Notice that this study also illustrates movement through the zone of proximal development.

From various studies with the blocks, Vygotsky inferred three stages of conceptual development: (1) unorganized categories (for example, a random heap), (2) complexes (for example, a chain in which a large red block is next to a large blue block because of their identical size, which is next to a small blue block because of their identical color, and so on, so that each block is similar in some concrete way to the block next to it but no single abstract characteristic unites all the blocks), and (3) concepts (correct sorting on the basis of height and size, possible because the child can use the nonsense word to abstract out dimensions and detect similarities along these dimensions among the blocks). Note the Vygotskian emphasis on how language helps direct the child's problem-solving activities.

Another example of the double-stimulation method is the so-called "forbidden colors" task. Children must not use certain color words to answer questions posed by the experimenter and must not say any color twice. Colored cards (potential stimulus means) were provided as possible memory aids—as psychological tools for achieving the goal. From age 8 or 9 on, children construct new means to the goal by separating out the cards with the forbidden colors to help themselves avoid saying the colors. Younger children did not do this, even with help, as shown in the following protocol from a 4-year-old (forbidden colors were red and blue).

What color are houses?	Red [without looking at forbidden colors].
Is the sun shining brightly?	Yes.
What color is the sky?	White [without looking at card; but after replying, searches for white card]. Here it is! [Picks it up and keeps it in his hand.]
What colors are tomatoes?	Red. [Glances at cards.]
And what color are exercise books?	White—like this [pointing to white card]!
What color are balls?	White [looking at card].
Do you live in the town?	No.
. . .	. . .
Do you think you have won?	Don't know—yes.
What must you not do if you want to win?	Mustn't say red or blue.
And what else?	Mustn't say the same word twice.

[Vygotsky, 1978, p. 42]

Vygotsky was particularly interested in what he called *scientific concepts*—logically defined concepts that can have social as well as scientific and mathematical content. Children can use them consciously and deliberately because they are "distanced" from them. In contrast, *spontaneous concepts* refer to intuitive, concrete concepts based on everyday experience. For example, "grandmother," a spontaneous concept, is defined as "She has a soft lap" (Vygotsky, 1978, p. 50). As a scientific concept it is understood as an abstract familial relationship that is expressed by many different specific people, some of whom may not have soft laps.

Vygotsky thought that scientific concepts formed one of the most powerful psychological tools developed by modern society. Children enter into this type of thinking with their teachers at school and subsequently internalize it. However, "development in children never follows school learning the way a shadow follows the object that casts it" (Vygotsky, 1978, p. 91). Rather, children's minds are "ready" to accept this overlay; abstract thinking simply formalizes their preexisting intuitive concepts based on everyday experience. Scientific concepts handed down from above by teachers meet children's intuitive concepts halfway and become intertwined with them. Scientific concepts become more concrete and spontaneous concepts become more logical and abstract. Vygotsky gives the example that when teachers introduce the abstract concept of class conflict, children use their concrete personal knowledge ("spontaneous concept") of poor and rich people to assimilate this new concept. As intuitive concepts are transformed into scientific concepts, they are decontextualized—taken from the child's concrete experience into a context-free formal system. Children become conscious of these concepts and skills and consequently can voluntarily make use of them in a variety of contexts. This "meeting of the minds" that characterizes the interaction between teachers and students during the process of acquiring scientific concepts is yet another example of movement through the zone of proximal development.

Vygotsky argued that instruction in school requires children to form concepts by thinking about speech in a new way: children no longer can simply think about words as ways of communicating meaning; the words themselves become the objects of communication. Teachers direct children's attention explicitly towards the meanings of words and the relations among these words—a system of knowledge. For example, children are taught to examine the logical consistency of written statements isolated from their referents. Moreover, children become conscious of their own thought processes—a harbinger of what today is called "metacognition." Again, a new form of social dialogue leads to a new form of thought.

Contemporary contextualists have studied the effects of schooling more generally (e.g., Cole, 1990; Rogoff, 1990). Western schooling tends to teach cognitive skills removed from the practical contexts in which they will be used. These decontextualized activities include memorizing unrelated pieces of information, learning procedures for mathematical calculation, and mastering a written language system. It is difficult to conclude whether schooling has significant effects on general cognitive development, because unschooled children, who appear to perform poorly, may simply be unfamiliar with the language and procedures of testing—the "rules of the game" of testing. In many cultures children are taught not to talk back to a person of higher status, not to act in such a way that would draw attention to themselves, not to initiate a conversation, not to appear to be a fool by giving an obvious answer, and not to produce information that the questioner might not have (Rogoff, 1990).

GUIDED PARTICIPATION IN THE ZONE OF PROXIMAL DEVELOPMENT

Present-day contextualists have devoted only moderate research efforts to Vygotskian views on language and concept formation. However, they have shown a great deal of interest in the two research areas presented next: guided participation in the zone of proximal development and cross-cultural research. Many examples of the zone have appeared in earlier pages. Thus, the basic principles of the zone will be illustrated in a single study by Freund (1990). Children aged 3 and 5 helped a puppet move his furniture into his new house—basically a sorting task in which dollhouse furniture was sorted into a living room, kitchen, and so on. The experimenter told the children to put the objects into the rooms in which they belonged. A child could, for example, place a sofa, chair, small table, and lamp into one room and label it a living room. In the same way children formed other rooms as well. This procedure assessed how well they could perform on their own—their current level of functioning. Next, half of the children interacted with their mothers on easy and difficult versions of the task. The latter had more rooms and more objects. The experimenter instructed the mothers to help their children but not explicitly teach them. The other half of the children spent this time working on the tasks by themselves rather than with their mothers; the experimenter did, however, give them the correct solution at the end. In a posttest, the children once again performed a similar task on their own.

The children who had worked on the problem with their mothers performed at a more advanced level on the posttest than the children who had practiced on their own, even though the latter had been given the correct solution by the experimenter. Mothers acted in the way advocated by Vygotsky for optimal movement through the zone. In particular, they adjusted their behavior to the child's cognitive level. For example, they gave more specific content (e.g., "That stove goes in a kitchen") to the 3-year-olds than to the 5-year-olds. Mothers gave the older children more general help, such as planning and keeping the goal in mind (e.g., "Let's make the bedroom and then the kitchen"). Mothers' sensitivity to the 3-year-olds' greater potential on the easy task than on the hard one led them to give general prompts to some extent on the easy task. Mothers tended to talk more in the difficult version. Thus, the mothers were giving their children as much responsibility as they thought they could handle, given their age and the difficulty of the particular task. They tried to structure their children's activities so that the children could move through the zone and gradually take on more responsibility for placing the objects. The dyads also showed intersubjectivity and use of their shared past experience in mothers' statements such as "Where do we keep our refrigerator at home?" Finally, the children also contributed to the exchange by actively attempting to solve the problems and adjusting their behavior in response to feedback.

CROSS-CULTURAL RESEARCH

Cross-cultural research contributes to our understanding of development in two main ways. First, it identifies universal characteristics of development and mechanisms by which culture affects development. Second, it shows us that certain child behaviors, stages, and child-rearing activities are not universal. Rather, they are the product of particular cultural–social–historical circumstances. In this way, our attention is drawn to what is "invisible" in our own culture because we are so accustomed to its presence. For example, nearly all middle-class babies in the United States sleep in their own bed and often in a different room from the parents. And U.S. parents encourage their babies to sleep through the night. In contrast, parents do not push babies toward sleeping through the night in cultures where parents and infants share a bed so that nursing on demand is possible, where parents need not live by the clock, and where babies are strapped to their mothers' backs while they work during the day—all true of rural Kenyan children (Super & Harkness, 1983). Families in each culture consider their sleeping arrangement as the only reasonable one. Mayan mothers, for example, expressed pity for babies in the United States when told that they slept in their own rooms (Morelli, Rogoff, Oppenheim, & Goldsmith, 1992). They considered this harmful for the babies. Japanese parents believe that babies are born separate beings who must be taught feelings of interdependence with other people, and sleeping with parents is thought to encourage this process (Caudill & Weinstein, 1969). In contrast, parents in the United States (and most Western social developmental theorists) believe that babies are born dependent and must develop independence; a separate bed is thought to facilitate this. It is interesting to think about this cultural difference in light of the discussion of bonding and attach-ment in Chapter 5.

Cross-cultural studies describe many striking cultural differences in verbal interaction patterns between parents and their children (Rogoff, 1990). In some cultures, children are expected to play a passive role in this activity—responding when spoken to but not initiating verbal interactions or participating equally in conversations. Mayan adults, for example, think that a child is challenging adults with her greater knowledge if she tells them something. In many cultures most of the care of young children comes from older sisters, who consequently may be the young children's main conversational partners. In these cultures, children still may learn a great deal from adults through nonverbal interactions—observing them in adult work settings in particular. Although this interaction pattern may work quite well in everyday settings, it may not prepare them for the verbal discourse expected by teachers in formal schooling, such as asking questions and making eye contact with the teacher. Navajo children, for example, sit quietly and observe their teachers more than twice as much as do Caucasian children in the same classroom (Guilmet, 1979).

Another cultural difference in adult-child interaction patterns is that North American middle-class mothers usually hold their infants facing toward them, whereas in many cultures, such as in the Marquesas Islands in the South Pacific, mothers hold their infants facing away from them (Martini & Kirkpatrick, 1981). Facing babies outward may reflect both the deemphasis on parent-child verbal interaction described above and an attempt to encourage children to observe and interact with older siblings and other members of the community. This orientation of children away from the parent to the larger community may indicate the sense of community typically found in such villages. Community members may share in the socialization of the young, reprimanding misbehavior in other people's children.

Bornstein and his colleagues (Bornstein, Toda, Azuma, Tamis-Le-Monda, & Ogino, 1990; Bornstein, Tal, & Tamis-LeMonda, 1991) have observed American and Japanese (Tokyo) mothers interacting with their 5-month-old infants. At this point infants in both cultures show equal amounts and types of orientation to their mothers and to physical objects in the environment. However, their mothers respond differently in the two cultures. American mothers are more responsive when babies orient to physical objects; Japanese mothers are more responsive when their babies orient to them. Mothers even tried to change their babies' attention to fit their preferences—toward themselves for the Japanese and toward objects for Americans. Japanese mothers in general continue to encourage their young children's dependence on them. These specific behaviors are a concrete expression of a very general cultural belief system. The Japanese culture values social ties and dependency; American culture values autonomy and independence. Culture clearly is directing development.

When Japanese children enter preschool, the value placed on group harmony continues to be instilled in them (Cole, 1992b). For example, American educators viewing a videotape of Japanese preschool were shocked that there were 30 preschoolers and only one teacher. In contrast, Japanese educators viewing the American classroom with only a few students per teacher expressed concern for the children: "A class that size seems kind of sad and underpopulated" and "I wonder how you teach a child to become a member of a group in a class that small" (Tobin, Wu, & Davidson, 1989). In the Japanese mind, "A child's humanity is realized most fully not so much in his ability to be independent from the group as [in] his ability to cooperate and feel part of the group" (Tobin et al., 1989, p. 39). As Markus and Kitayama (1991) observe, in America "the squeaky wheel gets the grease" and in Japan "the nail that stands out gets pounded down."

Even something as universal-sounding as mathematics is touched by culture. First, numerical symbol systems differ. Certain cultures in New Guinea, for example, use the names of parts of the body for their counting system. Counting begins with the thumb of one hand and progresses through 29 separate locations (each finger, wrist, elbow, shoulder, right ear, right eye, nose, left eye, and so on) through the far side of the other hand (Saxe, 1981). Second, the form of mental calculation varies as a function of the culture's symbol system. In the Orient, people often use abacuses to solve math problems. At least among older children who achieve expertise, these devices encourage people to solve calculation problems in their head by forming a mental image of the abacus (Stigler, 1984). As evidence, when they make an error, it is of the type that would be expected if they were reading from such a mental image rather than the type made by people in cultures where the abacus is not used. Third, certain social-cultural contexts encourage the development of mathematical skills. One example comes from Saxe's (1988) research on child candy vendors on the streets of Brazil. They must very quickly perform various numerical activities—purchase candy, decide on a sale price, negotiate the price, make change, and so on. Despite their generally disadvantageous childhood environment, they develop impressive mental calculation abilities. Interestingly, when child street vendors are asked to solve similar math problems outside the vending context, they perform much more poorly (Carraher, Carraher, & Schliemann, 1985). Another example is that Asian children surpass American children in their mathematical prowess. One cause may be that Asian mothers generally attribute mathematical performance to trying hard and not giving up, and instill these behaviors in their children. In contrast, American mothers tend to emphasize inherent ability, an attribution that does not encourage studying hard (Stevenson, Lee, & Stigler, 1986). Moreover, the Japanese language system encourages attention to the quantitative aspect of reality. There are separate words for counting people, birds, four-legged animals, broad thin objects such as sheets of paper, and long thin objects such as sticks. And Japanese mothers encourage even very young children to play counting games, such as "Let's count birds" (Hatano, cited in Siegler, 1991, pp. 163–164; 1989).

MECHANISMS OF DEVELOPMENT

Vygotsky and the contextualists focus on change and the mechanisms it involves rather than the outcome, or performance, of the child. For Vygotsky, development follows a dialectical process of thesis (one idea or phenomenon), antithesis (an opposing idea or phenomenon), and synthesis (resolution), which produces a higher-level concept or more advanced functioning. Examples of these two opposing ideas, phenomena, forces, or events are spontaneous, intuitive concepts versus scientific concepts (see "Development of Concepts"), children's level of cognitive functioning with and without an adult's help (see "Zone of Proximal Development"), the child versus the problem to be solved, and nature versus nurture. These opposing elements confront each other, intertwine, and become transformed into a new and higher level.

Klaus Riegel (1976) identified four sources of developmental change in a dialectical process: (1) inner biological, (2) individual psychological, (3) cultural–sociological, and (4) outer physical. Conflict can occur within each dimension, for example, parent–child conflict in the individual–psychological dimension or conflict between racial groups in the cultural–sociological dimension. In addition, as each of these four factors undergoes change, it affects and is affected by changes in the other three factors. These various causes are not simply added together; they interact. A serious illness (inner biological change) may thwart one's career and cause family tensions (individual psychological dimension). Changing a child's schooling from a traditional classroom to an "open" classroom (cultural–sociological change) may cause confusion and insecurity (individual psychological dimension).

Riegel emphasized that life is a sequence of *concrete* interacting events and episodes as the individual grows within a sociohistorical context. At any point in time, the four factors may be in or out of synchrony, but a lack of synchrony is much more common. Development is a lifelong process of trying to resolve the inevitable conflicts among these factors and within each factor. An active individual tries to cope with an active world and learns to live with a certain amount of contradiction. In fact, conflict plays a major role in bringing about successful development: "Rather than regarding these critical episodes in a negative manner or from a fatalistic point of view, they provide the fundamental basis for the development of the individual and for the history of society" (Riegel, 1976, p. 695).

The idea that there is continual conflict punctuated by momentary stable structures is similar to Piaget's notion of equilibration. Both Vygotsky and Piaget saw a dialectical process at work. However, Piaget did not include a changing society or changing physical environment as possible sources of disequilibrium; he saw an active organism but a somewhat passive environment. Vygotsky, of course, assigned a greater role to social forces, such as parental guidance, teacher instruction, and language, in this process than did Piaget. Another difference is that Vygotsky emphasized the collaboration of people or ideas in this process, whereas Piaget emphasized conflict between one's own concepts and those of a peer or adult.

The dialectical process proceeds through various means. Verbal and nonverbal interaction with adults or more advanced peers, play, and using technological and psychological tools are all important. Engaging in progressively more complex activities and tasks and internalizing social interaction and psychological tools bring about much of the change during development. Modern contextualists emphasize that children engage in an increasingly diverse set of contexts during development, which permits them to acquire many kinds of skills.

The specific processes of change during the dialectical process of adult–child interaction were described earlier in this chapter. During the internalization (or appropriation) process the intermental becomes intramental. Through guided participation, children respond to support and instruction from others and actively contribute to the instructional process. A child and an adult collaborate, and the child gradually takes on more responsibility for problem solving and other activities. Language (or other cultural tools) and observation of other people's activities contribute to the process of change. Once inner speech and various skilled activities are acquired, they in turn stimulate more advanced thinking.

Vygotsky emphasized change resulting from interaction between a child and a more skilled person, usually an adult, perhaps because he was interested in formal instruction and other settings in which children are taught how to use psychological tools to develop the higher mental functions. More recently, contextualists have also been interested in cognitive progress resulting from interaction between peers with comparable knowledge and skill levels. Such dyads permit a more equal contribution and avoid the imbalance inherent in adult–child dyads. Peers often *coconstruct* new (to them) knowledge that is a product of their collaboration. The novel outcome does not clearly belong to one child or the other. In contrast, Piaget thought that cognitive conflict more than cooperation between peers was responsible for any cognitive progress resulting from the interaction.

POSITION ON DEVELOPMENTAL ISSUES

HUMAN NATURE

Contextualism, not surprisingly, falls within the contextualist world view. Human nature can be understood only in context. Humans are not independent entities that engage their environment; they are part of it—a person-in-context. A child is an active, inherently social organism in a broad system of interacting forces in the past, present, and future. A child's actions occur in the context of others' actions. Children actively seek out and respond to a variety of social and physical contexts. These activities in turn change children cognitively, which subsequently changes the nature of their future activities. As Rogoff observes, this problem-solving approach "places primacy on people's attempts to negotiate the stream of life, to work around or to transform problems that emerge on the route to attaining the diverse goals of life" (1990, p. 9).

QUALITATIVE VERSUS QUANTITATIVE DEVELOPMENT

In Vygotsky's view, development is both quantitative and qualitative, with periods of calm alternating with periods of crisis or "turning points. . . spasmodic and revolutionary changes" (1978, p. 73). In a dialectical process two elements may develop in a quantitative way towards each other, but as a result of the process of synthesis a qualitatively new form emerges. As Vygotsky describes it, "child development is a complex dialectical process characterized by periodicity, unevenness in the development of different functions, metamorphosis or qualitative transformations of one form into another, intertwining of external and internal factors, and adaptive processes which overcome impediments that the child encounters" (1978, p. 73). Important examples of qualitative change are the acquisition of inner speech, moving from an intuitive, spontaneous concept to a scientific (logically defined) concept, and progressing from elementary mental functions to higher mental functions. During such qualitative changes the psychological system reorganizes itself.

Although contextualists typically do not posit stages of development, they are not opposed to them. One stage account is Cole and Cole's (1993) proposed universal biosocial–behavioral shifts—at birth (transition to life), then ages 2 1/2 months (formation of cortical–subcortical brain connections, social smiling, caretaker's new sense of communication with the baby), 7–9 months (wariness of novelty, fear of strangers, attachment), and 24–30 months (grammar-based language). Later shifts occur at 5–7 years (independent work responsibilities, formal instruction), 11–12 years (sexual maturation), and 19–21 years (responsibility for self). During each shift, a convergence of biological, social, and behavioral changes causes a reorganization in the way children interact with their environment. For example, the shift at age 2 1/2 months involves brain maturation and increased wakefulness (the "bio"), caretakers' growing emotional contact with their babies and a sense that they can communicate with them (the "social"), and increased visual acuity, social smiling, decreased fussiness, and improved learning and memory (the "behavioral"). Vygotsky had little interest in describing a set of specific stages but he and his colleagues did sketch out some possible themes for stages: affiliation (infancy), play (early childhood), learning (middle childhood), peer activity (adolescence), work (adulthood), and theorizing (old age).

NATURE VERSUS NURTURE

Vygotsky was an interactionist. He stated that biological and cultural forces "coincide and mingle with one another. . . . the two lines of change interpenetrate one another and essentially form a single line of sociobiological formation of the child's personality" (1960, p. 47). Cole (1992b) amends this stance by emphasizing that even biological influences are mediated by culture, as when the impact of a newborn's sex depends on the culture's social construction of the meaning of this biological fact. He notes, for example, that the birth of a girl often elicits comments from adults such as "It can't play rugby" and "I shall be worried to death when she's eighteen" (Macfarlane, 1977). Such cultural attitudes about the girl's future constrain and organize her present experiences and thus create a self-fulfilling prophecy.

Although the importance of biology is acknowledged, Vygotsky and the contextualists choose to concentrate on environmental forces—particularly cultural ones. The activities of others, such as communication, formal and informal instruction, and the use of technical and psychological tools, engage children in collaborative activities. Vygotsky, of course, also emphasized the sociohistorical forces expressed in the environment. Current contextualists pay less attention to these forces. Finally, Vygotsky and the contextualists point out that people change their environments to some extent through the use of technical and psychological tools.

The particular parts of the available environment that directly affect the child differ from child to child and from culture to culture. As Valsiner (1987) emphasizes, only certain areas of the environment, certain human and physical objects, and certain ways of interacting with those objects are available at a given time. Caretakers in a particular culture close off certain contexts from the child, for example, watching the birth of a sibling, attending school before a certain age, viewing certain television programs, and playing with certain peers. Moreover, within the culturally permitted contexts for children, parents permit or encourage only certain kinds of actions. Some cultures permit their children great freedom in choosing activities and ways of acting, whereas more restrictive or homogenous cultures give fewer choices.

What Develops

The Vygotskian view of what develops is very broad—a culture (sociocultural history), a species (phylogenesis), a child (ontogenesis), and a cognitive skill (microgenesis). Ontogenetically, an active-child-in-cultural-context is the unit that develops. This unit constructs a variety of cognitive skills, most importantly a system of meaning and its psychological tools—a culturally constructed system of knowledge. Goals, values, and motivation are inseparable from cognitive activity, so they follow a parallel developmental course. Development has no universal ideal endpoint; what constitutes an ideal endpoint depends on the goals of a particular culture. However, Vygotsky, like Piaget, clearly favored higher mental functions, particularly scientific concepts.

THEORETICAL NATURE OF THE THEORY

Contextualist theories typically are functional theories. There is continual interplay between theory and data, with changes in each leading to changes in the other. Vygotsky's theory is unique among those in this book in its explicit ties to Marxist political–social–economic theory. The latter generates many of the assumptions of Vygotskian theory.

Vygotsky also drew on spatial metaphors that serve as informal models. He referred to a *zone* of proximal development, the *distance* between actual and potential development. He also was fond of metaphors of technical tools, as both a general metaphor and a specific metaphor (e.g., telescopes and magnifying glasses) for mental activities. Vygotsky's Marxist beliefs, described earlier, obviously inspired use of a tool metaphor. Currently, a common metaphor is "scaffolding." Much as a temporary framework supports workers and materials involved in work on a building, more skilled people temporarily support a child's emerging skills. They adjust their degree of support to how much help the child needs. Finally, contextualists use the metaphor of a braided rope or woven tapestry to emphasize the continuity of past, present, and future, the intertwining of an object or person and its surroundings, the interconnectedness of contexts, and the intermingling of biology and culture (Cole, 1992a; Pepper, 1942).

EVALUATION OF THE THEORY

The many strengths of the contextualist approach are widely acknowledged today and were mentioned throughout this chapter. Thus, they can be described here rather quickly and attention can be focused on weaknesses, particularly limitations, with an eye toward needed future research. The strengths are the theory's attention to the social–cultural context, integration of everyday learning and development, and sensitivity to the diversity of development. Weaknesses include the vagueness of the notion of the zone of proximal development, insufficient attention to issues of development in the zone, difficulties of studying cultural–historical contexts, and failure to provide a legacy of prototypic tasks revealing interesting developmental phenomena.

STRENGTHS

Attention to Social–Cultural Context

Ethologists emphasize the evolutionary history of the species and adaptation to the immediate physical–social context, but neither they nor other developmental theorists seriously address the broader sociohistorical context of development. Vygotsky's theory is unique in developmental psychology in weaving together insights from history, sociology, economics, political science, linguistics, biology, art, and literature into psychology. This broader context is not simply another "influence" on children. Rather, it defines children and their activities. Thus, the Vygotskian–contextualist approach "corrects" other approaches.

Particularly useful for contemporary developmental psychology is Vygotsky's focus on the fluid *boundary* between self and others. Society and a child make cognitive exchanges at this boundary; society shares its cognitive goals with the child. The zone of proximal development, intersubjectivity, and internalization all refer to phenomena at this borderline.

Bronfenbrenner (1989a) argues for focusing on the specific *processes* involved in this interface between child and setting—the joint operation of forces in the child and in the environment. That is, what do a child and other people actually do together in a particular setting and how does this interaction affect the child's development? Why are certain ecological niches favorable for the development of particular types of children?

In a sense, development occurs at the child–society border rather than in the individual child. This notion is very difficult for the Western mind to assimilate. We tend to dichotomize the individual and the external world, including society, and to situate development within the individual. Vygotsky's view challenges our basic assumption about the nature of reality and, consequently, of psychological development.

Integration of Everyday Learning and Development

A main theoretical contribution is the account of the relation between development and learning—one of the most important issues of cognitive development. Vygotsky argued that learning drives development. As children learn (proceed through the zone of proximal development), they achieve a higher level of development. In turn, children's level of development affects their readiness to learn a new concept. This theoretical focus on change, along with the method of dynamic assessment, makes this a truly developmental theory (but see "Weaknesses").

Contextualists study what children actually do in their everyday environments. To a great extent children use their thinking to solve social and physical problems. They learn how to use materials and people in their specific circumstances to obtain goals: "Cognitive development consists of coming to find, understand, and handle particular problems, building on the intellectual tools inherited from previous generations and the social resources provided by other people" (Rogoff, 1990, p. 190).

Sensitivity to Diversity of Development

Most developmental theories focus on universal aspects of development. In contrast, the contextualists acknowledge both individual differences within a culture, such as wide versus narrow zones, and differences among cultures. This sensitivity to diversity is quite important, because much of the knowledge base of contemporary developmentalists comes from research on white, middle-class Western (mostly North American) children. What is true of this group may not be universally true. In particular, there may be no universal goal of development. Ideal thinking and behavior may differ for different cultures with their particular social and physical circumstances and types of tools available. And different historical and cultural circumstances may encourage different developmental routes to any given developmental endpoint.

WEAKNESSES

Vagueness of the Notion of the Zone of Proximal Development

Paris and Cross (1988) have noted two main ambiguities or limitations to Vygotsky's concept of the zone. First, knowing only the width of children's zones does not provide an accurate picture of their learning ability, style of learning, current level of development compared to other children of the same age, and degree of motivation. Children who have narrow zones may have so little inherent learning ability that they are unable to profit from assistance. These children may be functioning at a very low level. Or children with narrow zones may be successful independent learners who have achieved their potential. Consequently, social assistance helps them only slightly. Similarly, low-achieving children who have wide zones may be unable to solve problems independently and so rely on help from adults. Or high-achieving children may have wide zones because they have high learning ability but due to low motivation or lack of appropriate learning strategies rely on adults for help. Thus, having a wide zone (or a narrow zone) can be desirable or undesirable, depending on its causes. Moreover, children may appear to have a narrow zone simply because adults have failed to provide appropriate instruction. In short, simply assessing children's zones provides a very incomplete developmental picture.

Second, the zone has problems of measurement. Although the metaphor of a spatial zone implies a metric of distance, there currently is no metric for determining this "distance" (Paris & Cross, 1988). For example, one child needs help sounding out words during reading, a second child needs help connecting ideas across sentences, while a third only needs encouragement. Even if these children need an equal number of prompts, do they actually have equally wide zones? No common scale exists for answering this question. Vygotsky sometimes measured the zone in terms of age, such as when a child with an actual level of functioning of age 6 and a potential level of functioning of age 9 has a zone of 3 years. Yet, this is a very global metric, and it cannot be assumed that the difference of 3 years between 2 and 5 is equal to that between ages 6 and 9.

There are still other problems with the zone notion. One is that the exact psychological processes involved in internalization of the intermental to the intramental (Vygotsky) or appropriation of a shared activity (Rogoff) remain unclear. For example, what sorts of mental representations of social interaction are formed? Also, we know little about the generality and stability of an individual child's zone. Does a child tend to have a wide zone (or a narrow zone) across most domains? Is the size of the zone a stable individual characteristic that is constant over the years? Moreover, we know little about the developmental implications of the zone. Is guided participation from adults necessary or only helpful for development? Is improvement resulting from the zone long lasting? Can it generalize to other similar situations?

Another limitation is that most of our knowledge about the zone concerns mother–child and to a lesser extent peer dyads. Do father–child, adult–infant, sibling, and multiperson units operate in the zone in different ways? Not all parents are eager and competent guides, and many children in hostile environments may learn not to seek contexts with adults. Finally, we know little about the role of affect in the zone. Children seek out contexts that satisfy their needs for affection, food, stimulation, and so on. They enter contexts with their own emotion-laden agenda. Moreover, they often have a preexisting emotional (positive or negative) relationship with the people in these contexts that colors the nature of their social interaction. A child asks his mother to show him how to ride a bicycle because he wants to be able to engage in this activity with his friends. Another child is asked by a disliked relative to listen to instructions on using a vacuum cleaner so that she can help clean the house. The nature of learning in the zone will differ in these two cases. The general point is that our knowledge about zones must be broadened.

Perhaps because of these problems, Vygotsky's notion of dynamic assessment, despite its intuitive appeal, has had little impact on current intellectual assessment procedures. These procedures continue to assess current levels of ability rather than the ability to advance with help. Another reason for the lack of influence may be the difficulty of standardizing the tester's responses to the child's behaviors. Different children require different kinds of responses. This problem is similar to those discussed with respect to Piaget's clinical method in Chapter 1. Finally, dynamic assessments are difficult and time-consuming. There is, however, interest in dynamic assessment in school settings (e.g., Moll, 1990).

Insufficient Attention to Developmental Issues

Although Vygotskian–contextual theory is a quintessential developmental theory, in some ways the approach does not really seem very developmental, especially in work on the zone and other studies of the social context of problem solving. As Bronfenbrenner puts it, "In place of too much research on development 'out of context,' we now have a surfeit of studies on 'context without development'" (1986, p. 288). A more developmental account of child-in-context is needed for several reasons.

First, we have little *description* of differences in children-in-context at various ages or developmental levels. The characteristics of children at each age surely influence the nature of their contexts and the effect of a particular context on them. Vygotsky began to address this issue and suggested, for instance, that emerging speech and mobility after the first few months of life dramatically change children's potential for social interaction and the kinds of contexts they can enter. One example is

Luria's (1961) description of developmental changes in young children's ability to use language to regulate their behavior. But other developmental phenomena surely have an impact as well. For example, new needs and interests during development bring children to new contexts. Also, Vygotsky gave little attention to the role of physical maturation; specifically, the different neurological, sensory, cognitive, and motoric abilities of a 1-year-old and a 3-year-old surely affect which contexts are available to them and how people treat them in these contexts. Also, human infants are biologically predisposed toward acquiring some concepts more easily than others, as a result of phylogenesis (see Chapters 5 and 6). This puts constraints on the degree to which social experiences can influence various skills during infancy. Simultaneously, society's expectations differ for children of different ages. As children grow older, a culture puts new pressures on them and grants them new social freedoms. Society introduces older children to schooling, work responsibilities, clubs, and organized athletic and social activities. Thus, there is an interplay between the interests and abilities of a child at a particular developmental level and the social contexts that society allows or encourages. Cole and Cole's (1993) notion of bio-social-behavioral shifts is a recent promising attempt to add a developmental dimension to contextualism.

Second, we have little idea of the nature of developmental *processes* involved in moving through one's zone and whether they are the same at all ages. Contextual research rarely addresses the nature of the cognitive skills that are required for responding to prompts, joint attention, learning from observation, and collaborative dialogue. Developmental changes in these skills affect both the breadth of the zone and how quickly a child can move through it. Specifically, the most helpful hints, modeling, direct instruction, explanations, and motivators surely differ for children of different cognitive or social developmental levels. All of these require certain developing cognitive skills such as attention, memory for action sequences, mental imagery for comparing the actions of the self and others, verbal encoding, and inference of intentions. For example, at any age what children can acquire in the zone of proximal development is somewhat constrained by their developmental level. Among children who cannot count by themselves, 4-year-olds are more likely to shift to counting with their mother's help than are 2-year-olds (Saxe, Guberman, & Gearhart, 1987). As another example, preschoolers appear to profit less in the cognitive realm from peer-collaborative activities than do older children, and even when collaborating with skilled partners, preschoolers have difficulty engaging in certain cognitively sophisticated activities, such as abstract planning

(Rogoff, 1990). Without an account of these developmental differences we have no clear idea of how the processes of learning and development operate in, for example, a 2-year-old's zone compared to an 8-year-old's.

> It seems reasonable that naivete and lack of experience may underlie zones at some ages or in some domains and that poorly structured knowledge, lack of strategies, inappropriate expectations, and so forth may determine the widths of zones at other ages or in other domains.

[Paris & Cross, 1988, p. 35]

Tomasello, Kruger, and Ratner (1991) recently proposed a promising account of developmental changes in the capacity for acquiring culture through interacting with other people. As children's social cognition, particularly their ability to take the perspective of other people, matures they are capable of increasingly advanced forms of cultural learning. Nine-month-olds can acquire new behaviors through *imitation* because they understand that people are intentional agents. They know what goal the other person is trying to achieve through this behavior. Around age 4 children see others not only as intentional agents but also as mental ones. Their emerging understanding of representation allows them to represent someone else's representation of the situation and to try to reconcile it with their own. As a result, they can benefit from *instruction* from others and internalize instructions, which is similar to Vygotsky's notion of internalizing dialogue. By age 6 they can engage in *collaboration* with a peer at their level of competence because they can integrate the mental perspectives of two people who can think about each other's thinking. With a peer they coconstruct knowledge and internalize the coconstruction. In this model, intersubjectivity, because it permits social perspective taking, is central to cultural learning. Bronfenbrenner (1989a, 1992) and Azmitia and Perlmutter (1989) also have begun to develop process-person-context models that bring a developmental dimension to the person-context matrix.

Another important developmental difference affecting behavior in the zone may be a child's level of expertise or phase of stagelike development. For instance, children who are acquiring new skills or just entering a new stage may have a wider zone than children who are experts or are solidly in that stage. The inexperienced children may have a tenuous grasp of their new skills and concepts and need scaffolding from adults in order to perform at the level of the new stage. In contrast, the experienced children have a solid, stable understanding that allows them to function on their own, creating a narrow zone because they already have proceeded nearly as far as they can.

One problem resulting from inattention to developmental level is that different assessments of the zone (see "Methodology") may produce different zone widths because certain types of assessments are more developmentally appropriate. For example, modeling may be a more effective clue than verbal explanation for 4-year-olds because verbal explanation may be beyond their comprehension ability.

A third way in which a developmental dimension is needed is that the effects of major sociohistorical events depend on developmental characteristics of the child and other individual characteristics. For example, the Great Depression had its most negative effects on boys of preschool age (Caspi, Elder, & Herbener, 1989); both age and gender mediated this sociohistorical variable.

The overall point here is that the *developmental level* of the active-child-in-context influences (a) what contexts he enters, (b) the nature of the social–cognitive processes involved in the dyadic interaction, and (c) the effect of sociohistorical events on the child. "Developmental level" includes children's knowledge, motives, reasoning skills, attentional biases, metacognition, social skills, language ability, self-concept, and so on. Children of different developmental levels bring different things to a context.

Difficulties of Studying Cultural–Historical Contexts

Nearly all developmental psychologists would agree that it is important to examine the social, cultural, and historical contexts of development. Yet few studies examine or even vary the social and cultural context. And fewer still study the historical context. Why this discrepancy between attitudes and behavior? A main reason is the practical difficulty of conducting this type of research. Regarding social contexts, observing parent–child or older peer–younger peer dyads in action is difficult and time consuming. Investigators must develop a sensible classification system for coding the behaviors, use this system to code the videotaped interactions, establish interrater reliability, and so on. Regarding cultural contexts, it often is necessary to conduct cross-cultural research, which requires expensive travel, extensive learning about the other culture, careful translation of materials, and selection of appropriate testers. And cultural differences in the results often are uninterpretable because they could be caused by many differences between the cultures. Historical influences are even more difficult to study because the relevant events are no longer occurring. One historical moment can never be directly compared with another, and it is difficult to detect which of the many differing aspects of different historical moments is responsible for differences in behavior. Even Vygotsky conducted research mainly on adult–child dyads rather than larger historical–cultural forces such as class struggles, racial unrest, and alienation of certain groups. The same is true of current contextual researchers. The links between broad social–historical contexts and specific parent–child interactions need to be worked out better (see also Paris & Cross, 1988).

No Legacy of Prototypic Tasks Revealing Interesting Developmental Phenomena

One reason that Piaget's theory stimulated much productive research internationally is that he provided several tasks that revealed interesting, even surprising, developmental phenomena. The conservation, object permanence, spatial-perspective taking, class inclusion, and transitivity tasks come to mind. These served as arenas for empirical skirmishes for many years. Similarly, information-processing oriented investigators had these Piagetian tasks plus problem solving, attention, and memory tasks; ethology had imprinting, attachment, and peer dominance hierarchies; social learning had imitation paradigms; and Gibson had the visual cliff, reading, and traversability tasks. No such prototypic tasks from contextualism have caught the imagination of current developmentalists and stimulated an outpouring of research. Although Vygotsky developed several tasks to use with children, as described earlier, they have rarely been adopted in recent years. Even when Vygotsky did conduct experiments, he typically described his procedures in a very sketchy way and presented little or no data, relying instead on general summaries. His studies were more like pilot studies or demonstrations used to illustrate what he saw as the basic principles of cognition and development. Given the urgency of his mission and his chronically poor health, he directed his energy toward opening up new lines of research rather than fully examining any one area.

Contextualists use many different types of tasks. In a way this diversity is advantageous. The theory can be tested more generally, and research does not become the mindless, pedestrian varying of one factor after another on the same task. However, the lack of prototypic tasks and sets of interesting developmental findings connected with them makes an explosion of contextualist research unlikely. Moreover, a systematic, coherent, well-documented account of development in a single domain may never emerge. The body of contextual research may always seem scattered and unfocused and it may be difficult to compare findings from studies using different tasks.

CONCLUDING COMMENTS

Given this account of Vygotskian–contextual research, how much of the recent "Vygotskian" research is actually Vygotskian? The assimilation of Vygotsky into contemporary work on developmental psychology provides an interesting case study of the sociocultural influences on science. When researchers take a theory from a different culture and historical time, the theory usually is distorted in some way—much like the distortion that occurs when people assimilate, in the Piagetian sense, something into their current mental structure. In the case of Vygotsky, something is lost in the translation, so to speak. What contemporary developmental psychology needed from Vygotsky was a sensitivity to the social context of development. And that is what it took. In this sense there now have been quite a few Vygotskian studies. The prototypic current Vygotskian study is a mother helping her young child solve a problem and thus move through the zone of proximal development. However, there are three main aspects of Vygotsky's theory that do not fare as well in our individual-oriented world view and so have been relatively ignored. First, much current "contextual" research looks at how contexts influence behavior; it does not start with the child-in-context as its basic unit. The social context is grafted on to individual development rather than considered an inherent part of it. Second, the notion of the zone of proximal development has been plucked out of its social–political context. Vygotsky saw interactive learning processes in the zone as an expression of collectivism; society shares its mental skills during "shared consciousness" much as it shares its material goods. In contrast, current "Vygotskian" research still conveys the impression that an individual child is guided by an individual adult with the goal of furthering individual cognitive development, rather than society in general. Third, Vygotsky emphasized the culturally mediated nature of thinking, particularly through psychological tools provided by the culture. Contemporary contextual research and theorizing give little attention to this notion and instead study the influence of cultural contexts. These concepts are compatible and both are in the spirit of the Soviet sociohistorical school (Cole, 1988). Nevertheless, the fact of the differing weights assigned to the two concepts by researchers in two different times and cultures shows that science operates within a sociocultural niche.

Many recent studies of the zone that are presented as Vygotskian-inspired are little more than traditional studies of mother–child interaction. Researchers still view cognition as something that happens inside a child's head and an adult simply helps put it there. This research does not incorporate the principles that distinguish Vygotskian studies from any study of adult–child interaction (also see a critique by Lamb & Wozniak, 1990). Truly Vygotskian studies must (1) look at both adult and child behavior and at how each adjusts to the previous response of the other, (2) assess what a child can do both alone and with an adult's help, and (3) look at the gradual shift in responsibility from adult to child over the course of the session. Such studies must also (4) assess how the adult structures the learning process, tries to pull the child to a slightly higher cognitive level, relates the problem to the child's previous experience, and adjusts the amount of help to the difficulty of the task and (5) examine how the culture shapes the nature of the adult–child interaction. Some studies incorporate only certain aspects of this approach, such as looking at how adults "scaffold" (provide physical, social, or intellectual support for) children's emerging abilities (Griffin & Cole, 1984).

It is not necessarily "wrong" to selectively assimilate a theory. Scientific progress often comes from taking only what is most useful from a theory, in this case the surface features of zone research. But it should be recognized that Vygotsky's theory is often misunderstood.

SUMMARY

Contextualism has many roots, but Vygotsky was the main historical force for this approach in present-day developmental psychology. The theory currently has considerable influence on developmental psychologists, especially in the area of cognitive development. Unlike most theories, this approach focuses on the child-in-activity-in-context, rather than on the child alone. The higher mental functions are social; children use cultural tools, such as symbol systems, to solve problems in their everyday attempts to meet their goals within a social reality. Social contexts have many levels, ranging from interaction with other people in a microsystem to operating within an overarching cultural system in a macrosystem. Cultural beliefs, knowledge, values, artifacts, and physical settings influence what settings children are encouraged to enter and when they can enter them, what they learn in these settings, how they acquire skills, and who can enter particular settings.

Besides a child-in-activity-in-context as the unit of study, several other characteristics define contextualism. Children develop in a zone of proximal development—the distance between what a child can do without help and with help. A more skilled person uses prompts, discussion, modeling, explanation, and so on to guide and collaborate with children to move them through the zone. Because the child and a familiar adult share a past and have a common goal in the task, they have a shared understanding of the problem. Children actively contribute to their movement through the zone by seeking out contexts, influencing the course of the activity, and bringing personal qualities and developmental skills to the interaction. Vygotsky argued that only by looking directly at moment-to-moment change over time can we understand development; intelligence is not what you know but what you can learn with help.

As children engage in activities with others, intermental activities, particularly dialogue, become intramental. In this way individual mental functioning has sociocultural origins. Language between people eventually becomes spoken speech-for-self (egocentric speech), then silent, mental, speechlike inner speech. Children internalize (Vygotsky) or appropriate (Rogoff) information and ways of thinking from their activities with parents, teachers, other adults, and more skilled peers.

Technical and psychological tools provided by the culture mediate intellectual functioning. Language, in particular, helps children direct their own thinking efficiently; they plan, think logically, and so on. However, nonverbal interaction with others encourages cognitive skills as well. If culture constructs the mind and if culture changes, then it follows that we must study the mind by looking at how it changes.

Such theoretical considerations mandate a dynamic assessment of children's potential levels of development rather than a static assessment of current levels. The microgenetic method involves an analysis of moment-to-moment changes as a child moves through the zone of proximal development. In this approach, Vygotsky sometimes used the method of double stimulation to see if children could use materials as symbolic tools to solve a problem beyond their current ability. Because of their sensitivity to context, contextualists often study children in various contexts or compare children across cultures.

Prototypic Vygotskian–contextual research includes egocentric speech, the development of concepts (particularly "scientific" ones taught in school), guided participation in the zone of proximal development, and cross-cultural studies. For Vygotsky, the most general mechanism of development is the dialectical process in which two contradictory ideas or phenomena are synthesized into a new idea or phenomenon. Several types of forces enter into this dialectical process: inner biological, individual psychological, cultural–sociological, and outer physical change. The dialectical process operates mainly during interaction with adults, more skilled peers, or peers of equal ability and during play. Movement through the zone is a dialectical process as the child collaborates with another person and they coconstruct the meaning of the task, a goal, and a solution.

Regarding the theory's position on developmental issues, it holds a contextualist view of human nature; human nature develops in a social context. The temporal dimension (past, present, and future) is crosswoven with the spatial dimension (social context). Development is both quantitative and, when synthesis results in the dialectical process, qualitative. Nature and nurture also enter into a dialectical process, but contextualists focus on the social forces in this process. Finally, what develops is an active-child-in-context. The theory is primarily a functional theory, with a continual interplay between theory and data.

The strengths of the contextual approach are its attention to the social–cultural context of development, integration of everyday learning and development, and sensitivity to the diversity of development. Weaknesses are the vagueness (or limitations) of the notion of the zone of proximal development, insufficient attention to developmental aspects of the zone of proximal development, the difficulties of studying cultural–historical contexts, and the failure to provide prototypic tasks revealing interesting developmental phenomena. Although Vygotskian-contextual theory has stimulated more research on social influences, few studies have incorporated the aspects of the theory that do not fit easily into the contemporary Western cultural belief system.

Suggested Readings

The following two books by Vygotsky provide a good introduction to his theory.

Vygotsky, L. S. (1978). *Mind in society: The development of higher psychological processes* (M. Cole, V. John–Steiner, S. Scribner, & E. Souberman, Eds.). Cambridge, MA: Harvard University Press.

Vygotsky, L. S. (1962). *Thought and language.* Cambridge, MA: MIT Press.

The contemporary contextualist approach is well represented in the following volume.

Rogoff, B. (1990). *Apprenticeship in thinking: Cognitive development in social context.* New York: Oxford University Press.

For a recent overview of cultural influences on development, the following source is useful.

Cole, M. (1992). Culture in development. In M. Bornstein & M. Lamb (Eds.), *Developmental psychology: An advanced textbook* (3rd ed.). Hillsdale, NJ: Erlbaum.

8
REFLECTIONS

*The beginnings and endings of all human undertakings
are untidy, the building of a house, the writing of a
novel, the demolition of a bridge, and, eminently, the
finish of a voyage.*
[JOHN GALSWORTHY]

Although it is tempting to tidy up the assortment of theories presented here by offering an orderly set of conclusions, that aim is not realistic. Developmental psychology is a huge, multifaceted discipline that has produced a diverse group of theories. Some theories are bold and speculative, others are cautious and precise; some are large-scale and rambling, others are modest and systematic. Furthermore, they ask different questions about development. Consequently, they address different levels of reality, ranging from a simple motor response to a complex personality structure to a child-in-context. Any attempt to integrate all the theories would be foolish at best, and misleading at worst.

This chapter, then, offers several "untidy" thoughts that linger after we have delved into the theories of this book. The first section summarizes the theories' positions on the four developmental issues that were raised in each chapter. The second section views the history of developmental theory from two points of view. In the traditional view of scientific progress, research and theories build on previous work and thereby increase our knowledge base in a linear fashion. An opposing view, proposed by Thomas Kuhn, sees successive theories as supplanting previous theories rather than building on them and improving them. Third appears a list of common shortcomings of the theories that seem most serious in light of current needs of the field of developmental psychology. Critical areas for future theoretical and empirical work are identified. A final section proposes what roles theories of development can and should play today.

DEVELOPMENTAL ISSUES REVISITED

HUMAN NATURE

The distinction among organismic, mechanistic, and contextualist world views was a useful heuristic for understanding developmental theories, even though some theories do not fall neatly into one category. In particular, the dimension of active versus passive helped clarify the theories. All contemporary versions of the theories portray children as active agents in their own development, to varying degrees. Children assimilate, accommodate, and equilibrate (Piaget); strengthen ego processes

(Freud); construct a sense of identity (Erikson); and modify their environment and develop self-regulatory mechanisms (social learning). In addition, they activate control processes (information processing), search their environment and elicit reactions from others (ethology), explore environments for their affordances (Gibson), and seek out certain kinds of social settings (contextualism). One emerging theme regarding the active child is self-regulation. Social learning theory, Vygotsky, Piaget, Bowlby, information processing (control processes) and Freud emphasize processes of self-control and self-equilibration. Some of the theories include passive behaviors as well. Children are somewhat at the mercy both of drives (Freud, Erikson, ethology, early social learning theory) and of environmental stimuli (models and reinforcers in social learning theory, sign stimuli in ethology).

One of the main trends in developmental theorizing over the last 30 years is toward viewing children as active participants in their own development. However, we may have overcorrected the earlier view of children as passive. As Cairns remarked, "if [mother–infant] influence is a two-way street, one direction is a four-lane expressway, and the other an alleyway. Moreover, the weight of influence depends not only on the context and the interaction that is being assessed but also on the age–developmental status of the participants and their momentary status" (1991, p. 24).

One dimension separating mechanistic and organismic approaches ranges from antecedent causes of isolated behaviors to inherent causes within a whole structure. Antecedent causes operate in S–R associations (learning theory), fixed action patterns (ethology), and input–output procedures (information processing). Inherent causes are illustrated by cognitive structures (Piaget), the organization of the id, ego, and superego (Freud), the knowledge base or system of processing information (information processing), intrinsic motivation (Gibson), control systems of behavior (Bowlby's ethological theory) and dialectical systems (Vygotsky–contextualism).

Overall, Piaget's theory is the most clearly organismic theory, whereas traditional learning theory is the most clearly mechanistic. Later, learning theory added some organismic, self- regulatory features, especially as a result of Bandura's theoretical work.

In addition to differences in the theories' world views, there are striking differences in the theories' views of human nature: whether humans develop into rational, efficient "scientists" or into irrational beings whose thinking is colored by emotions. Piaget and information-processing theorists emphasize the rational; Freud and Erikson emphasize the irrational. Social learning theorists, ethologists, Gibsonians, and contextualists are more neutral on this issue. That is, social learning theorists believe that motivation influences thinking but also recognize that logical thinking is encouraged by models who present logical methods of solving problems. Ethologists, Gibsonians, and contextualists emphasize the adaptation required for survival in the particular environment. Rational, scientific thought is most adaptive for some settings, whereas sensitivity to interpersonal relationships and emotions may be more adaptive in other settings.

Our theorists' view of human nature is not a trivial matter, because it influences their theorizing. Developmentalists are influenced by their culture and need to be aware that both the field of developmental psychology and the definition of development are sociological phenomena to some extent. For example, society's emphasis on technology and interindividual competition encourages developmentalists to study the development of the child as a solitary, scientific thinker who accumulates knowledge (Meacham, 1983). In contrast, some societies are more concerned with interpersonal connections (Markus & Kitayama, 1991).

QUALITATIVE VERSUS QUANTITATIVE DEVELOPMENT

All the theorists see a number of ways in which development increases quantitatively—in amount, frequency, or degree. With increasing age, children strengthen and generalize their cognitive skills (Piaget), increase their ego strength (Freud and Erikson), imitate more accurately (social learning theory), and process information more efficiently (information processing). They also refine the interweaving of innate and learned components (ethology), detect more affordances (Gibson), and develop their skills gradually as they move through the zone of proximal development (Vygotsky). Although all the theories posit at least minor qualitative change, only Piaget, Freud, and Erikson—the stage theorists—make qualitative change a central part of their theory. In the other theories, the most common qualitative change is a new strategy of learning or problem solving. A major current question regarding the issue of qualitative, stagelike change concerns the apparent unevenness in a child's cognitive performance across tasks or content areas. Domain specificity, which is addressed by neo-Piagetian and information-processing theorists, poses a major challenge for developmental theorizing during the next decade.

NATURE VERSUS NURTURE

All the theorists agree that development springs from a complex inter-weaving of innate and experiential influences. However, they vary in their degree of concern with this issue and in which influences they choose to study. Piaget's theory most clearly is an interactionist theory. He sees development as an interaction of two innate factors (physical maturation and equilibration) and two types of experience (social and physical). Erikson also stresses both biological and social changes, showing that as drives change, they mesh (or conflict) with social in-stitutions. Moving from the middle of the spectrum toward one end, we see that social learning theory, Gibson's theory, and Vygotsky–contex-tualism examine the effects of experience. Toward the other end of the spectrum, ethologists and to a lesser extent Freud emphasize the effects of innate factors. In the remaining theory, information processing, this issue is not often addressed in the developmental work. Neurological development obviously increases the potential efficiency of the informa-tion-processing system, and problem-solving experience leads children to adopt new strategies when they receive feedback during attempts at problem solving.

WHAT DEVELOPS

The diverse answers to this question illustrate why an integration of theories is so difficult. The theorists attend to very different levels of behavior and select different content areas. The stage theorists look at stage-defining characteristics and therefore operate at a general level. In their view, the most important developments are cognitive structures (Piaget) or personality structures (Freud and Erikson). The other theorists focus on more specific acquisitions, often limited to certain situations or types of stimulation: rules (information processing and social learning theory), the perception of affordances (Gibson), adaptive behaviors (ethology), and culturally constructed systems of knowledge (Vygotsky-contextualism). With respect to content, the theories range from stressing social behaviors and personality (Freud, Erikson, social learning theory, ethology) to thinking (Piaget, information processing, Vygotsky) to perception (Gibson). The contextualists study a variety of skills. It is clear that development proceeds on several levels and in many content areas simultaneously. No one theory has unraveled this complex process. Finally, there is diversity between cultures and within a culture in what develops. The contributions of race, culture, gender, and social class are not well understood. There also may be various end points to development and various routes for reaching any end point.

HISTORICAL PROGRESS OF DEVELOPMENTAL THEORIES

A succession of developmental theories has waxed and waned in influence. Are we left with a sense of scientific progress? Has each successive theory been better than the one before it? The traditional view of scientific progress, also the commonsense view, sees the history of a discipline as a cumulative enterprise. Each new discovery or theory builds on previous work and is a refinement of it in the search for ultimate truth. Each theory stands until empirical observations cast doubt on its validity. It is believed that the evaluation of facts is totally objective: "There is only one established dogma in science—that scientists do not blindly accept established dogma" (Brush, 1976, p. 68).

Clearly, there is continuity and a sense of theory development between Freud and Erikson within the psychoanalytic tradition or between classical learning theory and social learning theory within learning theory. Over a longer period of time, however, the historical progression of theories in this volume does not seem to follow this pattern. One is struck more with discontinuity than with continuity in moving from Freud to learning theory to Piaget to information processing. Each theory challenged a previous one and proposed an attractive alternative conception of development more than it refined the earlier theory. Often a new theory is accepted because it corrects the excesses of an established theory, as when contextualism seems attractive because it addresses the social context of thinking, which is relatively ignored by information processing approaches. Furthermore, as discussed in the introductory chapter, there is less than complete objectivity to science, as when a theory is used to guide observations and interpret facts. This general view of the growth of scientific knowledge is proposed by Thomas Kuhn (1970).

Kuhn proposes the following historical sequence within any scientific discipline. First is a "preparadigmatic phase," in which no one theory or generally agreed-upon way of studying the discipline's subject matter has emerged. There is debate over fundamental issues within the discipline. Next comes a period of "normal science," in which one paradigm dominates the field or at least an important subarea of the field. A paradigm is a generally accepted set of assumptions as to what should be studied, what questions should be asked, how these questions can be studied, and how the results should be conceptualized. For example, the information-processing approach emerged from a general agreement among developmental psychologists to study the flow of information through a processing system that resembles the operations of a computer and, furthermore, to ask how that information is stored, not how it is repressed as a result of anxiety. An investigator using this paradigm therefore is likely to measure reaction time, types of errors, or number of items correct but probably not the frequency of the response during a particular time period or the mean length of an utterance, measures used by learning theorists. Thus, a paradigm serves as a working model of how to do science.

A paradigm is larger than a theory. It is both an intellectual framework and a sociological phenomenon. Examples of this intellectual framework are the organismic, mechanistic, and contextualist world views. One holding a mechanistic world view, for instance, would be more likely to develop a theory that posits external mechanical rather than internal cognitive causes of behavior. With respect to the sociological aspect of paradigms, Kuhn points to a "community" of scholars who share certain assumptions or ground rules. The scholars can make rapid progress during the period of normal science because, instead of questioning the assumptions of the approach, they can concentrate their efforts on gathering data and solving problems identified by the paradigm. It is a time for "mopping-up operations" (Kuhn, 1970) to tidy up the paradigm. The paradigm is maintained by training students to carry on the tradition. They absorb the conventions for solving problems in the field and thereby "step into the circle" of that paradigm. An old paradigm never dies immediately; it just fades away, as students trained in the new paradigm enter the field and believers in the old paradigm are ignored and left behind.

The change from one paradigm to another follows a typical pattern. At some point a crisis arises. Phenomena may be discovered that cannot be explained by the current paradigm and consequently cause a crisis of confidence in the paradigm. If a more promising alternative paradigm appears on the scene, it may win the allegiance of the field and begin its own phase of normal science. Thus, after a first paradigm emerges in a discipline, there is a continual back-and-forth movement between normal science (a time of stability) and scientific revolution (a time of change). The history of a science is cyclic more than continuous, according to Kuhn.

Obvious examples of scientific revolutions are Einstein's theory of relativity, Darwinian theory, and the Copernican revolution, which brought the view that the sun rather than the earth is the center of the universe. Each of these paradigms brought a gestaltlike shift in the way scientists looked at facts.

It is interesting that whether a new theory, set of findings, or method influences the field and eventually becomes a paradigm depends on many factors that have nothing to do with the work itself. A good case in point is the fact that Binet, the IQ pioneer, conducted experiments on conservation and other concepts of number before Piaget was even born. In fact he published over 200 books or papers on topics such as children's memory and cognitive styles that had nothing to do with IQ testing. Yet this work was, and still is, ignored for various historical and sociological reasons (Siegler, 1992; Wesley, 1989).

Kuhn's view has been extended and modified by others. In particular, Lakatos (1978) has proposed "research programs," a progressive series of related theories with a common hard core of shared commitments (world view). Each theory is more complex and adequate than those before it. As a result of research, each theory is modified and thereby improved, or it is replaced. The core commitments are kept, but dispensable features are changed. At any one time there are competing research programs. If a scientific research program has not made progress, then it should be abandoned in favor of a more efficacious program.

Psychologists disagree about the value of Kuhn's model for the social sciences and about where to locate psychology in this history-of-science model. Is psychology in a preparadigmatic phase, or has it entered the cycle of paradigms and scientific revolutions? There has never been a paradigm that was accepted by the entire field of psychology or even developmental psychology. Today, there is still a questioning of basic assumptions about development. However, a paradigm can be restricted to a subarea within the field. From this perspective, there are several candidates for paradigms in developmental psychology. In fact, each of the theories described in this book has won over a group of scholars who have accepted the assumptions and gone about the business of solving problems defined by these assumptions. The general orientation section of each chapter in this book roughly defines the paradigmatic characteristics (assumptions) of the theory. Each theory has had its community of productive investigators. One example is the Piagetian group in Geneva. A group of investigators accepted Piaget's intellectual framework and proceeded as though they were working out the details of this framework. Piaget's theory never quite reached this status among American researchers in cognitive development. Other paradigmatic communities can be identified for the computer-simulation approach at Carnegie-Mellon University and the Massachusetts Institute of Technology, for ethology in Germany, for psychoanalysis in certain clinical psychology or psychiatry departments, and for learning in the early 1960s in certain academic developmental psychology programs and in the early behaviorist movement in the United States.

Whether future generations look back on this period as a time of preparadigmatic or paradigmatic science, Kuhn's view of science as both continuous and discontinuous seems to have some validity in the history of theories of developmental psychology. Both continuity and discontinuity are apparent in information processing. It built on the precision and analytic posture of learning theory but won followers in part because of dissatisfaction within the ranks of learning researchers, rather than simply because it produced a better version of learning theory. Discontinuous change came when Piaget challenged learning theory rather than modified it. Continuous change came when Erikson built on, rather than replaced, Freudian theory.

The history of developmental psychology supports Kuhn's claim that when a theory cannot be modified satisfactorily, the stage is set for a revolution. A discipline seems to have a particular need for change at some point in history and embraces a new theory that offers a more satisfactory view of the discipline.

SHORTCOMINGS OF THE THEORIES

Although the theories vary in their strengths, there are common weaknesses that should be remedied in future research and theory construction. These weaknesses are (1) the failure to include all relevant sources of influence on development, (2) low ecological validity, and (3) the lack of adequate mechanisms of development.

FAILURE TO INCLUDE ALL RELEVANT INFLUENCES

Each theory identifies several sources of influence on development and then proceeds to emphasize one or two of these influences. Earlier chapters pointed out the ways in which each theory is incomplete. The Vygotsky–contextualist view, especially Riegel's version of the dialectical process, is the most encompassing of the theories in this book, though biological influences are not given much attention. The dialectical view points out various developmental influences ignored in the other theories. Of the various theorists, only Bandura and some of the contextualists (especially Bronfenbrenner) emphasize that children's behavior can change their environment. A cheerful, friendly child creates a positive, supportive social environment. Like Piaget, however, Bandura ignores sociohistorical changes. In fact, Freud, Gibson, the ethologists, and the information-processing psychologists also ignore the role of sociohistorical change. They all acknowledge or even emphasize that the environment influences development, but they see this influence as relatively constant, particularly during a person's lifetime. Ethologists emphasize changes in the physical environment but have not conceptualized the effect of changes in the social environment as well. Except for Vygotsky and the contextualists, Erikson comes closest to dealing adequately with sociohistorical changes. He points out that these changes lead to changes in social institutions, which in turn lead to changes in society's expectations of the child at each point in development. For this reason, he found it necessary to compare development in different cultures.

An adequate theory should include an account of the effects of past and current social change. Both technological innovations and changing social structures obviously have an impact on children. The automatic washing machine and disposable diapers made early toilet training less important to busy parents. Television and child-care centers brought a wider set of models to children. In particular, the television series "Sesame Street" brought academic instruction into the home of nearly every preschooler. Computers have made new forms of instruction and recreation possible. Mothers' employment outside the home, an increasing divorce rate, later first marriages, and the trend toward smaller families create a different environment from that of a child 30 years ago. Today only a minority of children live in a home with two parents in which the father works outside the home and the mother does not. Will attachment, identification, independence training, and other aspects of socialization proceed in the same way as they have before? It seems unlikely. Future theory building should take a broad perspective on development. Even if a theorist chooses to cover only one aspect of development—such as cognitive development—to be complete the theory should consider the interaction of physical maturation, psychological development, the changing physical environment, and the changing social environment over the entire life span.

Low Ecological Validity

Only Gibson, ethologists, Vygotsky, and the contextualists show a serious interest in the ecological validity of research. Although developmentalists acknowledge the importance of studying developmental tasks and problems as they actually operate in the lives of children, most research does not reflect this attitude. There is an understandable reluctance to give up the control and precision possible in the laboratory.

That low ecological validity can limit our understanding of a behavior is illustrated in the area of memory. The most common laboratory task is to recall a list of unrelated objects. Although there are some demands for rote memory in school or at home, it is likely that most material children need to remember is more meaningful. Preschoolers, in fact, accurately recall a substantial number of events in their lives, particularly social encounters (Fivush & Hudson, 1990).

Although Piaget's theory is high in ecological validity, in that he studied children interacting with objects commonly found in their environments, he paid less attention to the social context in which learning takes place. Other people affect the child's motivation to learn, and the social world itself consists of events that are interpreted by the child. Psychoanalytic accounts of the emotional relationships between parents and their child must be supplemented with information about the child's relationship with peers and teachers. Ethological theory emphasizes the need to examine carefully the meshing of the demands of the environment and the child's attempts to adapt to that environment. Thus far, however, this theory has been applied to a very narrow range of child behavior, primarily infant attachment and dominance in peer groups. Ethologists typically study the immediate environment, but not larger social settings, such as the school system or the economic system, that also influence children's development.

Both laboratory and naturalistic studies are needed because they can converge to make an ecologically valid statement. Laboratory studies show that X *can* cause Y, whereas studies in natural settings determine whether X and Y *are* in fact correlated. That is, are high levels of X associated with high levels of Y, and are low levels of X associated with low levels of Y? Better yet, a longitudinal study examines whether children naturally develop X before Y. To complete the picture, X is introduced into a naturalistic or quasinaturalistic setting to see whether it leads to Y.

An example of converging laboratory and naturalistic research comes from studies of whether viewing violent models on television (X) increases aggression (Y) in children. Work by Bandura and others documents that viewing aggressive models increases subsequent aggression in the laboratory. Other investigators, working in natural settings, have obtained a positive correlation between watching violent programs and exhibiting aggression. Some of these studies, in contrast to the laboratory studies, reveal a bidirectional pattern of cause and effect (Huesmann, Lagerspetz, & Eron, 1984). Viewing violence encourages aggression, and aggressive children tend to view violence. Finally, the few studies that have introduced X into natural settings by controlling the type of television viewed modify the conclusions drawn in the other types of studies. For example, Friedrich and Stein (1973) found that a preschool group that was shown Batman and Superman cartoons subsequently exhibited higher levels of aggression. But this was true only of the children who were high in aggression to begin with.

Such a program of research has ecological validity, in that it examines a problem of great concern to society and studies this problem in natural situations. The laboratory studies suggest that the television programs have their influence through modeling, the naturalistic studies show bidirectionality, and the final experimental–naturalistic phase adds qualifiers to the results of the other studies. Both laboratory and naturalistic studies are needed.

Even cognitive-assessment research performed in a laboratory setting can have greater ecological validity than it often does. The situation need not be artificial and unfamiliar. First of all, the task chosen can be familiar or meaningful to the child. Shatz and Gelman (1973) found that young children's communications are less egocentric when they are explaining how a toy works (for example, a truck dumping station) than if they are to communicate about less familiar objects or events. Another way to increase ecological validity in experimental tasks is to allow the usual situational variables to operate. If children sometimes rely on parents to remind them of what to take to school or what activity they are to do after school (Kreutzer, Leonard, & Flavell, 1975), then perhaps the development of this strategy should be studied in addition to the usual laboratory memory strategies, such as verbal rehearsal.

One of the main messages of the more ecologically oriented theories is that we should take an event as our unit of analysis. Children do something in some setting with some goal in mind. They move about, explore their world, and interact with other people. Developmentalists are becoming aware that we have looked at cognition, personality, and perception separated from meaningful motoric behavior for too long.

LACK OF ADEQUATE MECHANISMS OF DEVELOPMENT

A third common weakness of developmental theories is the lack of an adequate account of mechanisms of development. It was stated in the Introduction that a developmental theory must *describe* development within one domain and the relationship among simultaneously developing domains, and it must *explain* the course of development that has been described. Piaget, Freud, and Erikson have given us a rich description of development, but their mechanisms of development—equilibration and the invariant functions for Piaget, drives for the psychoanalysts—are vague. These mechanisms are not easily observed and studied. In contrast, social learning theory, information processing, ethology, Gibsonian theory, and Vygotsky–contextual approaches emphasize processes of change but are weaker at describing development. Even these process theories, however, do not provide satisfactory mechanisms of development. Social learning theory posits observational learning, which includes verbal instruction and imitation of models, and cognitive processes. However, it is not clear how these processes actually operate. The processes have been given labels but do not really serve as explanations of development. Acquisition of a new behavior by observing a model, listening to instructions, or reading involves a number of further processes. These processes include symbolically representing the sequence of behaviors to be imitated, constructing an image of a new behavior from printed words, integrating new information into previous knowledge, and translating new information into a course of action. One must still explain how these processes operate to cause change. In other words, it is not enough to identify the conditions facilitating observational learning and list the components involved (attention, retention, motor reproduction, and motivation). The identification step merely pushes the explanation back to another level.

The same problem arises with the information-processing, ethological, Gibsonian, and Vygotsky–contextual theories. Exactly how do we acquire new strategies, encode new information, develop control processes, overcome production deficiencies, integrate individual innate behaviors into a system, detect affordances, and learn new skills in social contexts? The precise cognitive, neurophysiological, or perceptual processes are still unspecified.

Future theories need to examine two roles of developmental mechanisms: (1) facilitating the acquisition of new skills and (2) making these skills readily accessible. Any given mechanism may play one or both roles. Examples of mechanisms proposed by theorists to explain acquisition are the equilibration process, the dialectical process, changes in biologically based drives, identification, ego development, observational learning, acquisition of strategies of information processing, automatization, and perceptual learning. Theorists have given much less attention to how new acquisitions become readily accessible and expressed in performance. This is a critical issue, particularly in the area of cognitive development, because recent research suggests that much of development involves children's learning to use the skills they have already acquired. Children can verbally mediate long before they spontaneously verbally rehearse a list of items to be remembered. Young children have a rudimentary understanding of number, but they are easily diverted from using this understanding by distracting stimuli or a large amount of information to process. Adolescents use formal operations in some content areas but not others. Social learning, contextual, neo-Piagetian, and information-processing theorists have identified a number of situational variables that facilitate or discourage the application of knowledge, but they have not satisfactorily explained why or how these variables have an effect on performance.

None of the theories have successfully addressed some of the more subtle aspects of mechanisms of development. These include the following (Flavell, Miller, & Miller, 1993). It may be that at different points in development, different mechanisms are important. And different aspects of development may involve different mechanisms. Language development and the acquisition of prosocial behavior, for example, may have different causes. Moreover, many of the mechanisms themselves are developing (Flavell, 1984, 1992). For example, exploratory behavior, speed of processing, encoding, and observational learning all have their own developmental trajectories. Finally, theories need to address whether the same mechanisms bring about short-term, moment-to-moment change and longer-term, sometimes qualitative change.

On a more optimistic note, recent theoretical and empirical advances in the study of mechanisms of development may preview exciting breakthroughs in the next few years. Siegler (1989), for example, identifies five types of mechanisms of developmental change and provides examples of each.

1. Neural pathways: increasing the number of synapses (connections between neurons), strengthening heavily used synapses while pruning others, and differentiating one neural pathway into two. These changes have been related to cognitive and perceptual changes during infancy.

2. Associative competition: strengthening associations between various aspects of input (for example, syntactic information) and output (for example, German articles for nouns). Learning in areas such as language, recall, and problem solving may involve changes in this pattern of associations.

3. Encoding: increasing the encoding of relevant information and relational information (for example, heavier rather than heavy) and forming new encodings; these are involved in developmental changes in problem solving.

4. Analogy: transferring knowledge from a familiar problem to a novel, but related, problem. As children grow older, they make this leap with fewer or more subtle cues and less perceptual similarity.

5. Strategy choice: adapting to the particular task by choosing from among several available strategies. Children may select faster strategies when these can yield accurate performance but slower strategies on certain problems that require these strategies for an acceptable level of accuracy.

Siegler concludes that underlying all these mechanisms is some type of competition, whether among synaptic connections, associations, information, cognitive rules, or strategies. Just as the fittest survive, the most adaptive processing units are retained. It is important that developmental psychologists understand mechanisms of change because, as Siegler notes, these mechanisms increase the generalizability of theories by showing that apparently unrelated developmental acquisitions may reflect the same underlying mechanisms of development.

CURRENT VALUE OF DEVELOPMENTAL THEORIES

A knowledge of the developmental theories in this volume can prevent tunnel vision in researchers or professionals working with children. A rigid, egocentric perspective on children's behavior can be avoided if one shifts from theory to theory in an attempt to understand behavior. There are many examples of this amalgamated approach. Freud's rich accounts of unconscious, irrational thinking made Piagetian-based research on logical concepts of physical phenomena seem incomplete. We have little work on the cognitive development underlying the defense mechanisms, emotional relationships with parents or peers, and identification. More generally, combining Freud's concern with emotions, Piaget's concern with cognitive structures, and contextual and learning theories' concern with performance in specific situations would produce a powerful perspective for understanding children's behavior.

Another example of how a multitheoretical approach broadens our view is the application of ethologists' methodology to social learning theory. By observing children in the environments to which they must adapt, we can see what role imitation plays. Is imitation most likely in situations where the child is uncertain about what the social environment is demanding? Does a peer dominance hierarchy involve imitation of the children higher in the hierarchy by children lower in the hierarchy?

It is important to realize that our use of some of the earlier theories may require certain modifications. Freud's notion of the powerful unconscious can be accepted without also accepting his claim that it is primarily sexual impulses that are repressed in the unconscious. As cultural conditions change and new information about development comes to light, we must select what is useful from the theories and ignore the rest.

As Beilin comments, "History makes every theory look deficient in some way" (1985, p. 9). Because no one theory satisfactorily explains development, it is critical that developmentalists be able to draw on the content, methods, and theoretical concepts of many theories. The various theories supply multiple levels of analysis, from the physiological to the sociological level. This proposed eclectic approach would most likely lead to small-scale, problem-oriented research and theories: a set of organized hypotheses concerning one area—for example, attachment, identification, or reasoning about quantity. Ideally, within this problem area the concepts and methods selected would capture most of the diverse variables. There probably will be few large-scale, grand theories of development in the future, but there could be a number of minitheories with a broad perspective.

In summary, it is proposed that developmental researchers and practitioners use various theories as heuristics to guide their problem solving. This does not mean, however, that there is no place for developmentalists who operate within a single theory. There is value to pushing a single theory to its limits. As Kuhn noted in his discussion of paradigms, sometimes rapid progress is most likely when investigators do not question the assumptions of their field. Finding out where a theory breaks down can be very informative. As the English logician Augustus De Morgan commented, "Wrong hypotheses rightly worked from have produced more useful results than unguided observation." Given the current level of knowledge in developmental psychology, we need both eclectics and true believers.

"Where shall I begin?" asked the White Rabbit.

"Begin at the beginning," the King said gravely, "and go on till you come to the end, then stop."

[Lewis Carroll]

BIBLIOGRAPHY

Ainsworth, M. D. S.
    1973   The development of infant–mother attachment. In B. M. Caldwell and H. N. Ricciuti, eds., *Review of child development research.* Vol. 3. Chicago: University of Chicago Press.

    In press   Attachments and other affectional bonds across the life cycle. In C. M. Parkes, J. Stevenson-Hinde, and P. Marris, eds., *Attachment across the life cycle.* New York: Routledge.

Ainsworth, M. D. S., M. C. Blehar, E. Waters, and S. Wall
    1978   *Patterns of attachment.* Hillsdale, NJ: Erlbaum.

American Psychologist
    1981   *36,* 27–34.

    1982   *37,* 74–85.

Anastasi, A.
    1958   Heredity, environment, and the question "How?" *Psychological Review, 65,* 197–208.

Anderson, J.
    1991   Comments on *Foundations of cognitive science. Psychological Science, 5,* 283–287.

Antinucci, F., ed.
    1989   *Cognitive structure and development in nonhuman primates.* Hillsdale, NJ: Erlbaum.

Ardrey, R.
    1966   *The territorial imperative.* London: Anthony Blond.

Atkinson, R. C., and R. M. Shiffrin
    1969   Storage and retrieval processes in long-term memory. *Psychological Review, 76,* 179-193.

Averill, J. R.
1976   Patterns of psychological thought: A general introduction. In J. R. Averill, ed., *Patterns of psychological thought*. Washington, DC: Hemisphere.

Azmitia, M., and M. Perlmutter
1989   Social influences on children's cognition: State of the art and future directions. In H. W. Reese, ed., *Advances in child development and behavior*. Vol. 22. San Diego: Academic Press.

Bahrick, L. E., and J. S. Watson
1985   Detection of intermodal proprioceptive-visual contingency as a potential basis of self-perception in infancy. *Developmental Psychology, 21,* 963–973.

Baillargeon, R.
1987   Object permanence in 3.5– and 4.5–month-old infants. *Developmental Psychology, 23,* 655–664.

Baker-Sennett, J., E. Matusov, and B. Rogoff
In press   Planning as developmental process. In H. W. Reese, ed., *Advances in child development and behavior*. Vol. 24. New York: Academic Press.

Baltes, M. M. and E. M. Barton
1979   Behavior analysis of aging: A review of the operant model and research. *International Journal of Behavioral Development, 2,* 291–320.

Bandura, A.
1965   Influence of model's reinforcement contingencies on the acquisition of imitative responses. *Journal of Personality and Social Psychology, 1,* 589–595.

1967   Behavioral psychotherapy. *Scientific American, 216,* 78–86.

1971   Vicarious and self-reinforcement processes. In R. Glaser, ed., *The nature of reinforcement*. New York: Academic Press.

1977   *Social learning theory.* Englewood Cliffs, NJ: Prentice-Hall.

1986   *Social foundations of thought and action.* Englewood Cliffs, NJ: Prentice Hall.

1989   Social cognitive theory. In R. Vasta, ed., *Annals of child development*. Vol. 6. Greenwich, CT: JAI Press.

Bandura, A., J. E. Grusec, and F. L. Menlove
1966   Observational learning as a function of symbolization and incentive set. *Child Development, 37,* 499–506.

Bandura, A., and F. J. McDonald
1963   The influence of social reinforcement and the behavior of models in shaping children's moral judgments. *Journal of Abnormal and Social Psychology, 67,* 274–281.

Bandura, A., D. Ross, and S. A. Ross
1961   Transmission of aggression through imitation of aggressive models. *Journal of Abnormal and Social Psychology, 63,* 575–582.

Bandura, A., and R. H. Walters
  1959   *Adolescent aggression.* New York: Ronald Press.

  1963   *Social learning and personality development.* New York: Holt, Rinehart
            & Winston.

Barash, D. P.
  1973   Personal space reiterated. *Environment and Behavior, 5,* 67–72.

Barker, R. G., and H. F. Wright
  1955   *Midwest and its children: The psychological ecology of an American
            town.* Evanston, IL: Row-Peterson.

Barnett, S. A.
  1963   *A study in behavior.* London: Methuen.

Baron-Cohen, S.
  1991   The theory of mind deficit in autism: How specific is it? *British Journal
            of Developmental Psychology, 9,* 301–314.

Bateson, P. P. G.
  1973   The imprinting of birds. In S. A. Barnett, ed., *Ethology and develop-
            ment.* Philadelphia: Lippincott.

  1976   Rules and reciprocity in behavioral development. In P. P. G. Bateson
            and R. A. Hinde, eds., *Growing points in ethology.* Cambridge: Cam-
            bridge University Press.

  1978   Early experience and sexual preferences. In J. B. Hutchison, ed., *Bio-
            logical determinants of sexual behavior.* London: John Wiley.

Baumrind, D.
  1973   The development of instrumental competence through socialization. In
            A. D. Pick, ed., *Minnesota Symposia on Child Psychology.* Vol. 7.
            Minneapolis: University of Minnesota Press.

Baylor, G. W., and J. Gascon
  1974   An information processing theory of aspects of the development of
            weight seriation in children. *Cognitive Psychology, 6,* 1–40.

Baylor, G. W., and G. Lemoyne
  1975   Experiments in seriation with children: Towards an information pro-
            cessing explanation of the horizontal décalage. *Canadian Journal of
            Behavioral Science, 7,* 4–29.

Beer, C. G.
  1973   Species-typical behavior and ethology. In D. A. Dewsbury and D. A.
            Rethlingshafer, eds., *Comparative psychology: A modern survey.* New
            York: McGraw-Hill.

Beilin, H.
  1971   The training and acquisition of logical operations. In M. F. Rosskopf, L.
            P. Steffe, and S. Taback, eds., *Piagetian cognitive-developmental re-
            search and mathematical education.* Washington, DC: National Coun-
            cil of Teachers of Mathematics.

1985   Dispensable and core elements in Piaget's research program. *The Genetic Epistemologist, 13,* 1-16.

1989   Piagetian theory. In R. Vasta, ed., *Annals of child development.* Vol. 6: *Developmental theory.* Greenwich, CT: JAI Press.

1992   Piaget's new theory. In H. Beilin and P. B. Pufall, eds., *Piaget's theory: Prospects and possibilities.* Hillsdale, NJ: Erlbaum.

Berk, L. E., and R. A. Garvin
1984   Development of private speech among low-income Appalachian children. *Developmental Psychology, 20,* 271–286.

Berland, J. C.
1982   *No five fingers are alike: Cognitive amplifiers in social context.* Cambridge, MA: Harvard University Press.

Berlyne, D. E.
1965   *Structure and direction in thinking.* New York: John Wiley.

Berman, P.
1980   Are women more responsive than men to the young? A review of developmental and situational variables. *Psychological Bulletin, 88,* 668–695.

Bhaskar, R.
1983   Beef, structure and place: Notes from a critical naturalist perspective. *Journal for the Theory of Social Behaviour, 13,* 81–97.

Bijou, S. W., and D. M. Baer
1961   *Child development.* Vol. 1. New York: Appleton-Century-Crofts.

Bivens, J. A., and L. E. Berk
1990   A longitudinal study of the development of elementary school children's private speech. *Merrill-Palmer Quarterly, 36,* 443–463.

Bjorklund, D. F.
1987   How age changes in knowledge base contribute to the development of children's memory. *Developmental Review, 7,* 93–130.

Bjorklund, D. F., ed.
1990   *Children's strategies: Contemporary views of cognitive development.* Hillsdale, NJ: Erlbaum.

Bjorklund, D. F., and B. L. Green
1992   The adaptive nature of cognitive immaturity. *American Psychologist, 47,* 46–54.

Bjorklund, D. F., and B. R. Zeman
1982   Children's organization and metamemory awareness in their recall of familiar information. *Child Development, 53,* 799–810.

Blurton-Jones, N.
1972   *Ethological studies of child behavior.* Cambridge: Cambridge University Press.

Bornstein, M. H.
1989   Sensitive periods in development: Structural characteristics and causal interpretations. *Psychological Bulletin, 105,* 179–197.

Bornstein, M. H., J. Tal, and C. S. Tamis-LeMonda
1991   Parenting in cross-cultural perspective: The United States, France, and Japan. In M. H. Bornstein, ed., *Cultural approaches to parenting.* Hillsdale, NJ: Erlbaum.

Bornstein, M. H., S. Toda, H. Azuma, C. S. Tamis-LeMonda, and M. Ogino
1990   Mother and infant activity and interaction in Japan and in the United States: II. A comparative microanalysis of naturalistic exchanges focused on the organization of infant attention. *International Journal of Behavioral Development, 13,* 289–308.

Bower, T. G. R.
1974   *Development in infancy.* San Francisco: W. H. Freeman.

Bowers, K. S.
1973   Situationism in psychology. *Psychological Review, 80,* 307–336.

Bowlby, J.
1958   The nature of the child's tie to his mother. *International Journal of Psychoanalysis, 39,* 350–373.

1969   *Attachment and loss.* Vol. 1: *Attachment.* New York: Basic Books.

1980   *Attachment and loss.* Vol. 3: *Loss, sadness and depression.* New York: Basic Books.

1991   *Charles Darwin: A new life.* London: Hutchinson.

Brannigan, C. R., and D. A. Humphries
1972   Human nonverbal behavior, a means of communication. In N. G. Blurton-Jones, ed., *Ethological studies of child behavior.* Cambridge: Cambridge University Press.

Breland, K., and M. Breland
1961   The misbehavior of organisms. *American Psychologist, 16,* 681–684.

Bretherton, I.
1991   Pouring new wine into old bottles: The social self as internal working model. In M. R. Gunnar and L. A. Sroufe, eds., *Minnesota Symposia on Child Psychology.* Vol. 23. *Self processes and development.* Hillsdale, NJ: Erlbaum.

Bringuier, J.
1980   *Conversations with Jean Piaget.* Chicago: University of Chicago Press.

Bronfenbrenner, U.
1977   Toward an experimental ecology of human development. *American Psychologist, 32,* 513–531.

1986   Recent advances in research on human development. In R. K. Silbereisen, K. Eyferth, and G. Rudinger, eds., *Development as action in context: Problem behavior and normal youth development.* New York: Springer-Verlag.

1989a   Ecological systems theory. In R. Vasta, ed., *Annals of child development.* Vol. 6: *Six theories of child development.* Greenwich, CT: JAI Press.

1989b   The developing ecology of human development: Paradigm lost or paradigm regained. In R. Vasta (Chair), *Theories of child development.* Symposium conducted at the meeting of the Society for Research in Child Development, Kansas City, MO, April.

1992   *The process-person-context model in developmental research: Principles, applications, and implications.* Unpublished manuscript, Cornell University.

Brown, A. L.
1975   The development of memory: Knowing, knowing about knowing, and knowing how to know. In H. W. Reese, ed., *Advances in child development and behavior.* Vol. 10. New York: Academic Press.

1978   Knowing when, where, and how to remember: A problem of metacognition. In R. Glaser, ed., *Advances in instructional psychology.* Vol. 1. Hillsdale, NJ: Erlbaum.

1979   Theories of memory and the problem of development: Activity, growth, and knowledge. In L. S. Cermak and F. I. M. Craik, eds., *Levels of processing in human memory.* Hillsdale, NJ: Erlbaum.

Brown, A. L., and J. S. DeLoache
1978   Skills, plans, and self-regulation. In R. S. Siegler, ed., *Children's thinking: What develops?* Hillsdale, NJ: Erlbaum.

Brown, A. L., and S. S. Smiley
1978   The development of strategies for studying texts. *Child Development, 49,* 1076–1088.

Brown, J. S., and R. B. Burton
1978   Diagnostic models for procedural bugs in basic mathematical skills. *Cognitive Science, 2,* 155–192.

Brückner, G. H.
1933   Untersuchungen zur Tiersoziologie, insbesondere der Auflösung der Familie. *Zeitschrift für Psychologie, 128,* 1–120.

Bruner, J. S.
1987   The artist as analyst. A review of *A way of looking at things: Selected papers from 1930 to 1980,* by E. Erikson. *The New York Review,* Dec. 3, 8–13.

1990   *Acts of meaning.* Cambridge, MA: Harvard University Press.

Brunk, M. A., and S. W. Henggeler
1984   Child influences on adult controls: An experimental investigation. *Developmental Psychology, 20,* 1074–1081.

Brush, S. G.
1976   Fact and fantasy in the history of science. In M. H. Marx and F. E. Goodson, eds., *Theories in contemporary psychology.* 2nd ed. New York: Macmillan.

Bryant, P. E.
1986   Theories about the causes of cognitive development. In P. L. C. Van Geert, ed., *Theory building in developmental psychology.* Amsterdam: North Holland.

Byrne, R. W., and A. Whiten
1988   Toward the next generation in data quality: A new survey of primate tactical deception. *Behavioral and Brain Science, 11,* 267–283.

1991   Computation and mindreading in primate tactical deception. In A. Whiten, ed., *Natural theories of mind: Evolution, development and simulation of everyday mindreading.* Oxford: Basil Blackwell.

Cairns, R. B.
1979   *Social development: The origins and plasticity of interchanges.* San Francisco: W. H. Freeman.

1991   Multiple metaphors for a singular idea. *Developmental Psychology, 27,* 23–26.

Campos, J. J., A. Langer, and A. Krowitz
1970   Cardiac responses on the visual cliff in prelocomotor human infants. *Science, 170,* 196–197.

Carey, S.
1985   *Conceptual change in childhood.* Cambridge, MA: MIT Press.

Carey, S., and R. Gelman, eds.
1991   *The epigenesis of mind: Essays on biology and cognition.* Hillsdale, NJ: Erlbaum.

Carr, M., B. E. Kurtz, W. Schneider, L. A. Turner, and J. G. Borkowski
1989   Strategy acquisition and transfer among American and German children: Environmental influences on metacognitive development. *Developmental Psychology, 25,* 765–771.

Carraher, T. N., D. W. Carraher, and A. D. Schliemann
1985   Mathematics in the streets and in schools. *British Journal of Developmental Psychology, 3,* 21–29.

Case, R.
1985   *Intellectual development: Birth to adulthood.* Orlando: Academic Press.

1992   *The mind's staircase: Exploring the conceptual underpinnings of children's thought and knowledge.* Hillsdale, NJ: Erlbaum.

Caspi, A., G. H. Elder, and E. S. Herbener
1989   Turning points in the life course. In A. Caspi (Chair), *Surmounting*

childhood disadvantage: Pathways to change. Symposium conducted at the meeting of the Society for Research in Child Development, Kansas City, MO, April.

Cassirer, E.
1951 *The philosophy of the enlightenment.* Boston: Beacon Press.

Caudill, W., and H. Weinstein
1969 Maternal care and infant behavior in Japan and America. *Psychiatry, 32,* 12–43.

Cazden, C. B., and V. P. John
1971 Learning in American Indian children. In M. L. Wax, S. Diamond, and F. O. Gearing, eds., *Anthropological perspectives in education.* New York: Basic Books.

Ceci, S. J.
1990 *On intelligence, more or less: A bioecological theory.* Englewood Cliffs, NJ: Prentice Hall.

Ceci, S. J., R. D. Caves, and M. J. A. Howe
1981 Children's long-term memory for information that is incongruous with their prior knowledge. *British Journal of Psychology, 72,* 443–450.

Cernoch, J. M., and R. H. Porter
1985 Recognition of maternal axillary odors by infants. *Child Development, 56,* 1593–1598.

Charlesworth, W.
1979 Ethology: Understanding the other half of intelligence. In M. von Cranach, K. Foppa, W. Lepenies, and D. Ploog, eds., *Human ethology: Claims and limits of a new discipline.* Cambridge: Cambridge University Press.

1983 An ethological approach to cognitive development. In C. Brainerd, ed., *Recent advances in cognitive developmental theory.* New York: Springer-Verlag.

1988 Resources and resource acquisition during ontogeny. In K. B. MacDonald, ed., *Sociobiological perspectives on human development.* New York: Springer-Verlag.

1992 Darwin and developmental psychology: Past and present. *Developmental Psychology, 28,* 5–16.

Chi, M. T. H.
1978 Knowledge structures and memory development. In R. S. Siegler, ed., *Children's thinking: What develops?* Hillsdale, NJ: Erlbaum.

Chi, M. T. H., R. Glaser, and M. J. Farr, eds.
1988 *The nature of expertise.* Hillsdale, NJ: Erlbaum.

Chi, M. T. H., and R. D. Koeske
1983 Network representation of a child's dinosaur knowledge. *Developmental Psychology, 19,* 29–39.

Chomsky, N.

1959   A review of *Verbal behavior*, by B. F. Skinner. *Language, 35,* 26–58.

1965   *Aspects of the theory of syntax.* Cambridge, MA: MIT Press.

Cohen, D.

1977   *Psychologists on psychology.* New York: Taplinger.

Cohen, L. B., and P. Salapatek

1975   *Infant perception: From sensation to cognition.* Vol. 1. New York: Academic Press.

Cohen, R., and A. W. Siegel, eds.

1991   *Context and development.* Hillsdale, NJ: Erlbaum.

Cole, M.

1988   Cross-cultural research in the sociohistorical tradition. *Human Development, 31,* 137–157.

1990   Cognitive development and formal schooling: The evidence from cross-cultural research. In L. C. Moll, ed., *Vygotsky and education.* Cambridge: Cambridge University Press.

1992a   Context, modularity, and the cultural constitution of development. In L. T. Winegar and J. Valinser, eds., *Children's development within social context.* Vol. 2: *Research and methodology.* Hillsdale, NJ: Erlbaum.

1992b   Culture in development. In M. Bornstein and M. Lamb, eds., *Developmental psychology: An advanced textbook.* 3rd ed. Hillsdale, NJ: Erlbaum.

Cole, M., and S. R. Cole

1993   *The development of children.* 2nd ed. New York: W. H. Freeman.

Cole, M., J. Gay, J. A. Glick, and D. W. Sharp

1971   *The cultural context of learning and thinking.* New York: Basic Books.

Cole, M., and S. Scribner

1974   *Culture and thought: A psychological introduction.* New York: Wiley.

1978   Introduction. In L. S. Vygotsky, *Mind in society: The development of higher psychological processes.* Cambridge, MA: Harvard University Press.

Collins, J. L.

1982   *Self-efficacy and ability in achievement behavior.* Paper presented at the meeting of the American Educational Research Association, New York, March.

Coté, J. E., and C. Levine

1987   A formulation of Erikson's theory of ego identity formation. *Developmental Review, 7,* 273–325.

Craik, F. I. M., and R. S. Lockhart

1972   Levels of processing: A framework for memory research. *Journal of Verbal Learning and Verbal Behavior, 11,* 671–684.

Darwin, C.
1877   A biographical sketch of an infant. *Mind, 2,* 285–294.

Decarie, T.
1965   *Intelligence and affectivity in early childhood.* New York: International Universities Press.

Dekker, E., and J. Groen
1956   Reproducible psychogenic attacks of asthma: A laboratory study. *Journal of Psychosomatic Research, 1,* 58–67.

DeLoache, J. S., D. J. Cassidy, and A. L. Brown
1985   Precursors of mnemonic strategies in very young children's memory. *Child Development, 56,* 125–137.

DeMarie-Dreblow, D.
1991   Relation between knowledge and memory: A reminder that correlation does not imply causality. *Child Development, 62,* 484–498.

Demetriou, A., and A. Efklides, and M. Platsidou
In press   Experiential structuralism: A frame for unifying cognitive developmental theories. *Monographs of the Society for Research in Child Development.*

Dewsbury, D. A.
1978   *Comparative animal behavior.* New York: McGraw-Hill.

1991   "Psychobiology." *American Psychologist, 46,* 198–205.

Diamond, A.
1991   Neuropsychological insights into the meaning of object concept development. In S. Carey and R. Gelman, eds., *The epigenesis of mind: Essays on biology and cognition.* Hillsdale, NJ: Erlbaum.

Diamond, A., ed.
1990   *The development and neural bases of higher cognitive functions.* New York: The New York Academy of Sciences.

Diaz, R. M., and L. E. Berk, eds.
1991   *Private speech: From social interaction to self-regulation.* Hillsdale, NJ: Erlbaum.

Dodge, K. A.
1986   A social information processing model of social competence in children. In M. Perlmutter, ed., *Minnesota Symposia on Child Psychology.* Vol. 18: *Cognitive perspectives on children's social and behavioral development.* Hillsdale, NJ: Erlbaum.

Dollard, J., L. W. Doob, N. E. Miller, O. H. Mowrer, and R. R. Sears
1939   *Frustration and aggression.* New Haven, CT: Yale University Press.

Dollard, J., and N. E. Miller
1950   *Personality and psychotherapy.* New York: McGraw-Hill.

Dornbusch, S. M., P. L. Ritter, P. H. Leiderman, D. F. Roberts, and M. J. Fraleigh
1987   The relation of parenting style to adolescent school performance. *Child Development, 58,* 1244–1257.

Dorr, D., and S. Fey
   1974   Relative power of symbolic adult and peer models in the modification
           of children's moral choice behavior. *Journal of Personality and Social
           Psychology, 29,* 335–341.

Drake, S. G.
   1834   *Biography and history of the Indians of North America.* Boston: Per-
           kins and Hilliard, Gray.

Dunbar, K., and D. Klahr
   1989   Developmental differences in scientific discovery processes. In D. Klahr
           and K. Kotovsky, eds., *Complex information processing: The impact of
           Herbert A. Simon.* Hillsdale, NJ: Erlbaum.

Dunn, J.
   1988   *The beginnings of social understanding.* Oxford: Basil Blackwell.

Edelman, M. S., and D. R. Omark
   1973   *The development of logical operations: An ethological approach.* Paper
           presented at the meeting of the Society for Research in Child Develop-
           ment, Philadelphia, March.

Eibl-Eibesfeldt, I.
   1975   *Ethology: The biology of behavior.* 2nd ed. New York: Holt, Rinehart
           and Winston. 1st ed., 1970.

   1989   *Human ethology.* New York: Aldine de Gruyter.

Elkind, D.
   1968   Giant in the nursery—Jean Piaget. *New York Times Magazine,* May 26.

Ellis, S., and M. Gauvain
   1992   Social and cultural influences on children's collaborative interactions. In
           L. T. Winegar and J. Valsiner, eds., *Children's development within social
           context.* Vol. 2: *Research and methodology.* Hillsdale, NJ: Erlbaum.

Erikson, E. H.
   1950a   *Childhood and society.* New York: Norton. 2nd ed., 1963.

   1950b   In M. J. E. Senn, ed., *Symposium on the healthy personality.* New York:
           Josiah Macy, Jr., Foundation.

   1951   The California loyalty oath: An editorial. *Psychiatry, 14,* 244–245.

   1958   *Young man Luther.* New York: W. W. Norton.

   1959   Identity and the life cycle. *Psychological Issues,* Monograph 1. New
           York: International Universities Press.

   1968   *Identity: Youth and crisis.* New York: W. W. Norton.

   1969   *Gandhi's truth.* New York: W. W. Norton.

   1973   The wider identity. In K. Erikson, ed., *In search of common ground: Con-
           versations with Erik H. Erikson and Huey P. Newton.* New York: W. W.
           Norton.

1977   *Toys and reasons.* New York: W. W. Norton.

Erikson, E. H., J. M. Erikson, and H. Q. Kivnick
 1986 *Vital involvement in old age.* New York: W. W. Norton.

Eron, L. D.
 1987 The development of aggressive behavior from the perspective of a developing behaviorism. *American Psychologist, 42,* 435–442.

Evans, R. I.
 1967 *Dialogue with Erik Erikson.* New York: Harper & Row.

 1973 *Jean Piaget: The man and his ideas.* New York: Dutton.

 1989 *Albert Bandura: The man and his ideas—A dialogue.* New York: Praeger.

Fabricius, W. V., and J. W. Hagen
 1984 Use of causal attributions about recall performance to assess metamemory and predict strategic memory behavior in young children. *Developmental Psychology, 20,* 975–987.

Feldman, D. H.
 1980 *Beyond universals in cognitive development.* Norwood, NJ: Ablex.

Fentress, J. C.
 1973 Specific and nonspecific factors in the causation of behavior. In P. P. G. Bateson and P. H. Klopfer, eds., *Perspectives in ethology.* Vol. 1. New York: Plenum.

Ferrara, R. A., A. L. Brown, and J. C. Campione
 1986 Children's learning and transfer of inductive reasoning rules: Studies of proximal development. *Child Development, 57,* 1087–1099.

Ferretti, R. P., and E. C. Butterfield
 1986 Are children's rule-assessment classifications invariant across instances of problem types? *Child Development, 57,* 1419–1428.

Fifer, W. P., and C. Moon
 1988 Auditory experience in the fetus. In W. Smotherman and S. Robinson, eds., *Behaviors of the fetus.* West Caldwell, NJ: Telford Press.

Fischer, K. W.
 1980 A theory of cognitive development: The control and construction of hierarchies of skills. *Psychological Review, 87,* 477–531.

Fivush, R., and J. A. Hudson, eds.
 1990 *Knowing and remembering in young children.* Cambridge: Cambridge University Press.

Flavell, J. H.
 1963 *The developmental psychology of Jean Piaget.* Princeton, NJ: Van Nostrand.

 1971a First discussant's comments: What is memory development the development of? *Human Development, 14,* 272–278.

1971b   Stage-related properties of cognitive development. *Cognitive Psychology, 2,* 421–453.

1982   On cognitive development. *Child Development, 53,* 1–10.

1984   Discussion. In R. J. Sternberg, ed., *Mechanisms of cognitive development.* New York: W. H. Freeman.

1986   The development of children's knowledge about the appearance-reality distinction. *American Psychologist, 41,* 418–425.

1992   Cognitive development: past, present, and future. *Developmental Psychology, 28,* 998–1005.

Flavell, J. H., D. R. Beach, and J. M. Chinsky
1966   Spontaneous verbal rehearsal in a memory task as a function of age. *Child Development, 37,* 283–299.

Flavell, J. H., A. G. Friedrichs, and J. D. Hoyt
1970   Developmental changes in memorization processes. *Cognitive Psychology, 1,* 324–340.

Flavell, J. H., and J. Hill
1969   Developmental psychology. In P. H. Mussen and M. R. Rosenzweig, eds., *Annual review of psychology.* Vol. 20. Palo Alto, CA: Annual Reviews.

Flavell, J. H., P. H. Miller, and S. A. Miller
1993   *Cognitive development.* 3rd ed. Englewood Cliffs, NJ: Prentice Hall.

Flavell, J. H., and H. M. Wellman
1977   Metamemory. In R. V. Kail and J. W. Hagen, eds., *Perspectives on the development of memory and cognition.* Hillsdale, NJ: Erlbaum.

Flavell, J. H., and J. F. Wohlwill
1969   Formal and functional aspects of cognitive development. In D. Elkind and J. H. Flavell, eds., *Studies in cognitive growth: Essays in honor of Jean Piaget.* New York: Oxford University Press.

Fodor, J. A.
1983   *The modularity of mind.* Cambridge, MA: MIT/Bradford Books.

Fox, R. and C. McDaniel
1982   Perception of biological motion by human infants. *Science, 218,* 486–487.

Freud, S.
1900*   The interpretation of dreams. Vols. 4 and 5. (1953)

1901   The psychopathology of everyday life. Vol. 6. (1960)

---

* The first date is that of the original German edition. The second date is that of the translation: J. Strachey, ed. and trans., *The standard edition of the complete psychological works of Sigmund Freud.* 24 vols. London: Hogarth Press, 1953–1966.

1905a   Fragment of an analysis of a case of hysteria. Vol. 7. (1953)

1905b   Three essays on the theory of sexuality. Vol.7 (1953)

1909a   Analysis of a phobia in a five-year-old boy. Vol. 10. (1955)

1909b   Notes upon a case of obsessional neurosis. Vol. 10. (1955)

1913   Totem and taboo. Vol. 13. (1955)

1914   The Moses of Michelangelo. Vol. 13. (1955)

1915   Instincts and their vicissitudes. Vol. 14. (1957)

1916, 1917   Introductory lectures on psycho-analysis. Vols. 15 and 16. (1963)

1918   From the history of an infantile neurosis. Vol. 17. (1955)

1920   Beyond the pleasure principle. Vol. 18. (1955)

1923   The ego and the id. Vol. 19. (1961)

1925a   An autobiographical study. Vol. 20. (1959)

1925b   Some psychical consequences of the anatomical distinction between the sexes. Vol. 19. (1961)

1927   The future of an illusion. Vol. 21. (1961)

1928   Dostoevsky and parricide. Vol. 21. (1961)

1930   Civilization and its discontents. Vol. 21. (1961)

1933a   New introductory lectures on psycho-analysis. Vol. 22. (1964)

1933b   Why war? Vol. 22. (1964)

1940   An outline of psycho-analysis. Vol. 23. (1964)

Freund, L. S.
1990   Maternal regulation of children's problem-solving behavior and its impact on children's performance. *Child Development, 61,* 113–126.

Friedrich, L. K., and A. H. Stein
1973   Aggressive and prosocial television programs and the natural behavior of preschool children. *Monographs of the Society for Research in Child Development, 38* (4, Serial No. 151).

Furth, H. G.
1987   *Knowledge as desire.* New York: Columbia University Press.

Garcia, J., and R. A. Koelling
1966   Relation of cue to consequences in avoidance learning. *Psychonomic Science, 4,* 123–124.

Gardner, R., and K. G. Heider
1969   *Gardens of war: Life and death in the New Guinea Stone Age.* New York: Random House.

Garmezy, N., and A. Tellegen
    1984   Studies of stress-resistant children: Methods, variables and prelimi-
             nary findings. In F. Morrison, C. Lord, and D. Keating, eds., *Applied
             developmental psychology.* Vol. 1. New York: Academic Press.

Gelman, R.
    1969   Conservation acquisition: A problem of learning to attend to rele-
             vant attributes. *Journal of Experimental Child Psychology, 7,* 167–
             187.

    1972   Logical capacity of very young children: Number invariance rules.
             Child Development, 43, 75–90.

    1991   Epigenetic foundations of knowledge structures: Initial and transcedent
             constructions. In S. Carey and R. Gelman, eds., *The epigenesis of mind:
             Essays on biology and cognition.* Hillsdale, NJ: Erlbaum.

Gelman R., and C. R. Gallistel
    1978   *The child's understanding of number.* Cambridge, MA: Harvard Uni-
             versity Press.

Gesell, A.
    1945   *The embryology of behavior.* New York: Harper & Row.

Gewirtz, J. L., and D. M. Baer
    1958   The effect of brief social deprivation on behaviors for a social reinfor-
             cer. *Journal of Abnormal and Social Psychology, 56,* 49–56.

Gewirtz, J. L., and W. M. Kurtines, eds.
    1991   *Intersections with attachment.* Hillsdale, NJ: Erlbaum.

Ghiselin, M. T., and F. M. Scudo
    1986   The bioeconomics of phenotypic selection. (Comment on D. Vining,
             *Social versus reproductive success: The central theoretical problems
             of human socio-biology.)* The Behavioral and Brain Sciences, 9,
             194–195.

Ghuman, P. A. S.
    1981   An evaluation of Piaget's theory from a cross-cultural perspective. In S.
             Modgil and C. Modgil, eds., *Jean Piaget: Consensus and controversy.*
             New York: Praeger.

Gibson, E. J.
    1969   *Principles of perceptual learning and development.* New York: Ap-
             pleton-Century-Crofts.

    1977   How perception really develops: A view from outside the network. In
             D. LaBerge and S. J. Samuels, eds., *Basic processes in reading: Percep-
             tion and comprehension.* Hillsdale, NJ: Erlbaum.

    1982   The concept of affordances in development: The renascence of
             functionalism. In W. A. Collins, ed., *The concept of development.*
             Hillsdale, NJ: Erlbaum.

1988   Exploratory behavior in the development of perceiving, acting, and the acquiring of knowledge. In M. R. Rosenzweig and L. W. Porter, eds., *Annual review of psychology.* Vol. 39. Palo Alto, CA: Annual Reviews.

1991   *An odyssey in learning and perception.* Cambridge, MA: Bradford/MIT Press.

1992   How to think about perceptual learning: Twenty-five years later. In H. L. Pick, Jr., P. Van den Broek, and D. C. Knill, eds., *Cognition: Conceptual and methodological issues.* Washington, DC: American Psychological Association.

Gibson, E. J., J. J. Gibson, A. D. Pick, and H. Osser
1962   A developmental study of the discrimination of letter-like forms. *Journal of Comparative and Physiological Psychology, 55,* 897–906.

Gibson, E. J., and H. Levin
1975   *The psychology of reading.* Cambridge, MA: MIT Press.

Gibson, E. J., C. J. Owsley, and J. Johnston
1978   Perception of invariants by five-month-old infants: Differentiation of two types of motion. *Developmental Psychology, 14,* 407–415.

Gibson, E. J., and N. Rader
1979   The perceiver as performer. In G. Hale and M. Lewis, eds., *Attention and cognitive development.* New York: Plenum.

Gibson, E. J., G. Riccio, M. Schmuckler, T. Stoffregen, D. Rosenberg, and J. Taormina
1987   Detection of the traversability of surfaces by crawling and walking infants. *Journal of Experimental Psychology: Human Perception and Performance, 13,* 533–544.

Gibson, E. J., and R. D. Walk
1960   The "visual cliff." *Scientific American, 202,* 64–71.

Gibson, E. J., and A. S. Walker
1984   Development of knowledge of visual-tactual affordances of substance. *Child Development, 55,* 453–460.

Gibson, J. J.
1979   Foreword: A note on E. J. G. by J. J. G. In A. D. Pick, ed., *Perception and its development: A tribute to Eleanor J. Gibson.* Hillsdale, NJ: Erlbaum.

Gibson, K. R., and A. C. Petersen, eds.
1991   *Brain maturation and cognitive development.* New York: Aldine de Gruyter.

Gigerenzer, G.
1991   From tools to theories: A heuristic of discovery in cognitive psychology. *Psychological Review, 98,* 254–267.

Gill, M. M.
1959   The present state of psychoanalytic theory. *Journal of Abnormal and Social Psychology, 58,* 1–8.

Gilligan, C.
1982   *In a different voice: Psychological theory and women's development.*
Cambridge, MA: Harvard University Press.

Ginsburg, H., and S. Opper
1988   *Piaget's theory of intellectual development.* 3rd ed. Englewood Cliffs,
NJ: Prentice Hall.

Ginsburg, H. J., V. A. Pollman, and M. S. Wauson
1977   An ethological analysis of nonverbal inhibitors of aggressive behavior in
male elementary school children. *Developmental Psychology, 13,* 417–418.

Goldberg, S., S. L. Blumberg, and A. Kriger
1982   Menarche and interest in infants: Biological and social influences. *Child
Development, 53,* 1544–1550.

Gottlieb, G.
1979   Comparative psychology and ethology. In E. Hearst, ed., *The first century of experimental psychology.* Hillsdale, NJ: Erlbaum.

Gould, S. J.
1980   *The Panda's thumb.* New York: W. W. Norton.

Greco, P.
1967   Logique et connaissance. In J. Piaget, ed., *Encyclopédie de la Pléiade.*
Paris: Gallimard.

Griffin, P., and M. Cole
1984   Current activity for the future: The Zo-ped. In B. Rogoff and J. V.
Wertsch, eds., *Children's learning in the "zone of proximal development."* San Francisco: Jossey-Bass.

Guilmet, G. M.
1979   Navajo and Caucasian children's verbal and nonverbal-visual behavior
in the urban classroom. *Anthropology and Education Quarterly, 9,* 196–
215.

Guttentag, R. E.
1984   The mental effort requirement of cumulative rehearsal: A developmental study. *Journal of Experimental Child Psychology, 37,* 92–106.

Gzesh, S. M., and C. F. Surber
1985   Visual perspective-taking skills in children. *Child Development, 56,*
1204–1213.

Hale, S.
1990   A global developmental trend in cognitive processing speed. *Child
Development, 61,* 653–663.

Halford, G. S.
In press   *Children's understanding: The development of mental models.* Hillsdale, NJ: Erlbaum.

Hall, C. S.
1954   *A primer of Freudian psychology.* New York: World.

Hall, C. S., and G. Lindzey.
1957   *Theories of personality.* New York: John Wiley.

Hall, G. S.
1904   *Adolescence.* New York: Appleton.

Harris, B.
1979   Whatever happened to little Albert? *American Psychologist, 34,* 151–160.

Harris, F. R., M. M. Wolf, and D. M. Baer
1967   Effects of adult social reinforcement on child behavior. In W. W. Hartup and N. L. Smothergill, eds., *The young child: Reviews of research.* Washington, DC: National Association for the Education of Young Children.

Hartmann, H.
1958   *Ego psychology and the problem of adaptation.* New York: International Universities Press.

Hartup, W. W., and A. Yonas
1971   Developmental psychology. In P. H. Mussen and M. R. Rosenzweig, eds., *Annual review of psychology.* Vol. 22. Palo Alto, CA: Annual Reviews.

Hayes, C.
1951   *The ape in our house.* New York: Harper & Row.

Hebb, D. O.
1949   *The organization of behavior.* New York: John Wiley.

1960   The American revolution. *American Psychologist, 15,* 735–745.

1980   *Essay on mind.* Hillsdale, NJ: Erlbaum.

Hess, E. H.
1970   Ethology and developmental psychology. In P. H. Mussen, ed., *Carmichael's manual of child psychology.* 3rd ed. Vol. 1. New York: John Wiley.

1973   *Imprinting: Early experience and the developmental psychobiology of attachment.* New York: Van Nostrand.

Hicks, V. C., and H. A. Carr
1912   Human reactions in a maze. *Journal of Animal Psychology, 2,* 98-125.

Hilgard, E. R.
1965   *Hypnotic susceptibility.* New York: Harcourt Brace Jovanovich.

Hinde, R. A.
1974   *Biological bases of human social behavior.* New York: McGraw-Hill.

1989   Ethological and relationships approaches. In R. Vasta, ed., *Annals of child development.* Vol. 6. Greenwich, CT: JAI Press.

In press   Developmental psychology in the context of other behavioral sciences. *Developmental Psychology.*

Hintzman, D. L.
1974 Psychology and the cow's belly. *Worm Runner's Digest, 16,* 84–85.

Horney, K.
1967 *Feminine psychology.* New York: W. W. Norton.

Horowitz, F. D.
1983 A behavioral alternative to an ecological approach to understanding the development of knowing in infancy: A commentary. *Developmental Review, 3,* 405–409.

Hudson, J. A.
1990 The emergence of autobiographical memory in mother-child conversation. In R. Fivush and J. A. Hudson, eds., *Knowing and remembering in young children.* Cambridge: Cambridge University Press.

Huesmann, L. R., K. Lagerspetz, and L. D. Eron
1984 Intervening variables in the TV violence-aggression relation: Evidence from two countries. *Developmental Psychology, 20,* 746–775.

Hutchins, E.
1991 The social organization of distributed cognition. In L. A. Resnick, R. Levine, and A. Behrend, eds., *Perspectives on socially shared cognition.* Washington, DC: American Psychological Association.

Hutt, S. J., and C. Hutt
1970 *Direct observation and measurement of behavior.* Springfield, IL: Charles C Thomas.

Inhelder, B., and J. Piaget
1980 Procedures and structures. In D. R. Olson, ed., *The social foundations of language and thought: Essays in honor of Jerome S. Bruner.* New York: W. W. Norton.

Inhelder, B., H. Sinclair, and M. Bovet
1974 *Learning and the development of cognition.* Cambridge, MA: Harvard University Press.

Johnston, M. K., H. N. Sloane, and S. W. Bijou
1966 A note on the measurement of drooling in free-ranging young children. *Journal of Experimental Child Psychology, 4,* 292–295.

Jones, E.
1953 *The life and work of Sigmund Freud.* New York: Basic Books. Vol. 1.

1955 Vol. 2.

1957 Vol. 3.

1961 Complete work, edited and abridged by L. Trilling and S. Marcus.

Jones, M. C.
1924 A laboratory study of fear: The case of Peter. *Pedagogical Seminary, 31,* 308–315.

Justice, E. M.
  1989   Preschoolers' knowledge and use of behaviors varying in strategic effec-
            tiveness. *Merrill-Palmer Quarterly, 35,* 363–377.

Kail, R.
  1991   Development of processing speed in childhood and adolescence. In H.
            W. Reese, ed., *Advances in child development and behavior.* Vol. 23.
            San Diego: Academic Press.

Kearins, J. M.
  1981   Visual spatial memory in Australian Aboriginal children of desert re-
            gions. *Cognitive Psychology, 13,* 434–460.

  1986   Visual spatial memory in Aboriginal and white Australian children.
            Australian Journal of Psychology, 38, 203–214.

Keeney, T. J., S. R. Cannizzo, and J. H. Flavell
  1967   Spontaneous and induced verbal rehearsal in a recall task. *Child
            Development, 38,* 953–966.

Keil, F. C.
  1989   *Concepts, kinds, and cognitive development.* Cambridge, MA: MIT
            Press.

Kellman, P. J., and E. S. Spelke
  1983   Perception of partly occluded objects in infancy. *Cognitive Psychology,
            15,* 483–524.

Kendler, H. H.
  1987   *Historical foundations of modern psychology.* Chicago: Dorsey
            Press.

Kerkman, D. D., and J. C. Wright
  1988   An exegesis of two theories of compensation development: Sequential
            decision theory and information integration theory. *Developmental
            Review, 8,* 323–360.

Kessler, K., G. M. White, T. L. Rosenthal, and J. Phibbs
  1973   *Modeling and overt practice in training a rule-creating rubric.* Paper
            presented at meeting of the Rocky Mountain Psychological Association,
            Las Vegas, May.

Kimble, G. A.
  1961   *Hilgard and Marquis' conditioning and learning.* 2nd ed. New York:
            Appleton-Century-Crofts.

Klahr, D.
  1982   Nonmonotone assessment of monotone development: An information
            processing analysis. In S. Strauss, ed., *U-shaped behavioral growth.*
            New York: Academic Press.

  1984   Transition processes in quantitative development. In R. J. Sternberg,
            ed., *Mechanisms of cognitive development.* New York: W. H. Freeman.

1985   Solving problems with ambiguous subgoal ordering: Preschoolers' performance. *Child Development, 56,* 940–952.

1989   Information processing approaches to cognitive development. In R. Vasta, ed., *Annals of child development.* Vol. 6. Greenwich, CT: JAI Press.

Klahr, D., and R. S. Siegler
1978   The representation of children's knowledge. In H. W. Reese and L. P. Lipsitt, eds., *Advances in child development and behavior.* Vol. 12. New York: Academic Press.

Klahr, D., and J. G. Wallace
1976   *Cognitive development: An information-processing view.* Hillsdale, NJ: Erlbaum.

Klaus, M. H., and J. H. Kennell
1976   *Maternal-infant bonding.* St. Louis: Mosby.

Klein, G. S.
1970   *Perception, motives, and personality.* New York: Alfred A. Knopf.

Klopfer, P. H.
1971   Mother love: What turns it on? *American Scientist, 59,* 404–407.

Koenig, O.
1951   Das Aktionsystem der Bartmeise *(Panurus biarmicus L.). Oesterreichische Zoologische Zeitschrift, 1,* 1–82.

Kohlberg, L.
1969   Stage and sequence: The cognitive-developmental approach to socialization. In D. A. Goslin, ed., *Handbook of socialization theory and research.* Chicago: Rand McNally.

Kreutzer, M. A., C. Leonard, and J. H. Flavell
1975   An interview study of children's knowledge about memory. *Monographs of the Society for Research in Child Development, 40* (1, Serial No. 159).

Kris, E.
1952   *Psychoanalytic explorations in art.* New York: International Universities Press.

Kuhl, P., and A. N. Meltzoff
1982   The bimodal perception of speech in infancy. *Science, 218,* 1138–1141.

Kuhn, D.
1989   Children and adults as intuitive scientists. *Psychological Review, 96,* 674–689.

Kuhn, T.
1970   *The structure of scientific revolutions.* 2nd ed. Chicago: University of Chicago Press. 1st ed., 1962.

Lachman, R., J. L. Lachman, and E. C. Butterfield
1979   *Cognitive psychology and information processing: An introduction.* Hillsdale, NJ: Erlbaum.

Lakatos, I.
  1978   *The methodology of scientific research programs.* Cambridge: Cambridge University Press.

Lamb, M.
  1978   Social interaction in infancy and the development of personality. In M. E. Lamb, ed., *Social and personality development.* New York: Holt, Rinehart and Winston.

Lamb, S., and R. H. Wozniak
  1990   Developmental co-construction: Metatheory in search of method [review of *Child development within culturally structured environments,* Vols. 1 and 2 by J. Valsiner]. *Contemporary Psychology, 35,* 853–854.

Langer, J.
  1969   *Theories of development.* New York: Holt, Rinehart & Winston.

Langlois, J. H., R. G. Cooper, and R. H. Woodson
  1985   The child: Many views, many fields. A review of *Handbook of child psychology,* ed. P. H. Mussen. *Contemporary Psychology, 30,* 357–369.

Langlois, J. H., L. A. Roggman, R. J. Casey, J. M. Ritter, L. A. Rieser-Danner, and V. Y. Jenkins
  1987   Infant preferences for attractive faces: Rudiments of a stereotype? *Developmental Psychology, 23,* 363–369.

Leon, M.
  1980   Integration of intent and consequence information in children's moral judgments. In F. Wilkening, J. Becker, and T. Trabaso, eds., *Information integration by children.* Hillsdale, NJ: Erlbaum.

  1984   Rules mothers and sons use to integrate intent and damage information in their moral judgments. *Child Development, 55,* 2106–2113.

Lepper, M. R., D. Greene, and R. E. Nisbett
  1973   Undermining children's intrinsic interest with extrinsic rewards: A test of the "overjustification" hypothesis. *Journal of Personality and Social Psychology, 28,* 129–137.

Leslie, A. M.
  1988   The necessity of illusion: Perception and thought in infancy. In L. Weiskrantz, ed., *Thought without language.* Oxford: Clarendon Press.

Levy, R. I.
  1969   On getting angry in the Society Islands. In W. Caudill and T. Y. Lin, eds., *Mental health research in Asia and the Pacific.* Honolulu: East-West Center Press.

Liben, L. S.
  1977   Memory from a cognitive-developmental perspective: A theoretical and empirical review. In W. F. Overton and J. M. Gallagher, eds., *Knowledge and development.* Vol. 1. New York: Plenum.

Liben, L. S., and C. J. Posnansky
1977   Inferences on inferences: The effects of age, transitive ability, memory load, and lexical factors. *Child Development, 48,* 1490–1497.

Lindsay, R. K.
1991   Symbol-processing theories and the SOAR architecture [review of *Unified theories of cognition* by A. Newell]. *Psychological Science, 2,* 294–302.

Looft, W. R., and C. P. Svoboda
1971   *Structuralism in cognitive developmental psychology: Past, contemporary, and futuristic perspectives.* Unpublished manuscript, Pennsylvania State University.

Lorenz, K. Z.
1931   Beiträge zur Ethologie sozialer Corviden. *Journal für Ornithologie, 79,* 67–127.

1937   Über die Bildung des Instinktbegriffes. *Die Naturwissenschaften, 25,* 289–300, 307–318, 325–331.

1943   Die angeborenen Formen möglicher Erfahrung. *Zeitschrift für Tierpsychologie, 5,* 235–409.

1950   *So kam der Mensch auf den Hund.* Vienna: Verlag Borotha-Schoeler.

1952   *King Solomon's ring.* New York: Thomas Y. Crowell.

1959   Psychologie und Stammesgeschichte. In G. Herberer, ed., *Evolution der Organismen.* Stuttgart: Fischer.

1963   *Das sogenannte Böse.* Vienna: Verlag Borotha-Schoeler.

1966   *On aggression.* New York: Harcourt, Brace and World.

Luria, A. R.
1961   *The role of speech in the regulation of normal and abnormal behavior.* New York: Liveright.

1976   *Cognitive development: Its cultural and social foundations.* Cambridge, MA: Harvard University Press.

1979   *The making of mind: A personal account of Soviet Psychology,* eds. M. Cole and S. Cole. Cambridge, MA: Harvard University Press.

McCain, G., and E. M. Segal
1969   *The game of science.* Belmont, CA: Brooks/Cole.

McCall, R. B., and C. B. Kennedy
1980   Attention to babyishness in babies. *Journal of Experimental Child Psychology, 29,* 189–201.

McClelland, J. L.
1989   Parallel distributed processing: Implications for cognition and development. In R. G. M. Morris, ed., *Parallel distributed processing: Implication for psychology and neurobiology.* Oxford: Clarendon Press.

McClelland, J. L., and E. Jenkins
  1991   Nature, nurture, and connections: Implications of connectionist models for cognitive development. In K. Van Lehn, ed., *Architectures for intelligence*. Hillsdale, NJ: Erlbaum.

MacDonald, K. B., ed.
  1988   *Sociobiological perspectives on human development*. New York: Springer-Verlag.

Mace, W. M.
  1977   James J. Gibson's strategy for perceiving: Ask not what's inside your head, but what your head's inside of. In R. Shaw and J. Bransford, eds., *Perceiving, acting, and knowing*. Hillsdale, NJ: Erlbaum.

McFarland, D. J.
  1976   Form and function in the temporal organization of behavior. In P. P. G. Bateson and R. A. Hinde, eds., *Growing points in ethology*. Cambridge: Cambridge University Press.

Macfarlane, A.
  1977   *The psychology of childbirth*. Cambridge, MA: Harvard University Press.

McGrew, W. C.
  1972   *An ethological study of children's behavior*. New York: Academic Press.

MacWhinney, B., ed.
  1987   *Mechanisms of language acquisition*. Hillsdale, NJ: Erlbaum.

Mahler, M. S.
  1968   *On human symbiosis and the vicissitudes of individuation*. Vol. 1: *Infantile psychosis*. New York: International Universities Press.

Mahler, M. S., F. Pine, and A. Bergman
  1975   *The psychological birth of the human infant*. New York: Basic Books.

Malinowski, B.
  1927   *Sex and repression in savage society*. New York: Harcourt Brace.

Mandler, G.
  1979   Emotion. In E. Hearst, ed., *The first century of experimental psychology*. Hillsdale, NJ: Erlbaum.

Mandler, J. M.
  1988   How to build a baby: On the development of an accessible representational system. *Cognitive Development, 3*, 113-136.

  1990   Recall of events by preverbal children. In A. Diamond, ed., *The development and neural bases of higher cognitive functions*. New York: The New York Academy of Sciences.

Marcia, J. E.
  1967   Ego identity status: Relationship to change in self-esteem, "general maladjustment," and authoritarianism. *Journal of Personality, 35*, 118–133.

1980   Identity in adolescence. In J. Adelson, ed., *Handbook of adolescent psychology.* New York: John Wiley.

Markus, H. R., and S. Kitayama
1991   Culture and the self: Implications for cognition, emotion, and motivation. *Psychological Review, 98,* 224–253.

Martini, M., and J. Kirkpatrick
1981   Early interactions in the Marquesas Islands. In T. M. Field, A. M. Sostek, P. Vietze, and P. H. Leiderman, eds., *Culture and early interventions.* Hillsdale, NJ: Erlbaum.

Marx, M. H.
1976   Formal theory. In M. H. Marx and F. E. Goodson, eds., *Theories in contemporary psychology.* 2nd ed. New York: Macmillan.

Meacham, J. A.
1977   Soviet investigations of memory development. In R. V. Kail and J. W. Hagen, eds., *Perspectives on the development of memory and cognition.* Hillsdale, NJ: Erlbaum.

1983   Wisdom and the context of knowledge: Knowing that one doesn't know. In D. Kuhn and J. A. Meacham, eds., *On the development of developmental psychology.* Basel: S. Karger.

Meacham, J. A., and N. R. Santilli
1982   Interstage relationships in Erikson's theory: Identity and intimacy. *Child Development, 53,* 1461–1467.

Mehler, J., P. W. Jusczyk, G. Lambertz, N. Hallsted, J. Bertoncini, and L. Amiel-Tison
1988   A precursor of language acquisition in young infants. *Cognition, 29,* 143–178.

Meltzoff, A. N., and M. K. Moore
1983   Newborn infants imitate adult facial gestures. *Child Development, 54,* 702–709.

Michaels, C. F., and C. Carello
1981   *Direct perception.* Englewood Cliffs, NJ: Prentice Hall.

Miller, N. E., and J. Dollard
1941   *Social learning and imitation.* New Haven, CT: Yale University Press.

Miller, P. H.
1978   Stimulus variables in conservation: An alternative approach to assessment. *Merrill-Palmer Quarterly, 24,* 141–160.

1990   The development of strategies of selective attention. In D. F. Bjorklund, ed., *Children's strategies: Contemporary views of cognitive development.* Hillsdale, NJ: Erlbaum.

Miller, P. H., V. F. Haynes, D. DeMarie-Dreblow, and J. Woody-Ramsey
1986   Children's strategies for gathering information in three tasks. *Child Development, 57,* 1429–1439.

Miller, S. A.
1976   Nonverbal assessment of Piagetian concepts. *Psychological Bulletin, 83,* 405–430.

1982   On the generalizability of conservation: A comparison of different kinds of transformation. *British Journal of Psychology, 73,* 221–230.

Moll, L. C., ed.
1990   *Vygotsky and education.* Cambridge: Cambridge University Press.

Moltz, H., and T. M. Leon
1983   The coordinate roles of mother and young in establishing and maintaining pheromonal symbiosis in the rat. In L. A. Rosenblum and H. Moltz, eds., *Symbiosis in parent-offspring interactions.* New York: Plenum.

Montagu, A.
1973   The new litany of "innate depravity," or original sin revisited. In A. Montagu, ed., *Man and aggression.* New York: Oxford University Press.

Morelli, G. A., B. Rogoff, D. Oppenheim, and D. Goldsmith
1992   Cultural variation in infants' sleeping arrangements: Questions of independence. *Developmental Psychology, 28,* 604-613.

Morris, D.
1967   *The naked ape.* New York: McGraw-Hill.

Mosier, C., and B. Rogoff
1991   *Infants' instrumental use of their mothers to achieve their goals.* Unpublished manuscript.

Munn, N. L.
1954   Learning in children. In L. Carmichael, ed., *Manual of child psychology.* 2nd ed. New York: John Wiley.

Murray, F. B.
1983   Learning and development through social interaction and conflict: A challenge to social learning theory. In L. Liben, ed., *Piaget and the foundations of knowledge.* Hillsdale, NJ: Erlbaum.

Myers, B. J.
1984   Mother-infant bonding: The status of this critical-period hypothesis. *Developmental Review, 4,* 240–274.

Neisser, U.
1985   Toward an ecologically oriented cognitive science. In T. M. Shlechter and M. P. Toglia, eds., *New directions in cognitive science.* Norwood, NJ: Ablex.

Nelson, K.
1978   How children represent knowledge of their world in and out of language: A preliminary report. In R. S. Siegler, ed., *Children's thinking: What develops?* Hillsdale, NJ: Erlbaum.

Nelson, K., ed.
1986   *Event knowledge.* Hillsdale, NJ: Erlbaum.

Newcomb, A. F., and W. A. Collins
1979   Children's comprehension of family role portrayals in televised dramas: Effects of socioeconomic status, ethnicity, and age. *Developmental Psychology, 15,* 417–423.

Newell, A., and H. A. Simon
1961   Computer simulation of human thinking. *Science, 134,* 2011–2017.

Noelting, G.
1980   The development of proportional reasoning and the ratio concept. *Educational Studies in Mathematics, 11,* 217–253, 331–363.

Noirot, E.
1974   Nest-building by the virgin female mouse exposed to ultrasound from inaccessible pups. *Animal Behavior, 22,* 410–420.

Ormiston, L. H.
1972   *Factors determining response to modeled hypocrisy.* Ph.D. dissertation, Stanford University.

Ornstein, P. A., and M. J. Naus
1985   Effects of the knowledge base on children's memory strategies. In H. W. Reese, ed., *Advances in child development and behavior.* Vol. 19. Orlando, FL: Academic Press.

Ornstein, P. A., M. J. Naus, and C. Liberty
1975   Rehearsal and organizational processes in children's memory. *Child Development, 46,* 818–830.

Overton, W. F.
1984   World views and their influence on psychological theory and research: Kuhn-Lakatos-Laudan. In H. W. Reese, ed., *Advances in child development and behavior.* Vol. 18. Orlando, FL: Academic Press, 1984.

Palincsar, A. S., and A. L. Brown
1984   Reciprocal teaching of comprehension-fostering and comprehension-monitoring activities. *Cognition and Instruction, 1,* 117–175.

1988   Teaching and practicing thinking skills to promote comprehension in the context of group problem solving. *RASE, 9(1),* 53–59.

Paris, S. G., and A. Y. Carter
1973   Semantic and constructive aspects of sentence memory in children. *Developmental Psychology, 9,* 109–113.

Paris, S. G., and D. R. Cross
1988   The zone of proximal development: Virtues and pitfalls of a metaphorical representation of children's learning. *The Genetic Epistemologist, 16(1),* 27–37.

Parke, R. D.
    1977   Parent-infant interaction: Progress, paradigms, and problems. In G. P. Sackett, ed., *Observing behavior*. Baltimore, MD: University Park Press.

Parkes, C. M., J. Stevenson-Hinde, and P. Marris, eds.
    1991   *Attachment across the life cycle*. London: Tavistock/Routledge and Kegan Paul.

Parton, D.
    1976   Learning to imitate in infancy. *Child Development, 47*, 14–31.

Pascual-Leone, J.
    1970   A mathematical model for the transition rule in Piaget's developmental stages. *Acta Psychologica, 32*, 301–345.

    1987   Organismic processes for neo-Piagetian theories: A dialectical causal account of cognitive development. *International Journal of Psychology, 22*, 531–570.

Patterson, G. R.
    1980   Mothers: The unacknowledged victims. *Monographs of the Society for Research in Child Development, 45* (5, Serial No. 186).

Patterson, G. R., and C. L. Bank
    1989   Some amplifying mechanisms for pathologic processes in families. In M. R. Gunnar and E. Thelen, eds., *Minnesota Symposia on Child Psychology*. Vol. 22: *Systems and development*. Hillsdale, NJ: Erlbaum.

Patterson, G. R., and J. B. Reid
    1984   Social interactional processes within the family: The study of the moment-by-moment family transactions in which human social development is imbedded. *Journal of Applied Developmental Psychology, 5*, 237–262.

Peery, J. C., and P. M. Crane
    1980   Personal space regulation: Approach-withdrawal-approach proxemic behavior during adult-preschool interaction at close range. *Journal of Psychology, 106*, 63–75.

Pepper, S. C.
    1934   A contextualistic theory of possibility. *University of California Publications in Philosophy, 17*, 177–197.

    1942   *World hypotheses: A study in evidence*. Berkeley: University of California Press.

Perner, J., S. R. Leekam, and H. Wimmer
    1987   Three-year-olds' difficulty with false belief: The case for a conceptual deficit. *British Journal of Developmental Psychology, 5*, 125–137.

Perry, D. G.
    1989   Social learning theory. In R. Vasta (Chair), *Theories of child development*. Symposium conducted at the meeting of the Society for Research in Child Development, Kansas City, MO., April.

Piaget, J.

1923* *The language and thought of the child.* New York: Harcourt Brace. (1926)

1924 *Judgment and reasoning in the child.* New York: Harcourt Brace. (1928)

1926 *The child's conception of the world.* New York: Harcourt Brace. (1929)

1927 *The child's conception of physical causality.* London: Kegan Paul. (1930)

1932 *The moral judgment of the child.* London: Kegan Paul. (1932)

1936 *The origins of intelligence in children.* New York: International Universities Press. (1952)

1937 *The construction of reality in the child.* New York: Basic Books. (1954)

1945 *Play, dreams and imitation in childhood.* New York: W. W. Norton. (1951)

1946a *The child's conception of time.* London: Routledge and Kegan Paul. (1969)

1946b *The child's conception of movement and speed.* London: Routledge and Kegan Paul. (1970)

1947 *The psychology of intelligence.* New York: Harcourt Brace. (1950)

1952 Autobiography. In E. G. Boring et al., eds., *A history of psychology in autobiography.* Vol. 4. Worcester, MA: Clark University Press.

1962 Comments. Supplement to L. S. Vygotsky, *Thought and language.* Cambridge, MA: MIT Press.

1964 Development and learning. In R. E. Ripple and V. N. Rockcastle, eds., *Piaget rediscovered.* Ithaca, NY: Cornell University Press.

1970 *Psychology and epistemology: Towards a theory of knowledge.* Harmondsworth, England: Penguin. (1972)

1971 The theory of stages in cognitive development. In D. R. Green, M. P. Ford, and G. B. Flamer, eds., *Measurement and Piaget.* New York: McGraw-Hill.

1974 *Experiments in contradiction.* Chicago: University of Chicago Press. (1980)

1978 *The equilibration of cognitive structures.* Chicago: University of Chicago Press. (1985)

1979 Correspondences and transformations. In F. B. Murray, ed., *The impact of Piagetian theory: On education, philosophy, psychiatry, and psychology.* Baltimore: University Park Press.

---

* The first date given is that of the original edition in French. The second date (in parentheses) is that of the translation.

1981   *Possibility and necessity.* Vol. 1: *The role of possibility in cognitive development.* Vol 2: *The role of necessity in cognitive development.* Minneapolis: University of Minnesota Press. (1987)

1983   Piaget's theory. In W. Kessen, ed., *Handbook of child psychology.* Vol. 1: *History, theory, and methods.* 4th ed. P. H. Mussen, series ed. New York: John Wiley.

Piaget, J., and R. Garcia
1991   *Towards a logic of meanings.* Hillsdale, NJ: Erlbaum.

Piaget, J. and B. Inhelder
1968   *Memory and intelligence.* London: Routledge and Kegan Paul. (1973)

Pick, H. L.
1992   Eleanor J. Gibson: Learning to perceive and perceiving to learn. *Developmental Psychology, 28,* 787-794.

Plomin, R., J. C. DeFries, and J. C. Loehlin
1977   Genotype-environment interaction and correlation in the analysis of human behavior. *Psychological Bulletin, 84,* 309–322.

Poincaré, J. H.
1908   *Science and hypothesis.* New York: Dover. (1952)

Premack, D., and G. Woodruff
1978   Does the chimpanzee have a theory of mind? *Behavioral and Brain Sciences, 1,* 515–526.

Pressley, M.
1982   Elaboration and memory development. *Child Development, 53,* 296–309.

Price-Williams, D. R., W. Gordon, and M. Ramirez III
1969   Skill and conservation: A study of pottery-making children. *Developmental Psychology, 1,* 769.

Quillian, M. R., P. M. Wortman, and G. W. Baylor
1964   *The programmable Piaget: Behavior from the standpoint of a radical computerist.* Unpublished manuscript, Carnegie Institute of Technology.

Rajecki, D. W., M. E. Lamb, and P. Obmascher
1978   Toward a general theory of infantile attachment: A comparative review of aspects of the social bond. *Behavioral and Brain Sciences, 3,* 417–464.

Rapaport, D.
1960   The structure of psychoanalytic theory: A systematizing attempt. *Psychological Issues,* Monograph 6. New York: International Universities Press.

Ratner, C.
1991   *Vygotsky's sociocultural psychology and its contemporary applications.* New York: Plenum.

Recht, D. R., and L. Leslie
1988   Effect of prior knowledge on good and poor reader's memory for text. *Journal of Educational Psychology, 80,* 16–20.

Reddy, V.
1991   Playing with others' expectations: Teasing and mucking about in the first year. In A. Whiten, ed., *Natural theories of mind: Evolution, development and simulation of everyday mindreading.* Oxford: Basil Blackwell.

Reese, H. W.
1991   Contextualism and developmental psychology. In H. W. Reese, ed., *Advances in child development and behavior.* Vol. 23. San Diego: Academic Press.

Renninger, K. A., S. Hidi, and A. Krapp, eds.
1992   *The role of interest in learning and development.* Hillsdale, NJ: Erlbaum.

Reyher, J.
1967   Hypnosis in research on psychopathology. In J. E. Gordon, ed., *Handbook of clinical and experimental hypnosis.* New York: Macmillan.

Rieber, R. W., and A. S. Carton, eds.
1987   *The collected works of L. S. Vygotsky.* Vol. 1. New York: Plenum.

Riegel, K.
1972   Influence of economic and political ideologies on the development of developmental psychology. *Psychological Bulletin, 78,* 129–141.

1976   The dialectics of human development. *American Psychologist, 31,* 689–700.

Robson, K. S.
1967   The role of eye-to-eye contact in maternal-infant attachment. *Journal of Child Psychology and Psychiatry, 8,* 13–25.

Roediger, H. L.
1979   Implicit and explicit memory models. *Bulletin of the Psychonomic Society, 13,* 339–342.

Rogoff, B.
1990   *Apprenticeship in thinking: Cognitive development in social context.* New York: Oxford University Press.

Rogoff, B., and W. P. Gardner
1984   Guidance in cognitive development: An examination of mother–child instruction. In B. Rogoff and J. Lave, eds., *Everyday cognition: Its development in social context.* Cambridge, MA: Harvard University Press.

Rogoff, B., and A. Goncu
1987   Vygotsky and beyond [review of *Vygotsky and the social formation of mind* by J. Wertsch]. *Contemporary Psychology, 32,* 22–23.

Rosenblatt, J. S.
   1976   Stages in the early behavioral development of altricial young of selected
             species of non-primate mammals. In P. P. G. Bateson and R. A. Hinde, eds.,
             Growing points in ethology. Cambridge: Cambridge University Press.

Rosenthal, T. L., and B. J. Zimmerman
   1978   *Social learning and cognition.* New York: Academic Press.

Russell, M. J., T. Mendelson, and H. V. S. Peeke
   1983   Mothers' identification of their infants' odors. *Ethology and Sociobiol-
             ogy, 4,* 29–31.

Samuel, J., and P. Bryant
   1984   Asking only one question in the conservation experiment. *Journal of
             Child Psychology and Psychiatry, 25,* 315–318.

Savin-Williams, R. C.
   1976   An ethological study of dominance formation and maintenance in a
             group of human adolescents. *Child Development, 47,* 972–979.

Saxe, G. B.
   1981   Body parts as numerals: A developmental analysis of numeration
             among the Oksapmin in Papua New Guinea. *Developmental Psychol-
             ogy, 52,* 306–316.

   1988   The mathematics of child street vendors. *Child Development, 59,*
             1415–1425.

Saxe, G. B., S. R. Guberman, and M. Gearhart
   1987   Social processes in early number development. *Monographs of the
             Society for Research in Child Development, 52* (2, Serial No. 216).

Scarr, S.
   1985   Cultural lenses on mothers and children. In L. Friedrich-Cofer, ed.,
             Human nature and public policy. New York: Praeger.

Schank, R. C., and R. Abelson
   1977   *Scripts, plans, goals and understanding.* Hillsdale, NJ: Erlbaum.

Schlein, S., ed.
   1987   *A way of looking at things: Selected papers from 1930 to 1980. Erik H.
             Erikson.* New York: W. W. Norton.

Schmuckler, M.
   1987   *The effect of imposed optical flow on guided locomotion in young
             children.* Paper presented at the meeting of the Society for Research in
             Child Development, Baltimore, April.

Schneider, W., J. Korkel, and F. E. Weinert
   1989   Domain-specific knowledge and memory performance: A comparison
             of high- and low-aptitude children. *Journal of Educational Psychology,
             81,* 306–312.

Schneider, W., and F. E. Weinert
   1989   Memory development: Universal changes and individual differences. In

A. de Ribaupierre, ed., *Transitional mechanisms in child development: The longitudinal perspective.* Cambridge: Cambridge University Press.

Schneirla, T. C.
1966   Behavioral development and comparative psychology. *Quarterly Review of Biology, 41,* 283–302.

Schrödinger, E.
1958   *Mind and matter.* Cambridge: Cambridge University Press.

Schweder, R. A.
1991   *Thinking through cultures: Expeditions in cultural psychology.* Cambridge, MA: Harvard University Press.

Sears, R. R., L. Rau, and R. Alpert
1965   *Identification and child rearing.* Stanford: Stanford University Press.

Shapley, H., S. Rapput, and H. Wright, eds.
1965   *The new treasury of science.* New York: Harper & Row.

Shatz, M., and R. Gelman
1973   The development of communication skills: Modifications in the speech of young children as a function of listener. *Monographs of the Society for Research in Child Development, 38* (5, Serial No. 152).

Shaw, R., and J. Bransford
1977   Introduction: Psychological approaches to the problems of knowledge. In R. Shaw and J. Bransford, eds., *Perceiving, acting, and knowing: Toward an ecological psychology.* Hillsdale, NJ: Erlbaum.

Shotter, J.
1989   Vygotsky's psychology: Joint activity in a developmental zone. *New Ideas in Psychology, 7,* 185–204.

Siegler, R. S.
1978   The origins of scientific reasoning. In R. S. Siegler, ed., *Children's thinking: What develops?* Hillsdale, NJ: Erlbaum.

1983   Information processing approaches to cognitive development. In W. Kessen, ed., P. H. Mussen, series ed., *Handbook of child psychology.* Vol. 1: *History, theory, and methods.* New York: John Wiley.

1986   *Children's thinking.* Englewood Cliffs, NJ: Prentice Hall.

1987   Strategy choice in subtraction. In J. Sloboda and D. Rogers, eds., *Cognitive processes in mathematics.* Oxford: Oxford University Press.

1988   Strategy choice procedures and the development of multiplication skills. *Journal of Experimental Psychology: General, 117,* 258–275.

1989   Mechanisms of cognitive development. In M. R. Rosenzweig and L. W. Porter, eds., *Annual review of psychology.* Vol. 40. Palo Alto, CA: Annual Reviews, Inc.

1991   *Children's thinking.* 2nd ed. Englewood Cliffs, NJ: Prentice-Hall.

1992   The other Alfred Binet. *Developmental Psychology, 28,* 179–190.

Siegler, R. S., and K. Crowley
    1991   The microgenetic method: A direct means for studying cognitive development. *American Psychologist, 46,* 606–620.

Siegler, R. S., and E. Jenkins
    1989   *How children discover new strategies.* Hillsdale, NJ: Erlbaum.

Sigel, I. E.
    1986   Mechanism: A metaphor for cognitive development? A review of Sternberg's *Mechanisms of cognitive development. Merrill-Palmer Quarterly, 32,* 93–101.

Signorella, M. L., and L. S. Liben
    1984   Recall and reconstruction of gender-related pictures: Effects of attitude, task difficulty, and age. *Child Development, 55,* 393–405.

Simon, H. A.
    1972   On the development of the processor. In S. Farnham-Diggory, ed., *Information processing in children.* New York: Academic Press.

Simon, T., A. Newell, and D. Klahr
    In press   Q-Soar: A computational account of children's learning about number conservation. In D. Fisher and M. Pazzani, eds., *Concept formation: Knowledge and experience in unsupervised learning.* San Mateo, CA: Morgan-Kauffman.

Skinner, B. F.
    1948   *Walden Two.* New York: Macmillan.

    1967   Autobiography. In E. G. Boring and G. Lindzey, eds., *A history of psychology in autobiography.* Vol. 5. Englewood Cliffs, NJ: Prentice-Hall.

    1971   *Beyond freedom and dignity.* New York: Alfred A. Knopf.

    1980   The experimental analysis of operant behavior: A history. In R. W. Rieber and K. Salzinger, eds., *Psychology: Theoretical–historical perspectives.* New York: Academic Press.

Smith, P. K., and K. Connolly
    1972   Patterns of play and social interaction in preschool children. In N. G. Blurton-Jones, ed., *Ethological studies of child behavior.* Cambridge: Cambridge University Press.

Snarey, J., L. Kohlberg, and G. Noam
    1983   Ego development in perspective: Structural stage, functional phase, and cultural age-period models. *Developmental Review, 3,* 303–337.

Spelke, E. S.
    1976   Infants' intermodal perception of events. *Cognitive Psychology, 8,* 553–560.

    1991   Physical knowledge in infancy: Reflections on Piaget's theory. In S. Carey and R. Gelman, eds., *The epigenesis of mind: Essays in biology and cognition.* Hillsdale, NJ: Erlbaum.

Spiker, C. C.
  1966   The concept of development: Relevant and irrelevant issues. In H. W. Stevenson, ed., Concept of development. *Monographs of the Society for Research in Child Development, 31* (5, Serial No. 107).

Spitz, R. A.
  1945   Hospitalism: An inquiry into the genesis of psychiatry conditions in early childhood. *Psychoanalytic Study of the Child, 1,* 53–74.

  1957   Die Entstehung der ersten Objektbeziehungen. Stuttgart: Klett.

Sroufe, L. A.
  1983   Attachment and adaptation in preschool. In M. Perlmutter, ed., *Minnesota Symposia on Child Psychology.* Vol. 15: *Development and policy concerning children with special needs.* Hillsdale, NJ: Erlbaum.

  1985   Attachment classification from the perspective of infant-caretaker relationships and infant temperament. *Child Development, 56,* 1–14.

Stern, D.
  1974   Mother and infant at play: The dyadic interaction involving facial, vocal, and gaze behaviors. In M. Lewis and L. Rosenblum, eds., *The effect of the infant on its caretaker.* New York: John Wiley.

  1985   *The interpersonal world of the infant.* New York: Basic Books.

Sternberg, R. J.
  1979   The nature of mental abilities. *American Psychologist, 34,* 214–230.

  1985   *Beyond IQ: A triarchic theory of human intelligence.* Cambridge: Cambridge University Press.

  1986   *Intelligence applied.* San Diego: Harcourt Brace Jovanovich.

Sternberg, R. J., and B. Rifkin
  1979   The development of analogical reasoning processes. *Journal of Experimental Child Psychology, 27,* 195–232.

Stevenson, H. W., S. Lee, and J. W. Stigler
  1986   Achievement in mathematics. In H. Stevenson, H. Azuma, and K. Hakuta, eds., *Child development and education in Japan.* New York: W. H. Freeman.

Stigler, J. W.
  1984   "Mental abacus": The effect of abacus training on Chinese children's mental calculation. *Cognitive Psychology, 16,* 145-176.

Strauss, S., and I. Levin
  1981   Commentary. *Monographs of the Society for Research in Child Development, 46,* (2, Serial No. 189).

Strayer, F. F.
  1980   Social ecology of the preschool peer group. In W. A. Collins, ed., *Development of cognition, affect, and social relations.* Hillsdale, NJ: Erlbaum.

Strayer, F. F., and J. Strayer
1976   An ethological analysis of social agonism and dominance relations among preschool children. *Child Development, 47,* 980–999.

Streri, A., and M. Pecheux
1986   Vision-to-touch and touch-to-vision transfer of form in 5–month-old infants. *British Journal of Developmental Psychology, 4,* 161–167.

Super, C. M., and S. Harkness
1983   *Looking across at growing up: The cultural expression of cognitive development in middle childhood.* Unpublished manuscript, Harvard University.

Thatcher, R. W., R. A. Walker, and S. Giudice
1987   Human cerebral hemispheres develop at different rates and ages. *Science, 236,* 1110–1113.

Thayer, G. H.
1909   *Concealing coloration in the animal kingdom.* New York: Macmillan.

Thorndike, E. L.
1898   Animal intelligence: An experimental study of the associative processes in animals. *Psychological Review: Series of Monograph Supplements, 2* (4, Whole No. 8).

Tinbergen, E. A., and N. Tinbergen
1972   *Early childhood autism: An ethological approach.* Berlin: Parey.

Tinbergen, N.
1951   *The study of instinct.* London: Oxford University Press.

1958   *Curious naturalists.* New York: Basic Books.

1973   *The animal in its world: Explorations of an ethologist 1932–1972.* Vols. 1 and 2. Cambridge, MA: Harvard University Press.

Tobin, J. J., D. Y. H. Wu, and D. H. Davidson
1989   *Preschool in three cultures.* New Haven, CT: Yale University Press.

Tolman, E. C.
1959   Principles of purposive behavior. In S. Koch, ed., *Psychology: A study of a science.* New York: McGraw-Hill.

Tomasello, M., A. C. Kruger, and H. H. Ratner
1991   *Cultural learning* (Tech. Rep. No. 21). Atlanta: Emory University, Emory Cognition Project.

Toulmin, S.
1978   The Mozart of psychology. *New York Review of Books,* September.

Trabasso, T.
1977   The role of memory as a system in making transitive inferences. In R. V. Kail and J. W. Hagen, eds., *Perspectives on the development of memory and cognition.* Hillsdale, NJ: Erlbaum.

Trivers, R.
1985   *Social evolution.* Menlo Park, CA: Benjamin-Cummings.

Tuddenham, R. D.
1966   Jean Piaget and the world of the child. *American Psychologist, 21,* 207–217.

Tudge, J., and B. Rogoff
1989   Peer influences on cognitive development: Piagetian and Vygotskian perspectives. In M. H. Bornstein and J. S. Bruner, eds., *Interaction in human development.* Hillsdale, NJ: Erlbaum.

Tulviste, P.
1991   *Cultural-historical development of verbal thinking: A psychological study.* Commack, NY: Nova Science.

Uzgiris, I. C.
1968   Situational generality of conservation. In I. E. Siegel and F. H. Hooper, eds., *Logical thinking in children: Research based on Piaget's theory.* New York: Holt, Rinehart & Winston.

Valsiner, J.
1987   *Culture and the development of children's action.* Chichester: John Wiley.

1989   *Human development and culture.* Lexington, MA: D. C. Heath.

Valsiner, J. , ed.
1988   *Child development within culturally structured environments.* Vols. 1 and 2. Norwood, NJ: Ablex.

van den Daele, L.
1969   Qualitative models in developmental analysis. *Developmental Psychology, 1,* 303–310.

Van der Veer, R., and J. Valsiner
1991   *Understanding Vygotsky: A quest for synthesis.* Oxford: Basil Blackwell.

Vurpillot, E., and W. A. Ball
1979   The concept of identity and children's selective attention. In G. Hale and M. Lewis, eds., *Attention and cognitive development.* New York: Plenum.

Vuyk, R.
1981   *Overview and critique of Piaget's genetic epistemology, 1965–1980.* Vol. 1. London and New York: Academic Press.

Vygotsky, L. S.
1956   *Selected psychological investigations.* Moscow: IAPN-SSSR.

1960   *Development of the higher psychical functions.* Moscow: APN.

1962   *Thought and language.* Cambridge, MA: MIT Press.

1981   The instrumental method in psychology. In J. V. Wertsch, ed., *The concept of activity in Soviet psychology.* Armonk, NY: M. E. Sharpe.

Vygotsky, L. (and M. Cole, V. John-Steiner, S. Scribner, and E. Souberman, eds.)
1978   *Mind in society.* Cambridge, MA: Harvard University Press.

Waddington, C. H.
1957   *The strategy of the genes.* London: Allen and Unwin.

Wallace, I., D. Klahr, and K. Bluff
1987   A self-modifying production system model of cognitive development. In
          D. Klahr, P. Langley, and R. Neches, eds., *Production system models of
          learning and development.* Cambridge, MA: MIT Press.

Wallbank, T. W., and A. M. Taylor
1960   *Civilization past and present.* Chicago: Scott, Foresman.

Wason, P. C., and P. N. Johnson-Laird
1972   *Psychology of reasoning.* Cambridge, MA: Harvard University Press.

Watson, J. B.
1924   *Behaviorism.* New York: W. W. Norton.

1928   *Psychological care of infant and child.* New York: W. W. Norton.

Watson, J. B., and R. Rayner
1920   Conditioned emotional reactions. *Journal of Experimental Psychology,
          3,* 1–14.

Wegman, C.
1985   *Psychoanalysis and cognitive psychology: A formalization of Freud's
          earliest theory.* Orlando, FL: Academic Press.

Wellman, H. M., and S. A. Gelman
1992   Cognitive development: Foundational theories of core domains. In M.
          R. Rosenzweig and L. W. Porter, eds., *Annual review of psychology.*
          Vol. 43. Palo Alto, CA: Annual Reviews.

Wertsch, J. V.
1979   From social interaction to higher psychological processes: A clarifica-
          tion and application of Vygotsky's theory. *Human Development, 22,*
          1–22.

1985b   *Vygotsky and the social formation of mind.* Cambridge: Harvard Uni-
          versity Press.

1991   *Voices of the mind: A sociocultural approach to mediated action.* Cam-
          bridge, MA: Harvard University Press.

Wertsch, J. V. , ed.
1985a   *Culture, communication, and cognition: Vygotskian perspectives.* New
          York: Cambridge University Press.

Wertsch, J. V., and M. Hickmann
1987   Problem solving in social interactions: A microgenetic analysis. In M.
          Hickmann, ed., *Social and functional approaches to language and
          thought.* Orlando, FL: Academic Press.

Wertsch, J. V., and P. Tulviste
    1992   L. S. Vygotsky and contemporary developmental psychology. *Developmental Psychology, 28,* 548-557.

Wesley, F.
    1989   Developmental cognition before Piaget: Alfred Binet's pioneering experiments. *Developmental Review, 9,* 58–63.

Weston, D. R., and E. Turiel
    1980   Act-rule relations: Children's conceptions of social rules. *Developmental Psychology, 16,* 417–424.

White, B. L.
    1969   Child development research: An edifice without a foundation. *Merrill-Palmer Quarterly, 15,* 47–78.

White, R. W.
    1963   Ego and reality in psychoanalytic theory: A proposal regarding independent ego energies. *Psychological Review,* Monograph 11. New York: International Universities Press.

White, S. H.
    1970   The learning theory approach. In P. H. Mussen, ed., *Carmichael's manual of child psychology.* 3rd ed. Vol. 1. New York: John Wiley.

    1976   The active organism in theoretical behaviorism. *Human Development, 19,* 99–107.

Whiting, J. M., and I. L. Child
    1953   Child training and personality. New Haven, CT: Yale University Press.

Willatts, P.
    1989   Development of problem-solving in infancy. In A. Slater and G. Bremner, eds., *Infant development.* Hillsdale, NJ: Erlbaum.

Wilson, E. O.
    1975   *Sociobiology. The new synthesis.* Cambridge, MA: Belknap Press of Harvard University Press.

    1978   *On human nature.* Cambridge, MA: Harvard University Press.

Winegar, L. T., and J. Valsiner
    1992   *Children's development within social context.* Vol. 1: *Methodology and theory.* Vol. 2: *Research and methodology.* Hillsdale, NJ: Erlbaum.

Winnicott, D. W.
    1953   Transitional objects and transitional phenomena. *International Journal of Psychoanalysis, 34,* 89–97.

    1971   *Playing and reality.* New York: Basic Books.

Wober, M.
    1972   Culture and the concept of intelligence: A case in Uganda. *Journal of Cross-Cultural Psychology, 3,* 327–328.

Wohlwill, J. F.
 1973 The concept of experience: S or R? *Human Development, 16,* 90–107.

Wozniak, R. H.
 1980 Theory, practice, and the "zone of proximal development" in Soviet psychoeducational research. *Contemporary Educational Psychology, 5,* 175-183.

Yando, R., V. Seitz, and E. Zigler, eds.
 1978 *Imitation: A developmental perspective.* Hillsdale, NJ: Erlbaum.

Yussen, S. R.
 1974 Determinants of visual attention and recall in observational learning by preschoolers and second graders. *Developmental Psychology, 10,* 93–100.

Zajonc, R. B.
 1980 Feeling and thinking: Preferences need no inferences. *American Psychologist, 35,* 151–175.

Zimmerman, B. J.
 1974 Modification of young children's grouping strategies: The effects of modeling, verbalization, incentives, and praise. *Child Development, 45,* 1032–1041.

 1985 The development of "intrinsic" motivation: A social learning analysis. In G. J. Whitehurst, ed., *Annals of child development.* Vol. 2. Greenwich, CT: JAI Press.

Zivin, G.
 1979 *The development of self-regulation through private speech.* New York: John Wiley.

INDEX OF NAMES

INDEX OF TOPICS